Mothers Wh

Edited by Charlotte Beyer
and Josephine Savarese

Mothers Who Kill

Edited by Charlotte Beyer and Josephine Savarese

Copyright © 2021 Demeter Press

Individual copyright to their work is retained by the authors. All rights reserved. No part of this book may be reproduced or transmitted in any form by any means without permission in writing from the publisher.

Demeter Press
2546 10th Line
Bradford, Ontario
Canada, L3Z 3L3
Tel: 289-383-0134
Email: info@demeterpress.org
Website: www.demeterpress.org

Demeter Press logo based on the sculpture "Demeter" by Maria-Luise Bodirsky www.keramik-atelier.bodirsky.de

Printed and Bound in Canada

Cover design and typesetting: Michelle Pirovich
Proof reading: Jena Woodhouse

Library and Archives Canada Cataloguing in Publication
Title: Mothers who Kill / edited by Charlotte Beyer and Josephine L. Savarese.
Names: Beyer, Charlotte, 1965- editor. | Savarese, Josephine, 1962- editor.
Description: Includes bibliographical references.
Identifiers: Canadiana 20210364394 | ISBN 9781772583571 (softcover)
Subjects: LCSH: Filicide. | LCSH: Infanticide. | LCSH: Homicide. | LCSH: Women murderers. | LCSH: Mothers.
Classification: LCC HV6542 .M68 2022 | DDC 364.3085/2—dc23

Acknowledgments

We are very grateful to Demeter Press for the opportunity to create this unique and necessary book, which will help to redress the complex subject of mothers who kill their own children from the perspective of mothers. Thank you to chief editor and motherhood scholar supreme, Andrea O'Reilly, and her entire team at Demeter Press.

Greatest thanks to all our contributors for their wonderful work on this most troubling of topics. Your creativity, engagement, meticulousness, and originality have helped generate a book filled with fascinating chapters that contribute in vital ways to motherhood scholarship.

Along with the contributors, Josephine wishes to thank Charlotte for being a bright light, equal parts professionalism and warmth, as this manuscript addressing an area described as a dark one took shape. She wishes to acknowledge the newcomer families and children she came to know during this period, and the bright lights as well as demonstrations of love they also offered. Josephine acknowledges the memory of "Alice" and "Adam" who died in early 2020 through maternal filicide and suicide.

Charlotte wishes to thank Josephine for her great friendship and collegiality and for all her hard work in helping this book come into existence. Charlotte dedicates this book to her daughter, Sif, and husband, Stuart, with all her love and appreciation of their support. Grateful thanks go to Sif for her technical assistance with Charlotte's photograph, which became this book's cover.

This book is dedicated to narratives of, by, and about mothers who kill their children. May all find peace.

Contents

Acknowledgments
3

Introduction
Uncovering the Complexities and Silences: Mothers Who Kill
Charlotte Beyer and Josephine Savarese
9

Part I.
Creative Explorations
23

1.
Hopes and Dreams
Chevelle Malcolm
25

2.
baby girl // medea
Amy Lynne Hill
29

3.
So Sing! Sister Hildegard of Bingen Comforts Marijoy
Josephine Savarese
53

Part II.
Legal Perspectives Now and Silenced Histories
59

4.
"I Wasn't Normal": Reading Illegibility into
Canadian Infanticide Law, a Wild Reading
Josephine Savarese
61

5.
"Stories Too Painful for the Light of Day":
Narratives of Neonaticide, Infanticide, and Child Murder
Judith Broome
83

6.
Claiming the Infanticidal Space: An Analysis of
King v. Lottie DesRoches, 1904, Prince Edward Island
Sharon Myers
103

7.
Baby Farming and Betrayal: Foster Mothers Who Murder
Rachel Franks and Caitlin Adams
125

8.
Storytelling and the Personification of Oppression
During US Feminism's First Wave:
The Infanticide Case of Hester Vaughn
Andrea S. Walsh
145

9.
The Ambivalent Monstrosity:
Museum Interpretation of the Infanticidal Mother
Meighen S. Katz
167

10.
"A Crown of Martyrdom": Infanticide, Insanity,
and Capital Punishment in Colonial Victoria
Georgina Rychner
189

**Part III.
Global Literary and Cultural Narratives**
209

11.
"She Cut Her Hair and Changed Her Name,
from Fair Elinor to Sweet William": Constructions
and Reconstructions of Female Identity in Early Modern
Infanticide Ballads
Chrissie Andrea Maroulli
211

12.
The Wicked Stepmother in the Age of Maternalist Politics
Sace Elder
235

13.
Assia Djebar's *La Soif*: Abortion and Crime
Anna Rocca
253

14.
Image Shatterer: Delores Phillips's *The Darkest Child*
Trudier Harris
275

15.
Smother Love:
Maternal Filicide in Veronique Olmi's *Beside the Sea*
Amy B. Hagenrater-Gooding
293

16.
From Murderous Monster to Loving Mother:
Reconsidering and Rewriting the Legend of
La Llorona in Children's Literature and Film
Anne McGee
311

17.
"I Never Made Those Marks on My Girl":
Challenging Cultural Narratives about Mothers Who Kill
in Sara Paretsky's Crime Novel *Brush Back*
Charlotte Beyer
333

Notes on Contributors
355

Introduction

Uncovering the Complexities and Silences: Mothers who Kill

Charlotte Beyer and Josephine Savarese

This book investigates the figure of the mother who kills and, for the first time, provides a matricentric, mother-focused examination of the topic. Rather than perceiving the mother who kills as Other—a monster or figure so far removed from social and cultural norms for mothering that there can be no retrieval or recovery—our book challenges and counters these discourses. To account for the complexity and nuance of infanticide and mothers who kill, we explore and investigate significant alternative interpretations, representations, and case studies found within historical, literary and cultural texts. Instead of presenting mothers who kill as unredeemable monsters, the varied chapters in this book explore the myths and the possibilities of reclaiming this area for motherhood studies. Our study looks at these mothers from a different and less one-dimensional angle. As readers will note, the case studies and true crime narratives examined in our book highlight the importance of re-examining material from the distant and recent past through a new, feminist, and mother-focused perspective.

The importance of the book is even clearer when one notes that the association of mothers and motherhood with care and nurturing is dramatically at odds with the figure of the mother who kills her child. There is a strong impulse in society towards silencing and erasing maternal filicide, as the idea of a mother killing her child presents one of the greatest cultural taboos. Maternal filicide or infanticide is often regarded as the most disturbing, pathological, and upsetting aspect of maternal experience. Critics Betty L. Alt and Sandra K. Wells examine the reasons for this erasure: "Most people either aren't aware or don't wish to be made aware of the number of mothers who kill their children. Society attempts to discover the motives behind all cases of child murder by mothers, but the reasons provided are never simple" (23). The trope of the mother who murders her child is frequently used to undermine the struggles of mothers who are fighting against different forms of social and cultural exclusion. Precisely because of this erasure, scholars and artists, including the writers showcased in this text, urgently challenge these narratives, interrogating cultural, historical, and literary representations of filicide and infanticide. Breaking new ground and subjecting this contentious area to feminist scrutiny, this book offers the first interdisciplinary academic and creative companion to this emerging and vital field of study. The complex motivations of mothers who kill are made prominent in Toni Morrison's 1987 acclaimed novel *Beloved*. In the novel, escaped slave mother, Sethe, addresses her daughter Beloved, whom she murdered out of desperation, in order to avoid her returning to a life of slavery and sexual abuse. Sethe reflects on how to tell Beloved of her reasons for this violent and transgressive act and explains that her actions were driven by love: "I'll explain to her, even though I don't have to. Why I did it. How if I hadn't killed her she would have died and that is something I could not bear to happen to her. When I explain it, she'll understand" (200). The mother's impassioned attempt to explain the seemingly inexplicable, to justify that which seems beyond comprehension, contrasts sharply with conventional cultural representations of mothers who kill.

Significant scholarship in the field and its main findings have focused on criminology, psychology, sensationalized true crime, and legal aspects. An overview of these findings is useful in terms of situating our study within a scholarly context, thereby foregrounding the book's innovative and ground-breaking contribution, and clarifying how it extends the current terms of academic and creative enquiry. Examining the critical parameters of existing texts treating the topic of maternal filicide, Cheryl Meyer et al. in their book *Mothers who Kill Their Children: Understanding the Acts of Moms from Susan Smith to Prom*

Mom (2001) take a sociopsychological approach to the topic. An important dimension of Meyer et al.'s study is the attempt to identify and detail a typology that will help to increase understanding of the various cases and to identify commonalities and patterns that may eventually lead to further prevention. In their book *When Caregivers Kill: Understanding Child Murder by Parents and Other Guardians* (2010), Betty L. Alt and Sandra K. Wells argue that cases abound of mothers killing their new-born babies and infants (23). Exploring a range of historical but sensationalized cases, the authors examine the circumstances around each killing and the context for the mother's actions; they argue that authorities disregard the context of the mother who kills her child—for example, other parent, health visitors and doctors, friends and family (36)—in order to concentrate solely on the figure of the mother, thereby enhancing and magnifying the enormity of her act. In their article, "Blurring Reality with Fiction: Exploring the Stories of Women, Madness, and Infanticide," Diana Jefferies, Debbie Horsfall, and Virginia Schmied investigate the narrativization of mothers who kill their children and the centrality of the trope of madness to those narratives, which is a central theme in several of the chapters in this book.

Their analysis differs, however from the examinations offered in our book, as their emphasis is on preventative measures—identifying signs and symptoms displayed by mothers in distress and developing intervention strategies or measures to be adopted that could help to ameliorate these problems before they lead to child murder or infanticide (Jefferies, Horsfall and Schmied 1). As we shall see, the different historical case studies and true crime narratives examined in our book highlight the importance of re-examining material from the past through a new, feminist, and mother-centred perspective. Emily G. Thompson's book, *Unsolved Child Murders: Eighteen American Cases, 1956-1998* (2017), also investigates real-life child murders—albeit not all by mothers—and retells the narrative of each child's killing and the context around it. Such examination of the affective and emotional dimensions of true crime taps into readers' fascination with true crime and real-life historical or present-day events.

This book highlights the difference in emotional and affective impact of such true crime and insists on the key distinction between the narratives that feature the mother as the child killer as opposed to the narratives in which the killer is another person. True crime is defined by Jean Murley as a crime narrative that is based on real-life events— "the story of real events, shaped by the teller and imbued with his or her values and beliefs about such events" (6). According to Rachel Franks, true crime narratives are often based on murder, which foregrounds the connection to maternal filicide (239). True crime is an important growth area in textual, media as well as filmic formats, albeit at times sensationalized and/or exaggerated for audience manipulation. The proliferation of short popular articles and book reviews on popular crime website Crimereads—on topics such as the terrifying mother, the monstrous mother, mothers suffering from Munchausen by proxy syndrome—suggests a rising interest in and preoccupation with the dark underbelly of mothering and with maternal violence and transgression. Such works call attention to gaps in knowledge and representation—gaps that our book specifically accounts for, challenges, and critically evaluates.

Legal perspectives also foreground current debates around maternal filicide. In their 2012 article, Susan Hatter Friedman, James Cavney, and Phillip J. Resnick list several nations with infanticide laws, including Austria, Brazil, Colombia, Finland, Germany, Greece, Hong Kong, Italy, Japan, Korea, Norway, the Philippines, Sweden, Switzerland, and Turkey (587). The crime of infanticide remains as a provision in Canadian criminal law and is modelled on the English law. Australia and New Zealand are former Commonwealth countries with infanticide prohibitions (587). Scotland parallels the United States in lacking a statute (587). Although this book's chapters focus largely on Western nations, including the United States, Canada, Australia and the United Kingdom, infanticide occurs throughout the world. While not meant to be a comprehensive list, studies are available discussing infanticide in other contexts, such as Malaysia (Razali, Fisher and Kirkman), Hong Kong (Tang and Siu), Albania (Myftari and Vyshka), South Africa (Stevens), Finland (Rautelin 2013), India and Nepal (Vickery and Van Tejilingen), Japan (Yasumi and Kageyama), Croatia, (Marcikić, et al.), and Rwanda (Mushumba, et al.).

Current Canadian scholarship maintains that the infanticide provision should be abolished and be replaced by a defence of diminished responsibility (Anand 705-728); others have argued that the infanticide section violates the Canadian *Charter of Rights and Freedoms* by disregarding young infants' human rights (Mair 241-280). Infanticide laws are objectionable to some because they allow women who might ordinarily be convicted of a more serious offence like murder to be prosecuted for a crime with less stigma and a lesser penalty. In the Albanian context, Kreshnik Myftari and Gentian Vyshka worry that a crime described as "horrendous" and that is "universally condemned from all ethical, juridical and moral standpoints" is treated with leniency and "excessive empathy" (1). They state that successfully prosecuting an infanticide charge in an Albanian court is largely "an impossible enterprise" given the strong likelihood that a defendant will achieve an acquittal on "mental insanity grounds" (1). Comparable arguments are also presented in texts on the suitability of infanticide laws in the United States. In "Murderous Madonna: Femininity, Violence, and the Myth of Postpartum Mental Disorder in Cases of Maternal Infanticide and Filicide," Heather Leigh Stangle reasons that such laws denied women's "agency and power" by reinforcing outdated sociobiological arguments (734).

Margaret Spinelli's conclusion that better resources for women are needed is affirmed by a 2018 study by Margarita Poteyeva and Margaret Leigey, in which they found that poor mental health was influential in a woman's decision to kill a child (6). The preventative policies Poteyeva and Leigey recommend include counselling and parenting programs as well as measures to address income inequality and social inclusion. Meda Chesney Lind (407 - 422) also endorses wholistic approaches. She urges scholars and activists to prioritize reproductive health, of which infanticide is a component, as an urgent human right in their advocacy. These legal perspectives provide important context to the chapters featured in this book that specifically examine legal cases and their implications and provide useful insight into current legal debates around maternal filicide.

Turning to the structure of this book, we present the material in three parts: Creative Explorations; Legal Perspectives Now and Silenced Histories; and Global Literary and Cultural Narratives. These three thematic parts also broadly describe the academic approaches informing the individual chapters presented within them. Rather than imposing an overly complicated structure on the wide-ranging material in this book, we opted for a presentation that gives the reader maximum scope to make their own creative and scholarly connections between various chapters and perspectives. We felt that this freedom to make connections across diverse forms of materials generates a textual space or site where voices and perspectives can be heard and where they may chime, echo, contrast, and reverberate in order to create new connections and creative possibilities in their evaluations of maternal filicide.

Part One: Creative Explorations

Part One explores creative writing as a means of researching the topic of maternal filicide. Chevelle Malcolm's poem, "Hopes and Dreams," imagines a mother in anguish over the thought that her child, like her, would be forced into slavery, a system that only recognized her as property and devoid of humanity. As the poem narrates, the mother looks at her child and sees the epitome of innocence, hope, and freedom, a direct contrast to a future in slavery. As a result, she decides that the only way to preserve her child's innocence is by making the decision to kill her baby. Amy Lynne Hill's play, "baby girl // medea," delivers a creative re-imagining of Medea in the German context, producing an original stage play based on the figure of Medea in order to illustrate the longstanding influence this myth has had on cultural representation of mothers who kill and infanticide. Importantly, Hill's play offers both academic reflection and creative representation of the mythical figure of Medea and her legacy of filicide. The poem "*So Sing! Sister Hildegard of Bingen Comforts Marijoy*" by Josephine L. Savarese unites words of Hildegard of Bingen, the German Benedictine abbess, writer, composer, philosopher, and Christian mystic and visionary, with the facts of a criminal case in which a newborn's remains were found in a recycling waste bin. The poem imagines Sister Hildegard offering blessings and forgiveness to the distraught mother.

Part Two: Legal Perspectives Now and Silenced Histories

Opening Part Two, Josephine Savarese investigates whether arguments that infanticide is best prevented by addressing the structural causes of crime and the adoption of restorative based proceedings might apply to infanticide in Canada. Savarese's chapter, "'I Wasn't Normal':

Reading Illegibility into Canadian Infanticide Law, a Wild Reading," explores a recent case, *R. v. Borowiec* (2016), to frame the arguments. Rather than a text offering clarity on the infanticide law and its socio-legal implications, Savarese reads the Supreme Court of Canada's infanticide decision through a lens of illegibility or madness, what Mishra Tarc has called a "wild reading." Writing with Tarc, this chapter moves away from a pretence of sensemaking regarding the crime of infanticide and the level or type of mental disturbance that is required for a conviction. The facts of the few reported cases are troubling, varied, and complex. Many commentators, including feminist legal advocates, have convincingly argued that what is commonly deemed a mental disturbance in an individual woman may in fact be read as a response to oppressive gendered conditions or may even be attributable to other reasons indecipherable by judicial reasoning.

In her chapter, "'Stories Too Painful for the Light of Day': Narratives of Neonaticide, Infanticide, and Child Murder," Judith Broome also draws from a historical account. On March 2, 1670, Mary Cook was hanged for the murder of her youngest and allegedly favourite daughter, two-year-old Elizabeth. The lurid details of Elizabeth's death and the melancholy years of Mary's life preceding her violent crime were detailed in at least three pamphlets, low-cost news publications that circulated in the streets of London. Mary Cook's story is one of many narratives of maternal filicide in the long eighteenth century that have been extensively written about. As Broome points out, our current attempts to account for filicide and infanticide through stories of madness, religious frenzy, despair, or indifference are comparable to those told in the eighteenth century. Broome focuses on cases that cannot be explained by shame, fear of losing one's position, or a scarcity of resources; lacking any material explanation, these murders are attributed to other causes, such as despair, madness, religious frenzy, or rage. Where no clear motive for the murder of a child can be found, narratives proliferate in what Broome argues is an effort to explain the unexplainable: how could a mother kill her own child?

In "Claiming the Infanticidal Space: An Analysis of *King v. Lottie DesRoches*, 1904, Prince Edward Island," Sharon Myers's chapter analyses a real historical case, namely the 1904 case of Lottie Des Roches, and uses it to examine how women could and did attempt to resist attempts to regulate and punish their reproductive choice.

Drawing from this case, Myers focuses on themes of agency and resistance and considers DesRoches's individual circumstances; she proposes that DesRoches practiced a kind of agency and resistance that crafted a physical space and moral space free from patriarchal moral regulation and law where she could exercise her reproductive choice. This important reassessment of a historical case sheds light on cultural narratives about mothers who stand accused of killing their children.

In their chapter, "Baby Farming and Betrayal: Foster Mothers Who Murder," Rachel Franks and Caitlin Adams investigate the practice and representation of the practice of baby farming in nineteenth-century Australia. Defining baby farmers as latter-day foster mothers, Franks and Adams show that the publicity surrounding foster mothers who murdered babies generated sufficient public pressure for legislators to bring in child protection laws across Australia. Through this research, Franks and Adams raise important questions about the representation and reading of baby farmers, infanticide and social change.

Andrea S. Walsh's chapter, "Storytelling and the Personification of Oppression During US Feminism's First Wave: The Infanticide Case of Hester Vaughn," examines a specific example of infanticide. She looks at the conflict between the legal authorities' need to make an example of women whom they deemed guilty of infanticide and American first-wave feminists who highlighted the discrimination and exploitation of women generally and mothers specifically. Hester Vaughn was convicted of infanticide in Philadelphia in 1868 by a male jury and sentenced to hang. Walsh persuasively argues that Vaughn's narrative personified the need for gender equality in marriage, sexual standards, healthcare, employment, and the courts.

In her chapter, "The Ambivalent Monstrosity: Museum Interpretation of the Infanticidal Mother," Meighen S. Katz begins with an examination of an 1876 Catalogue from Madame Tussaud & Sons waxworks. Katz uses this overview to remind us that the infanticidal mother continues to create quandaries of display even though modern museums resist language in which infanticide is compared to the utilitarian killing of chickens. Although the sense of the monstrous has been removed, it is often not replaced with a substantial interrogation of either circumstances or the act itself. Katz's chapter considers the ways in which the museum interpretation of infanticide raises issues of women's agency and of the interpretation of mental illness.

In her chapter, "'A Crown of Martyrdom': Infanticide, Insanity, and Capital Punishment in Colonial Victoria," Georgina Rychner examines how different parties conceived of and advanced theories of mental illness as they related to offenders of capital crime who were tried in the colony of Victoria in the late nineteenth century. Her chapter conducts a micro-analysis of the trial of Rosanna Plummer (1884), in which doctors, judges, jurors, journalists, and a significant number of lay men and women put forward theories regarding her mental state at the time of committing the crime of infanticide on her infant son. Rychner pro-vocatively argues that insanity was central to the way society grappled with guilt and responsibility in these cases and crucial to sentencing outcomes.

Part Three: Global Literary and Cultural Narratives

Part Three investigates global literary and cultural narratives about maternal filicide. Chrissie Andrea Maroulli's chapter, "'She Cut Her Hair and Changed Her Name, from Fair Elinor to Sweet William': Constructions and Reconstructions of Female Identity in Early Modern Infanticide Ballads," examines the compelling but underresearched topic of the treatment of infanticide in early modern literature and particularly balladry. Maroulli's chapter argues that the recurrent appearance of murderous mothers in popular ballads of the time was aimed at emphasizing the purity of Elizabethan women and to contrast the qualities of the fictitious characters to the actual women in early modern England.

Focusing on the late nineteenth and early twentieth centuries, Sace Elder's chapter, "The Wicked Stepmother in the Age of Maternalist Politics," examines stepmothers accused of violence against their stepchildren. Elder's chapter shows how the stepmother occupies a paradoxical position. On the one hand, she completes the normative nuclear family, but, on the other, she is also perceived to lack natural nurturing instincts ascribed to mothers. Focusing largely on continental Europe and Germany, Elder's chapter draws on a range of material from social welfare, legal, medical, and popular literature as well as press accounts of child abuse. She argues that the stepmother was the focus of contestation over the meaning of motherly love and the role of violence in the modern family.

Anna Rocca's thought-provoking chapter, "Assia Djebar's *La Soif*: Abortion and Crime," focuses specifically on Algeria and the Global South. Her chapter highlights the significance of cultural and religious difference in examining infanticide and mothers who kill. Analysing the representation of motherhood and termination of pregnancy in Algerian author Assia Djebar's earliest literary work *La Soif* (1957), Rocca investigates the question of abortion through cultural, gender-political, moral and religious perspectives, demonstrating how Global South women remain oppressed, isolated and unheard, and highlighting the complex politics of representing motherhood and abortion in such contexts.

Trudier Harris's chapter, "Image Shatterer: Delores Phillips's *The Darkest Child*", focuses on Delores Phillips's only published novel, *The Darkest Child*, which has been overlooked by critics and scholars, and Harris investigates possible reasons for this. She argues that historical and folk traditions have mostly romanticized the relationships between African American mothers and their children, and that the primary defining feature of African American mothers is their willingness to sacrifice their physical and mental health for their children. However, Delores Phillips's *The Darkest Child* (2004) is an anomaly among these texts, as it portrays a monstrous and violent mother who does not fit neatly into existing categories and perceptions.

In "Smother Love: Maternal Filicide in Veronique Olmi's *Beside the Sea*," Amy B. Hagenrater-Gooding analyzes French author Veronique Olmi's 2001 novel, *Beside the Sea*. By focusing on a story of filicide, this acclaimed novel examines the script of societal expectations of how a lone mother should act versus how a mother performs in reality. For Hagenrater-Gooding, examining the intersection of real and fictional mothers promotes understanding of the power of the image of the ideal mother. She suggests that we must take in the whole narrative and process the entirety of the mother's story. Instead, in her analysis of Olmi's novel, Hagenraater-Gooding highlights the complexity of motherhood through the consideration of fallibility, conflict and responsibility. Her chapter persuasively argues that we should all care enough about the future to want to improve it.

Anne McGee's chapter, "From Murderous Monster to Loving Mother: Reconsidering and Rewriting the Legend of La Llorona in Children's Literature and Film," explores the trope of the Weeping or

Wailing Woman as one of the key representations of Mexican maternity. La Llorona is traditionally represented in both Mexican and Chicane cultural production as a woman who kills her own children, yet as McGee shows, there are alternative Llorona narratives in Mexican and Chicano folklore that have been silenced by patriarchal society. Her important retrieval of these narratives adds significant fresh insight on this topic.

Finally, Charlotte Beyer examines the representation of filicide in crime fiction in her chapter, "'I Never Made Those Marks on My Girl': Challenging Cultural Narratives about Mothers Who Kill in Sara Paretsky's Crime Novel *Brush Back*." Beyer examines the representation of this crime from a feminist perspective and argues that crime fiction has the capacity to represent maternal perspectives with complexity, but fairly and empathetically. Paretsky's novel offers a key case study of the capacity of crime fiction to confront cultural narratives through its challenging of popular and literary stereotypes of mothers who kill their children. *Brush Back* shows instead how maternal crime is shaped and defined by inequalities of class, race/ethnicity, religion, and social and cultural deprivation.

Given that crimes of violence, particularly murder, are seldom perpetrated by women, it is not surprising that when mothers commit murder "they attract more media and public attention, the image created of them is more powerful, and they leave a more long-lasting impression" (Jewkes 134). Taken together, the chapters in this book provide detailed insight into the representations, cases and policies that govern the treatment of mothers, as well as challenging their outcomes and portrayals. This opportunity to place mothers at the centre of the account is the key dimension that has often been missing from representations of mothers who kill their children. The studies provided in this book offer an opportunity to scrutinise important debates around the representation of mothers who kill, including the issue of how to restore justice for victims from the perspective of mothers, thus considering hitherto overlooked aspects of filicide. This book also underscores the clear need for developing new methodologies as well as further intersectional analyses and representations of this complex topic. It is clear from the material presented in this book that creative, fictional, as well historical and legal examinations of maternal filicide help increase understanding of the topic. With this book, it is our aim to generate further debate, research, academic study, and various forms of creative engagement concerning infanticide and mothers who kill.

Works Cited

Alt, Betty L., and Sandra K. Wells. *When Caregivers Kill: Understanding Child Murder by Parents and Other Guardians*. Rowman & Littlefield Publishers, 2010.

Anand, Sanjeev. "Rationalizing Infanticide: A Medico-Legal Assessment of the Criminal Code's Child Homicide Offence." *Alberta Law Review*, vol. 47, no. 3, 2010, pp. 705-728.

Chesney Lind, Meda. "Feminist Criminology in an Era of Misogyny." *Criminology*, vol. 58, no. 3, 2020, pp. 407-22.

Franks, Rachel. "True Crime: The Regular Reinvention of a Genre." *Journal of Asia-Pacific Pop Culture*, vol. 1, no. 2, 2016, pp. 239-54.

Friedman, Susan Hatters, James Cavney, and Phillip J. Resnick. "Mothers Who Kill: Evolutionary Underpinnings and Infanticide Law." *Behavioral Sciences and the Law*, vol. 30, no.5, 2012, pp. 585-97.

Jewkes, Yvonne. *Media and Crime*, 3rd ed. SAGE, 2015.

Kumari, Arunima, Wangshitula Longchar, and Parul Saini. "Female Foeticide, Infanticide and Girl Child Trafficking–Challenges and Strategies to Overcome." *Journal of Health Science*, vol, 7, 2019, pp. 110-14.

Mair, Scott. "Challenging Infanticide: Why Section 233 of Canada's Criminal Code Is Unconstitutional." *Manitoba Law Journal*, vol. 41, no. 3, 2018, pp. 241-80.

Marcikić, Mladen, et al. "Infanticide in Eastern Croatia." *Collegium Antropologicum*, vol. 30, no. 2, 2006, pp. 437-42.

Matias, T., F. H. Dominski, and D. F. Marks. "Human Needs in COVID-19 Isolation." *Journal of Health Psychology*, vol 25, no. 7, 2020, pp. 871–882. Print.

Morrison, Toni. *Beloved*. Plume, 1988.

Murley, Jean. *The Rise of True Crime: 20th-Century Murder and American Popular Culture*. ABC-CLIO, 2008.

Mushumba, H., et al. "Trends and Patterns of Suspected Infanticide Cases Autopsied at the Kacyiru hospital, Rwanda: A Case Report."

Rwanda Medical Journal, vol 73, no. 3, 2016, pp. 21-23.

Myftari, Kreshnik, and Gentian Vyshka. "Mission Impossible: Upholding Successfully a Charge of Infanticide in the Albanian Legal Practice." *Journal of Medical Ethics and History of Medicine,* vol. 7, no. 3, 2014, pp. 1-4.

Peterman, A., A. Potts, and M. O'Donnell, et al. "Pandemics and Violence against Women and Children." *Center for Global Development,* Working Paper 528, April 2020, iawmh.org/wp-content/uploads/2020/04/pandemics-and-vawg-april2.pdf. Accessed 6 Nov. 2021.

Poteyeva, Margarita, and Margaret Leigey. "An Examination of the Mental Health and Negative Life Events of Women Who Killed Their Children." *Social Sciences,* vol. 7, no. 9, 2018, pp. 168-184.

Rautelin, Mona. "Female Serial Killers in the Early Modern Age? Recurrent Infanticide in Finland 1750–1896." *The History of the Family* 18, no. 3, 2013, pp. 349-70.

Razali, Salmi, Jane Fisher, and Maggie Kirkman. "'Nobody Came to Help': Interviews With Women Convicted of Filicide in Malaysia." *Archives of Women's Mental Health,* vol. 22, no.1, 2019, pp. 151-58.

Spinelli, Margaret G. "Infanticide: Contrasting Views." *Archives of Women's Mental Health,* vol. 8, no. 1, 2005, pp. 15-24.

Spencer, Brittany, and Sally Pit. "Lawyers Recommend Prison for Woman Who Killed 3 of Her Newborn Babies." *CBC News,* 30 Sept. 2019, www.cbc.ca/news/canada/prince-edward-island/peiinfanticide-shannon-rayner-sentencing-hearing-1.5302454. Accessed 6 Nov. 2021.

Stangle, Heather L. "Murderous Madonna: Femininity, Violence, and the Myth of Postpartum Mental Disorder in Cases of Maternal Infanticide and Filicide." *William and Mary Law Review,* vol. 50, no. 2, 2009, pp. 699-734.

Thompson, Emily G. *Unsolved Child Murders: Eighteen American Cases, 1956-1998.* Exposit Books, 2017.

Stevens, Geert Philip. "A Mother's Love? Postpartum Disorders, the DSM-5 and Criminal Responsibility–A South African Medicolegal Perspective." *Psychiatry, Psychology and Law,* vol. 25, no. 2, 2018, pp. 186-96.

Tang, Dorothy, and Bonnie Siu. "Maternal Infanticide and Filicide in a Psychiatric Custodial Institution in Hong Kong." *East Asian Archives of Psychiatry*, vol. 28, no. 4, 2018, pp. 139-43.

Toebes, Brigit. "Sex Selection under International Human Rights Law." *Medical Law International*, vol 9, no. 3, 2008, pp. 197-225.

Vickery, Michelle, and Edwin Van Teijlingen. "Female infanticide in India and its relevance to Nepal." *Journal of Manmohan Memorial Institute of Health Sciences*, vol. 3, no. 1, 2017, pp. 79-85.

Yasumi, K., and J. Kageyama. "Filicide and Fatal Abuse in Japan, 1994–2005: Temporal Trends and Regional Distribution." *Journal of Forensic Legal Medicine*, vol. 16, no. 2, 2009, pp. 70-75.

Part I
Creative Explorations

Chapter 1

Hopes and Dreams

Chevelle Malcolm

As I was writing this poem, I imagined a mother in anguish over the thought that her child, like her, would be forced into slavery, a system that only recognized her as property and essentially void of humanity. As she looked at her child and saw in the child the epitome of innocence, hope, and freedom, a direct contrast to a future in slavery, she decided that the only way to preserve her child's innocence was to ensure that she never knew the horrors of being in captivity, both physically and metaphorically. From this enslaved mother's perspective, being in captivity limits one's ability to move; in addition, it distorts the carefree nature of one's hopes and dreams, an essential part of being human.

Freedom.
My hope,
My little dream,
Twinkle, twinkle, little star.
Those tiny hands and brown eyes like gravity,
Twinkle, twinkle, little star.
Those tiny hands and that sunshine smile,
My hope,
My little dream,
These shackles will never know you.

Oh, tiny hands!
Oh, tiny feet!
Innocent,
These shackles will never hold you.
As I heard your first cry,
As I clasped your tiny hands with mine,
As your bright eyes searched my soul,
As your warm smile beckoned for hope,
As I clasped your tiny hands with mine
I decided,
My hope, my little dream,
These shackles will never hold you.

I'd rather,
I'd rather you find a space to shine in the night's sky,
I'd rather,
I'd rather you find a space at heaven's table,
I'd rather,
I'd rather these shackles never know you.
I'd rather you be branded by your shine in the night's sky,
Twinkle, twinkle, little star.

As I made your bed in the deep blue sea, I hoped that freedom would find you,
I dreamt that you would shine,
Twinkle, twinkle, little star.
As I laid you to rest in the open arms of the ocean, I hoped that you would find a brighter life,
I dreamt that you would shine,
Twinkle, twinkle, little star.

Oh, tiny hands!
Oh, tiny feet!
Precious.
Oh, innocent and sweet soul,
Oh, innocent and sweet soul, forgive me
But these shackles will never taint you.
My hope,
My little dream,
How I wonder, would you shine for me?

Chapter 2

baby girl // medea

Amy Lynne Hill

I am using neither the Greek, nor the Latin, nor the French, nor the German Medea. This work here and in this form is my own.

Dramatis Personae

Eudora | Nanny to Medea
Carson | Babysitter to Medea's children
Baby Girl | Medea
Al-Anon Group | Chorus of Defeated Creek Women
Jason | Jason
O'Conner | Pastor, Defeated Creek Baptist Church
Ambrosia | Pastor's Daughter
Elvis, Scarlett | Children of Medea

A Note on Staging

Defeated Creek is a lush, green oasis in the foothills 100 miles outside a booming Southern metropolis. The yards of Defeated Creek are an appropriate balance of neat and overgrown, with just a hint of whimsy, neglect, and despair. While the pastor's house, a lovely A-frame wood cabin with picture windows, is surrounded by a white picket fence and overlooks the lake, the other houses, many either doublewides on cement foundations or well-loved old farm homes, are dotted among the forested hills of the small unincorporated township. Like many old forgotten and wayward communities in the South, there is no proper town center, just an old brick city hall, the church with its modest white steeple, a general store popular with tourists driving through, and a Waffle House adjacent to a family owned gas station at the interstate exit. ACT I

Eudora stands alone in the backyard of an average home in Defeated Creek in the late afternoon.

Eudora   I've been with this foolish child for too many years and taught her too damn well to see her go this cuckoo for a man without even the sense God gave a drowning goose. I've followed her stupid, lovesick ass all the way here to Hicksville just to watch him follow his pecker to the first patch of unshaved pubis he'd yet to comb his dirty, cheating fingers through. After all she's done for him, after all the kin she's lost—her daddy, her brother, both dead. Burnt up with all their worldly belongings, not even her Great-Granny's mink fur coat left to her name. And for what? So Jason and those friggin' Argos could score some more dadgummed dope.

And that sonofabitch dragged us here, said it would be for the best. Swore he was done running with those damnable turds, swore he was clean, swore the last detox stuck, he just needed somewhere quiet, somewhere safe. Somewhere they don't know us. A fresh start, he said. More like a fresh pile of steaming bullcrap. I know for a fact he's stopped going to group, claims he's repented instead. Says he's confessed his sins, seen the error of his ways, he doesn't need help, just the Lord Almighty, and that friggin' Pastor is eatin' Jason's righteous lies right up out the hand that was just coochie-deep in his precious little daughter. No sir, that pastor is so convinced of his own glory, bestowed to him by God himself, that he can't smell the fish through the shit.

And where does that leave us? What about me, my baby girl Medea, and her babies? Those precious babies whose momma can't even look at them no more, whose daddy can't stop fucking and praying to an empty sky long enough to teach his children the dadgummed alphabet or how to tie their little shoes. Praise be they ain't nursing anymore. I don't know what I'd do if I had to coax milk from Medea now. She's so dried up—no milk, no love, nothing left in her at all, 'cept that rage I never could tame out of her.

Eudora collapses like a snipped marionette onto an ancient swinging bench. She swings a few beats as the fight and breath seem to leave her frail body.

That temper, oh God, my baby girl's temper. Not even her momma could calm that girl down when she'd decided on fighting the world around her. And now here we are, all decisions made for her already, death decided for her daddy and brother, Jason decided for his new piece of ass, these dumb friggin' hicks decided for the pastor's new prodigy, and nothing left at all for my baby girl to decide on, except for that fearsome loathing of a woman left alone with nothing but her own despair and the hateful ignorance of a bunch of God-fearing rednecks.

Carson and the children enter from the woods behind the house. Eudora stops swinging.

And oh Jesus, those babies. They ain't never seen a place so beautiful. They spend their days fishing for crawdads in cool creeks, swimming at the shore of the lake, sucking on fresh dewy honeysuckle. I'm too damned rickety to be out in those woods, but I pick the ticks off their wriggly little bodies every night before bed, and I see how they're darker now than they've ever been, looking more like Medea than they ever have, and their dumb gummy smiles and big golden eyes stare back up at me, and I think to myself, if there is a God who cares, he cares for these babies, who don't understand their momma's pain or their pigheaded daddy's moods, and when I tuck their little warm honey bodies into bed at night, I roll my eyes up to whoever listens to tired old women in the dark, and I pray that they wake up happy and that my baby girl wakes up at all.

Eudora turns to smile at the children as they approach with Carson; her short blonde hair is hidden under a ratty snapback, a bag of dead crawfish in her hand.

Carson   Lord, Eudora, you goin' crazy? Out here talking to yerself after only a few weeks among us poor country folk? I see how it is. None of us are good enough for you and your highness, huh? Where is she, by the way? She don't need you to wipe her royal ass for her right this second?

Eudora   You hush your mouth, Carson. You know what's got my blood up, and you know it ain't just Medea. These damn hicks don't have nothing better to do than sit around the fellowship hall gossiping. What? They think just 'cause she comes from money she's the devil? Or let me guess, they don't know what to do with all this melanin running in their hills all the sudden?

Carson   Aw, hell, Eudora, why you always gotta make such a big deal outta everything? They're poor, not dumb, and they ain't all the incorrigible racists you think they are.

Eudora   Incorrigible, oh my, what a big word; don't go getting it get stuck in your mouth like that snuff you think I don't see stuffed there in your lip.

Carson spits.

You're such a barbarian.

Carson   Fine, be like that, you salty old hag. Go on, kids, go on in the house. Take these to your momma, bet she ain't never seen nothin' like 'em before.

Elvis and Scarlett take the bag of crawfish carcasses inside. Carson waits until they're inside to speak.

Now, see, I had planned on telling you what I heard down at the Waffle House this morning, but you're being so damned sour. I don't think I will.

Immediately on edge, Eudora lifts her body from the swing to face Carson, as if ready to take a swing at her instead.

Eudora	Don't you play me like this, Carson. Don't you dare. I don't have any patience for no more friggin' nonsense than what I'm already putting up with. Now either you tell what you came here to tell me, or you can leave right now, and you can bet your ass you won't see one pretty penny of all that rich-city-folk money you and all these rednecks seem to hate as much as you need.
Carson	Alright, alright. Point taken.

Carson spits.

Now listen, I was at the WaHo this morning gettin' bait when I heard O'Conner's yard boy runnin' his mouth about the baptism planned for this weekend. Apparently, they're bringin' the whole congregation down to the lake, and O'Conner's gonna dunk Jason right there for the whole town to see. It's all anyone can talk about, and apparently, the only way Jason done convinced the old man to do it is by promisin' he'd get your girl to leave town an' "go back where she came from."

Carson rolls her eyes skywards, and Eudora's body stiffens.

He's got the whole lot of 'em convinced Medea's the reason Jason turned to the bottle and was runnin' dope, and that if he wants to be fully reborn, she's gotta get gone. Too much of that old evil spirit trying to drag him back down, s'what O'Conner says.

Carson spits again.
Eudora blanches and throws her hands in the air.

Eudora	Of course! Of friggin' course. As if things weren't already shitty enough. Now what are we supposed to do? The only reason we even came to this God forsaken waste of space was to get away from all that ailed us, and now here we are, thicker in it than we ever were before. And what about the babies? Huh, what does your Christian love say about abandoning children?

Carson	Well, now, Eudora, you see, that's where things get complicated.
Eudora	What the hell you call all this, Carson, if not complicated already?
Carson	Jason wants to keep the kids. Says he wants to be the father to Elvis and Scarlett he never could be before. Says he's turned over a new leaf and he's ready to raise them in the church, like he should have all along.

Carson speaks with air quotes, and Eudora stares before laughing, wiping tears from her eyes.

Eudora	That dumbass ain't ever stepped foot in a church before we came here, except maybe to steal from the collection plate. What a bunch of bull. And what about a momma? How's he plan on raisin' those babies without Medea?
Carson	Well, he wasn't planning on doing it by hisself, is what I heard. 'Parently he wants to set up house with Ambrosia. Give those kids a proper momma, one who'll hug 'em and kiss him, sing 'em bedtime stories and the like.
Eudora	Fan-friggin-tastic. How's that girl supposed to raise babies when she ain't but a child herself? From what I hear, she just finished school last year and now what—she thinks just 'cause Jason's taught her how to lay with a man, she's ready to take on the world and raise a real woman's children? She ought to be ashamed of her damned self.
Carson	I don't exactly disagree with you, Eudora, but what the hell did you expect to happen once O'Conner found those two fools in bed together, naked as the day they first sinned? He had to make it all proper somehow and looks like betrothin' 'em was the only way he saw fit. Besides, it ain't like Medea's winning any mother of the year awards as it is.
Eudora	Carson, I swear to God, if you say one more word against my baby girl, they'll be fishing your dead 'n bloated body out the lake when they baptize that fool Jason.

Carson	Jesus an' Mary, woman. I didn't do nothing but speak the truth. When's the last time she even touched those kids? Tucked 'em in at night, fixed 'em breakfast in the morning, huh? You tell me, when she ever show an ounce of love to them babies?
Eudora	What love does your fool ass think she has left to give, after all that's been done to her?
	I fear for her, Carson, and I fear for those babies. If you're only half as sensible as I think you are, you'll take them now, and you'll keep them from her. You hear me, Carson? You protect them best you can, however you have to.

Eudora wrings her aged boney hands and takes a step towards the house, Carson following her as she does.

Carson	From what, Eudora? Protect them from what?

Medea enters from the house, carefully but absentmindedly twisting her hair into a single, thick braid.

Medea	Thought I heard your dulcet tones, Carson. Only you would deem it appropriate to send my children to me bearing miniscule corpses.

Carson grins. Spits. Tips her hat playfully.

Carson	You didn't like the gift, I take it?

Finished with her braid, Medea steps closer to Carson. She flicks the rim of her baseball cap.

Medea	It had a certain charm to it, I must admit. Now, why are you still here? Shouldn't you be in town with the others, lighting the torches with which you aim on chasing me out of town?
Carson	Christ, Medea. Forget to take your meds today or something?

Medea smiles, still looking at her hands.

Medea	Or something.

Carson	Fine, message received. I was just about to show the kids how to hunt for mushrooms anyway.
Medea	Wonderful. Don't forget to demonstrate the side effects of the poisonous ones on yourself, will you?

Carson rolls her eyes. Spits.

Carson	Goodbye, you crazy, evil witch.

Carson calls for the children. They emerge, laughing, from the house. Carson leads them back into the woods, Medea waving her fingers coyly after them. She turns to Eudora.

Medea	Well there's nothing for it, I suppose.
Eudora	For what? Your plan to make everyone in this town think the absolute worst of you, even the one person who's shown us any sort of kindness?
Medea	So you call what Carson does to me at night now that Jason's gone "a kindness"?

Medea quirks her lips and flips her braid.

Eudora	No, I call that another stupid friggin' mistake on your part. Think, girl. Think.

Eudora steps up to Medea and flicks her forehead.

These people already believe it was you who got your daddy and brother killed in that fire. They don't know that it was Jason's dumb drunk ass who fell asleep on the couch with a lit friggin' cigarette. They don't know the only reason the Argos were even in the house that night was to steal that damned mink coat just so they could go chasin' another high. All they know is you let him in, and now that pastor has them all believin' you're the dark temptress who damned him to sex, drugs, and God only knows what else because you were too stupid in love to let Jason take the fall when the police came calling. Now here you are, acting like those babies don't need you, like nobody's gonna bat an eye when they find out what you're

	really doin' with the woman watchin' them little ones now that I can't? Baby girl, didn't I raise you better than to fuck where you shit? Didn't I do better than this?
Medea	You mean shit where I eat? Besides, Nanny, what you did or didn't do doesn't matter now.
Eudora	Well then, tell me, baby girl. What matters?

Medea is silent. She brings a shaking hand to her face and wipes at delicate hairs of her forehead. Eudora waits. Medea takes a deep breath, lowers her hands to her sides, and squares her shoulders.

Medea	What matters is that Jason has a lovely new bride-to-be, and what kind of respectable woman would I be if I didn't personally congratulate the happy couple on their engagement? And you know, Nanny, it would be simply indecent if I dared show my face without a proper gift. Just because we're forced to make do here in dear Defeated Creek doesn't mean it's acceptable to let the proper etiquette slip.

Medea exits back in to the house.

Eudora	God damn you, Medea. Damn that fool Jason, that stupid girl Ambrosia, that witless old O'Conner, this trash town full of trash people. Damn them all, and damn you, and God damn me, Medea, if ever I did doubt that creeping, filthy sickness I felt come up over me when they sliced that first baby out of you. Let me burn eternal if I tried to numb that pain when the hurt seeped in my bones the first time I heard your baby cry, and cry and cry, and you, baby girl—you sat there. You let that itty-bitty thing wail himself to sleep, and wail himself awake, and wail himself hungry until I just couldn't take it. I pumped that sweetness from your breast myself. I took that baby in my arms and I fed him, just as I fed you.
	And you, baby girl. You, Medea. You slept, for days and days and days, until I wondered if you'd ever wake again. I wondered what land you'd gone to, what place you'd found for yourself where maybe Jason loved you, where

maybe your momma stayed, and maybe she taught you how to hold a hissing, fussing little monster to your teat until he latched and suckled and you felt not empty but full, full of love for that little human made from your own guts. But, you, Medea, you slept.

And when you finally, finally woke and let me take your milk, and give it to that hungry little boy, you turned your back, Medea. You washed your hair, rouged your cheeks, and wet your lips, and you went to Jason. You wouldn't take a bottle in your own hand, but you coaxed one from his and led his rotten mouth to your body, let his nasty love slip right back inside you, and before that first baby shed his first teething tear, you were already full up with the next baby. And you, Medea—You. Mother?

No, Medea.

God damn you, Medea, and God damn me, Medea, if ever I did doubt the mean whispers of the wicked furies when they decide to snatch an angry, aching woman with child.

Eudora exits, shaking her head.

ACT II

Medea enters the church and encounters a group of women gathered in the parlour. A sign on the door reads "Al-Anon, Friday Friends group. Support group for friends and family of problem drinkers." The women talk and chatter among themselves but go silent when Medea enters.

Medea, dressed elegantly in a seafoam green pantsuit, her hands clutching a neatly wrapped garment box, attempts to walk past the women, but they stop her.

Chorus   We see you, Medea.

Medea   Yes, you do. And?

Chorus   We see you, and we know you.

Medea   Well now, that, I highly doubt.

Chorus	Girl, please. Do you really think we're all so naïve? We know women like you. We've heard your cries and lamentations, and we've suffered the same joyless misfortunes: We know what it means when he says he's serious this time, when he promises he won't do it again, not another drop, no ma'am, it's different now, hand to God. Don't you trust me, baby? It was just a few beers. How many? What you mean how many? Well hell, how should I know? Aw, sugar, don't be like that. Come on, sweetheart, let me make it better.
	Any of that sound familiar? We know bull when we see a steer, and we know addiction when it's steering a man wrong. It's all over your man Jason, and not even a bath in the tears of the Lord himself will wash away those sins. Jesus turned water in to wine, girl, not the other way around.
Medea	If that's the case, then please, do enlighten me: How did I end up here, in this church, looking for the girl about to marry the father of my children? What have I done to be cast in this role, the homewrecker without a home, the mistress to her own man, the skeleton in a closet already full of broken bones? I knew Jason when he was just a stupid boy, when he made mistakes, not choices, and bed girls, not women. I took it upon myself to take him not just on but in me. I taught him how to live in polite company, introduced him to fine things, nice things you don't just trade for pills. I cleaned him up. I made him into a man. I gave him children. They call him daddy. And what does he call me now?
Chorus	Sin.
Medea	One night. One last night with those foul-mouthed hooligans, his damned precious Argos. One night is all it took for everything to burn. And he got what he wanted, and my father, and my brother, they got one last night, too. A final night, a final breath, a final resting place for the burnt ash and brittle bone Jason left for me to sweep up after him, as always. What then did I have left? If you

	know me, then you tell me what choice I had than to follow him here, to a place where Medea was not Medea and Jason was not Jason. Of course, now I know how foolish I was. We will never escape the ugly inevitability of Jason and Medea, Medea and Jason. And now Medea is just Medea, and Jason is no longer Jason, oh no. Jason has repented, and he's to be reborn. And Medea? Who is she?
Chorus	She is a mother.
Medea	Medea? A mother? To whom? To the children who look nothing like her? To the children whose tanned, freckled faces and curly amber hair look not at all like the black hair on her brown head? Haven't you heard? Apparently, Medea is just the nanny to those children she bore, those children who ripped her, made her sag, sucked her dry, left her empty. Mother to those children whose father made her fatherless, whose daddy burned her brother? No, that is not Medea.
Chorus	She is a lover.
Medea	Who does Medea love? That despicable man and his wilting tenderness, or is it his back she loves? She sees it often enough. What about that new wickedness gracing her bed, who charms her children when the sun shines, and then her thighs when the moon glows? Must we be so trite as to so easily conflate lust with love? Or does Medea love that nanny who worries alone in the dark and weeps over little babies at night when she thinks her lady is sleeping? What about those beloved men, the ones Jason took from her? Can Medea love what wasn't even left to rot?
Chorus	She is a survivor.
Medea	A survivor? Of what? Of Jason and his stinking breath? Of her children and their clawing cries? Or perhaps of that fire that exiled her here or of the people here who, in the privacy of their homes and depravity of their minds, call her names they would never dare let pass their lovely Leviticus lips?

Chorus	She is a woman.
Medea	Is that not precisely my point?

The parlour falls to silence.

Chorus	Then why are you here?
Medea	I only wish to do the right thing. Where is the lovely lady of the hour?
Chorus	Who are we then to stop you, but women ourselves? You'll find Ambrosia in the sanctuary. We wish you well, Medea. We hope to see you next Friday. We'll be here when you're ready to admit and accept the power of your powerlessness.
Medea	All that I accept is that which I have been given: To be Medea.

Medea exits the parlour and goes to Ambrosia in the sanctuary. The girl rises with a perky smile.

Ambrosia	Medea! Hi! Medea. Medea—oh, what a beautiful name and so fun to say: Medea! Does it mean anything?
Medea	Woman spurned.
Ambrosia	Really? That's not very romantic.
Medea	No, not really.
Ambrosia	Oh. Well, now surely it means something! Or comes from somewhere? It's so exotic!
Medea	Is there a point to this line of questioning, or was there just some air in your lungs that needed out?

Ambrosia giggles, taking a step closer. She reaches out to touch Medea's hair.

Ambrosia	And your hair, oh gosh, Medea! Oh! It's so soft! Like cotton. I wasn't expecting that!
Medea	Cotton? Like the cotton of your Walmart Fruit-of-the-Loom panties? Or like the raw, unprocessed cotton your great-granddaddy's slaves picked? Child, do you ever think before you speak?

Ambrosia	Oh hush! You and your city girl manners, Medea, you ought to know better than to speak of such things! If Daddy were here, he'd say that's too much scandal for the daylight. Speak of the devil—Daddy!

O'Conner enters from a door off to the side of the sanctuary.

O'Conner	This is a place of worship, girls, not idle chatter.
Medea	Of course, sir. I was just here to offer my congratulations to your daughter. And Jason, of course. Here, a token of my affection. Every bride needs something borrowed, but don't worry, love, I don't expect this back any time soon.

Medea presents the wrapped box to the girl.
Ambrosia unwraps the paper and gleefully
lifts a wispy veil woven of fine silk lace out of the box.

Ambrosia	Oh, Medea! That's just too kind! Oh, look, Daddy! It's so beautiful! I've never felt anything so delicate in my whole life!

Medea smiles.

Medea	It was my mother's. One of the only things we managed to save in the fire. I'd planned on wearing it on my wedding day, but now—well. It always was destined for Jason's bride, and who am I to fight the fates?
O'Conner	That's awfully generous of a woman in your position, Medea. Ambrosia, honey. Go see to it that you put that somewhere safe. Run along now.

The girl, still clutching the veil and gently rubbing the soft silk to her cheek, turns to leave with a serene smile on her face. Alone in the sanctuary, Medea and the Pastor turn to face one another.

My daughter may be too sweet and simple for this world, but I've seen enough, even in this small town, of the bitter sacraments women like you are forced to swallow. I've seen the scowling rage of all the women like you for all the Jasons of this earth, and I've come to expect the stealthy poison of your words, not the gracious gifts your hands

	have offered today. I don't trust a lioness who demurs like a lamb.
Medea	And this is why you want me gone? Please. I don't trust a donkey who brays like a stallion.
O'Conner	You think I want you near my daughter, with the illness of your will, or near Jason, with the hostility of your whims, tempting him away from the gospel he so clearly needs to heal his misguided soul?
Medea	You think me, Medea, to be the reason his liver fails, his skin yellows, and his veins collapse?
O'Conner	Who else is there?
Medea	His name is Jason. And the children—what about them? You wish me banished, but the children you'll allow to stay?
O'Conner	Those children are an abomination.
Medea	Because they were born out of wedlock? Or because they're mine?
O'Conner	Those children are an abomination, but my daughter has taken to them and wishes to save them and raise them as her own in the Lord's house.
Medea	And who are you to deny your daughter? Tell me, though, old man: What would you have done if they hadn't taken after Jason? If they weren't fair like you and yours, if their tan didn't fade with the summer sun?
O'Conner	I'm sure I don't know what you mean.
Medea	Of course you don't, you dirty old creon. As long as they can pass as Ambrosia's, what does it matter to you who falls in your wake?
O'Conner	What did you dare call me?
Medea	King doesn't suit you?
O'Conner	We are in his Kingdom, not mine, and you're trespassing regardless of who reigns here. Jason is to be baptized on Sunday, and he and my daughter will marry at the altar in one week's time. You have seven days, Medea, to make

	peace with your children and their father and be gone. This is the kindness I extend to you. Don't make me regret it.
Medea	It's not my aim to spit in the face of kindness.
O'Conner	So you'll leave?
Medea	I'll do what's right.
O'Conner	I'm glad to hear that, girl. Very glad, indeed. Now, if you'll excuse me. I've got preparations to attend to, as do you, I'm sure. Goodbye, Medea. May peace be with you.
Medea	And peace be with you as well, old man. Lord knows you'll be needing it soon enough.

INTERLUDE I

Medea lays in bed and watches Carson as she dresses in the early morning light.

Carson	You goin' today?
Medea	Now why on earth would I do that?
Carson	Who knows, maybe O'Conner'll miscalculate, hold Jason under for too long. Or better yet—maybe the lake's been infested with piranhas! They'll nibble his ass right up.
Medea	That's awfully sweet of you, but we both know the chances of that happening are about as likely as Jason crawling back to me on his knees and begging for forgiveness. Besides, one taste of his unsavory unmentionables, and the fish will be asking for their own baptism.
Carson	Well if you're not going, the kids should at least. He may be one of the dumbest wastes of space on God's green earth, but Jason's still their daddy. On the off chance that he's serious about all this, they should be there for him.
Medea	Yes, we wouldn't want to deprive Jason of his fatherhood, now would we?
Carson	Hush, you witch. Want me to take 'em?

Medea	No, that won't be necessary. Nanny can do it. She says she won't believe all this foolishness is actually happening unless she sees it with her own two eyes. Now shoo, if you're to make it home and shower before the blessed event, then you need to not be here very soon. Unless you plan on taking a holy splash today, too?
Carson	Nah, I'll leave the watersports up to the men.

She returns to the bed to give Medea a lingering kiss goodbye and then quietly retreats. After some time, Medea rises, dresses in a white robe, and goes to join Eudora in the kitchen.

Eudora	Why're you awake at this wretched hour? I know you don't plan on watchin' this dumpster fire today.
Medea	No, I'm awake at this wretched hour because Carson didn't let me sleep one wink last night. Sinning is hard work, haven't you heard?
Eudora	It is far too early in the fucking morning to be hearing about your sex life, baby girl.
Medea	Would you rather hear the word of God? Because if you don't leave soon, you're going to miss it.
Eudora	Are the babies ready?
Medea	Almost. Carson's stopping by to pick them up later.
Eudora	I suppose that's for the best. They've grown wild in these woods. I can hardly keep up with them anymore.
Medea	You can hardly keep up me.
Eudora	Ain't that the gospel truth. Alright, baby girl, I'm gone. Stay out of trouble. I know it feels like your bosom friend these days, but don't let that mean melancholy hug you too close.
Medea	I won't, Nanny. You worry too much.
Eudora	Nah, I reckon I don't worry enough.

Eudora shakes her head, kisses Medea's cheeks, and then shuffles out the door.

Medea watches her leave and then goes to the kitchen. She pulls out oats, berries, yogurt, sausages, eggs, milk, cheese, and tomatoes. She whisks the eggs lazily in an old wooden bowl and prepares a large breakfast over the miniature flames of the ancient gas stove. She sets the table, carefully arranging each piece of silverware with her long, graceful fingers.

As a finishing touch, she sprinkles finely diced wild mushrooms, precisely portioned, atop the children's eggs.

Medea   Come, babies. It's time to eat.

ACT THREE

The evening sun is warm and pink in the sky, and Medea sits at the base of the tallest tree in the yard as dragonflies dance around her. The sound of a truck's squealing tires echoes across the lonely yard, followed by the slamming of metal, and Jason emerges around the side of the house.

Jason   You fuckin' bitch.

Medea   Hello to you, too, sweetheart.

Jason   Don't give me that shit, Medea. This is you. I know it is.

Medea   Yes, this is me. Very astute observation, dear.

Jason   You!—I just can't with you anymore!

Medea   Use your words, honey.

Jason   I know I ain't done right by you, but she was innocent! She never crossed you once in her life, and now she's laid up in the ICU—she just stopped breathing, just like that, out of nowhere, and her face, oh Christ, her face—I've never seen a thing like it my whole life, and the doctors, they said—And O'Conner, he's all but dead of a broken heart already. His only daughter, Medea. His only child, how could you do such an ugly, evil thing?

Medea   I assume you're rambling about that vile girl, Ambrosia. How, indeed.

Jason   She's not a girl. She's the woman I was set to marry, and you knew that, and now you've good as killed her!

Medea	If she's a woman it's only because you made her so.
Jason	Are you out of your damned mind? How can you sit there calm as can fuckin' be and act like you didn't just take a girl's life, just because I couldn't stand to be with you anymore!
Medea	Oh, so she's a girl now?
Jason	You're crazy! How did I never see it before? You're absolutely fucking crazy! And to think, I actually thought I loved you, I gave you children, I—The kids. Medea. Tell me right now—where are my children?
Medea	Oh yes, that's right. Rumour has it your new goal in life is to be a father. In his name, and what not.
Jason	God damn it all, Medea. I already am a father. I'm Daddy to those two babies you never could be Momma to. I'm not stupid, Medea. You think I don't know what Eudora did? How she kept them alive when you couldn't even bathe yourself, wouldn't eat a thing, just completely checked out? You think it was easy for me to see that? Why do you think I couldn't stay clean, Medea? You think I didn't want to? Hell, Medea, all I wanted was you, and a family, with you, but you weren't there. You were just—gone.
	So yeah, I fucked up. I did a lot of stupid shit, and I know I never did do right by you, and I know I did you a world of hurt when you were already hurtin', but I am sorry, Medea. I am. I am sorry for every sin I ever committed with, for, and against you, and I'll be sorry for the rest of my damned life now. You've made sure of that by hurting Ambrosia like you did. And if she lives, I'll spend every last day of my life apologizing to you however you see fit— so you answer me right fucking now, Medea: Where are they?
Medea	They're safe.
Jason	What does that mean, safe? Where are they? Elvis! Scarlett!
Medea	They're inside, but don't worry, they can't hear you.

Jason	What do you mean? Where are they?
Medea	You really should work on your attention span, sugar. I already told you—they're safe, probably for the first time in their lives. I've protected them from you. From you and from me. I did it to keep them safe from Jason and Medea.

Understanding slowly stretches across Jason's features. He runs into the house while Medea lounges against the tree. His pained wailing echoes from the house, and he returns to the yard.

Jason	Oh, God. Oh, Christ. You're their mother, Medea! What have you done, Medea?
Medea	Only what I said I would.
Jason	God damn you, Medea. Just do it, then! Just kill me! That's what you want isn't it? And if not, then at the very least, after all the unspeakable evil you've already done, you can spare me this one kindness?
Medea	I'm afraid you're mistaken.
Jason	Please, Medea, please! Just kill me!

Medea stands.

Medea	No! If I have to live, then so do you!
Jason	And who says you do?
Medea	Didn't you know, Jason? That's how the story always ends.
Jason	I'll kill you with my bare hands!
Medea	No, you won't. What would your God say then?

Jason drops to his knees. His head hangs.

Jason	You're insane!
Medea	I'm a woman.
Jason	You're evil!
Medea	I'm human.
Jason	You're a murderer!
Medea	I am Medea.

The End

Afterword

Since first being recorded for the ages by Euripides in 431 BC, the myth of Medea, the prototypical mother who kills, has both enraged and enthralled audiences. Medea is half goddess and half mortal woman, the princess of a foreign barbarian king who sacrifices her home and kin, even murdering her own brother, in order to help Jason, leader of the Argonauts, steal the Golden Fleece. After they flee to Corinth and Jason spurns her for a Corinthian princess, Medea murders the children she bore Jason, a revengeful act so terrible it obscures all her other crimes, including killing her own uncle as well as the woman she was jilted for, among many others.

The myth of Medea was poorly received by ancient audiences, but due in part to its early feminist themes has nonetheless gone on to be adopted and adapted into the cultural consciousness of many Western European societies, where she has found a special home in German literature. From Friedrich Maximilian Klinger and Franz Grillparzer in the eighteenth and nineteenth centuries, to Christa Wolf and Dea Loher in the twentieth century, the figure of Medea has been written into German literature as a figure onto which debates surrounding, for example, otherness, feminism, and postcolonialism can be projected and thematized. Yet no matter what each author's vision brings to the myth of Medea and regardless of how they portray the marriage of Jason and Medea, one thing never changes: The children always die.

This creative project is an homage to, reflection on, and adaptation of the Medea myth as it has been conceptualized in German literature, as executed by myself, a Southern American Germanist. Through a close reading of the key Medea texts in the German context, I have written a stage play of the Medea myth that borrows structural features of the German tradition in order to adapt Medea from the ancient Greek to the contemporary American South. My dramatis personae is a call back to the Euripides myth, as are two of the critical feminist aspects of my play: the opening monologue by the nanny Eudora, much like the original nurse's opening speech, as well as the modern-day chorus of women in the form of an Al-Anon support group. From the start, female voices have resonated throughout the Medea myth, and I honour this as well in my own work. Much later, at the end of the eighteenth century, Klinger critically claims *Medea in Korinth* as not the French or Greek adaptation but rather his own unique one, thereby invoking the intertextuality of the myth as it had developed through the centuries with his opening statement. This too I have done with my own work, which in its intertextuality draws a key characteristic from Grillparzer's Medea trilogy, published in the first quarter of the nineteenth century: in his adaptation, Grillparzer calls into question the very nature of the drama by including elaborate stage directions, at once making the world rich and steeped in detail, yet impossible to bring to the stage as imagined. I borrow this approach to stage directions to highlight the precarious role of place in the Medea myth. He additionally overtly others Medea as not just an outsider but a woman of colour, as do other later adaptations, including my own.

Later, in 1996, Christa Wolf created one of the better known contemporary adaptations of Medea in her novel *Medea: Stimmen (Medea: Voices)*, which tells the story of Medea through the inner thoughts of the protagonists in chapters that alternate point of view. Wolf also critically investigates underlying motives in the tragedy, troubling the idea that Medea only murdered her children out of vengeance. I wished to further trouble this tradition in my own adaptation with the suggestion that Medea was suffering from postpartum depression and there was more to her motives for murder than meet the eye. Then in 1999, Dea Loher brought Medea to America in the absurdist drama *Manhattan Medea*, which inspired me to bring Medea down south in order to explore how the particular setting of the American South would create conflict for Medea and her biracial children. Finally, like others before me, I made my own contribution to the intertextual myth of Medea: in transforming the original role of Tutor to Medea's children in the Euripides drama into the role of Carson, a masc-presenting gender queer character with whom Medea has an affair, I offer readers a glimpse at a Medea capable of something like affection and further trouble Medea's status as the Other.

Equal parts academic reflection and creative expression, this drama once again submits Medea to her inescapable fate: mythical murdering mother.

Works Cited

Euripides. *Euripides: Cyclops, Alcestis, Medea*. Translated by David Kovacs. Harvard University Press, 1994.

Grillparzer, Franz. *Medea: Trauerspiel in fünf Aufzügen*. P. Reclam, 1994.

Klinger, Friedrich Maximilian, et al. *Medea in Korinth; Medea Auf Dem Kaukasos ; Aristodymos*. Walter De Gruyter, 2012.

Loher, Dea. *Manhattan-Medea*. Verlag der Autoren, 2015.

Müller, Heiner. *Verkommenes Ufer, Medeamaterial, Landschaft mit Argonauten*. Editions Phi, 1988.

Wolf, Christa, and Sonja Hilzinger. *Medea: Stimmen: Roman*. Suhrkamp, 2010.

Chapter 3

So Sing! Sister Hildegard of Bingen Comforts Marijoy

Josephine Savarese

> Don't let yourself forget ...
> God's grace rewards not only those who never slip,
> but also those who bend and fall. So sing!
> —Hildegard of Bingen, Christian Mystic[1]

Water Broke (After the Evening Shift Restocking Shelves)[2]

Marijoy, collapsed,
Relieved to feel cool
Bathtub against
      her back,
Marijoy, gasped
Purplish, bloody blue/round ball
Cradled in vernix,
Baby held to chest for
      one breath, one *shudder.*
umbilical cord cut

Shrouded remains
Encased in plastic
for disposal.
    Marijoy, held her breath,
    while the world divided into miniscule planets,
    each one a fiery ball, hurling sparks at her soft, cowering body.
    Observed scowling angels overhead,
    moving to the discordant symphony
    notes repeated in her bloodied mind.

1. While Sister Hildegard Sings Encouragement

Marijoy Tells Her Story:
I was in a dream like state during the "commission of the offence"
Glance at the Sun, Marijoy

They said I acted:
    Contrary to Section 243, Disposing of the Dead Body
    With the intent to conceal the fact I was delivered of it.
Behold the Moon and Stars

Did not know I was pregnant
Now, think.

Shock when I woke up, did not know how to react,
All of creation is a song to the praise of God

During the birth, things were unreal
God hugs you.

They called it: "depersonalization and derealization"
A nightmare or a dream
You are encircled by....

Cried throughout the two hour interview
Especially when describing the birth.
And the blue aftermath, when
I buried Baby
in a waste bin.

> *...God's*
> *mystery.*

2. Hildegard Offers Healing

Sets out three cups
    For tansy tea.
Bends to wash
    Marijoy's scalded feet.
The remains gleam
Underneath a burning orange tree.
Douses the frightened earth
    With parsley wine.
Chants the world's glory,
In every glistening note.

3. Marijoy Joins the Ceremony

Scalded mouth
Silently murmuring
Prayers in Tagalog.
Recites Hildegard:
You're a World,
Everything is Hidden
in you.

Feet move slowly
To the mourning *hum*
Of harpsichords
Strung by white moths.

My Flesh Held Joy[3]

Like the dew that
falls on the grass.

Greenness poured
Into me and grew.

Hildegard offers:

Forgiveness

Hides my shame
Among her trees.

My new song rooted

In Hildegard's forest.

Endnotes

1. Quotes by Hildegard of Bingen, https://healthyhildegard.com/hildegard-bingen-quotes/
2. The details are drawn from *R v Geraldizo,* 2016 BCPC 484 (CanLII).
3. Passages from Hildegard of Bingen quoted in Bruce Wood Holsinger, "The Flesh of the Voice: Embodiment and the Homoerotics of Devotion in the Music of Hildegard of Bingen (1098-1179)." *Signs: Journal of Women in Culture and Society* 19.1 (1993): 92-125.

Works Cited

"Hildegard of Bingen Quotes." Hildegard of Bingen, 2020, healthyhildegard.com/hildegard-bingen-quotes. Accessed 7 Nov. 2021.

Holsinger, Bruce Wood. "The Flesh of the Voice: Embodiment and the Homoerotics of Devotion in the Music of Hildegard of Bingen (1098-1179)." *Signs: Journal of Women in Culture and Society,* vol. 19, no. 1, 1993, pp. 92-125.

R v Geraldizo, 2016 BCPC 484 (CanLII).

Part II

Legal Perspectives Now and Silenced Histories

Chapter 4

"I Wasn't Normal" Reading Illegibility into Canadian Infanticide Law, a Wild Reading

Josephine L. Savarese

> Through readings that attend to the wild desires driving our true attempts to know anything at all about the world, scholars might begin to reread and represent humanity as profoundly dependent on our felt response to others and objects – a humanity that acknowledges its debt to "this madness" that guides our deeply affected thinking and being with others in the world.
> —Mishra Tarc "Wild Reading" 549

Opening

Dr. Karen Brennan, a senior lecturer in law at the University of Essex, has summarized sentencing practices in infanticide prosecutions. In *Murderous Mothers & Gentle Judges: Paternalism, Patriarchy, and Infanticide*, Brennan presents the "first critical study" of Irish sentencing judgments involving women convicted under the Infanticide Act 1949 between 1950 and 1975, a time when Ireland was a "deeply conservative and patriarchal society" (140). The women were typically granted noncustodial sentences rather than terms of imprisonment. However, Brennan questioned the interests that even these more lenient sanctions served. In her conclusion, she notes that "mercy"—whether it was attributed to "gender constructions" that examined femininized ideals or owing to "paternalism"— affirmed patriarchy rather than freeing women from oppression (185).

Brennan reasons that the courts in Ireland and elsewhere would better serve public interests by being transparent about "the structural causes of crime," which she identifies as "gender inequality and the denial of reproductive autonomy" (142). Brennan identifies positive outcomes that would result from her recommendations: "[They] would provide a more honest account of the reasons for mitigation, and possibly help shift focus away from placing the blame for infanticide solely on individual women and towards recognizing the contribution of socio-political inequality to the offense" (142).

In this chapter, I explore whether this approach might advance women's rights and work to prevent infanticide. I investigate whether similar arguments might be made regarding infanticide decisions in Canada by investigating a recent case, *R. v. Borowiec* (2016). The *Borowiec* case is significant because the Supreme Court of Canada provided clarification on the legal meaning of "her mind is then disturbed," a phrase not specifically defined in Section 233 or clarified in prior judgements. Infanticide convictions are often lauded because they result in more lenient treatment than would result from murder conviction. However, I describe the law as an illustration of the reach of the carceral state. Rather than benevolent, the shortened custodial or community sentences that the women prosecuted for infanticide tend to receive are part of the racialized, class-based, and punishment-oriented system rooted in colonialism and accomplished through the continued occupation of Indigenous land (Shahshahani and Kates).

This chapter addresses ways that the criminal law threatens certain communities at the intersections of race, gender, and class. During the contemporary period characterized by a global pandemic, societal breakdown, protests, reactions to the devaluing of lives—particularly Black and Indigenous lives—and the resulting openings for change, scholars and activists like prominent Black feminist, sociologist, and lawyer, Dorothy Roberts are encouraging us to take up the "urgent social justice issues" related to "policing, family regulation, science, medicine, and biopolitics" (Haymarket Books). Rather than a text offering clarity on the infanticide law and its socio-legal implications, I read the Supreme Court of Canada's infanticide decision through a lens of illegibility or madness, what Mishra Tarc calls a "wild reading" (537-52). She defines this qualitative method as one that engages the "promiscuous aspects of human existence and difference" ("Wild Reading" 537). Tarc draws from poststructural, decolonial, and psycho-analytic theories as well as literature, including Coetzee's 2003 short story "The Humanities in Africa," to remind us that "wild reading" is insufficiently acknowledged in "ordinary and scholarly interpretive practice" (539). This includes the interpretative practices adopted in the cases and legal forums that this chapter analyzes in relation to Canadian infanticide law's more clinical, individualized focus on the mental disturbance that propels the offence. Writing with Tarc, this chapter moves away from sensemaking regarding infanticide and the level or type of mental disturbance that is required for a conviction.

The facts of the few reported cases are troubling, varied, and complex. Many feminist legal advocates, including Rosanna Langer, have convincingly argued that what is commonly deemed a mental disturbance in an individual woman may in fact be interpreted as a response to oppressive gendered conditions. The factors underlying a mental disturbance may even be attributable to other reasons indecipherable by judicial reasoning (358-88). While acknowledging that cases of infanticide are often deeply troubling and tragic, this chapter suggests that the crime of infanticide is a warning sign that signals to social inequities that lead to the over-prosecution of marginalized women more generally. With Elizabeth Rapaport, I argue against "our excessive preoccupation with female deviance" (530). This chapter reasons that we need to recognize "other causes of child homicide," which are deeper and more structural, thereby realizing the overall aims of developing successful prevention policies and equitable criminal law responses (Rapaport 530).

Borowiec at the Supreme Court of Canada

At trial, Meredith Katharine Borowiec was convicted of two counts of infanticide and acquitted of two counts of second-degree murder. Crown appeals against the trial results were unsuccessful at the Alberta Court of Appeal and at the Supreme Court of Canada. Reporters described the decision as "the first time that the highest court has examined Canada's infanticide law" (Grant, "Infanticide"). This legal consideration was "something [the Supreme Court] had declined to do in past cases" (Grant, "Infanticide").

Borowiec's statement that she was not "normal" when the offences occurred supported the finding she was mentally destabilized (Graveland, "'I Wasn't Normal'"). The Attorney General of Alberta was unsympathetic to her plight and asked the Supreme Court to rule that the "vague" and "outdated" law left "too much room for new mothers to kill their babies, no matter their moral culpability" (Grant, "Meredith Borowiec"). The Crown argued that the ordinary stresses experienced by all mothers of newborns could provide a defence to more culpable forms of homicide. While affirming Ms. Borowiec's acquittal, the Supreme Court of Canada denounced the crime, noting that infanticide law was "a particularly dark corner of the criminal law" (par. 1).

Intervenors presented a range of views to the court. A feminist advocacy organization, the Women's Legal Education and Action Fund (LEAF), favoured the reduced penalty tied to the infanticide charge. Rather than an affront to newborns, the offence of infanticide, which carries a maximum sentence of five years imprisonment, ensured "the complex interaction of social, economic, psychological, biological, and cultural factors" that influence the mental state of the very small number of women who kill their newly born children was considered during the prosecution (Women's Legal Education and Action Fund, par. 12).

LEAF argued that the section on infanticide aided women in achieving substantive equality (par. 1). It was justified by Parliament's aim of creating a "flexible legal standard that accounts or the diverse array of factors—medical, social and economic—that may arise upon birth and/or lactation" (par. 2). The section appropriately recognized diminished blameworthiness as well as the uniquely gendered context of the offence. The Criminal Lawyers' Association of Ontario, another intervenor, argued for a review of the infanticide law by Parliament, if necessary, rather than by a panel of justices (Criminal Lawyers' Association of Ontario, par. 2).

A Wild Reading

This chapter is inspired by Tarc's argument that the less predictable qualities that emerge through "a wild reading" are foreclosed by "established research methods and representations" ("Wild Reading" 537). To illustrate her points, Tarc explores the maternal-infant relationship, an example directly relevant to this chapter. She relies on the "not known of knowledge" within "the unconscious time of the maternal relation"—a time when the infant is required to "wildly and without symbolic resources make sense of others and the world around her" ("Wild Reading" 537).

Notably, Tarc cites Toni Morrison's acclaimed novel *Beloved* in later writing (Tarc, "Literacy"). *Beloved* is used to illustrate ways that language education and acquisition are projects informed by hidden texts of colonial power and privilege. In *Beloved*, the ghost baby killed by the mother, Sethe, serves as the symbolic representation of the inner wounds, outrage, and desolation wrought by slavery. As Tarc reasons in "*Literacy of the Other*," reclaiming the self through renarration is the way to "repair and renew representations that fail to do justice to our lives" (124). Tarc maintains that it is through "creative word work" that we can most ably perform the work of mourning ("Literacy" 124). Literary work can repair "meaning and renew significance, to remake out of the other's ruinous words a story of our own" ("Literacy" 124). Because Tarc aims to destabilize "dominant representations of human existence", her writing has importance for this chapter ("Wild Reading" 537). Tarc's encouragement to feminist researchers who adopt "unorthodox" methods to "commune with the less rational processes of thinking and being driving representation" was taken up ("Wild Reading" 537). Treating legal cases as a type of literature enables this chapter "to heed the creative and destructive potential of the wildness inherent in interpretive practice" while also promoting "ethical attentiveness to the lived realities" of subjugated persons, which might include mothers prosecuted for infanticide ("Wild Reading" 539).

While affirming feminist-oriented, intersectional arguments on the infanticide provision, I work to circumvent the more typical conversations favouring one of two solutions—either repealing the infanticide law or upholding it in its current form. This chapter expands on scholarship that analyzes the retributive features of Canadian infanticide law. Statements in *R v. Borowiec* (2015) are intriguing in what they reveal about the motivations for infanticide prosecutions. The Honourable Mr. Justice Côté and the Honourable Mr. Justice Mc Donald, justices with the Alberta Court of Appeal, upheld the convictions on infanticide. In support of their conclusion, they affirm the importance of the infanticide provision to facilitate convictions, thereby eliminating "outright acquittals, either directly or via fewer charges of infanticides" (par. 89).

Their assertion suggests that the infanticide section offers a way to avoid acquitting women given the preference for punishment. In its ruling, the Alberta Court of Appeal made further statements that are important in the context of this chapter, which seeks to understand the standard against which mothers are measured. As Dorothy Roberts and others have established, prosecutions of mothers involving their children, whether in the criminal or family regulation context, are informed by stereotypical ideals of good and bad mothers. In keeping with this view, the Alberta Court stated:

> The death of a child is always extremely upsetting and a difficult matter to adjudicate dispassionately, even for those who are engaged in the administration of criminal justice on a fulltime basis. Such cruel and unnatural acts are hard to comprehend, particularly when they are committed by the child's mother, whose instincts should be to protect and nurture. (R. v. Borowiec, 2015 ABCA 232 [CanLII], par. 52, quoting *R v Effert*, 2011 ABCA 134 at para 33)

Without diminishing the harm of infanticide, this chapter argues that alternative justice reforms through restorative justice, transformative justice, and community-based interventions offer a more satisfactory way to address these crimes. By exposing systemic harm that underpins women's offending, the complexity and horror that both accompany and tend to propel these deaths may be more adequately addressed.

Given the numerous reports documenting the rising number of women serving time in Canada's prisons and jails, particularly Indigenous women, the need to rethink the criminalization and demonization of women appears urgent. This is the case, even in the seemingly innocuous forms of carceral control—the relatively short sentences imposed following infanticide convictions. Radhe S. Hegde, a professor at New York University, has studied female infanticide in South India. She conducted interviews with women who had disposed of their newborn daughters. About infanticide, she states: "Only by interrupting the ideological logic that naturalizes violence can we begin to reclaim the marked bodies of women" (520). Her insights inform this chapter.

Although Canada is often praised for its role in promoting women's human rights, both domestically and internationally, its actual track record is often discriminatory and inequitable, particularly in relation to Indigenous women and others disciplined within the justice system. As part of this chapter's exercise in reading wildly, I argue that although the criminalization of infanticidal mothers is softer, with shorter prison sentences accompanied by probation, as seen in *Borowiec*, it perpetuates stereotypes informed by colonialism and patriarchy. The infanticide section criminalizing women's marginality is part of the embedded logics of punishment. These logics are most evident in relation to Indigenous women and women of colour, who disproportionately bear the brunt of carceral oversight and state regulation (Savarese; Park). In her seminal 1993 text, *Motherhood and Crime*, Roberts states: "We must condemn mothers' violence against their children. However, their violence may force us to confront the complexity of women's subordination and the radical measures we must take to eradicate it" (141). This text acknowledges women's violence while calling for a reconsideration of criminal justice beyond the binary of punishment and leniency, which often appears in infanticide discussions.

In "Languages of Injustice: The Culture of 'Prize-Giving' and Information Gathering on Female Infanticide in Nineteenth-Century India," Padma Anagol helps identify the retributive tendencies that we might look for in Canadian law (429-445). She writes that attempts to raise public awareness on infanticide through essay contests, while seemingly "gentle and persuasive" techniques, were "actually quite violent in gendering the practice of female infanticide" (442). The outcome was that the focus shifted from "a community-specific 'custom' of female infanticide" where 'heads of households' were accountable to a characterization of female infanticide as a crime "committed by women (principally mothers and midwives)" (442).

While located in a different context and time period, Anagol's writing aids in this skeptical read of Canadian infanticide law. In a 2002 text, Anagol describes how the imposition of colonial law in India displaced traditional legal systems such as caste courts and village councils, meaning that women were judged by an impersonal system with limited knowledge of local practices ("The Emergence" 73). I assert similar findings in the Canadian context where colonial legal systems displaced Indigenous justice mechanisms and law, leading to a current crisis in over-incarceration, particularly among Indigenous women.

Background Facts in *Borowiec*

According to the case facts, the accused, Meredith Katharine Borowiec, was originally charged with second-degree murder in 2010 after the baby she gave birth to was rescued from a trash bin. A bystander heard whimpers and contacted emergency personnel. In a sad twist of fate, one of the persons who discovered the disregarded infant was the newborn's biological father. When the support persons arrived, they observed Meredith Borowiec sitting close by, wrapped in a blanket stained in blood. Under police questioning, Ms. Borowiec revealed she had disposed of two other infants in the same way, leading to further charges. Unlike the baby discovered in 2010, which survived, the remains of the newborns delivered in 2008 and 2009 were never discovered.

Concerning the last pregnancy, Borowiec informed law enforcement officers that she was unaware she was pregnant and that "she never wanted to hurt the baby" (R v Borowiec, 2015 ABCA 232 (CanLII), par. 9). She reported being "terrified" and feeling as though she "could not control anything." She was disassociated and unaware of her thoughts. She wished things "were different" (ABCA, par. 9). Several minutes of the original interview in 2011 with Detective Karka Malsam-Dudar, then a Calgary law enforcement officer, are available on YouTube (*Calgary Herald*).

Borowiec made a further statement when she was sentenced. Tearing up, she expressed remorse for her actions. In her statement, she read that it hurt her daily reflecting on her actions. She commented that she accepted what happened and felt "horrible about it all." (Slade, "Crown") She also said that she could not "express in words" her level of sorrow (Slade "Crown"). Justice Peter McIntryre, the sentencing judge, described the case as "terrible", as one where the woman "shocked the community" and "shamed" herself (Slade, "Crown"). Ultimately, he rejected the Crown's calls for a custodial sentence of eight or nine years, favouring a sentence of eighteen more months in addition to the eighteen months served while waiting for trial combined with three years of probation (Slade, "Crown").

The convictions for the lesser offences of infanticide turned on the finding that Ms. Borowiec was in a confused state of mind at the time of the births. According to the Supreme Court, the word "disturbance" was to be given its "grammatical" and "ordinary" meaning, determined by *The Oxford English Dictionary* (2nd ed. 1989), given it was not a legal term of art (par. 19). Accordingly, the judges held that the defence was not required to prove the presence of a mental disorder or a specific mental illness. The Crown was unsuccessful at all court levels in arguing for Borowiec's legal culpability to the level of murder.

The expert witness testimony at the trial from Dr. Smith on Borowiec's experience of depersonalization was deemed sufficient. Dr. Smith examined hospital records and police statements in addition to interviewing Ms. Boroweic for seven hours in 2013 before the trial. In her view, the respondent had low self-esteem and avoided facing difficult decisions. Dr. Smith confirmed that the respondent's descriptions of "not being in control, not being normal, being unable to think clearly and observing from outside her body" aligned with depersonalization, confirming her mind was disturbed in the required manner (ABCA par.14). The births caused high levels of panic and anxiety, which fostered the depersonalization and subsequent abandonments (ABCA par. 14). The lower appeal court held that Borowiec was "operating in a sort of individualized pocket of unreality that persisted in the period shortly following the births" (ABCA par. 75).

Debating the Meaning of Mental Disturbance

At the Supreme Court hearing, Ms. Borowiec's legal counsel recommmended a less restrictive interpretation of the infanticide section. The defence counsel opposed the Crown's view that the trial ruling, which convicted Ms. Borowiec of the lesser infanticide offense, was unwarranted, thereby opening "floodgates" and operating to "disparage" the lives of the individuals "that were taken" (Respondent's factum par. 17). The Crown argued that a limited interpretation was warranted by what was labeled as a shift in "modern societal values" and a discernment that the infanticide label was only rarely justified. According to defence counsel, the Crown's plea to the Court's "moral and legal obligation" to reject an expansive view of infanticide was ill founded (Respondent's factum par. 4). In the legal documents filed with the Supreme Court of Canada, Ms. Borowiec's counsel described infanticide and neonaticide as part of the "human condition" (Respondent's factum par. 66). Although times had changed and women's circumstances had improved, with fewer neonaticides, counsel for Borowiec stated that "prototypical offenders, of which the Respondent is the most recent, are and probably always will be amongst us" (Respondent's factum par. 66). In making this pronouncement, counsel for Borowiec seems to be reminding us that eradicating infanticide is unlikely, especially given the inequities that tend to drive the commission of the offence. Meredith Borowiec's frailties are those of the typical infanticidal mother in that they included mental health concerns and the lack of social support.

The Canadian Provision on Infanticide

On July 9, 1892, the first Criminal Code of Canada received royal assent and later came into force on July 1, 1893. Notably, this code, which was enacted by the governing settlers, included culpable homicides as wrongful behaviour that could be publicly prosecuted. Although criminal law textbooks typically cite this information as neutral, the move away from the more wholistic approaches to wrongdoing characteristic of the Indigenous legal systems that were displaced is a subject pertinent to critiques of infanticide law. As Indigenous scholars have pointed out, the *Criminal Code's* implementation supplanted the varied justice practices that maintained peace and order in Indigenous communities (Mandamin, et al.).

The administration of justice in Indigenous communities was eroded by the affirmation of colonial law. The limitations of the Western justice system inform this analysis of the criminalization on infanticidal mothers. In contrast to Western legal systems, Indigenous laws and practices adopted a "more flexible response to misconduct, and reliance on the local community" (Mandamin, et al. 8) Indigenous councils determined remedies in the absence of codified rules (Mandamin, et al.).

More recently, scholars have pointed out that restorative oriented justice was a characteristic of the Indigenous justice systems, which many are seeking to revitalize (Mandamin, et al.). In the infanticide context, particularly noting Anagol's work in India, I argue for a restorative approach to allow cases to be adjudicated outside of the formal justice system. Alternative models might promote individualized assessments focused on healing and harmonization as well as community involvement in the woman's reintegration.

R. v. Coombs (2003): The Prosecution of an Indigenous Offender

Importantly, the only reported case involving infanticide located involving an Indigenous woman, *R. v. Coombs* (2003), resulted in a conviction for the more serious crime of manslaughter. The *Coombs* case is often cited in cases including *Borowiec* as part of the infanticide jurisprudence. Krystal Ann Coombs was sentenced as though her crime were one of infanticide. The case seems to illustrate the differing treatment granted to racialized offenders in the family law context, as written about by Dorothy Roberts.

After the trial, Krystal Ann Coombs's attempts to attribute the fatality to her partner's actions were unsuccessful. Ultimately, she was convicted of manslaughter for the death of her ten-week-old baby daughter, Hazel Ann, who died from her injuries after being shaken vigorously and thrown against a wall. Although Coombs was convicted of the more serious offence, the sentencing decision uses the infanticide standards as a reference. Coombs's diminished responsibility for the crime and the time spent in custody during the prosecution justified relying on the infanticide sentencing guidelines. Considering the time already served, the court imposed a briefer period of custody followed by a term of probation.

Importantly, the court stated that Krystal Ann Coombs was entitled to sentencing treatment in accordance with her status as an Indigenous person given that she was Métis. The court recognized this fact even though it also noted that Ms. Coombs had not been part of a cultural Métis community. The child's father, Michael Krywohyza, was also

Métis. Beyond this acknowledgment, the court does not engage in any analysis on the historical trauma of Métis communities, nor does it address how hardship might have informed the offence.

The treatment of Krystal Coombs, an Indigenous offender convicted of an infanticide related offence, offers a useful comparator. The more punitive approach taken in her case is noteworthy given that Ms. Coombs did not, in contrast to Borowiec, cause multiple infant deaths. According to the general criminal law, her actions are less serious, although the physical injuries inflicted are alarming. In addition, Coombs was just over eighteen years old when Hazel Ann died. Krystal experienced physical problems after the birth and required a dilation and curettage. She suffered from addictions and was in a violent relationship.

In a 2004 decision that reviewed the conditions of Coombs's probation, the judge noted that Ms. Coombs was a "young, new, and first-time mother, with no extended family support but with institutional support" (par. 14). She had been placed in state care at a young age and "had been a ward of the state through her teenage years" (par. 14). Coombs was described as "an admitted drug addict", albeit one without a criminal record for crimes of violence (par. 14). On the day of Hazel Ann's death, Coombs had smoked several marijuana joints and had consumed a considerable quantity of alcohol, followed by a heated argument with the baby's father.

Given her period of pretrial custody, it was determined that Coombs had served a sentence of about four years, which was considered an appropriate sanction for the infant death. The relatively harsher treatment afforded to Ms. Coombs is noteworthy, given that racialized injustice in Canada is a pressing consideration. In the decision, the Honourable Madam Justice J.B. Veit described Krystal Ann Coombs in ways that stress her incorrigibility, descriptions that align with typical depictions of Indigenous mothers (Savarese). Coomb's prior criminal record was cited with disapproval and used to "rebut the presumption of good character" at the time her ten-week-old daughter, Hazel Ann, was killed (2003 ABQB par. 41).

The Infanticide Law and Women's Criminalization

The main points of the law have been carefully reviewed elsewhere. Consequently, this section points out a few brief highlights.[1] Canada enacted the infanticide provision in 1948 due to problems obtaining convictions, a challenge that mirrored the reticence observed in the United Kingdom. Canadian juries hesitated to cast mothers as murderers, particularly since many were young, emotionally distressed, and in severe social and economic circumstances at the time of the homicide. In Canada, like the United Kingdom, the death penalty was the required sentence for all murders in 1948, thus the consequences were significant for even sympathetic defendants, like distraught young mothers (Mitchell).

The current infanticide section reflects the series of amendments described elsewhere. The prohibited behaviour and mental elements of infanticide are described in what is now Section 233 of the Criminal Code, RSC. 1985, c. C-46. The section states that the application of the provision is limited to a "female person" who engages in either a "wilful act" or an "omission" that results in the death of a "newly-born child." At the time of the act or omission, it must be established that the accused was not "fully recovered from the effects of giving birth to the child" (Section 233). The accused must be suffering from a mind that is "then disturbed" in the aftermath of the birth or as a result of "the effect of lactation consequent on the birth of the child her mind is then disturbed" (Section 233).

Methodology: A Wild Reading

In this text, I question and work to destabilize the Supreme Court's findings on mental disturbance. Tarc's "wild reading" offers a methodology that moves analysis beyond more predictable frames to attend to the urgent project of renarrating the infanticidal mother beyond the stereotypes of the bad or deviant mother, the mad or psychotic mother, or the sad or depressed mother, as described in earlier texts (Appignanesi).

With statements like these in mind, I engage in a close and wild read of *Borowiec* to disrupt the supposed clarification of the mental disturbance needed to support an infanticide conviction and its direction on infanticide law, more generally.

Making Space for the Wild Horse in Us

As the summaries stated, opinions on infanticide law are varied and largely incompatible, even irreconcilable. Tarc reimagines societal institutions, namely education. When she cites Derrida's writings and his suggestions that we "begin the difficult and complex task of re-envisioning an altered humanism," she offers instructions for this chapter and its quest to reimagine the infanticidal mother. Tarc calls for "a humanism founded on the call of the Other" (Tarc, "Education as Humanism" 833). This revitalized humanism would be realized in such institutional sites as education, whereas the goal of this chapter is to reconsider the administration of justice.

She praises what she labels "an incredible insight" made by Derrida (Tarc, "Wild Reading" 537). In an interview conducted by François Ewald, Derrida shared his understanding that an individual's "reasonable means of faithfully representing the world defend against unfathomable dimensions of human thought and action" (qtd. in Tarc 537). Tarc highlights Derrida's realization that what Virginia Woolf labels "the wild horse in us" is renounced when the scientific methods underlying normative humanistic inquiries are adopted as tools for knowing the world (qtd. in Tarc 537). Derrida's reasoning has insights for this chapter, given that we are invited to consider ways to reinvent terminology, including infanticide. As Tarc points out, Derrida recommends that we engage in work without any reassurance yet with "an ethic of the other" that aims towards "the invention of a language that does not make the other suffer" (548). This new language should disrupt or deconstruct "the folly of interpreting the other's existence through the very objective and scientific modes of thought that, in the first place, over-determine, subjugate, injure, and eviscerate her humanity" (548). These lessons offer insight on infanticide law and our persistence in probing the mind of the accused to impose a certain sense making on her reasoning and level of disturbance.

In *"Mother of Sorrows": Post-Partum Mental Disorder and the Law across Five Jurisdictions*, Langer offers an alternative reading of infanticide law. Langer examines cases from five common law jurisdictions—namely Canada, the United States, the United Kingdom, Australia, and New Zealand—where mothers were showing signs of mental distress due to postpartum factors or owing to "desperate social and economic circumstances" (358). Langer analyzes unsettling cases and the challenges that the erratic behaviour by the accused presents for professionals trained in mental health and law. The cases are uneasy in their alignment with the criminal law doctrine of voluntariness. They defy more clinical assessments on physical and mental wellness as well as more standard determinations on appropriate sanctions. From the case analysis, Langer found that mental disorders following childbirth meet with "an ambivalent mix of compassion, dismissiveness and outrage" (538). She reasons that the disjointed social and legal responses to new mothers' mental states leaves women's actions and mental status open to narrow interpretations of what it means to be debilitated by mental illness. Furthermore, the prosecutions expose the women facing infanticide charges to the "narrative authority" of others—namely, experts and legal professionals—who control the women's stories, thereby limiting their ability to author their own accounts of wrongdoing and silencing their voices (360).

In her review, Langer discerns that "gendered assumptions about idealized motherhood" were influential in the cases (374). While these "sad and desperate actions" warranted a societal response, the case studies demonstrate "the idealization, social isolation, structural and institutional deficiencies that form the modern social context of mothering" (387). Treating depression as an individual pathology offers limited instruction on "intentionality and agency" (381). Furthermore, it diverts attention away from the necessity of improving community resources for mothers. As Langer points out, "sympathy, discretion, and the exercise of mercy" are capricious grounds for decision making, which often fail to offer reliable and just outcomes for the women prosecuted for this crime (381).

The Women's Legal Education and Action Fund and a Wild Reading

This alternative reading of infanticide resonates with the arguments presented by LEAF during the Supreme Court of Canada ruling. In their factum, they observed that the Crown's position for a narrow interpretation of the law was based on an "imagined flood of women who might otherwise invoke the infanticide defence" (par. 13). LEAF acknowledged that infanticide cases were rare. While an atypical crime, the motivations for enacting a section on infanticide remain "pressing social concerns" (par. 9). The wish to infuse "a compassionate understanding of the unique inequalities" experienced during pregnancy, childbirth, and childrearing were not outdated relics. In fact, this thinking corresponded with "contemporary social norms and values" irrespective of the appellant's claims. As LEAF states: "Women continue to disproportionately experience the negative effects of continuing inequality in relation to childbirth and child-rearing. Social, economic, cultural, psychological and biological factors intersect to cause some mothers of newly-born children to experience a disturbance of the mind" (par. 9).

Infanticide cases usually involve young women who are marginalized and socially isolated; they cause the death of their newborns in conditions that are often marked by desperation and tragedy. LEAF's observations have some application to the accused in the *Borowiec* case, given her relative youthfulness, gender, and mental health challenges.

"Sweep It Under the Carpet; It will Go Away"

In her statement to a Calgary police detective in 2011, Borowiec offered further details on her deterioration. She stated that she had always had low "self-esteem" and had "no self-worth." She felt she was a "terrible" person. The officer reassured her that she was a "beautiful young lady" who was "nice" and "articulate." The officer describer her upbringing as "crappy" and one in which she was taught to "sweep it under the carpet" with the hope that "it would go away" (qtd. in *Calgary Herald*). Regardless of Borowiec's revelations, the officer presses on to probe the other newborn abandonments, quickly switching from a reassuring to a more clinical, authoritative tone. When Meredith begins to tear up, stating that she knows she "is in a lot of trouble," the officer advises that they "get this over with today" and that they "get it all on the table" (qtd. in *Calgary Herald*).

A further example where a wild reading may be advantageous relates to a detail shared in news report in 2012. It was reported that Meredith Borowiec, who was then thirty-one, gave birth to a fourth baby known to be a boy while being held at the Southern Alberta Forensic Psychiatric Centre at the end of July in 2012. The baby was adopted. The father, whose identity was not disclosed, reported that he intended to fight for custody. The executive director of the Calgary

Elizabeth Fry Society, Barbara Hagen, urged readers not to reach conclusions too easily about Meredith's fourth pregnancy. Hagan stated that her "biggest hope" was that people "take a very long, deep breath" and that they "consider that this is something that they will never really know the truth about" (qtd. in CBC). In Barbara Hagan's view, there was "nothing to be gained in judgment." Hagan acknowledged that it was "human nature to want to make sense of a tragedy." She explained, however, that the *Borowiec* case was "an absolute tragedy on so many levels for so many people" (qtd. in CBC). In Hagan's advocacy for Meredith Borowiec, we might see an intuitive impulse to "reread and represent humanity as profoundly dependent on our felt response to others and objects" (Tarc, "Wild Reading", 549). Hagan's pleas seem to embody some of the wild reading that this chapter recommends as a starting point towards reclaiming the representation of the Other as an act of justice.

From the vantage point of this scholarship, and in this site of reimaging relations, the conversation with the police and the response to the fourth pregnancy present an opportunity to move into a different relational realm. It is suggested that we use these narrative opportunities to "forge a creative attendance to the madness of our methods for writing the self, other, and the world" (Tarc, "Wild Reading" 547). The view that attentive approaches offer "a means to repair the damage done through wild and potentially demeaning interpretations of the other's humanity" was accepted in this scholarship (547).

Conclusion

While supporting the retention of the infanticide provision as an interim measure, this text has argued for reformative and restorative oriented solutions beyond the current system of punishment and regulation, which seems to offer limited healing to women and communities; it forecloses spaces for mothers, however murderous, and others to grieve and commemorate the deceased infants and to comprehend their passing (Malacrida).

Throughout this text, I have challenged the logic of punishment. I proposed that we use this period of change, this broken moment of pain and possibility, to thoughtfully reimagine systems of justice through using the infanticide law as one example of the need for reform

(Benjamin and Roberts). In this vein, I have attempted to write in creative ways that reinterpret and challenge existing discourse on infanticide in ways that may align with the words of the lauded writer, scholar, and author of *Beloved*, , Toni Morrison, who wrote in 2015 the following: "I know the world is bruised and bleeding, and though it is important not to ignore its pain, it is also critical to refuse to succumb to its malevolence. Like failure, chaos contains information that can lead to knowledge—even wisdom. Like art" (qtd. in Tarc, "Engaging Texts Today" 37).

While critically analyzing the jurisprudence and commenting on the infanticide section in the criminal law, this chapter has also located concerns about infanticide within broader debates regarding criminal justice reform, women's criminalization, and abolitionist advocacy. This context is currently being urgently vocalized as the world faces a global pandemic. Furthermore, this chapter argued for measures to address the systemic racism embedded in criminal justice systems and issued a call to end colonial regimes and their violent practices, propelled by capitalism, racism, and heteropatriarchy (Benjamin and Roberts). It was argued that social justice oriented preventive strategies could address the systemic injuries, which manifest in forms of individual violence, including infanticide.

Endnotes

1. As the Supreme Court of Canada stated in its decision in its 2016 Borowiec decision, the background details on the infanticide provision were summarized by the only other appellate decision on infanticide, R. v. L.B., 2011 ONCA 153, 274 O.A.C. 365, leave to appeal refused, [2011] 4 S.C.R (par. 12).

Works Cited

Anagol, Padma. "The Emergence of the Female Criminal in India: Infanticide and Survival under the Raj." *History Workshop Journal*, vol. 53, no. 1, March 2002, pp. 73-93.

Anagol, Padma. "Languages of Injustice: The Culture of 'Prize-Giving' and Information Gathering on Female Infanticide in Nineteenth-Century India." *Cultural and Social History*, vol. 14, no. 4, 2017, pp. 429-445.

Appignanesi, Lisa. *Mad, Bad and Sad: A History of Women and the Mind Doctors from 1800 to the Present*. Hachette UK, 2011.

Attorney General of Alberta. "Factum of the Appellant." *Supreme Court of Canada,* www.scc-csc.ca/WebDocuments-DocumentsWeb/36585/FM010_Appellant_Her-Majesty-the-Queen.pdf. Accessed 8 Nov. 2021.

Benjamin, Ruha, and Dorothy E. Roberts. Haymarket Books, "Policing Without the Police: Race, Technology and the New Jim Code", 8 July, 2020, climatechallenge.ca/events-campaign/policing-without-the-police-race-technology-and-the-new-jim-code/. Accessed 10 July 2020.

Brennan, Karen. "Murderous Mothers & Gentle Judges: Paternalism, Patriarchy, and Infanticide." *Yale Journal of Law and Feminism*, vol. 30, no. 3, 2018, pp. 139-96.

Brennan, Karen. "Social Norms and the Law in Responding to Infanticide." *Legal Studies,* vol. 38, no. 3, 2018, pp. 480-99.

Calgary Herald. "Meredith Borowiec Police Confession Tape." *YouTube*, 28 Feb. 2018, youtu.be/J84R2ue3L54. Accessed 8 Nov. 2021.

Canadian Broadcasting Corporation, "Mom Charged in Baby Deaths Gives Birth in Custody." *CBC News*, 30 Oct. 2012, www.cbc.ca/news/canada/calgary/mom-charged-in-baby-deaths-gives-birth-in-custody-1.1279319. Accessed 8 Nov. 2021.

Criminal Lawyer's Association of Canada. "Factum of the Intervener." *Supreme Court of Canada*, www.scc-csc.ca/WebDocuments-DocumentsWeb/36585/FM030_Intervener_Criminal-Lawyers-Association-Ontario.pdf. Accessed 8 Nov. 2021.

Grant, Meghan. "Meredith Borowiec Infanticide Appeal Heard by Supreme Court." *CBC News*, 20 Jan. 2016, www.cbc.ca/news/canada/calgary/meredith-borowiec-supreme-court-dumpster-babies-infanticide-1.3409214. Accessed 8 Nov. 2021.

Grant, Meghan. "Infanticide Convictions Upheld for Meredith Borowiec, Who Dropped 3 Babies in Dumpster." *CBC News*, 27 Mar. 2016, www.cbc.ca/news/canada/calgary/meredith-borowiec-supreme-court-infanticide-murder-1.3504383. Accessed 8 Nov. 2021.

Graveland, Bill. "'I Wasn't Normal:' Calgary Woman Guilty of Infanticide in Deaths of Her Newborns." *The Canadian Press*, 26

Nov. 2013, www.macleans.ca/news/i-wasnt-normal-calgary-woman-guilty-of-infanticide-in-deaths-of-her-newborns. Accessed 8 Nov. 2021.

Graveland, Bill. "Meredith Borowiec, Mother Who Tossed Out Newborns, Gets 18 Months In Jail." *Huffington Post*, 29 Jan. 2014, www.huffingtonpost.ca/2014/01/29/meredith-borowiec-sentence_n_4690065.html. Accessed 8 Nov. 2021.

Hegde, R.S. "Marking Bodies, Reproducing Violence: A Feminist Reading of Female Infanticide in South India." *Violence Against Women*, vol. 5, no. 5, 1999, pp. 507-24.

Langer, Rosanna. "'Mother of Sorrows': Post-Partum Mental Disorder and the Law across Five Jurisdictions." *Psychiatry, Psychology and Law*, vol. 3, no. 19, 2012, pp. 358-88.

Malacrida, Claudia. *Mourning the Dreams: How Parents Create Meaning from Miscarriage, Stillbirth, and Early Infant Death*. Routledge, 2016.

Mandamin, Leonard, Dennis Callihoo, Albert Angus, and Marion Buller, "The Criminal Code and Aboriginal People," *University of British Columbia Law Review*, vol. 26, Special Edition, 1992, pp. 5-40.

Mitchell, Teresa. "Infanticide: Such a Sad and Sorry Crime." *LawNow*, vol. 36, 2011, pp. 25-27.

Ottawa Agent for Counsel for the Respondent. "Factum for the Respondent, Meredith Borowiec." *Supreme Court of Canada*, www.scc-csc.ca/WebDocuments-DocumentsWeb/36585/FM020_Respondent_Meredith-Katharine-Borowiec.pdf. Accessed 8 Nov. 2021.

Park, Hijin. "Racialized Women, the Law and the Violence of White Settler Colonialism." *Feminist Legal Studies*, vol. 25, no. 3, 2017, pp. 267-90.

Rapaport, Elizabeth. "Mad Women and Desperate Girls: Infanticide and Child Murder in Law and Myth." *Fordham Urban Law Journal*, vol. 33, no. 2, 2005, ir.lawnet.fordham.edu/ulj/vol33/iss2/8/. Accessed 8 Nov. 2021.

Roberts, Dorothy E. *Killing the Black Body: Race, Reproduction, and the Meaning of Liberty*. Vintage, 1999.

Roberts, Dorothy E. "Motherhood and Crime." *Iowa Law Review*, vol. 79, no. 1, Oct. 1993, pp. 95-142.

Savarese, Josephine L. "Theorizing Soft Criminalization and Surveillance in the Saskatchewan Child Welfare System: Analyzing Re S.F." *Within Criminalized Mothers, Criminalizing Motherhood*, edited by J. Minaker and B. Hogeveen, Demeter Press, 2015, pp. 88-111.

Shahshahani, Azadeh, and Charlotte Kates. "How Settler States Use Incarceration as a Tool of Dehumanization During the COVID Crisis." *Canadian Dimension*. 10 July 2020, canadiandimension.com/articles/view/how-settler-colonial-states-use-incarceration-as-a-tool-of-dehumanization-during-the-covid-crisis. Accessed 8 Nov. 2021.

Slade, Daryl. "Crown Seeks New Murder Trial for Mom Found Guilty of Infanticide." *Calgary Herald*, 4 Dec. 2014, calgary herald.com/news/crime/crown-seeks-new-murder-trial-for-mom-found-guilty-of-infanticide. Accessed 14 July 2020.

Tarc, Aparna Mishra. "Education as Humanism of the Other." *Educational Philosophy and Theory*, vol. 37, no. 6, 2005, pp. 833-49.

Tarc, Aparna Mishra. "Engaging Texts Today or How to Read a Curriculum Poem." *Journal of Curriculum Theorizing*, vol. 35, no.1, 2020, pp. 32-45.

Tarc, Aparna Mishra. *Literacy of the other: Renarrating humanity.* State University of New York Press, 2015.

Tarc, Aparna Mishra. "Wild Reading: This Madness to Our Method." *International Journal of Qualitative Studies in Education*, vol. 26, no. 5, 2013, pp 537-52.

Women's Legal Education and Action Fund (LEAF). "Memorandum of Argument of the Intervenor, Women's Legal Education and Action Fund (LEAF)." *Supreme Court of Canada*, www.scc-csc.ca/Web Documents-DocumentsWeb/36585/FM040_Intervener_Womens-Legal-Education-Action-Fund.PDF. Accessed 8 Nov. 2021.

Cases Cited

R. v. Borowiec, 2016 SCC 11 (CanLII).

R. v. Borowiec, 2015 ABCA 232 (CanLII).

R. v. Coombs, 2003 ABQB 818 (CanLII).

R. v. Coombs, 2003 ABQB 567 (CanLII).

R v. Coombs, 2004 ABQB 621 (CanLII).

Chapter 5

"Stories Too Painful for the Light of Day": Narratives of Neonaticide, Infanticide, and Child Murder

Judith Broome

On March 2, 1670, Mary Cook was hanged for the murder of her youngest and allegedly favourite daughter, two-year-old Elizabeth. The lurid details of Elizabeth's death and the melancholy years of Mary's life preceding her violent crime were detailed in at least three cheap news pamphlets that circulated in the streets of London.[1] A married woman and mother of eight, living in comfortable circumstances, Mary denied any religious frenzy and refused her husband's attempt to attribute her crime to insanity, insisting only that her husband and his family were unkind to her and that she feared that Elizabeth would be neglected should she be left motherless after Mary's own suicide; moreover, Mary knew that her own death would certainly follow her crime (Dolan 147). Whereas historical examinations of neonaticide and infanticide[2] in the long eighteenth century (1660-1815) have often pointed to the social and economic circumstances of murdering mothers, many of whom were unmarried servants who risked dismissal and disgrace, in this chapter, I will focus on those cases—like that of Mary Cook—that cannot be explained by shame, fear of losing one's position, or a scarcity of resources. Lacking any material explanation, these murders are attributed to other causes, such as despair, madness, religious frenzy, or rage. These are the cases that generate the narratives and stories that cultures must tell themselves to explain—and maintain distance from—horrific, unthinkable crimes. Where no clear motive for the murder of a child can be found, narratives proliferate in an effort to explain the unexplainable: How could a mother kill her own child? Such narratives, as Paul Stoller has observed, construct a reality that reveals our own "human vulnerabilities" and "bring to the surface deep fears about how we construct misfortune, illness, and death" (para. 3). Through the examination of primary sources—such as the Old Bailey Sessions Papers (the trial transcripts from the Old Bailey, London's criminal court) and "Accounts" by the ordinary, or chaplain, of Newgate Prison,[3] as well as a review of the literature examining the history of infanticide in England during the long eighteenth century, and critical studies of the narratives about the murder of infants and children that emerged from England during this period—I will argue that the stories told to explain child murder reveal more about the cultures themselves than they do about an individual woman's motives.

Mary Cook's story is one of many narratives of maternal filicide in the long eighteenth century that have been the subject of a proliferation of research by such scholars as Gregory Durston, Mark Jackson, Anne-Marie Kilday, Laura Gowing, Josephine McDonagh, Robert Malcolmson, Susan C. Staub, and Jennifer Thorn, among others.[4] The preponderance of scholarship on this topic—both within and without the long eighteenth century—seems to be an indication of the anxiety and fascination that we feel for mothers who murder their children, particularly when not explainable by socioeconomic factors. The Old Bailey Sessions Papers record facts and testimonies, while the ordinary's "Accounts" allow for some interpretation. Both frequently emphasize the socioeconomic conditions of women brought before the court: most often a woman charged with killing her newborn was young, nulliparous, employed as a domestic servant, and lacked family support or resources; she would lose her position if she gave birth to an illegitimate child.[5] As a result, she would often conceal her pregnancy and give birth in private, without assistance.

At the start of the seventeenth century, there were difficulties attendant on prosecutions of women who were suspected of neonaticide: In order to obtain a conviction, the court would have to prove the baby was born alive and had been intentionally killed. Often, the courts had to rely on circumstantial evidence, and witnesses sometimes presented contradictory testimonies; without definite marks of violence on the infant's body, juries were often hesitant to convict a woman of murder. In 1624, the *Act to Prevent the Destroying and Murthering of Bastard Children* (21 James I, cap 27) was passed. This special statute reversed the burden of proof:

> Whereas many lewd women that have been delivered of bastard children, to avoid their shame and escape punishment, do secretly bury or conceal the death of their children, and after, if the child is found dead, the said women do alledge, that the said child was born dead, whereas it falleth out sometimes (although hardly is it to be proved) that the said child or children were murthered by their lewd mothers, or by their assent or procurement.[6]

Because murder was difficult to prove, and juries were loath to convict a young woman of a capital offense, concealment of the birth became the crime, and the burden of proof was placed on the accused woman. Three conditions had to be met: The woman must have concealed her pregnancy; she must not have called for help during delivery; and the newborn was dead or missing.[7]

There were a number of narratives engendered by this legislation, as Laura Gowing has observed. Witnesses were called, such as neighbours, who would report that a certain woman had gained weight, appearing to be pregnant—known as "the rising of the apron"—and then had suddenly regained her previous figure. It was not uncommon for neighbouring women to ask to examine another woman's breasts for evidence of lactation or engorgement, which would indicate pregnancy or recent childbirth. In cases of suspected neonaticide, bed linens were examined for blood evidence, and midwives were called to examine the woman's body (91). These witnesses were often hostile towards the suspected woman. In addition to judging the woman's guilt or innocence, the object was frequently to determine paternity—to discover who was chargeable in order to relieve the parish of the economic burden of support for the child. In cases where single women had made their pregnancies known and had planned for delivery, the attending midwives frequently testified to eliciting the name of the father just at the moment when the labouring woman's pain was greatest—even withholding their aid until the father was named (Gowing 100).

The childbirth narratives of the suspected mothers are similar throughout cases reported in the Old Bailey Sessions Papers. Young and inexperienced, many claimed no knowledge of the pregnancy, which at the time was not easily determined. Many of these young women would be unfamiliar with the particulars of giving birth and would report stories of sudden illness or pain, "griping" of the intestines, followed by "something dropping" from their bodies.[8] As Laura Gowing observes, once an investigation of a newborn's death began, the testimonies of both suspects and witnesses produced narratives that "obscure as much as they reveal" (89). She further notes that all parties had their own agendas and that stories of pregnancy, labour, and childbirth, possibly including suspected newborn murders, were often secret, part of the oral culture maintained by women (89). Such stories might have been shared among women at a "lying-in," the rest period before and after birth where a woman received visits from her female friends who discussed their own childbirth experiences and offered advice. It is unlikely that young girls, even those employed as servants, would be included in these gatherings.

With the requirement of a witness to prove that a child was stillborn or a witness to testify that the woman had requested help during delivery or had indeed laid in child linen in preparation for the birth, a proliferation of narratives surrounded suspected neonaticides. The requirement of a witness presented a dilemma for an unmarried woman who found herself pregnant. If she asked for help, she would have a witness but would suffer social disgrace, the loss of her position if she were a domestic servant, and the real possibility of destitution; if she kept her pregnancy secret, even if the child were premature, stillborn, or died of natural causes, she would be charged with concealment, which presumed premeditated neonaticide. There was seldom a question of motive: The women brought to trial were trying to avoid the shame of an illegitimate birth, which would result in the loss of position without a character or reference to obtain future employment; greatly reduced opportunities to achieve a good marriage; and corporal punishment, such as whipping; and/or a subsequent sentence to the workhouse. Married women, in contrast, were seldom tried for neonaticide; with no reason to hide a pregnancy, a married woman could kill a child by simple neglect or exposure or by "overlaying"—that is, accidentally smothering the infant as they slept in the same bed. So while the cases of unmarried women appeared to have obvious motives, those of married women did not, and so most often went unquestioned and undetected, except in cases of obvious violence.

The Case of the "Woman of the Parish of St. Martins in the Fields"

Neither married women nor men could be tried for concealment, although they could be tried for murder, as in the case of an unnamed "Woman of the Parish of St. Martins in the Fields." The Old Bailey record attests that she was married to a man "of good repute, and credit" with whom she lived "contentedly and well." She stood accused of killing her infant by throwing it into a fire, according to the narrative of her servant. During her postnatal confinement, when the woman was "newly Siting up[9] ... she was observed for some time before to be some what discomposed and distempered in her mind, the ground of which is Variously reported but not certainely [sic] known," causing those around her to fear leaving her alone. One day, the woman ordered her nurse to make a "Sea-coal" fire in her room and to "blow it up well pretending she was cold." She then sent the nurse out on an errand; left alone, the mother "thrust" the infant into the fire, covering it with hot coals. When the nurse returned, she was horrified at finding the remains of the infant in the fire and asked who had placed the baby there; the mother then confessed. In such a case, the evidence was clear. But lacking any motive for a "contented" married woman to kill her child, it was determined that it had "pleased God (whose Judgments are unaccountable to his Creatures) so for the Devil to prevail upon this poor wretch." The jury found her "not to be of sound mind before, and at the time of doing the fact," and she was subsequently acquitted. In this case, we see an attempt to explain a crime that lacks the ambiguity of concealment of a birth and lacks any socioeconomic explanation of poverty, shame, or ignorance of the signs and symptoms of pregnancy. The explanation offered for this heinous crime was based on religious belief, resting on the will of God and the workings of the devil to cause her to be "discomposed and distempered in her mind" (Old Bailey Proceedings Online t16755Ol15).

"Weary of Her life": The Case of Mary Cook

The search for an explanation of the death of a child at the hand of a married mother, as in the case above, is similar to that of the 1670 case of Mary Cook.[10] In the pamphlets that told the sensational story of her crime, Mary is described as "civil" and "sober," with "a melancholy temper" (*Blood for Blood*, qtd. in Staub, *Stepdames* 198). The authors of the pamphlets credit her "melancholy" for making her susceptible to the workings of the devil, who encouraged Mary to take her own life, leading her to two failed suicide attempts. After the second attempt, in which Mary tried to hang herself, her husband, Thomas, removed all the hooks and nails from the basement walls. On another day, Thomas returned home to find Mary threatening to throw their daughter Elizabeth into the fire if he left her alone again. When Mary once again began to think of suicide, she planned to slash her own throat, but when she considered that there would be no one to take care of Elizabeth, she decided that she should kill Elizabeth first, thereby guaranteeing her own death by hanging. So, one day, she served Elizabeth breakfast, and then she slit her daughter's throat.

As an explanation, Mary declared that "her Husband and Kindred were unkind to her" (*Inquest after Blood* 9) and that despite her request for help when she was feeling unwell, his family did not offer any assistance. Faced with a crime so gruesome and a mother so apparently lacking in compassion for her child, the pamphleteers depicted her as possessed by the devil, and Thomas sought to have her declared insane and thereby pardoned (*Inquest after Blood* 10). But Mary herself objected to the suggestion that she was insane and strenuously denied any religious cause for the murder of Elizabeth. She insisted that the general neglect of her husband and his relatives was the reason for her extreme despair and that she was "weary of her life" (*Blood for Blood* 202)—an explanation that might have been judged insufficient or difficult to comprehend in the context of contemporary expectations for wives and mothers. While the mother who threw her child into the fire was acquitted by reason of insanity, Mary Cook, who refused to say that she had been insane, was sentenced to death. Because she eventually repented, albeit on her own terms, and prayed for forgiveness, she was, as Marilyn Francus argues, "rehabilitated ... into the Christian community sufficiently to let her story be told" (*Monstrous Motherhood* 107). The idea of a woman giving into her anger or despair in an act of violence towards her own child is a transgression that society cannot tolerate or integrate into the narrative we tell ourselves about the so-called natural desire for motherhood and the gentle, passive, and domestic roles expected of women ("Monstrous Mothers" 147-48).

As we can see from this story, a number of narratives circulated around the murder of Elizabeth Cook: Mary's, her husband's, her husband's family's, her neighbours', the court's, and those of the pamphleteers. Everyone claimed the right to tell Mary's story and to attempt to make sense of a child's murder that could not be explained by insanity, religious frenzy, poverty, or social stigma.

Narratives surrounding infanticide contain embedded social and cultural beliefs about the nature of women—that they are less violent, more passive, and naturally nurturing. A woman who kills her own child shatters all of those gender norms and challenges the patriarchal structure on which society is structured. The family was considered the nation in microcosm, and whereas a woman who killed her husband was accused of petty treason, a woman who killed her child was deemed monstrous or inhuman. Susan C. Staub explores the "ambiguous" construction of motherhood in the seventeenth century in "Early Modern Medea: Representations of Child Murder in the Street Literature of Seventeenth-Century England." She observes that while mothers were increasingly authorized with the spiritual and emotional, in additional to physical, upbringing of their children, within the patriarchal family they remained subordinate to their husbands, posing "a potential site of conflict between motherly authority and wifely submission" (333-34). Whereas contemporary conduct books[11] presented an idealized version of motherly behaviour, street literature (which seldom discussed cases of unmarried women) focused on those "instances when motherhood [had gone] awry, on those cases when maternal nurture transmutes into maternal violence" (Staub, *Stepdames* 45). Committed within the domestic sphere, such crimes were seen as highly disruptive, even "threatening," to patriarchal models of motherhood and family (Staub, *Stepdames* 45-46). In the face of inexplicable violence, street literature sought to reveal the motives for infanticides by married women, who were treated with some respect (for their married status) and occasionally some sympathy. Lacking shame as a motive, married mothers might have killed their children out of a sense of maternal duty. "In a perversion of the responsible mother of the conduct manuals," Staub notes, "these mothers kill[ed] their children in order to save them from religious falsehood, from starvation, and occasionally, from the mother's own desperate state" (*Stepdames* 47). Mary Cook asserted her authority, however misguided, within her household and claimed agency by insisting on her own story; she made her voice heard in a context that no one could understand, since contemporary cultural beliefs denied the potential violence of women. Had she agreed to her husband's intent to have her declared insane or if she had insisted that the devil told her to kill Elizabeth, she might have escaped punishment for the capital crime. But by insisting on her own narrative, she was hanged.

"An Unaccountable Prosecution": Anna Maria Thorne, the Elder

Brought before the Old Bailey on December 10, 1735, Anna Maria Thorne, a widow, was indicted for the second time for the alleged murder of her fifteen-year-old daughter, Anna Maria, known as "Nanny." Thorne was accused of forcing Nanny to sleep in a cold room, occasionally locking her in, for nearly eight months, during which time Thorne failed to provide the girl with sufficient food and drink. Upon the death of her husband, Sir George Rivers, Thorne had found it necessary to move from her home in Tottenham and take up lodgings in the house of Thomas Falkner, a silk dyer. At this time, she removed her two youngest daughters, Charlotte and Nanny, from the care of their nurse, Susan Robinson, and brought them to live with her and her eldest daughter, Dorothy, who had remained at home while her sisters were sent away. Thomas Falkner, his wife Ann Falkner, and their servant, Mary Scot, all testified to instances when Nanny would steal food from their pantry or ask them for food, saying that she had not eaten in several days, all the while begging them not to tell her mother, who would beat her if she found out. When Ann Falkner questioned Nanny about why she did not cry out during the beatings, she alleged that her mother stuffed a handkerchief into her mouth. Ann Falkner testified that when she once gave Nanny some bread and cheese, the girl hid the food in her petticoat fearing that her sister would find it.

Mary Scot, the servant, would occasionally hide food for Nanny under a dust tub and noted that when the older sisters would occasionally come down to have tea with her, they would always lock Nanny upstairs. Moreover, Scot reported that Thorne's son, Charles Rivers, was also locked up and deprived of food when he returned home after having run away from his master, a jeweller, for the second time. Charles Rivers eventually left his mother's home and went to board at the home of Susan Robinson, Nanny's and Charlotte's former nurse (11). Nurse Robinson testified that Nanny had lived with her from the age of one month until she was thirteen and had always been a healthy child. After being removed from Robinson's care in the month of August, Nanny ran away from her mother and returned to Robinson's home in March. According to Robinson, "She came to my house at Edmonton. She looked like a Beggar, and very thin and Poor, 'tho she was a healthy plump Girl before. She complain'd that she had nor her belly full, I gave her some Victuals, and she Eat it very well, but as if she had been Starved (11-12)." The prosecution suggested that Thorne's "circumstances" had been reduced due to the death of her husband, as if to explain the lack of food, but Robinson replied: "I can't say to that. But while I kept the Children, she saw them two or three times a year, and then behaved as a Mother should do" (12). Witnesses for the defense included Nanny's two older sisters, Dorothy and Charlotte Thorn [sic]; Mr. Holloway; Mr. Freake, a surgeon; Mr. Buxton, a witness to Holloway's and Freake's examination of the body; as well as several acquaintances from Anna Maria Thorne's former life in Tottenham. Testimonies from Buxton, Holloway, and Mr. Freake were brief. Buxton reported that upon opening the body, Freake found "two or three Ounces of something in the Stomach, which he said looked like a Cordial Draught."[12] Holloway said that "he found the Body much distempered," but believed Nanny died from "Natural Causes" and not from starvation. Freake, the surgeon, "depos'd to the same Effect, as Mr. Holloway had done" (12).

Dorothy testified at length that her mother had shown "like Favour and Affection" to all her children, that Nanny "had the same food as we," and that "the Victuals was never lock'd up from her" (12). Nanny was never locked in and slept with Charlotte on a "good warm Feather-Bed, in the warmest Room in the House" (12). Dorothy claimed to know nothing about Nanny's alleged requests for food from the Falkners and acknowledged that although her mother's "Circumstances were reduced ... we always had Victuals enough" (12). She then detailed a brief illness that had come upon Nanny and her mother's various ministrations. Believing the illness was merely a cold, they did not call the apothecary for treatment, and Nanny died within a day. The subsequent witnesses, including Anna Maria Thorne's minister and an apothecary, all knew her from the time she lived in Tottenham with her husband, where, the witnesses claimed, she entertained the finest people in the Parish, regularly attended church, and was highly respected by the community. William Evans, the apothecary, testified that all the children had been under his care, that Thorne was an "indulgent" and "solicitous" mother, and treated all her children equally (13). Ralph Harwood, Esq., said he knew Thorne to be a modest woman, and "company for the best in the parish," declaring "'Tis an unaccountable Prosecution" (12). The transcript then notes that "Several others were ready to speak to her Character, but it was thought unnecessary" (13). Anna Maria Thorne was acquitted (Old Bailey Proceedings Online, t17351210-37).

I cannot agree with the assessment of Anne-Marie Kilday and Katherine D. Watson that the death of the younger Anna Maria was a "desperate and pitiful" murder "carried out due to financial hardship" ("Child Murder in Georgian England" 44). The prosecution's questioning in the trial transcript attempts to create a narrative of a sensible and kindly gentlewoman of reduced circumstances, by frequently bringing up the question of her lowered finances; moreover, when Thomas Falkner testified that Nanny had not sufficient food, the prosecution suggested that she may have been given food that he did not know about. When Ann Falkner testified that Nanny hid food in her pocket, the prosecution asked, "And would she have done so if she had been ready to starve[?]" (11), ignoring Ann's testimony that Nanny lived in fear of her mother's and sisters' cruelty if they found her hiding food. Despite the prosecution's attempt to prove otherwise, financial hardship does not explain Thorne's exceptional cruelty to her youngest daughter. Kilday and Watson note that Thorne's "[social] status meant that she could not simply turn the child out on the streets" (44), but certainly other alternatives existed: the belt-tightening required could have been shared among the family members or, despite possible social stigma, she might even have sent Nanny into domestic service, surely a better option than starving her to death.

Stories We Tell Today

A twenty-four-hour television news cycle and rapid dissemination of information via the internet leave few stories of child murder untold. The more violent or shocking the crime, the more it is retold, sensationalized, and reported yet again, with the narrative eventually becoming crystallized in any number of in-depth investigative news programs or true crime television series. On Sunday, October 8, 2006, *The Dallas Morning News* ran a feature article that seemed almost too improbable to believe: Dena Schlosser, found not guilty by reason of insanity of killing her infant daughter by cutting off her arms, had become the roommate—and friend, according to the article—of Andrea Yates, who had murdered her five children by drowning them, one by one, in a bathtub. "At night, after lights out, they whisper stories too painful for the light of day," the article states. "Tales of fear and guilt and memories of how life used to be."[13] While we may not have access to the stories allegedly whispered in the dark between Dena Schlosser and Andrea Yates, there is no shortage of public narratives surrounding women who kill their children. The sensational stories of Schlosser and Yates stayed in the news because of Schlosser's extreme violence and the magnitude of Yates's crime. Yet as horrific as these child murders were, there was no mystery, no lack of explanation, as there was in the case of Mary Cook or Anna Maria Thorne. Both Schlosser and Yates had long and well-documented histories of mental illness and postpartum depression and psychosis.[14]

"Childbirth is a complex event" as Ian Brockington observes, "packed with somatic and psychological incident":

> It is a period of rapid biological, social and emotional transition. It is a social and psychological crisis, requiring intrapsychic adaption and interpersonal reorganisation, especially after the first child. There is physical discomfort, and there may be loss of employment, financial pressures, changes in the social network, decreased recreation, confinement to the house and boredom. Marriage and other relationships may come under strain.... Although there are examples of extreme stress, such as bereavement, imprisonment and battle, the psychiatry of childbirth is probably more complex than any other human situation. (138)

Research, beginning with that of Philip Resnick in 1970, has identified indicators and risk factors for some potentially murderous mothers: for example, girls or young women who commit neonaticide or women with histories of mental or emotional illness that put them at higher risk for severe postpartum depression or psychosis.

It is important to note, however, that there are seldom tidy explanations in cases of child killing. Carl P. Malmquist notes that "for some individuals different combinations of factors become controlling" (405). And Michelle Oberman, in her carefully detailed studies of child-murder, or filicide, by mothers in the United States, observes that there is quite often a failure of society to support mothers who are single, impoverished, and isolated. Oberman cites the case of Mary Pixley, a nineteen-year-old mother of two, who suffocated her six-week-old infant "because no one was helping . . . take care of it" ("Coming to Terms" 44), an echo across centuries of Mary Cook's lament that her husband and his family did not provide the help she had requested. Most significantly, Oberman observes, the killing of a child by its mother is "a reflection on the individual mother's experience of *the conditions under which she [is] expected to raise her child*" (my emphasis, "Cross-Cultural Patterns" 493). Such conditions may vary across time, culture, and geography, but by looking at the specific circumstances of a mother's filicide, Oberman asserts, it is apparent that "maternal filicide is not a random, unpredictable crime committed predominantly by mentally ill women. Instead, it is deeply imbedded in and responsive to the societies in which it occurs" (494). The constant among these crimes is that they are "committed by mothers who cannot parent their child under the circumstances dictated by their particular position in place and time" (493). Often, the expectations of motherhood are "unwritten norms that govern womanhood and motherhood" (494), such as essentialist beliefs about women's natural desire for motherhood and instinctual mothering abilities—beliefs that have been in place since the early modern period and before. Having internalized these societal expectations, women are "reluctant to discuss their feelings of failure, shame, and desperation" because they fear familial and social disapproval and "because they fear losing their babies," a very real possibility in the United States, where children may be removed from the home by state child protective services for a wide variety of reasons (Jefferies et al. e24). Our collective impulse, as a society, is to seek an explanation for an unthinkable crime. Although each incident of maternal child murder may possibly be understood by a thorough analysis of the specific social and material conditions of the crime, such analysis rarely, if ever, takes place. Instead, the narratives created fall into patterns of the mad or bad mother—that is, the mentally ill woman, or the heartless, incompetent, or improper mother who does not satisfy society's expectations of a good mother (Meyer and Oberman 68-94).[15]

Christine Alder and June Baker agree. Contemporary research suggests that neonaticide, especially in young girls, is generally not premeditated, but the result of powerful emotions: shock, fear, shame, and guilt. They argue the following: "It would be inappropriate and unenlightening to depict these events as moments of anger or rage, or eruptions of extreme uncontrolled aggression. These scenarios do reveal the burden of responsibility borne by women in our society, and the continuing negative consequences for young women of single parenthood" (30-31). Despite the reduction of stigma regarding unwed mothers in contemporary society and the availability of safe havens—such as hospitals, fire stations, or police stations where a new mother can drop off a newborn infant with no questions asked[16]—women and girls continue to discard unwanted newborns in trash containers; bury or abandon them in backyards; stuff them in suitcases that they leave in the trunk of a car or throw into a body of water; burn or dismember the bodies; or occasionally hide the body in a closet. It may be time, as Michelle Oberman has suggested, that instead of asking why women kill their children, we examine the lives and conditions in which these women live, the social expectations of motherhood in their worlds, and their roles as women in society and within the family. "Only when we come face-to-face with the desperation of these mothers," notes Oberman, "can we begin to devise effective manners of protecting both them and their children" ("Cross-Cultural Patterns" 514). But although desperation is a constant among women across historical periods and cultures, the causes of that desperation vary, and a deeper understanding of neonaticide, infanticide, and child murder would require the united efforts of education, health, and social services, as well as legal and judicial systems to prevent unwanted pregnancies, to support mothers and families in both material ways and through social safety nets, and to adjudicate fairly the killing of children when those systems fail. But until our society—and all societies—work to reduce income inequality, stigma, unrealistic models of motherhood, violence within the family, and the unequal treatment of women—in other words, to cure all social ills—we are left asking, "How could she do that?"

The mad or bad roles described by Meyer and Oberman have no legal definitions, and a twenty-four-hour news cycle that often thrives on highly disturbing crimes generates narratives that interpret maternal filicide by inserting these mothers into recognizable stories that will make sense to the public. There are outliers, however: Women like Mary Cook who claim agency and insist on their own narratives. This subset of women who kill their children does not fit easily into either category, that of the mad or bad mother. Theirs are the stories that generate narrative.[17] The examples provided here are only a very few of the stories of neonaticide, infanticide, or child murder in the long eighteenth century. Every period and every culture tells its own stories of infanticide—stories that are attempts to make sense of child murder and stories that insist we think about the unthinkable: killing one's own child. Although advances in psychiatry have given us tools to help us understand the actions of some mothers who kill their children, as Anne-Marie Kilday notes, "regardless of the historical period, it is *context* that holds the key to an understanding of this crime as it can reflect nuances in how and why the offence was carried out. The context can also impact how the crime was regarded and how the perpetrator was treated" (my emphasis, "Desperate Measures" 72). The narratives generated to explain the killing of a child by its mother in each culture reflect the concerns and anxieties of the culture itself. The stories we tell ourselves today—of madness, religious frenzy, despair, or indifference—are not terribly different from those told in the eighteenth century. Just as the story of Mary Cook was circulated in Restoration-era pamphlets, the stories of our modern Medeas are circulated on the internet, in tabloids, on twenty-four-hour news networks, or in true crime television programs—replete with lurid details and expert testimony but ultimately devoid of convincing explanation for a crime that continues to resist interpretation.

Endnotes

1. Pamphlets were made of cheap paper folded into several pages; broadsides were single-page publications. Both were sold on London streets, frequently recounting news of horrid crimes, as well as prisoners' confessions and dying speeches. For more information regarding pamphlets in general, see Joad Raymond, *Pamphlets and Pamphleteering in Early Modern Britain*. For a discussion of ballads and pamphlets in the dissemination of news of domestic crime, see Frances E. Dolan, *Dangerous Familiars: Representations of Domestic Crime in England*, esp. "Introduction" (6-9); Jennifer Thorn, ed., *Writing British Infanticide: Child-Murder, Gender, and Print, 1722-1859*; and Susan C. Staub, "Early Modern Medea: Representations of Child Murder in the Street Literature of Seventeenth-Century England."

2. In this essay, I will use "neonaticide" to refer to a newborn within the first 24 hours of life; "infanticide" to refer to a child under the age of one year; and "child murder" or "filicide" to refer to a child above the age of one year.

3. As the spiritual advisor to prisoners who had been sentenced to death, the ordinary of Newgate was permitted to publish accounts of prisoners' behaviour at their hanging, a record of their final speeches, and brief biographies and descriptions of their crimes. These publications were quite popular, and resulted in print runs of several thousand copies. See "The Ordinary and His Account," www.oldbaileyonline.org/static/Ordinarys-accounts.jsp.

4. See, among others, Malcolmson; Hoffer and Hull; Jackson; Francus; Staub; Thorn; Durston; Kilday; Porter and Gavin.

5. Current research shows that characteristics of neonaticide are consistent over history and geography. Since Philip Resnick's extensive 1970 study of neonaticide, many researchers have confirmed his findings that in Westernized cultures, the majority of babies killed within twenty-four hours of birth are born to inexperienced, emotionally immature teens or young women, frequently living at home with their families, who conceal or deny (often to themselves) their pregnancies, seek no prenatal care, and give birth outside a hospital. In the long eighteenth century in Britain and elsewhere in Europe, newborns could be killed or abandoned and left to die of exposure, most often by young live-in

servants, who knew little about pregnancy or childbirth, concealed their pregnancies, and gave birth in secret without asking for help.

6. Virtually identical statutes were adopted in Scotland in 1690 and in Ireland in 1707.

7. After an initial increase in convictions and executions of women accused of killing their newborns, attitudes towards women accused of infanticide gradually softened, and by the middle of the eighteenth century, the statute was not regularly enforced, unless there were obvious marks of violence on the infant's body (Kilday, "Desperate Measures" 63-64).

8. The description of unanticipated childbirth as "something dropping" or "falling" from the body is found in thirteen of the cases examined by Marilyn Francus in "Monstrous Mothers, Monstrous Societies: Infanticide and the Rule of Law in Restoration and Eighteenth-Century England" (153n25).

9. The "traditional sequence" of recovery from childbirth entailed remaining prone in bed for the first week, sitting up in bed in the second week, moving about the bedroom in the third week, remaining at home in the fourth week, followed by "churching," a woman's first public appearance after childbirth and an occasion of "ritual purification and thanksgiving" (Vickery 105).

10. Because *The Proceedings of the Old Bailey* date from 1674, there is no record of Mary Cook's trial in this source.

11. Conduct books, beginning in the medieval period and continuing through the eighteenth century, advised young people on proper behaviour in society as well as within marriage and family, thus reinforcing traditional gender roles.

12. A cordial draught was an early modern remedy made of herbs, berries, sugar, brandy, or any assortment of substances believed to relieve a variety of physical or even emotional complaints. Testimony that a cordial draught was present in Nanny's stomach may have suggested that care was taken to treat her final illness.

13. "Schlosser and Yates Find Solace in Friendship." *The Dallas Morning News*, 8 April 2006.

14. Despite her history of mental illness, in 2002, Andrea Yates's insanity plea was denied; she was convicted of two counts of capital murder and sentenced to life in prison. In 2005, her conviction was

reversed on appeal; in 2006, she was found not guilty by reason of insanity and committed to a Texas state mental hospital, where she remains today. Dena Schlosser was also found not guilty by reason of insanity and was sent to the psychiatric facility where Andrea Yates resided. In 2008, Schlosser was released into outpatient care, under the conditions that she not see her children and that she comply with a prescribed medication regimen, including doctor-approved birth control. She was recommitted in 2010, and after a brief course of treatment, she was once again released to outpatient treatment.

15. See, for example, the story of Darlie Routier, a wife and mother of three, who in 1997 was sentenced to death for the stabbing death of one of her two murdered sons, despite her insistence that she was the innocent victim of an unknown intruder; her own nearly fatal injuries in the attack; and a careless investigation that unearthed no significant evidence against Routier. *The Last Defense,* a documentary that includes interviews with the prosecuting attorney, her appellate lawyers, and jurors reveals that Routier was largely judged by her appearance and behaviour. As of 2019, Routier remains on Texas's death row awaiting the results of additional and more technologically advanced fingerprint and DNA testing.

16. Requirements for safe haven surrender exist throughout the United States, with state-by-state variations: see safehavenalliance.org.

17. The multiple narratives surrounding the 2008 death of three-year-old Caylee Anthony are still in circulation. Her death remains unsolved. Although her mother, Casey Anthony, was charged with the crime, there was no clear motive, as Anthony and her daughter lived with her parents, who supported them financially and cared for Caylee much of the time. The only motive for Casey Anthony to kill her child appeared to be a desire for more personal freedom and relief from the responsibilities of motherhood. Despite having lied to her family and the police on numerous occasions regarding Caylee's disappearance, Casey Anthony was acquitted on charges of first-degree murder, aggravated manslaughter of a child, and aggravated child abuse—to intense public outrage. Journalist John Cloud, writing in *Time* magazine, has called the case the "social-media trial of the century." Found guilty of several misdemeanours for giving false information to police, she was sentenced to time served and released from jail in 2011.

Works Cited

Alder, Christine M., and June Baker. "Maternal Filicide: More Than One Story to Be Told." *Women and Criminal Justice*, vol. 2, 1997, pp. 15-39.

An Act to Prevent the Destroying and Murthering of Bastard Children. 1624, 21 James I cap. 27, Electronic facsimile.

Anonymous. *Blood for Blood, or Justice Executed for Innocent Blood-Shed. Being a True Narrative of That Late Horrid, Murder, Committed by Mary Cook, upon Her Own and Only Beloved Child*. Printed for F. Smith, 1670. Rpt. in Staub, *Nature's Cruel Stepdames*, pp. 180-215.

Brockington, Ian. *Motherhood and Mental Health*. Oxford University Press, 1996.

Cloud, John. "How the Casey Anthony Murder Case Became the Social-Media Trial of the Century." *Time* 16 June 2011, content.time.com/time/nation/article/0,8599,2077969,00.html. Accessed 11 Nov. 2021.

Dolan, Frances E. *Dangerous Familiars: Representations of Domestic Crime in England 1550-1700*. Cornell University Press, 1994.

Durston, Gregory. "Eighteenth-Century Infanticide: A Metropolitan Perspective." *Griffith Law Review*, vol. 13, no. 2, 2004, pp. 160-84.

Francus, Marilyn. *Monstrous Motherhood: Eighteenth-Century Culture and the Ideology of Domesticity*. Johns Hopkins University Press, 2013.

Francus, Marilyn. "Monstrous Mothers, Monstrous Societies: Infanticide and the Rule of Law in Restoration and Eighteenth-Century England." *Eighteenth-Century Life*, vol. 20, 1997, pp. 133-56.

Gowing, Laura. "Secret Births and Infanticide in Seventeenth-Century England." *Past and Present*, vol. 156, 1997, pp. 87-115.

Hoffer, Peter, and E.H. Hull, *Murdering Mothers: Infanticide in England and New England, 1558-1803*. New York University Press, 1984.

Jackson, Mark, editor. *Infanticide: Historical Perspectives on Child Murder and Concealment, 1550-2000*. Ashgate, 2002.

Jackson, Mark. *New-Born Child Murder: Women, Illegitimacy, and the Courts in Eighteenth-Century England*. Manchester University Press, 1996.

Jeffries, Diana, Debbie Horsfall, and Virginia Schmied. "Blurring Reality with Fiction: Exploring the Stories of Women, Madness, and Infanticide." *Women and Birth*, vol. 30, no. 1, 2016, pp. e24-e31.

Kilday, Anne-Marie. *A History of Infanticide in Britain, c. 1600 to the Present*. Palgrave Macmillan Limited, 2013.

Kilday, Anne-Marie "Desperate Measures or Cruel Intentions? Infanticide in Britain since 1600." *Histories of Crime: Britain 1600-2000*, edited by Anne-Marie Kilday and David Nash, Palgrave Macmillan, 2010, pp. 60-79.

Kilday, Anne-Marie. "Infanticide, Religion, and Community in the British Isles, 1720-1920: Introduction." *Family and Community History*, vol. 11, no. 2, 2008, pp. 84-99.

Kilday, Anne-Marie. *Women and Violent Crime in Enlightenment Scotland*. Boydell Press, 2007.

Kilday, Anne-Marie, and Katherine D. Watson. "Child Murder in Georgian England." *History Today*, vol. 55, no. 1, Jan. 2005, pp. 40-46.

The Last Defense. Executive producers Viola Davis, Julius Tennon, Andrew Wang, et al. ABC Television Network, 2018.

Malcolmson, Robert. "Infanticide in the Eighteenth Century." *Crime in England 1550-1800*, edited by J.S. Cockburn, Princeton University Press, 1977, pp. 187-209.

Malmquist, Carl P. "Infanticide/Neonaticide: The Outlier Situation in the United States." *Aggression and Violent Behavior*, vol. 18, 2013, pp. 399-408.

Meyer, Cheryl, and Michelle Oberman. *Mothers Who Kill Their Children: Understanding the Acts of Moms from Susan Smith to the "Prom Mom."* New York University Press, 2001.

Oberman, Michelle. "Mothers Who Kill: Coming to Terms With Modern American Infanticide." *American Criminal Law Review*, vol. 34, no. 1, 1996-1997, pp. 1-110.

Oberman, Michelle "Mothers Who Kill: Cross-Cultural Patterns in and Perspectives on Contemporary Maternal Filicide." *International Journal of Law and Psychiatry*, vol. 26, 2003, pp. 493-514.

Old Bailey Proceedings Online. "Trial of Woman." t16750115-1, www.oldbailey.org. Accessed 11 Nov. 2021.

Old Bailey Proceedings Online. "Trial of Anna Maria Thorn." t17351210-37. www.oldbailey.org. Accessed 11 Nov. 2021.

Porter, Teresa, and Helen Gavin, "Infanticide and Neonaticide: A Review of 40 Years of Research Literature on Incidence and Causes." *Trauma, Violence & Abuse*, vol. 11, no. 3, 2010, pp. 99-112.

Raymond, Joad. *Pamphlets and Pamphleteering in Early Modern Britain.* Cambridge University Press, 2003.

"Schlosser and Yates Find Solace in Friendship." *The Dallas Morning News*, 08 Apr. 2006. Page no longer available.

Staub, Susan C. "Early Modern Medea: Representations of Child Murder in Seventeenth-Century England." In *Maternal Measures: Figuring Caregiving in the Early Modern Period*, edited by Naomi J. Miller and Naomi Yavneh, Ashgate, 2000, pp. 333-47.

Staub, Susan C. *Nature's Cruel Stepdames: Murderous Women in the Street Literature of Seventeenth-Century England.* Duquesne University Press, 2005.

Stoller, Paul. "Commentary: Storytelling and the Construction of Reality." *Literature and Medicine*, vol. 32, no. 2, 2014, pp. 466-73, 495.

Thorn, Jennifer, editor. *Writing British Infanticide: Child-Murder, Gender, and Print, 1722-1859.* Cambridge University Press, 2003.

Vickery, Amanda. *The Gentleman's Daughter: Women's Lives in Georgian England.* Yale University Press, 2003.

Chapter 6

Claiming the Infanticidal Space: An Analysis of *King v. Lottie DesRoches*, 1904, Prince Edward Island

Sharon Myers

Introduction

This chapter highlights the case of Lottie DesRoches and what it reveals about how women tried to resist attempts to regulate and punish their exercise of reproductive choice. In the spring of 1904, DesRoches's dead infant was discovered buried in the sand of Blooming Point Beach on Prince Edward Island (PEI). Several of her coworkers confronted Lottie, admonished her, and quickly drew in legal officials with the formal force of law. This chapter analyzes the case of Lottie DesRoches and centres attention on themes of agency and resistance. I embed DesRoches's experience that spring in her contemporary context, and I consider her individual circumstances in order to illuminate the conditions that might have shaped her choices and explained the type of resistance she employed. DesRoches practiced a kind of agency and resistance that constructed and drew upon spatial boundaries, and her defence of her actions, or at least the action she was accused of, did so as well. I argue that DesRoches attempted to craft an infanticidal space—a location that was private and autonomously female. In other words, DesRoches engaged in a deeply political act of crafting a physical space and moral space free from patriarchal moral regulations and laws, where she could exercise her reproductive choice.

As DesRoches's case illustrates, the act of infanticide was one among a repertoire of reproductive choices women employed historically. Such choices were made in complex contexts that sometimes constrained women's choice making. Women's individual circumstances—such as their marital status, class position, and ethnicity—conditioned the limits and capaciousness of their agency. Additionally, the choices they made sometimes provoked responses from individuals or communities in the form of social control or moral regulation or from the state through the formal governance mechanisms of criminal law. Thus, while exerting some control over their own reproductive lives, women who committed infanticide exercised their agency in complex contexts, which were shaped by their experiences with impoverishment, marginalization, and other constraining forces. Additionally, their acts were sometimes met with complex regulatory responses that disciplined their actions without fully considering those contexts. Their agency was not, therefore, unfettered or unbounded, but neither were all women wholly constrained by the rules prohibiting infanticide.

Historians necessarily exercise some power when translating the lived experiences of people about whom we write. We locate, read, and consider records they have left behind or that they are included in. The historian's power comes both from reconstructing the person's experiences from those records—puzzle piecing lives back together from fragmented records—and from claiming that our reconstruction is accurate, reliable, and maybe even true. But whether or not our historical subjects would recognize themselves in our reconstructions of them is an important question to ask. It is also an ethically necessary question, most especially when writing from the feminist perspective that I attempt here (Jenkins 55). In crafting this text about Lottie, I am guided by scholar Radha Hegde who alerts us to the feminist responsibility to "preserve the dignity of the lives we expose" (276). This concern seems particularly important in the context of infanticide scholarship, in which the risk of slippage into sensation or judgment would be fraught.

I am equally cognizant that the story I tell of Lottie DesRoches is fragmentary and decidedly incomplete. In some measure, this results from the fragmentary historical sources that surround the DesRoches case. The bulk of the information that has survived is contained in the depositions to the coroner's jury and the grand jury, the first two formal steps that led to a criminal prosecution. The testimony at trial or a trial transcript appears not to have survived. This is not uncommon for the Supreme Court of PEI in that time period, when trial records seem to have been retained by luck and chance. As a result, we know little about what happened during the trial. Additionally, the only information we have from DesRoches directly is through a short statement she made to the coroner's jury. All else is filtered through one of the men with whom she worked, the others called upon to testify, a brief report in a newspaper, or recorded in note form by a member of the legal bureaucracy. To some extent, then, DesRoches is an elusive historical character whose traces in the historical record are only occasionally revealing and other times frustrating. For example, a form used by the crown attorney's office to gather biographical information about accused persons omitted DesRoches's place of birth, age, education, and drinking behaviour (Crown Causes, No. 43). Newspapers often reported extensively on criminal trials on PEI, but they barely made mention of *King v. DesRoches* in 1904. Vital statistics were not collected on PEI until 1906, leaving the simple matter of her place of birth, for example, unknown.

Despite these limitations, the case of Lottie DesRoches is a compelling one. It invites us to explore the ways in which the case was a usual one but also a less usual one and DesRoches a usual and less usual woman who might have committed infanticide. This in itself contributes to the Canadian historical literature on infanticide, if simply by reinforcing key themes already established by scholars but doing so for an early twentieth-century PEI context (Backhouse; Hanlon; Kramer; Lachance; Osborne; Pilarczyk; Wright). Much of the historical literature has focused on shared patterns among women who committed infanticide, the law surrounding infanticide and prosecutions under it, and the social regulation of gender and motherhood. Largely, the literature has taken a macro view, using particular cases as examples and illustrations within a more general examination of at least one of the above themes. I attempt to join others who have pursued a method more like that of microhistory in considering infanticide. One such practitioner, Lindsey Earner-Byrne, has argued "a careful (re)construction of [a woman's] … story serves to highlight that the individual in history can be resurrected to heighten our historical understanding of broader patterns and the unique 'otherness' of each protagonist, an approach that respects the complexity of experiences" (78). Tamar Hager, drawing on the work of Sandra Stanley Holton, has similarly noted "tracing the names of particular persons, formerly excluded from the larger narratives of mainstream academic history, is central to microhistory; this approach has special value for those who seek to write 'history from below,' such as women's history" (458). Moreover, she continues, "microanalysis provides a concrete description of a historical moment in which legal and administrative norms were challenged." (458). Microhistory, then, moves in opposite ways from traditional approaches, from the specific to the general. In this case, this means moving from the experience of Lottie DesRoches and then outwards to ask what her experience helps us to understand about the context in which she lived and the community's encounter with infanticide. Here, the emphasis is on what her story helps to illuminate and centring her experience as explanatory and instructive.

The Case of Lottie DesRoches

On the evening of Friday, April 29, 1904, two fishermen left S. C. Clark's lobster canning factory and walked west along the shoreline of Blooming Point, Prince Edward Island. This was not a casual after supper stroll after a hard day's work. Philip Smith and Donald James MacDonald were searching for evidence that would confirm their suspicions about the day's events.

Earlier in the day, they and the other Clark fishermen had arrived at the factory's cookhouse for the midday meal only to find the cook, Lottie DesRoches, was not there, and she would not return until about five o'clock. The absence of the sole cook in a bustling cannery would have been especially conspicuous as the workforce gathered and expected to be fed at regular intervals. But DesRoches's absence was granted even greater significance by a particular social dynamic at the factory: The men had been gossiping about her, suggesting she was "in the family way" as they had put it. Her return to the cookhouse around five, looking disheveled, ill, and "much reduced" in size, had prompted some men of the factory to encourage Smith and MacDonald's forensic investigation of the shoreline. Having followed footprints for about a mile, Smith and MacDonald discovered an imprint where someone had sat down and then a pile of sand with two stones atop. Smith removed the stones nestled between the high tideline and the cliff base and, with a bit of superficial scratching in the sand, revealed some cloth under the surface. According to their depositions, the men then left the scene and returned to the factory cookhouse, where they told others what they had discovered (Grand Jury Depositions: MacDonald, Smith). The next morning, Saturday, April 30, fellow fishermen John McCormack and Michael McDonald joined the other two men. Collectively, they returned to the suspect spot on the shore where they disinterred an infant body wrapped in a rag and apron, the outer layer of which was tied in two places. They slung what was thereafter referred to in depositions as "the parcel" on a lath, carried it back to the factory's paint shop, and placed the body in a box. Smith and Donald James MacDonald then went to the nearest magistrate to report their discovery and awaited the arrival of the constable and coroner (Grand Jury Depositions: McCormack, MacDonald, McDonald, Smith). The formal legal apparatus surrounding infanticide soon enveloped Lottie DesRoches, compounding the power of community regulation and local justice exercised by the fishermen.

While the fishermen unearthed and transported the infant body back to the factory on the cold April morning, Lottie DesRoches was back at work, newly laced up and cooking for the factory workers and fishermen. Her thirteen-year-old daughter, Josie (christened Mary Josephine), was with DesRoches. As the finger pointing at the thirty-five-year-old DesRoches began, and as word reached her that the body had been retrieved, she left the cookhouse and took refuge in a fisherman's shanty a quarter mile up the shore. Visited by the factory foreman and later a fisherman, she refused to leave the shanty. The factory owner soon had DesRoches and her daughter removed to a nearby neighbour's in a truck wagon lined with a straw mattress (Coroner's Inquest: Ferguson, McAuley; 1891 census; Baptismal Record). A coroner's inquest began in the cookhouse that same afternoon. Smith and McCormack recounted their experiences leading to the discovery of the body and noted their suspicions that the infant belonged to the cook. A day-long suspension in the proceedings followed that initial testimony, allowing the body to be delivered to Dr. James Walsh. In his postmortem on the neonate, Walsh determined it was an eight pound, twenty-two-inch long female, whose body showed no signs of violence and whose organs were fully developed. The umbilicus had been rightly tied, and there was no hemorrhaging. The hydrostatic test, or float test, performed on portions of the lungs led the examiner to conclude the infant had breathed even though the reliability of that test had been called into question by the medical literature for some time (Backhouse, *Petticoats* 129; Caron, 215). From his postmortem assessment, Walsh concluded the child had been born healthy and that the cause of death was exposure (Coroner's Inquest: Walsh).

The testimonies of six fishermen and canners to the coroner's inquest offered a consistent narrative about DesRoches's absence from the cookhouse at the Friday midday meal, her return late that afternoon looking decidedly ill, the discovery of the body of an infant that night, and its retrieval the next morning. Furthermore, there were observations about DesRoches's size and shape having changed in the course of those hours (Coroner's Inquest: McCormack et al.). The coroner's jury—an assemblage of community members tasked to determine the identity of a deceased person and the cause of death—found "that the infant whose body we viewed was the child of Lottie DesRoche and that said infant came to its death from exposure while the mother was endeavoring to conceal its birth" (Coroner's Inquest: Determination). Any ambiguity surrounding the provenance of the infant had been laid to rest by Lottie DesRoches, who acknowledged the child was hers. "I placed the baby there and covered it," she told the jury. According to DesRoches, she had walked down the shoreline, sat down, and the infant was born soon after. She tied the cord with some string in her pocket and cut it with scissors that she also carried in her coat pocket. "I swear positively that the baby did not breathe and that it was dead born," she reported (Coroner's Inquest: DesRoches). Her daughter arrived a short time after DesRoches wrapped the infant in an apron. Josie saw the infant lying on her mother's lap and, at her mother's urging, returned to the factory. According to DesRoches's testimony, she told Josie the infant was born dead. According to her daughter's testimony, DesRoches said nothing about the infant other than that she had given birth to it (Coroner's Inquest: L. DesRoches and J. DesRoches).

The grand jury depositions taken just two days after the coroner's jury did not significantly alter the narrative that had formed at the inquest. Two testimonies were added, those of the coroner and constable, who noted the body had been secured under lock and key in the paint shed and later conveyed to Dr. Walsh for the postmortem. Walsh changed his testimony slightly, concluding the cause of death was neglect as opposed to his earlier pronouncement of exposure (Grand Jury: Walsh, Toombs). Neither DesRoches nor her daughter gave testimony at the grand jury, but the same men of the factory largely repeated their earlier testimonies. In substance, the story remained the same (Grand Jury: Walsh et al.). Having been present for and having heard the statements against her, Lottie DesRoches was then indicted by the grand jury, which found sufficient grounds to proceed to trial, concluding that DesRoches "did willfully and with malice aforethought kill and murder her infant child contrary to the statute in such case." Nevertheless, the cover page to the grand jury testimonies records an indictment for neglecting to obtain assistance in childbirth. It is the latter charge, coupled with a concealment charge, that appears in the subsequent court records, limited though those records are. When asked by the stipendiary magistrate if she wished to speak to the indictment, DesRoches stated, "I have nothing to say" (Grand Jury: Determination).

The Legal Background

The charges against DesRoches of concealment and neglecting to obtain assistance in childbirth reflected the legal prescriptions of the 1892 Criminal Code of Canada. Canada's collection of laws around infanticide flowed from historical roots in Europe. Early manifestations of concealment laws appeared in mid-sixteenth-century France. By 1624, England's Jacobean Act defined the basis of what would eventually become the corpus of infanticide law—murder, concealment, and negligence—in British North America and early Canada. The Jacobean Act prescribed a death penalty to unmarried women who concealed the birth of a child that was later found dead. In essence, concealment was treated as murder, and only a witness to the birth of a stillborn child could provide a legal defense to women so charged (Backhouse, *Petticoats* 114-15; Kramer, 23-25). PEI adopted the tenets of the Jacobean Act in 1792, following the lead of other British

North American colonies (Kramer 29). The highly punitive prescription of capital punishment, however, prompted revisions to colonial legislation, as courts proved reluctant to sentence women to death for an infanticidal crime. In the early 1800s, moves to repeal the death penalty unless all elements of the crime of murder could be proven were successful and the punishment for the crime of concealment was reduced to two years imprisonment. (Backhouse, *Petticoats* 123, 133; Kramer, 28). At Confederation in 1867, the criminal laws of British North American colonies were consolidated, and married women then became chargeable for crimes of infanticide (Backhouse, *Petticoats* 133).

The creation of Canada's Criminal Code in 1892 revised some of the conditions of the crime of concealment and created a new crime within the corpus of infanticide law: failing to obtain reasonable assistance during childbirth. These were the very charges laid against DesRoches. The Code, Backhouse reminds us, defined concealment as follows: "Every one is guilty of an indictable offence, and liable to two years' imprisonment, who disposes of the dead body of a child in any manner, with intent to conceal the fact that its mother was delivered of it, whether the child died before, or during or after birth" (Backhouse, *Petticoats* 133). As Backhouse observes, this conceptualization of concealment meant that the cause of death was unimportant. Nevertheless, while the cause of death receded in importance, theoretically, juries continued to amplify the significance of a live birth in their considerations of the accused's guilt (Backhouse, *Petticoats* 133). Given the hesitancy of the courts to convict in cases of infanticide, the 1892 revisions therefore endeavoured to augment the meaning of concealment by expanding definitions of abandonment and exposure to include the failure to take care of an infant and leaving an infant at risk and without protection (Backhouse, "Desperate" 474). The 1892 Code also added the crime of failing to obtain reasonable assistance, reflecting the ascending power of the medical profession and their attempts to secure hegemony. Here, the maximum penalty was life imprisonment (Backhouse, *Petticoats* 133).

The Ordinary and …

The case of Lottie DesRoches fits into the historical literature in ways that are usual but, as I will later suggest, also noteworthy and less ordinary. American, British, and Canadian historians have established and largely agreed upon a number of themes around the historical practice of infanticide. These points of relative consensus and refrain allow us to make informed speculations about DesRoches and her experiences despite the dearth of direct information about her or her motivations. Three hallmarks of that relative consensus are discussed below. First, the perpetrators of infanticide and those most often charged with the crime were women, not husbands, male family members, nor purported fathers. Moreover, often, though not always, those women were relatively young and unmarried. Second, given their unmarried state, the prospect of having a child in tow threatened the respectable status of women, limiting their prospects for marriage, future employment, and the search for security that a clean moral reputation could partially facilitate. Third, the economic consequences of single motherhood were potentially devastating for many women because the associated stigma made them less likely to find employment or diminished the prospect of securing a job that could support a mother and child. Additionally, complications of securing childcare, rendered the choice to keep the child often unfathomable for such women. Taken together, the consensus goes, reputational and economic precarity—an intersection of gender and class experience—led an untold number of women to commit one of the crimes captured under the umbrella term infanticide (Backhouse, *Petticoats* 13; Farrell 65, 67; Green; Rattigan 142; Hemphill 437-38, 446-48; Kramer 26-27).

Does the case of Lottie DesRoches square with these elements of a relative historiographical consensus? Despite DesRoches's elusiveness and our inability to know all we might want to about her and her circumstances, her story seems quite usual when read in tandem with the historiography. A woman with a child aged thirteen already in tow (at least some of the time) and an older but absent daughter aged eighteen seems to have been trying to manage entirely by way of her own resources. DesRoches was married, yet Josie reported she did not know if her father, Joseph DesRoches, was alive or dead in 1904. Thirteen years earlier, census takers had recorded a family that appeared to be intact and living in Tignish, an Acadian fishing community on the northwest tip of the island. The census details are consistent with what is known about Lottie. Twenty-eight-year-old Joseph was a fisherman, and twenty-two-year-old Lottie was a mother to then four-month-old Josie and four-year-old Maggie (1891 Census; Coroner's Inquest: J. DesRoches). The details about when or why the family fractured, or about why Joseph and Lottie came to live separately are unknown. So too is the thirteen-year history of Lottie's life between the 1891 census and the events of 1904. In a sense, Joseph's status was immaterial; as Josie's testimony made clear, he was no longer present in their lives in 1904, making DesRoches, in practice, a single woman with a third child on the way.

After she became pregnant with the third child, Lottie DesRoches, née Charlotte Poirier (Baptismal Record) was hired out of a house on Water St. in Charlottetown, then a neighbourhood of wharves and train tracks and home to some of the rough and marginalized classes of the city's commercial waterfront (Coroner's Inquest: Ferguson; Grand Jury: Ferguson). At least eight months pregnant when hired, Des Roches made her way to PEI's central north shore, where she cooked from the predawn to dusk for just shy of three weeks before giving birth to the child on the shoreline. It seems reasonable to assume, that at least on the issue of economic vulnerability, DesRoches's circumstances corresponded with those of many other women who committed infanticide. Moreover, just two weeks into the fishing and factory season, DesRoches left her employment at the house on Water St. because she was granted the promise of room, board, and a small wage for the season for her and her daughter. In their seemingly peripatetic and precarious economic state, a spring stint at a canning factory promised short term security for them. The presence of a newborn would most certainly have wrecked that promise.

In regards to the law, historians point to a fourth area of relative consensus in relation to infanticide. Historians willingly concede the numbers of infanticides that became visible in the historical record were small compared to the actual number of infanticides in any given time and place. Many bodies were undoubtedly never discovered. Some infants were erroneously thought to have died from natural causes. Historians have concluded that infanticide was a far more common practice than captured in the historical record. They further note that even when an infant body was discovered and a woman suspected, the number of women actually charged was small, those tried and convicted even smaller, and those sentenced for anything other than the lesser crime of concealment, only fractional (Backhouse, *Petticoats* 113-14; Rattigan 135; Pilarczyk 575). In short, women who committed infanticide rarely encountered the full sanction of the law and often avoided prosecutions. *King v. DesRoches* adheres to common practice in this way, too. The substitution of the grand jury indictment for murder with the lesser charges of concealment and neglecting to obtain assistance in childbirth (*Morning Guardian*, July 5, 1904, 4; Crown Cases, No. 43; Supreme Court Minutes) squares the DesRoches case with the historically normative practices surrounding infanticide prosecutions in Canada—both after the consolidations of Canadian criminal law in 1867 and the articulations under the 1892 Criminal Code. The case of Lottie DesRoches seems usual or as some contemporaries termed such cases, "routine infanticide" or "infanticide of an ordinary character" (Hanlon; Farrel).

... and the Less Ordinary

At the same time, there is a distinctive element in the DesRoches case quite worthy of note. Much of the historical literature concludes that women who committed infanticide were driven to their crimes by desperation and contextual circumstances rooted in the intersection of class and gender. Desperate women, the argument goes, made desperate choices. In such interpretations, their actions read as reactions, less so the practice of rational and weighed choice making (Karlen, 126, 162-68). The DesRoches case seems to invite us to reconsider the relationship between reaction and agency and, indeed, women's claims over their bodily autonomy and the politics of infanticide. And this is why DesRoches's case provokes important reconsiderations. Charles Ferguson had hired DesRoches out of Charlottetown and served as a sealer of cans and foreman at the factory. He had visited DesRoches in the shanty after she took refuge there. Ferguson recounted that he closed the shanty door and said to her:

> This is a critical case or something with that meaning. She replied that no one had any business to interfere with it. I said that the law had to take hold of anything like that. She said the child was

dead born and a month before its time and that she and Josie intended to take it out of that or do something with it. She said that she came to the shore to work a month till she could get some money so that she could go somewhere to get looked after. (Coroners Jury: Ferguson)

Michael McDonald also visited DesRoches in the shanty where she told him he "had no business meddling with it" (Coroners Jury: McDonald). John Angus McAuley had been tasked to take Lottie DesRoches from the fisherman's shanty to the neighbour's house. Over the course of the journey, DesRoches confessed that the "parcel" found on the shore was hers and stated "the men had no business interfering with it." She went on to suggest, as she had to Ferguson, that she and her daughter were going to take care of the remains later that day and, incidentally, that the child had been born a month prematurely and was dead when she was delivered (Grand Jury: McAuley).

Claiming the Infanticidal Space

The feminist geographer Doreen Massey reminds us that places and spaces have politics and practices, and these characteristics help to create the character and meaning of a space (13). In this sense, spaces are not neutral containers but political ones, both constructing and reflecting a collection of power relations. As Altha Cravey has noted, part of the politics of places is that inequalities are inscribed upon them, so places become objects of power struggles around gender, class, and ethnicity (2). Such was true of DesRoches's infanticidal shoreline. As a space, what did that spot of sand a mile away from the factory mean, as Massey prompts us to consider? Certainly, it was an attempt to secure privacy—a common practice among infanticidal women who would act on their own and often return to work or chores hoping not to have raised suspicions (Backhouse, "Desperate" 114; Caron, 219; Williams, 70, 74-75). DesRoches demanded, however, a more capacious definition of the space. Not merely a space for acts in private, DesRoches characterized it as a place for the exercise of her autonomy, rights, and her power. The men of the factory, she claimed, had no business interfering with what happened in that space, in her chosen space, with her maternal property. While DesRoches claimed that space in her interests, she was drawing upon and reinforcing the idea that the politics of reproduction were within women's purview and thus a matter for the domestic and private (Campbell e42).

DesRoches's birthing space on the shore was intended to be private, but it was also a relational one that extended outwards to the protoindustrialized shore scape that encircled PEI and that was richly textured with class politics. The number of canneries had more than doubled in twenty years so that by 1900, 246 lobster canneries so densely populated PEI's coves and bays that one contemporary described the island as "polluted with factories." The quick multiplication of those seasonal proto-industries was accompanied by a new sort of workplace for some eight thousand islanders—one that drew sizeable numbers of women into paid employment preparing seafood in an untraditional setting and in a setting shared with nonfamilial men (Goveatt 10, 12; MacDonald 27). The shore-situated wharf, cannery, cookhouse, and (sometimes a) bunkhouse occupied a liminal space between a private world of hearth and home over which women claimed dominion and a public world in which men moved more freely (Johnson 578). The shore factory space necessarily brought private and public together—inasmuch as they were ever actually separate (Brenner and Elden 361, 371; Cravey 6; Poutanen 31). This sometimes left community members jostling to defend traditionally gendered terrain, such as the composition of a workplace or the authority of men therein as breadwinners. Indeed, in the shore factory context, the equations between gender divisions and spatial divisions were destabilized.

What did that mean for the woman who committed infanticide? Infanticide was most often regarded and practiced as a private act carried out by a woman alone in a private context. Indeed, that helps us to understand the (re)creation and legal value of the crime of concealment, which emphasized the solitariness of the act. Yet such women also lived in communities, liminal or not, where they were surveilled. Typically, such surveillance took the form of rumour and gossip that reinforced community morals, like the kind the men at the Clark factory had engaged in. This was accompanied by physical surveillance, again like that of the men at the Clark factory, where community members monitored a woman's size and sometimes carried out investigations after it was assumed she had given birth (Keenan

362; Rattigan 138-41; Williams 72). So the surveillance and regulation of DesRoches must necessarily be read through a gender lens, in which a public, carceral masculinity oriented towards disciplining errant women bore down upon DesRoches, who, they concluded, had rejected motherhood in relation to her third child and thus corroded traditional gender scripts (Hager 456, 462; Hedge 283; Pilarczyk 576, 581, 621).

But was there more to the power struggle between the men of the factory and DesRoches than the regulation of gender scripts and the erosion of spatial divisions? By 1904, PEI's lobster catch had declined 50 per cent, from five million pounds in 1881 to two and a half million in 1900 (MacDonald, 27). The striking decrease in the availability of the commercial product, accompanied by increased competition owing to the proliferation of canneries, heightened the economic vulnerability of fishermen and their families, like those of the Clark factory. That vulnerability, indeed poverty, was compounded by the common reliance on the merchant credit system, in which fishermen secured bait and gear on credit from the cannery owners. Fishermen were then indebted to merchants until they settled their credit in catch. In a context of limited catches, increased competition, and indebtedness, fishermen were at economic risk and their power was eroded. As historian Ed MacDonald has noted, "those who fished exclusively were among the poorest Islanders" (28).

Why is this contextual point meaningful to the DesRoches case, or the DesRoches case meaningful to it? At the turn of the century, the notion that the male head of household was the primary economic provider for the family was increasingly held up as the social ideal, even among the working class. That ideal was intertwined with ideas about masculinity and the notion that a good man was a good provider. When his ability to provide was threatened or thwarted, so too was the surety of a fisherman's masculinity. In this economic context, we can see experiences of class and gender intertwining. The men's struggle to wield what limited power they had may help us to understand why the men of the factory assertively sought to intervene, manage, and exercise control over DesRoches—the private space she claimed on the shore and the female world of reproduction. If the regulation of DesRoches's actions and space was a product of gender and class insecurity, it was also a product of ethnic relations. The men who intervened and testified against DesRoches were, in their entirety, anglophones of UK descent.

DesRoches was Acadian. As MacDonald has suggested: "From the perspective of the ruling culture, the Acadians came from the wrong racial stock, spoke the wrong language (French), and followed the wrong religion (Catholicism). Accordingly, they were generally tolerated, occasionally oppressed, but seldom respected" (15). MacDonald concludes that the Acadians of PEI "had taken up residence on the social and economic fringe" of island society (15). In short, Acadians had been effectively othered on PEI and essentialized as inferior. This too shaped the struggle between DesRoches's claim on the shoreline birthing place as hers and the men of the factory who may have felt especially entitled and empowered in such a context to meddle and intervene. DesRoches's claim on the infanticidal space for herself, and by proxy for women, was trampled upon by the power of the fishermen. The private space was re-written as a public space by the men of the factory who invoked not only surveillance, but also brought to bear the formal rule and apparatus of law, which was most certainly embedded in the public realm (Parker 7). This reminds us of the permeable boundaries of gendered space; spaces leak and permute, in this case, from liminal into private and private into public, spreading outwards from the liminal factory setting (Cravey 6; Lansing 233-34). In that politically charged space, DesRoches and the fishermen cast and then recast the spot on the shore, exerting competing claims in an effort to establish social and political authority.

The Outcome of the Trial

In late June 1904, a jury at the Supreme Court of PEI acquitted DesRoches of the crimes of concealment and neglecting to obtain assistance in childbirth (Crown Cases, 14, no. 43; *Morning Guardian*, July 6, 1904, 7). Without trial records, it is difficult to know the tone of the proceedings, the arguments that were presented, or the instructions offered by the judge that led the jury to their conclusion. The provincial daily, *Morning Guardian*, reported that DesRoches "testified that she had not expected the birth, and had only temporarily heaped sand around the body" (July 5, 1904, 4). In addition to DesRoches, the defense called the local sheriff, Charles Smith, who had walked the shoreline earlier than the other fishermen and saw nothing, and two physicians (Supreme Court Minutes; Coroner's Inquest: McDonald).

Perhaps the physicians offered evidence against the reliability of the float test and DesRoches's earlier claim that the infant was "dead born" carried the day, or perhaps DesRoches's testimony at trial was sufficiently persuasive. In either case, the acquittal reminds us, just as historians have argued, that juries adopted "a pervasive sense of tolerance and even compassion ... toward women accused of infanticide" (Backhouse, *Petticoats* 136). Backhouse has concluded that juries and courts understood the plight of the woman who committed infanticide and the limited options she faced (Backhouse, *Petticoats* 135-36; Pilarczyk 579, 630-631; Williams 81). And Kirsten Johnson Kramer has concurred. Early twentieth-century Canadians understood the economic and social hardships single mothers faced and accommodated the notion that women who committed infanticide were "victims of social circumstance" (Kramer 14, 20; Farrell 62; Hemphill 450, 455). The fishermen did not muster that compassion, grasping instead for shreds of power they could practice in a complicated context. But the jury, situated in Charlottetown, did. In a sense, the verdict validated DesRoches's claim on the infanticidal space that the fishermen sought to deny her—both the literal space of her shoreline birthing place and the figurative space claimed for the act of infanticide.

In her consideration of the work of Doreen Massey, Juliana DeVries asks us to consider a number of questions about spaces and people's relationships to them. In particular, she challenges us to contemplate "what does this place stand for" and "what does it mean to be of this space?" And we can ask those questions about a spot on a shoreline occupied and later politicized by Lottie DesRoches. So to address DeVries's questions—what did this space stand for, and what did it mean to be in that space—we might draw tentative conclusions. The spot on the shoreline where DesRoches chose to birth and abandon her child was intended to be a place that stood for privacy and to be a place that stood for autonomy and personal agency. It was both a physical space of isolation and also a moral space where difficult decisions were taken and acted upon. DesRoches's claim on the infanticidal space was both a physical and moral claim but also clearly a deeply gendered one that linked women to childbirth and defended women's agency over it and ownership of it. The men had no business inserting themselves physically, morally, or paternalistically into a space that was hers, DesRoches argued, because it was private and feminine.

Nevertheless, the fishermen of the factory successfully rewrote that piece of contested shoreline as a public space not only by invoking surveillance but also by bringing to bear the formal rule and apparatus of criminal law, the strong arm of the state. This recasting of a liminal space into a private rather than a public one—an individual one into a communitarian one and a feminine one into a masculine one—reminds us of the permeable boundaries of gendered space and the very leaky vessels that such spaces are. DesRoches's claim on the infanticidal space was made in a liminal context, where gender roles were destabilized. But in a case of infanticide, where arguably the central tenet of female gender ideology was rejected, the instability was too much for the fishermen to bear or tolerate, and they asserted their patriarchal privilege physically and morally, rendering DesRoches's infanticidal space ultimately a male and public one. But the court seemingly recognized the complex context that shaped DesRoches's life and choices, and following common practice of sidestepping convictions, it chose not to punish her for the reproductive choices she had made.

Conclusion

Claims that a neonate was born dead were common in infanticide cases (Hemphill 457). But a woman's claim of the infanticidal space by women, autonomous and free from male interference or meddling, is not a common theme in the historical literature. This is what makes the DesRoches case more compelling. It invites the more complicated and nuanced analysis that this chapter has pursued. DesRoches claimed that whatever happened on the shore that afternoon, it was her domain and that the men of the factory had no business intervening in the results. Indeed, she emboldened her stance when she told Michael McDonald that not only should the men let the situation be but that the object, the child, was hers and her property to control. In asserting this, DesRoches claimed the infanticidal space of women, highlighting women's agency and choice making, free from interference and patriarchal moral regulation. In staking that claim, DesRoches engaged in a significant political act of claiming and crafting the infanticidal space as women's space.

Endnotes

1. The spelling of her surname varies from document to document, occurring as DesRoches, DeRoches, DesRoche, and DeRoche, depending on the source. I have adopted the spelling recorded in the baptismal record for Lottie's daughter rather than the spellings in government records. Additionally, the baptismal record records Lottie as Charlotte Poirier, and the 1891 nominal census records her as Lauché DeRoche.

Works Cited

Primary Sources

Baptismal Record, Mary Josephine DesRoches, 1891, Public Archives and Records Office (hereafter PARO), Prince Edward Island, Canada, Nominal Census of Canada 1891, Prince Edward Island, Prince Co., Lot 1

Morning Guardian, Charlottetown, PEI, Prince Edward Island, Supreme Court fonds, RG 6.1, ser. 1, Minutes, subser. 2, Queens Co., Minutes 1835-1938, vol. 13, PARO

Prince Edward Island, Supreme Court fonds, RG 6.1, ser. 2, Crown Cases, vol. 2, PARO

Prince Edward Island, Supreme Court fonds, RG 6.1, ser.3, Dockets, subser. 2, Queens Co. Dockets, PARO

Prince Edward Island, Supreme Court fonds, RG 6.1, ser. 5, Case Files, subser. 2, K. v. DesRoche 1904, PARO

Prince Edward Island, Supreme Court fonds, RG 6.1, ser. 12, Sessional Papers – Grand Jury Presentments, subser. 3 file 73, PARO

Prince Edward Island, Supreme Court fonds, RG 6.1, ser. 14, Coroner's Inquests, file 790 DesRoche, PARO

Secondary Sources

Backhouse, Constance. "Desperate Women and Compassionate Courts: Infanticide in Nineteenth-Century Canada." *University of Toronto Law Journal* 478 (1984): 448-478. Online.

Backhouse, Constance. *Petticoats and Prejudice: Women and Law in Nineteenth-Century Canada*. Toronto: Women's Press, 1991. Print.

Caron, Simone. "'Killed by its Mother': Infanticide in Providence County, Rhode Island, 1870-1938." *Journal of Social History* 44.1 (2010): 213-237. Print.

Cravey, Altha J., Michael Petit. "A Critical Pedagogy of Place: Learning Through the Body." *Feminist Formation* 24.2 (2012): 100-119. Print.

DesVries, Juliana. "Place Re-imagined: A Review of Doreen Massey." *Minding Nature* 5.1 (2012). Online.

Earner-Byrne, Lindsey. "The Rape of Mary M.: A Microhistory of Sexual Violence and Moral Redemption in 1920s Ireland." *Journal of the History of Sexuality* 24.1 (2015): 75-98. Print.

Farrell, Elaine. "Infanticide of the Ordinary Character: An Overview of the Crime in Ireland, 1850-1900." *Irish Economic and Social History* 39 (2012): 56-72. Print

Gorveatt, Nancy. "'Polluted With Factories': Lobster Canning on Prince Edward Island." *The Island Magazine* 57 (2005): 10-21. Print.

Green, Elna C. "Infanticide and Infant Abandonment in the New South: Richmond, Virginia, 1865-1915." *Journal of Family History* 24.2 (1999): 187-211. Print

Hager, Tamar. "Justice, Morality or Politics: Why Did the British Legal System Execute Selina Wadge?" *Women's History Review* 26.3: 455-476. Print

Hanlon, Gregory. "Routine Infanticide in the West 1500-1800." *History Compass* 14.11 (2016): 535-548. Print.

Hedge, Radha S. "Fragments and Interruptions: Sensory Regimes of Violence and the Limits of Feminist Ethnography." *Qualitative Inquiry* 15.2 (2009): 276-296. Print.

Hemphill, Katie M. "'Driven to the Commission of This Crime': Woman and Infanticide in Baltimore, 1835-1860." *Journal of the Early Republic* 32 (2010): 437-461. Print.

Jenkins, Keith. "Ethical Responsibility and the Historian: On the Possible End of History 'Of a Certain Kind'." *History and Theory* 43.4 (2004): 55. Print.

Johnson, David A. "Vigilance and the Law: The Moral Authority of Popular Justice in the Far West." *American Quarterly* 33.5 (1981): 558-586. Print

Karlin, Molly. "Damned if She Does, Damned if She Doesn't: De-Legitimization of Women's Agency in Commonwealth v. Woodward." *Columbia Journal of Gender and Law* 18.1 (2008): 125-174. Print.

Keenan, Laura T. "Reconstructing Rachel: A Case of Infanticide in the Eighteenth-Century Mid-Atlantic and the Vagaries of Historical Research." *The Pennsylvania Magazine of History and Biography* 130.4 (2006): 361-385. Print

Kramer, Kirsten Johnson. *Unwilling Mothers, Unwanted Babies: Infanticide in Canada*. Vancouver and Toronto: UBC Press, 2005. Print

Lachance, André. "Women and Crime in the Early Eighteenth Century, 1712-1759." *Lawful Authority: Readings in the History of Criminal Justice in Canada*. Ed. R. C. Macleod. Toronto: Copp Clark Pitman, 1988. 9-21. Print.

Lansing, Michael. "Different Methods, Different Places: Feminist Geography and New Directions in US Western History." *Journal of Historical Geography* 29.2 (2003): 230-247. Print.

MacDonald, Edward. *If You're Stronghearted: Prince Edward Island in the Twentieth Century*. Charlottetown: Prince Edward Island Museum and Heritge Foundation, 2000. Print

Massey, Doreen. *World City*. Cambridge: Polity, 2007. Print.

Osborne, Judith A. "The Crime of Infanticide: Throwing Out the Baby With the Bathwater." *Canadian Journal of Family Law* 6 (1987): 47-59. Print.

Parker, Karen F. "Women and Crime in Context: Examining the Linkages Between Patriarchy and Female Offending Across Space." *Feminist Criminology* 3.1 (2008): 5-24. Print.

Pilarczyk, Ian C. "'So Foul a Deed': Infanticide in Montreal, 1825-1850." *Law and History Review* 30.2 (2012): 575-634. Print.

Poutanen, Mary Anne. "The Homeless, the Whore, the Drunkard, and the Disorderly: Contours of Female Vagrancy in Montreal Courts, 1810-1842." *Gendered Pasts: Historical Essays in Femininity and Masculinity in Canada*. Eds Kathryn McPherson, Cecilia Morgan, and Nancy M. Forestell. Toronto: UTP, 2003. 29-47. Print.

Rattigan, Clíona. "'I Thought From Her Appearance That She Was in The Family Way': Detecting Infanticide Cases in Ireland, 1900-1921." *Family and Community History* 11.2 (2008): 134-151. Print.

Williams, Samantha. "The Experience of Pregnancy and Childbirth for Unmarried Mothers in London, 1760-1866." *Women's History Review* 20.1: 67-86. Print.

Wright, Mary Ellen. "Unnatural Mothers: Infanticide in Halifax, 1850-1875." *Nova Scotia Historical Review* 7.2 (1987): 13-29. Print.

Chapter 7

Baby Farming and Betrayal: Foster Mothers Who Murder

Rachel Franks and Caitlin Adams

Introduction

By the mid- to late nineteenth century, those most at risk of being murdered in Australia were newborn babies. In New South Wales, for example, infants accounted for less than 3 per cent of the total population but were murdered at fifty-five times the rate of adults (Allen 31), with exnuptial children, in Australia's first colony and across the continent, having a far lower chance of survival than those born in wedlock (Swain and Howe 91). Infanticide was not just common but so normalized that one Sydney newspaper carried a regular column—"How the Babies Go"—which reported on the dead babies found in the city each week from the late 1880s up until the early 1900s. During this time, middle-class domesticity was becoming entrenched in England and its Australian colonies (Davidoff and Hall 175, 335-43; Davin, "Child Labour" 638-39; Grimshaw et al. 202, 117-21) with ideas of maternal duty increasingly fetishized. News coverage assumed these infants were illegitimate and so accepted their deaths as the natural solution to the challenge that unmarried mothers and their children posed to the conventional family (Swain and Howe 91-92).

This chapter uses newspaper accounts of infanticide in Australia to examine how the imagery of the good mother was both claimed by baby farmers and contested through public discussion. It uses three case studies concerning baby farming and its most tragic consequences in New South Wales, Victoria, and Western Australia. Print media coverage of the trials of John and Sarah Makin, Frances Knorr, and Alice Mitchell drew on ideas around virtuous motherhood, the social stigma attached to unmarried mothers, and the foster mothers who turned caring into a career. Shurlee Swain and Renate Howe note that in Victorian parliamentary debates, the spectre of the baby farmer obscured the reality that birth mothers commonly killed their infants (101). This chapter argues that, in turn, baby farmers drew on the imagery of good motherhood to obscure their own neglect.

Newspaper commentary reveals the social positioning of motherhood in the Australian colonies. This form of print media explicitly discussed the importance of motherhood and prescribed clear characteristics, duties, and behaviours for mothers. In 1878, the *Sydney Mail and New South Wales Advertiser* explained a mother "should live for duty, and teach her children to do the same" ("Mother's Love Reconsidered" 90). The *North Melbourne Courier* similarly claimed that mothering "is the most responsible work in the world" and counselled mothers to model "obedient, unselfish, and honorable" conduct to their children ("Responsibility of Motherhood" 3). Another example of the public exhortation of such sentiments was seen in the *Maitland Weekly Mercury*'s poem, published in 1894, which asserted that mothers were those women who "within her heart the knowledge of all good" resides ("Poetry" 9). Furthermore, newspapers reflected the ways that society-wide interest stopped short of society-wide responsibility for the poor, vulnerable, and weak (Davin, "Imperialism and Motherhood" 12).

With appalling repetition, the loss of life was noted in various newspapers in short narratives. The example below, from Sydney in 1891, contrasts a commitment to celebrate a great explorer and navigator with a complete failure to provide meaningful social security and protect the most at-risk members of society: "[T]he body of a newly-born female infant was discovered by Constable Flynn in Hyde Park, near Captain Cook's statue. Flynn removed the body to the South Sydney Morgue, where it was examined by a doctor, who expressed the opinion that the child had been born alive, and had died from exposure" ("How the Babies Go" 3).

Some of the most publicized infant deaths during the colonial period were at the hands of baby farmers. Baby farming was a practice that Australia inherited, alongside many traditional ideas of family and motherhood, from Britain. In a society with little tolerance for the unmarried mother or her illegitimate newborn, baby farming—the taking in of infants in exchange for payment—was commonplace. Baby farmers took in children for a small fee to offset the costs associated with raising a child and to secure a modest income. Some of these foster mothers—a few of whom were trained general nurses, qualified midwives, or wet nurses—betrayed their young charges and turned to manslaughter or murder. John E. S. McCulloch describes the practice as one in which women made a living "from tending to (usually illegitimate) children on a sort of reverse hire purchase basis—a lump sum deposit and so much per week—and generally used the profits to support their own families" (48). Thus, baby farming can be seen as a practice of sacrificing the children of others to ensure the survival of the baby farmer themselves or their own offspring. The term "baby farming" is thought to have been coined by the *British Medical Journal* as early as October 1867 ("Baby-Farming" 343).

To some extent, the public abandonment of infants was easier for politicians and their policy makers to respond to. For those children who were obviously the victims of wilful murder or died as a result of exposure—discovered in drains, in public parks, on street corners, and in waste grounds—there was, without identification of the mother, no immediate focus for blame. Rather, governments placed advertisements offering lucrative rewards in return for information and free pardons for accomplices ("Infanticide" 2073; "Infanticide" 11). Furthermore, birth mothers were rarely charged with infanticide and those who were often had their crimes commuted to the lighter sentence of "concealment of birth" (Swain and Howe 95-96; Stephen and Oliver 25)[1]. In instances of baby farming, however, public discussion considered whether the birth mothers or the foster mothers were to blame. These so-called bad mothers were responsible for the illegitimacy rates that drove the industry of baby farming. Underpinning broad discussions of baby farming are notions of class as well as ideals of femininity and motherhood. From the late eighteenth century, popular debates around which women were suited to the task of mothering agitated the Australian colonies. These ideas were expressed in anxiety around the morality of convict women and motivated the establishment of orphan schools (Damousi 120, 128)[2]. Issues around who could and should mother the colony's children continued throughout the nineteenth century and were driven by the newspapers of the day.

In both England and its antipodean colonies, working-class mothers came under growing scrutiny. Governments, upper- and middle-class philanthropists, and medical professionals all sought to manage the mothering practices of labouring women (Davin, "Imperial Motherhood" 26-27, 36-39; Kociumbas 144-47, 150). From the end of the century, anxieties around racial and Imperial fitness gave concerns around baby farming new impetus. This was particularly pronounced in Australia, where falling birth rates combined with concern that without sufficient population growth, white settlers would be inundated by "Asiatics" (Swain, "Toward a Social Geography" 153; *Official Report* 157).

Against this backdrop—concern for the falling birth rate and the elevation of motherhood—leading members of the medical profession proffered the view that women who took in babies to nurse were "engaged in a system of commercial infanticide" (Swain, "Toward a Social Geography" 152). In 1890, *The Contemporary Review* ran an essay by English social commentator Benjamin Waugh, who took pains to distinguish between the good foster mother and the baby farmer. This division, he claimed, could be traced to the pursuit of money and was between those women who wanted to adopt a child for the sake of "joy in children" and those who advertised for children "where a 'living' is the chief motive" (701). Nor were the women whose children suffered under this system exempt. Waugh compared mothers who knowingly left their infants to the mercy of baby farmers to "heathen" or "cannibal mothers," who allegedly ate their own children (700). He disqualified these working-class women from motherhood and even womanhood itself, calling them "mere she-things" (705).

This chapter looks at three of the most notorious baby farming cases in Australia: John and Sarah Makin who buried dead babies in Sydney backyards and were punished in 1893; Frances Knorr who murdered babies in Melbourne and was hanged in 1894; and Alice Mitchell who killed as many as forty of the fifty-two babies placed in her care in Perth and was sentenced to a term of hard labour in 1907. The significant publicity surrounding these foster mothers who murdered babies, across the entire colonial Australian press corps, assisted in generating sufficient public pressure for legislators to bring in child protection laws across the continent (Kociumbas 147-48). The coverage of these cases all debated issues surrounding child welfare and the idea of the good mother. Successful prosecutions of baby farmers not only highlighted the difficult choices forced upon unmarried mothers in the late nineteenth and early twentieth centuries but also illustrated the boundaries of mothering and motherhood.

John and Sarah Makin

Two Sydney-based baby farmers, and possibly the best-known child murderers in Australia, were John and Sarah Makin. John Makin was born on February 14, 1845, in Dapto in New South Wales; Sarah Sutcliffe was born later the same year on December 20, in Sydney. The pair married on August 27, 1871, and they eventually had a total of "five sons and five daughters" (Radi 257-58). This family swelled when the Makins took up baby farming. On June 24, 1892, a notice appeared on the front page of *The Evening News*. In between notices for a "kind Person to Adopt Baby Boy, 9 days old" and "LOAN of £2500 on security of Property valued at £7100" was an advertisement for a suitable carer for Amber Murray's child: "WANTED, kindly, motherly person, to adopt fair baby boy, 3 weeks, small premium" (1).

Such advertisements often appeared alongside notices that perpetuated, in part, the problem of baby farming. On the same page as the advertisement for Murray's baby, Horace, were notices for "respectable Girl, from 12 years, good home, clothing, in return for light services" and "useful Girl, 14, comfortable home and clothing in return for services" ("Wanted" 1). Annie Cossins explains "most illegitimate babies were born to servants. Domestic service was the most common form of employment for single women in cities and usually involved living-in" (*Baby Farming* 63). Such arrangements made women vulnerable to sexually-based abuses of power by employers or fellow employees, with gendered social expectations of the day ensuring that it was rare for men to face any consequences for the coercion of a girl or woman (Cossins, *Female Criminality* 60). Girls and women who fell pregnant under these conditions—needing to avoid the shame of a child born outside of marriage or needing to keep their paid position— had very few options. Turning to a baby farmer was legal and came with a promise of potentially taking a child back if the birth mother's circumstances changed.

The Makins responded to Murray under the name E. Hill (Cossins, *Baby Farmers* 173-74). This alias was one of many subterfuges, such as carefully worded advertisements and frequent changes of address, that were familiar to many nineteenth-century baby farmers (Swain, "Toward a Social Geography" 156). When deposed in court, Murray stated Mrs Makin assured her that: "If you give me your child I will bring it up as one of my own", and Mr Makin had said that for £2 10s or £3, a large sum to ask of a poor and single woman, the infant "would not be in better hands than ours" ("Great Baby Farming Case" 4). The couple came across as caring and genuine. By promising to treat the child as one of their own, Mrs Makin evoked ideas around a mother's natural duty towards her child, conveying that they were good people and good carers for Murray's baby. The truth was different. The Makins left their Macdonaldtown home in August 1892. In October, new drainage pipes were being laid in the property's rear yard when a small package was discovered by a labourer who, thinking it was a cat, reburied the bundle. The discovery of a second, similar package the next day revealed a baby, and authorities were quickly alerted (Cossins, *Baby Farmers* 70-71). Police went to Macdonaldtown to undertake a methodical dig of the yard:

> No. 1, found on Wednesday evening about 20 minutes past 5 o'clock: Female child, aged about 14 months, wrapped in a piece of white flannel with a red and blue stripe, and with a napkin pinned around. No. 2, found on Thursday at 9.30 a.m.: Male child, aged about six months, dressed in a coloured shirt, and wrapped in a napkin and a piece of white flannel covered with blood. No. 3, found on Thursday at 10.30 a.m.: Male child, aged about three months, wrapped in white calico, pinned up in several places, and in a white napkin worked with the letter "F" in black in one corner. No. 4, found on Thursday at 11.30 a.m.: Female child, aged about two months, dressed in a white flannel dress worked in fancy work, and scallops all round, striped pinafore, and petticoat. No. 5, found at 2.45 p.m. on Thursday: Female child, aged about two weeks, dressed in flannel wrapper. ("Discovery of Dead Infants" 10)

Babies A, B, C, and D ("Thursday, November 10" 4) were discovered in the yard of another inner-Sydney suburb, a Redfern address once occupied by the Makins. Two more bodies were discovered days later at the nearby suburb of Chippendale, where the Makins had lived the previous year ("Two Bodies Found" 5). Large, bold fonts signalled news of "Wholesale Infanticide in Sydney" (28); "Discovery of Infants' Remains" (7); and "Great Baby Farming Case" (4). The Makins's fate was sealed when Horace Murray's body was identified and declared to have "been killed by foul means" ("Thursday, December 22" 7). In the eyes of the press, and press readerships, the Makins ceased to be parents and were repositioned as killers.

The Makins certainly provided false hope to parents and grim fodder for the press in equal measure. The number and length of articles about the Makins marked a major shift in Australian reporting of infanticide. In the early part of the century, most information on criminal trials are from accounts in local newspapers. These reports "tend to give broad outlines of proceedings rather than minute accounts of testimony; moreover, many events such as the murder of a baby or spouse were deemed simply too gruesome and unsavoury for extensive reportage in the press" (Saunders 69). The trauma inflicted upon babies and their birth mothers profiled baby farming and its risks, in turn forcing wide-ranging conversations about the care of children in the colony.

Shortly after the case of the Makins was finalized, an advertisement appeared in a Sydney newspaper: "WANTED, Kind Couple Adopt nice little Boy, 6 years, father dead; no baby farmer need apply" ("Advertising" 1). The inference, here, of only a good mother being wanted is clear. The Makins were guilty of numerous crimes, and through their failure to repent and the sheer scale of their activities, they sparked a public furore. Most obviously, there was a failure to live up to the minimum expectations of caring for an infant and fulfil the basic duties of feeding, housing, clothing, and tending. That the Makins treated their foster children as garbage, throwing them out in their backyards, was extremely shocking. Both Makins were sentenced to death: John Makin was hanged on August 15 1893, and Sarah Makin's sentence was commuted to life in prison, but she was paroled in 1911 (Fitzgerald 279-80).

Frances Knorr

As the trials of John and Sarah Makin progressed in Sydney, similar crimes were being committed in Melbourne. One perpetrator of such criminal activity was Frances "Minnie" Thwaites, born on November 6, 1867, in Middlesex in England. Within two years of Thwaites landing in Sydney, in 1887, she had married a German-born man, Rudolph Knorr, and moved to Melbourne. Financial difficulties, the imprisonment of her husband for selling furniture he had not paid off (Laster 220) and her attempts to provide for her own children saw the young Mrs Knorr take to baby farming in an effort to stay solvent. Her crimes and her punishment would, like the Makins before her, dominate the press. Again, this case of baby farming was driven by a general, society-wide failure to accommodate the unmarried mother and her illegitimate baby, since "these girls [who had given up their babies] were not devoid of natural affection but were deluded into the belief that they were delivering their children into the hands of a motherly person, who would bestow on them the maternal care and love which their own circumstances rendered it impossible to provide" (Fitzgerald 281-82).

The scale of Knorr's baby farming was not nearly as extensive as the Makins' enterprise. There are, however, several similarities across the two cases that reinforce the known patterns of baby farming in Australia. Knorr used multiple names, she changed her address regularly and the babies thought to have died at her hand were anonymized as Babies 1, 2, and 3 ("Trial of Frances Knorr" 3). Knorr was also a mother, a role that could be mobilized by baby farmers with their own children serving as caring credentials in taking on the babies of other women. The most striking similarity is how the crimes were revealed. In the rear yard of a Brunswick home once occupied by Knorr, works uncovered the body of a baby (Saunders 135-36), with two more infant corpses subsequently found. These discoveries led to Knorr's arrest.

Knorr had been convicted of minor offences in Sydney before travelling to Melbourne with her husband, including multiple counts of larceny and false pretences ("Particulars of Frances Knorr's Career" 3). The husband and wife were also known to police in Adelaide. Nothing Knorr had done in Sydney or Adelaide compared to her Melbourne-based crimes. The Knorrs returned to Sydney where they were located and arrested. The idea of the good mother was again contested in this story, as Knorr had just given birth to her second child, a baby girl, (Laster 220). To outsiders, it may have initially seemed that she was a good mother—at least to her own children—as the birth of her daughter Reita Daisy generated a delay before Knorr could be remanded to Melbourne to face trial for murder. Yet whatever appearance of motherliness this may have created, Knorr was found, once again, to be an inappropriate carer. Shortly before Knorr's execution, Reita was "committed [by the courts] to the Department for Neglected Children" ("Frances Knorr's Baby" 1).

As for many instances of death at the hands of a baby farmer, the cause was cited as general neglect or as being from "unsuitable feeding" (Sutherland 6), with both types of findings carrying inferences of basic incompetence of the carer and placing blame at the feet of the unsuitable foster mother. Interestingly, as Knorr gave her last-minute confession she offered, also, an acknowledgment of the dire ramifications of being a bad person and a bad foster mother: "I confess to be guilty. Placed as I am now within a few hours of my death I express a strong desire that this statement be made public with the hope that my fate will not only be a warning to others but also act as a deterrent to those who are perhaps carrying on the same practice" ("Brunswick Murderer" 2). The case of Knorr was further complicated by her claims that one of her charges, for whom the cause of death had obviously been severe head trauma, had died simply of convulsions. Knorr then attempted to transfer guilt to Edward Thompson, who was a fish hawker who had at one stage been supporting her and her first child while her husband was in gaol and was the father of her second child. When this failed, Knorr implored Thompson to "get witnesses to come to court to swear falsely." The scheme was described as one "of villainy from beginning to end" ("Trial of Frances Knorr" 3). Knorr was sentenced to hang. Australia had hanged numerous felons since the first settlement in 1788, a practice of punishment that came with colonization. Yet comparatively few of those hanged were women. The execution proceeded despite several claims for clemency, including from Knorr's husband, who regardless of admissions of adultery quickly came to the woman's defence, "telling the government his wife was an epileptic given to strange irrational behaviour" (Saunders 141). This information further undermined Knorr's appropriateness to care for children. Not only was she an unsuitable mother but she was, too, an unfit wife. Attempts to explain Knorr's situation were heard but unheeded. The hanging took place, as scheduled, on January 15 1894, making Knorr one of only five women to meet the hangman's noose in Victoria (Laster 221). The event was duly reported, in detail, by the press:

> The execution of Frances Knorr for the perpetration of the Brunswick baby murders took place at the Melbourne Gaol on Monday morning, the gruesome proceedings passing off without the slightest hitch. In view of the fact that the hangman was comparatively inexperienced, and that the doomed woman had signified her intention of refusing to walk to the scaffold, it was dreaded that there would be a scene. Fortunately this did not happen, and the execution was accomplished without bungling, and with quietness and despatch. ("Execution of Frances Knorr" 24)

The professionalism of the executioner is offered in sharp juxtaposition to the unsuitable foster mother at the scaffold. John D. Fitzgerald, an early-twentieth-century legal scholar, wrote the following about baby farming in *Studies in Australian Crime*: "It only remains to say that the execution of Makin and Mrs Knorr effectively stamped out baby murder in Australia as a lucrative profession" (291). Fitzgerald, a former minister of justice and solicitor-general of New South Wales, was incorrect on two counts. First, the Makins and Knorr did not enjoy comfortable lives of financial stability as a result of their baby farming careers. Baby farming, as an industry, was often pursued to secure survival, with baby farmers taking on additional responsibilities not for the purposes of making large sums of money but to offset their own living costs and the costs of keeping their own families. In this way, the care of multiple infants in a single home did not promote personal wealth; rather, it saw the concentration of poverty and precarious living. Second, there would be one more major case of baby farming leading to the deaths of multiple infants in Australia. The case of Alice Mitchell horrified the nation.

Alice Mitchell

Notions of motherhood, and questions of who was qualified to care for children, were central in Australia's final major case of baby farming. When newspapers attributed the deaths of forty children to registered nurse Alice Mitchell, media coverage not only contested Mitchell's status as a good foster mother but also questioned the state's ability to protect children. A key difference between this case and its antecedents, including the Makins and Knorr, was that prior to Mitchell's crimes, legislators had actively sought to eliminate the practice of baby farming in Western Australia. Under the *Health Act 1898* (WA), nurses receiving money for the care of infants were required to register with their local board of health and to keep records of the children in their care (Part VII). In the wake of Federation, and the *Immigration Restriction Act 1901* (Cth), which marked the beginning of the White Australia Policy, Australian commentators fretted about infant mortality and declining birth rates, believing "a strong and sturdy white population was necessary to defend the newly colonised landscape" (Featherstone 446; "Slaughter of Innocents" 5).

Mitchell—a middle-aged nurse registered under the *Health Act* and so subject to departmental inspection—was ostensibly an appropriate carer. Yet when she enrolled as a child minder in 1903, she had already caused the deaths of at least six children. So when the public discovered in March 1907 that Mitchell had allowed numerous infants to die in her care, it was unsurprising that Perth's *Sunday Times* declared "the accused, wasn't the only person on trial, the Perth health board was also in the dock and the popular verdict is, unquestionably, 'Guilty of criminal neglect'" ("Certain Horrors" 4). Given that the case of "Mother Mitchell" and her "Slaughterhouse" ("Mitchell's Baby Farm" 8; "Certain Horrors" 4) was to dominate Western Australian press for over two months, it began prosaically enough. On February 4, 1907, Mitchell flagged a police constable passing her house to complain that a woman whose ailing child she was caring for had not paid maintenance. Without it, Mitchell claimed that she could not acquire the necessary medicine. As a result, the following day, Corporal O'Halloran and Dr. Davey visited Mitchell's house in Edward Street and discovered two emaciated infants, including Ethel Booth, who were quickly removed to the hospital. The filthy condition of the house and the death of Booth the next day prompted Mitchell's arrest and began a series of sensational discoveries about her operation ("Dead Baby [5 Mar.]" 8).

Press coverage of the inquest, and later the criminal trial, revealed dreadful details about how Mitchell treated the infants in her care. During the inquest, thirty-six witnesses were called (Hetherington 83), including the mothers of several of Mitchell's charges, undertakers, doctors, a clergyman, and Mitchell's lodgers, who provided a grim account of the infants' living conditions. Elizabeth Booth described a bleak picture of her daughter's decline. After denying Booth access to her daughter for several weeks, Mitchell finally allowed her to see the child. Booth stated that when she eventually saw the baby: "[S]he hardly knew her. She had sores on her head, sore eyes, and was very thin ... [on a subsequent visit she found that the child] smelt horribly" ("Boarded-Out Infants" 16). Lodger Carl Roux stated that: "Language could not picture the MISERY OF THE ROOM" ("Dead Baby [6 Mar.]" 8). Seven or eight children were kept in there together, healthy and sick alike, without anything to do but lie on disordered bedclothes, unprotected from flies crawling on their faces and around their infected eyes. The babies were attended by a woman named Susie, who had lice and was infected with syphilis.

In a growing climate of medicalized childcare in which hygienic practice came to differentiate good from bad mothers (Kociumbas 147-48), these reports conveyed to readers that Mitchell was a deficient foster mother. A Perth periodical, *Truth*, was more explicit, parodying "Mother Mitchell. The 'Heroine' of the East Perth Baby Farm" under the heading "The Jury's Verdict: Wilful Starvation and Negligence" ("Mitchell's Baby Farm" 8).

The details of Mitchell's neglect were accompanied by disturbing statistics. Throughout the coverage of the case, the number of children revealed to have died under her custody continued to rise ("Dead Baby [8 Mar.]" 8); the final estimate was that forty of fifty-two children had perished due to her lack of care ("Baby-Farming Case" 2). Yet Mitchell was only found guilty of manslaughter—caused by criminal negligence—for the death of one child: Ethel Booth ("Dead Baby" 4). The wealth of testimony surrounding Mitchell's treatment of the infants under her charge did not deter her from claiming she had primarily played the role of the caring mother. When one of the many periodicals interviewed Mitchell, she asserted that the allegations against her were lies and described a scene in which Roux "threw his arms around me and said: 'Never mind, mother. Your friends know you're innocent'" ("Interesting Interview!" 5). Indeed, when the reporter also asked Mitchell if she had frequently prevented mothers from visiting the infants in her care, she replied in the negative. Rather, Mitchell implied that she was the one with strong maternal feeling and that it was the women who had abandoned their children to her who were bad mothers. She exclaimed: "Most of the time I had trouble in getting them to come to the house to see their children" ("Interesting Interview!" 5).

The verdict of manslaughter—combined with what the *Daily News* described as a "comparatively light sentence" ("Dead Baby" 4) of five years hard labour ("Mrs Mitchell Sentenced" 7)—must have seemed a travesty of justice to the Western Australians who had followed the case. Perhaps it was for this reason that newspapers, such as *The Daily News* ("Dead Baby" 4) and *Coolgardie Miner* ("Baby Farming" 3), published the "death roll" of Mitchell's young victims, representing a trial by popular opinion. Indeed, public action commenced less than a fortnight after Mitchell was sentenced, sparking a popular infant life protection movement ("City Notes" 3). This case subsequently went on to drive the passage of the *State Children Act of 1907* (WA), which replaced the *Health Act* and provided more comprehensive measures to protect infants and their mothers (Hetherington 94-96). Although Mitchell was—prior to the discovery of her crimes—apparently an appropriate choice for a child carer, her status as a registered nurse and the media's claim that the Perth health board itself had been on trial did not lead to the conclusion that the state was inadequate to assume the role of mother. Rather, Mitchell was labelled a bad mother and the state assumed greater responsibility for parenting the nation's children.

Conclusion

The problem of baby farming in colonial Australia, and into the early twentieth century, was not a new development. Infanticide in England, in the seventeenth, eighteenth and nineteenth centuries, is well documented. Infanticide was an issue, too, in the United States (see, for example, Broder) as well as other countries around the world. As Cossins wrote in a scathing indictment of nineteenth-century Australian society:

No-one explained why the lives of illegitimate children mattered more when they were dead than when they were alive. The decision in the Makin case did nothing to change the short lives and quick deaths of countless babies in the city of Sydney in the 1890s and beyond. Baby farming was the inevitable outcome of the clash between poverty, morality and women's place in Victorian society. (*Baby Farmers* 229)

Parliamentarians debated the devastating problem but remained unable to reduce the "approximately 6,000 deaths of children under the age of five years each year in the New South Wales colony" (Cossins, *Baby Farmers* 76). Their peers in Victoria faced similar issues, as in late-nineteenth-century Melbourne, Australia's largest city at that time, babies in their first year of life consistently provided "over 40% of murder victims" (Swain, "Toward a Social Geography" 154). The history of women in Australia clearly reveals how the "unmarried pregnant woman was trapped by the twin gatekeepers of financial ruin on one side and moral ruination on the other. The thin space in between was occupied by the baby farmer" (Cossins, *Baby Farmers* 62). In the heyday of baby farming, it was easy to report, and read, of a black and white world in which evil villains preyed on the most vulnerable for profit.

The women who were involved in this trade in babies were thus bound by both patriarchal values and ideas around motherhood, its duties, as well as its characteristics. It is no coincidence that baby farmers used the language and imagery of motherhood to argue that they were appropriate carers or that newspaper coverage and public commentary condemned these women through the same terms. In this period when ideals of "good" and "hygienic" motherhood were prized, media coverage detailed these baby farmers' failures to demonstrate appropriate care in order to suggest that they were unsuitable foster mothers. Today, a review of the social contexts, with their myriad complexities, reveals issues of baby farming shown in shades of grey. As Swain argues: "Feminist historians, [for example], have sought to question assumptions of innate criminality amongst the key actors. The supposed baby farmers, they have argued, should be seen as one extreme of a continuum of out-of-home infant care, as much victims as were the mothers of the children under their care" ("Toward a Social Geography" 152). The idea of victimhood persists, with a focus on the child, and is seen in modern Australian histories exploring the foster care of children. Dee Michell has noted, for example, that regardless of a child's negative or positive experiences in care, there is always "the painful acquaintance with social stigma at an early age" (663). Importantly, in the context of this research, Michell acknowledges how the stigma attached to children who are given to, or taken by, the state are routinely victims of "injuries inflicted by a classed society" (669). Those babies and children with less resources suffer the broader stereotyping of "less", they were seen as less intelligent, less law-abiding, less loved. As early baby farmers were, themselves, looked down upon, recent studies reveal that modern-day foster mothers often feel powerless and undervalued. These mothers, in a continuation of the problems with press coverage highlighted here, also "report feeling stigmatized by the media," which is in addition to greater feelings of social isolation (Blythe et al. 235).

There were several legal changes realized across Australia in the response to public pressure to bring about better state control and regulation over infants and children after so many horrific cases of baby farming. The results included the *Infant Life Protection Act 1890* (Vic) and the *Act to Provide for the Protection of Children 1892* (NSW), which made unauthorized adoptions for payment unlawful, as well as several pieces of legislation in Western Australia, including the *State Children Act 1907* (WA). These, and associated pieces of legislation, began to replace the widespread system of institutionalizing infants and children which "essentially positioned the children as being in need of control rather than care" (Swain, "History of Child Protection Legislation" 6). Although the efficacy of such legislative protections has since been shown to be flawed, these, and similar, acts in colonies across Australia did put an end to the widespread practice of baby farming. Many babies died in the nineteenth and early twentieth century in Australia through basic—and in some poverty-based circumstances—unavoidable neglect. Some deaths were brought about much more deliberately. What makes the three cases, briefly explored here, so extraordinary is how the cover of the caring and suitable foster mother was utilized to betray, extort, neglect, and ultimately serve as a guise for manslaughter and murder.

Endnotes

1. *The Criminal Law Amendment Act 1883* (NSW), specified this crime as: "Where any woman has been delivered of a child, every person who, by any act after its death, wilfully conceals, or endeavours to conceal the birth of such child, whether it died before, or at, or after its birth, shall be liable to imprisonment ... any person tried for murder of a child may, if acquitted of such murder be convicted under this section" (s57).

2. The removal of "children from the age of three from their convict mothers" and sent to orphan schools, in the early years of the colony, reiterated traditional ideas around who could and could not mother and "established a precedent for legal seizure and separation of children" which was seen, across the country, into the late twentieth century (Bogle 78). It should be noted that First Nations parents were consistently targeted, and their children routinely taken and so placed at risk. This practice of removing children from their parents inflicted great trauma, which is still felt today, as Indigenous children were "forcibly separated from their families and communities since the very first days of the European occupation of Australia" (*Bringing Them Home Report*, Chapter 2).

Works Cited

Act to Provide for the Protection of Children 1892 (NSW).

"Advertising." *Evening News*, 13 Dec. 1893, 1, http://nla.gov.au/nla.news article112931856. Accessed 21 Nov. 2021.

Allen, Judith A. *Sex and Secrets, Crimes Involving Australian Women Since 1880*. Oxford University Press, 1990.

"Baby-Farming." *British Medical Journal*, vol. 2, no. 355, 1867, pp. 340-45.

"Baby Farming." *Coolgardie Miner*, 18 Apr. 1907, 3, http://nla.gov.au/nla.news-article217453605. Accessed 21 Nov. 2021.

"The Baby-Farming Case." *Coolgardie Miner*, 18 Apr. 1907, 2, nla.gov.au/nla.news-article217453590. Accessed 21 Nov. 2021.

Blythe, Stacy L., Debra Jackson, Elizabeth J. Halcomb, and Lesley Wilkes. "The Stigma of Being a Long-Term Foster Carer." *Journal of Family Nursing*, vol. 18, no. 2, 2012, pp. 234-60.

"Boarded-Out Infants." *Western Mail*, 9 Mar. 1907, 16, nla.gov.au/nla.news-article37399502. Accessed 14 May 2018.

Bogle, Michael. *Convicts: Transportation and Australia*. 1999. Historic Houses Trust of New South Wales, 2008.

Bringing Them Home Report: National Inquiry into the Separation of Aboriginal and Torres Strait Island Children from Their Families. Human Rights and Equal Opportunity Commission, 1997, humanrights.gov.au/our-work/bringing-them-home-report-1997. Accessed 21 Nov. 2021.

Broder, Sherri. "Child Care or Child Neglect? Baby Farming in Late-Nineteenth-Century Philadelphia." *Gender & Society*, vol. 2, no. 2, 1988, pp. 128-48.

"The Brunswick Murderer." *Express and Telegraph*, 16 Jan. 1894, 2, hnla.gov.au/nla.news-article208288619. Accessed 21 Nov. 2021.

"Certain Horrors." *Sunday Times*, 14 Apr. 1907, 4, nla.gov.au/nla.news-article57227567. Accessed 21 Nov. 2021.

Children's Protection Act 1892 (NSW).

"City Notes." *Eastern Districts Chronicle*, 27 Apr. 1907, 3.

Cossins, Annie. *The Baby Farmers: A Chilling Tale of Missing Babies, Shameful Secrets and Murder in 19th Century Australia*. Allen & Unwin, 2013.

Cossins, Annie. *Female Criminality: Infanticide, Moral Panics and the Female Body*. Palgrave Macmillan, 2015.

Criminal Law Amendment Act 1883 (NSW).

Damousi, Joy. *Depraved and Disorderly*. Cambridge University Press, 1997.

Davidoff, Leonore, and Catherine Hall. *Family Fortunes*. Century Hutchinson, 1987.

Davin, Anna. "Child Labour, the Working-Class Family, and Domestic Ideology in 19th Century Britain." *Development and Change*, vol. 13, no. 4, 1982, pp. 633-52.

Davin, Anna. "Imperialism and Motherhood." *History Workshop Journal*, vol. 5, 1978, pp. 9-66.

"Dead Baby." *The Daily News*, 5 Mar. 1907, 8, nla.gov.au/nla.news-article83316529. Accessed 21 Nov. 2021.

"Dead Baby." *The Daily News*, 6 Mar. 1907, 8, nla.gov.au/nla.news-article83317999. Accessed 21 Nov. 2021.

"Dead Baby." *The Daily News*, 8 Mar. 1907, 8, nla.gov.au/nla.news-article83316382. Accessed 21 Nov. 2021.

"Dead Baby." *The Daily News*, 15 Apr. 1907, 4, nla.gov.au/nla.news-article77616269. Accessed 21 Nov. 2021.

"Discovery of Dead Infants." *Sydney Morning Herald*, 5 Nov. 1892, 10, nla.gov.au/nla.news-article13885182. Accessed 21 Nov. 2021.

"Discovery of Infants' Remains." *Sydney Morning Herald*, 20 Dec. 1892, 7, nla.gov.au/nla.news-article13890455. Accessed 21 Nov. 2021.

"Execution of Frances Knorr." *The Leader*, 20 Jan. 1894, 24, nla.gov.au/nla.news-article196856411. Accessed 21 Nov. 2021.

Featherstone, Lisa. "'The Value of the Victorian Infant': Whiteness and the Emergence of Paediatrics in Late Colonial Australia." *Historicising Whiteness: Transnational Perspectives on the Construction of an Identity*, edited by Leigh Boucher, Jane Carey, and Katherine Ellinghaus, RMIT Publishing and University of Melbourne, 2007, pp. 445-53.

Fitzgerald, John D. *Studies in Australian Crime*, 2nd Series. Cornstalk, 1924.

"Frances Knorr's Baby." *The Herald*, 3 Jan. 1894, 1, nla.gov.au/nla.news-article241581477. Accessed 21 Nov. 2021.

"Great Baby Farming Case." *The Evening News*, 20 Dec. 1892, 4, nla.gov.au/nla.news-article113320316. Accessed 21 Nov. 2021.

Grimshaw, Patricia, Marilyn Lake, Ann McGrath and Marian Quartly. *Creating A Nation*. McPhee Gribble, 1994.

Health Act 1898 (WA).

Hetherington, Penelope. "Baby-Farming in Western Australia: The Case Against Alice Mitchell 1907." *Studies in Western Australian History*, vol. 25, 2007, pp. 75-97.

"How the Babies Go." *The Evening News*, 7 Sep. 1891, 3, nla.gov.au/nla.news-article111979890. Accessed 21 Nov. 2021.

Immigration Restriction Act 1901 (Cth).

Infant Life Protection Act 1890 (Vic).

"Infanticide, £50 Reward." *New South Wales Government Gazette*, 19

Sep. 1871, 2073, nla.gov.au/nla.news-article223717011. Accessed 21 Nov. 2021.

"Infanticide, £50 Reward." *The Australian Star*, 6 Aug. 1892, 11, nla.gov.au/nla.news-article227299685. Accessed 21 Nov. 2021.

"Interesting Interview!" *Truth*, 10 Mar. 1907, 5, nla.gov.au/nla.news-article206694736. Accessed 21 Nov. 2021.

Kociumbas, Jan. "Azaria's Antecedents: Stereotyping Infanticide in late Nineteenth Century Australia." *Gender & History*, vol. 13, no. 1, 2001, pp. 138-60.

Laster, Kathy. "Knorr, Frances Lydia (Minnie) (1867–1894)." *Australian Dictionary of Biography: Supplementary Volume*. Australian National University, 2005.

McCulloch, John E. S. "Baby-Farming and Benevolence in Brisbane, 1885–1915." *Hecate*, vol. 36, no. 1-2, 2010, pp. 42-56.

Michell, Dee. "Foster Care, Stigma and the Sturdy, Unkillable Children of the Very Poor." *Continuum: Journal of Media & Cultural Studies*, vol. 29, no. 4, 2015, pp. 663-76.

"Mitchell's Baby Farm." *Truth*, 17 Mar. 1907, 8, nla.gov.au/nla.news-article206694835. Accessed 21 Nov. 2021.

"Mrs Mitchell Sentenced." *The Advertiser*, 16 Apr. 1907, 7, nla.gov.au/nla.news-article5062143. Accessed 21 Nov. 2021.

"Mother's Love Reconsidered." *The Sydney Mail and New South Wales Advertiser*, 20 July 1878, 90, nla.gov.au/nla.news-article162695854. Accessed 21 Nov. 2021.

Official Report of the National Australasian Convention Debates, Sydney, 2 March to April 1891. Government Printer, 1891, in Raymond Evans, Clive Moore, Kay Saunders, and Bryan Jamison. *1901 Our Future's Past: Documenting Australia's Federation*. Macmillan, 1997.

"Particulars of Frances Knorr's Career." *Toowoomba Chronicle and Darling Downs General Advertiser*, 16 Jan. 1894, 3, nla.gov.au/nla.news-article218998545. Accessed 21 Nov. 2021.

"Poetry." *The Maitland Weekly Mercury*, 29 Sep. 1894, 9, nla.gov.au/nla.news-article126610560. Accessed 21 Nov. 2021.

Radi, Heather. "Makin, John (1845–1893) and Makin, Sarah Jane (1845–1918)." *Australian Dictionary of Biography: Supplement, 1580–1980*. Australian National University, 2005, pp. 257-58.

"Responsibility of Motherhood." *North Melbourne Courier and West Melbourne Advertiser*, 6 Aug. 1897, 3, nla.gov.au/nla.news-articlel 03235695. Accessed 21 Nov. 2021.

Saunders, Kay. *Deadly Australian Women*. ABC Books, 2013.

"Slaughter of Innocents." *Sunday Times*, 4 Mar. 1906, 5, nla.gov.au/nla.news-article57211194. Accessed 21 Nov. 2021.

State Children Act 1907 (WA).

Stephen, Alfred, and Alexander Oliver. *Criminal Law Manual: Comprising the Criminal Law Amendment Act of 1883, with An Introduction, Commentary and Index*. Thomas Richards Government Printer, 1883.

Sutherland, Miss. "Traffic in Babies." *The Argus*, 1 Jan. 1894, 6, nla.gov.au/nla.news-article8721430. Accessed 21 Nov. 2021.

Swain, Shurlee. *History of Child Protection Legislation, prepared for the Royal Commission into Institutional Responses to Child Sexual Abuse*, Australian Catholic University, 2014, safeguardingchildren.acu.edu.au/research-and-resources/history-of-child-protection-legislation. Accessed 21 Nov. 2021.

Swain, Shurlee. "Toward a Social Geography of Baby Farming." *The History of the Family*, vol. 10, no. 2, 2005, pp. 151-59.

Swain, Shurlee, and Renate Howe. *Single Mothers and Their Children: Disposal, Punishment and Survival in Australia*. Cambridge University Press, 1995.

"Thursday, December 22." *Sydney Morning Herald*, 22 Dec. 1892, 7, nla.gov.au/nla.news-article13890797. Accessed 21 Nov. 2021.

"Thursday, November 10." *Sydney Morning Herald*, 10 Nov. 1892, 4, nla.gov.au/nla.news-article13885631. Accessed 21 Nov. 2021.

"Trial of Frances Knorr." *The Bendigo Independent*, 2 Dec. 1893, 3, nla.gov.au/nla.news-article174519464. Accessed 21 Nov. 2021.

"Two Bodies Found in Chippendale." *Sydney Morning Herald*, 14 Nov. 1892, 5, nla.gov.au/nla.news-article13886199. Accessed 21 Nov. 2021.

"Wanted." *The Evening News*, 24 June 1892, 1, nla.gov.au/nla.news-article112944141. Accessed 21 Nov. 2021.

Waugh, Benjamin. "Baby-Farming." *The Contemporary Review*, 1 Jan. 1890, 700-14.

"Wholesale Infanticide in Sydney." *The Leader*, 3 Dec. 1892, 28, nla.gov.au/nla.news-article196894054. Accessed 21 Nov. 2021.

Chapter 8

Storytelling and the Personification of Oppression During US Feminism's First Wave: The Infanticide Case of Hester Vaughn

Andrea S. Walsh

> Let every heart by sorrow tried,
> Let every woman born,
> Feel that her cause stands side by side
> With that of Hester Vaughn.
> —Lizzie Doten, "Hester Vaughn" in *Poems of Progress*, 1871, 83

On July 2, 1868, in Philadelphia, Hester Vaughn, a young impoverished British immigrant, was convicted of first-degree murder for infanticide and sentenced to death by hanging. Judge James Reilly Ludlow of Philadelphia's Court of Common Pleas faced Vaughn directly at her sentencing and emphatically stated that since infanticide had become so common, "some woman must be made an example of" (Snodgrass). At that moment, little did Ludlow know that this death sentence would become a rallying cry for women's rights activists, such as Susan B. Anthony and Elizabeth Cady Stanton, who mobilized to save Vaughn and narrated her story to reveal the ways in which a woman could be "oppressed on all sides" by individual men and male-dominated institutions (Stanton, "Declaration"). With a sociological and historical focus on the power of feminist storytelling as a social movement practice, this chapter draws upon primary sources, such as legal documents, newspaper accounts, and activist biographies as well as contemporary scholarship on the first wave of US feminism and the Vaughn case. This piece explores the contested meaning of this case in its time and argues that the Vaughn narrative has continuing relevance for contemporary feminism, since it opens up rich possibilities for understanding complex and interrelated issues of reproductive, economic, and legal justice for women and girls. The feminist ideal of freely chosen motherhood lies at the heart and centre of the Vaughn case, then and now.

Storytelling has long played a key role in social justice movements. As sociologist Francesca Polletta argues, such dramatization can engage a wide public while also providing a framework for understanding social problems and mobilizing to change them. Narratives can inspire empathy for victims of injustice, anger at a system that denies human rights, and determination to change laws, institutions, and culture (Polletta). Many first-wave US women's rights advocates, such as Susan B. Anthony and Elizabeth Cady Stanton, regularly employed storytelling, personifying issues such as marital oppression, sexual violence, and workplace inequality to advance a broad reform agenda (Thomas, "Misappropriating"; Wellman). Sometimes activists shared stories from their own lives; other times they wove composite narratives from the experiences of many women. These storytellers employed hyperbole, crafted parables, and drew upon genre conventions of sentimental fiction popular with women (Thomas, "Misappropriating"). Through vivid, melodramatic, and sometimes confrontational narratives, women's rights leaders employed maternalist rhetoric[1] to appeal to female audiences (Dubois; Elbert; Ginzberg) while also invoking the ethos of democracy and justice. When a story featured a poor young immigrant woman sentenced to hang for infanticide, it possessed urgent movement appeal. From August 1868 through June 1869, the legal case of Hester Vaughn engaged the energies of activists—such as Susan B. Anthony and Elizabeth Cady Stanton, leaders in the radical wing of the movement—which focused not only on suffrage but also on a broader reform agenda (Dubois). These leaders saw Vaughn's case as an opportunity both to save an individual life and advocate for broader change.

In 1868, storytelling was not new to the women's rights movement. In shaping Vaughn's narrative, her advocates drew upon a rich legacy of activist storytelling. Antebellum female temperance, antiprostitution, and abolitionist groups, infused with Quaker tradition, employed narratives about everyday and family justice issues as well as the need for broader reform (Roth; Wellman). Temperance stories and songs dramatized the violence suffered by wives of alcoholics. Stanton saw herself as channelling the voices and stories of women unable to speak for themselves: "The drunkards' wives speak through us and they number 50,000" (Stanton, "The Rights of Married Women"). Autobiographies, such as ex-slave Harriet Jacobs's *Incidents in the Life of a Slave Girl* (1861), testify to the brutality of slavery and the sexual exploitation of female slaves. The 1848 Seneca Falls Convention, the first organized U.S. women's rights gathering, drew networks of upstate New York participants from these narratively rich and gender-conscious movements (Wellman). As the movement continued to press for change after Seneca Falls, activists continued their storytelling practices in advocating for marriage reform, educational opportunity, and suffrage. Twenty years after Seneca Falls, the strategy of feminist storytelling would intensify as the movement faced critical challenges after the Civil War. The radical wing of the movement, headed by Anthony and Stanton, split with some of its abolitionist colleagues; the campaign for female suffrage, after an 1867 Kansas defeat, faced an uncertain future (Dubois). At this time, activists such as Stanton, Anthony, and Anna Dickinson tried innovative strategies, such as supporting female defendants in high profile legal cases (Ginzberg). Veterans of temperance, abolition, and antiprostitution campaigns, these activists employed the narrative skills, frames, and language honed within those movements to advocate for these women.

Among the most controversial of these cases was the 1868 infanticide trial of Hester Vaughn. The decision to support Vaughn was fraught with political risk, since many Americans could have viewed Vaughn as a monstrous mother, an antithesis of the core values of the women's movement. Understanding the political vision and organizing style of Elizabeth Cady Stanton is key to understanding the decision to campaign for Hester Vaughn. As historian Lori Ginzberg notes, by 1868, Stanton, having risen to women's movement fame within an informal elite, saw herself as a vanguard leader rather than one democratically accountable to a membership. Never an "organization woman," Stanton disliked "dragging, vapid conventions" (Ginzberg 138).

Although often hypercritical of passive women, Stanton nevertheless saw herself as expressing their grievances and stories in her writing and speeches, often drawing on the imagery and narratives of temperance and abolition (Ginzberg). Her 1851 essay "Our Costume," for example, advocates for female dress reform by portraying conservative upper-class women as "parlor dolls" weighed down by clothing that felt like a "ball and chain" (Stanton, "Our Costume"). In 1868, she cofounded (with Anthony and Parker Pillsbury) *The Revolution*, a weekly with a circulation of three thousand, as well as the Working Women's National Association (WWNA), a small group of skilled female workers, primarily printers. In Ginzberg's words, "Now that Stanton had her own battleground, she could decide the rules of engagement" (136). Although *The Revolution* (1868–1872) and WWNA (1868–69) had brief lives, both proved central to the Vaughn campaign (S. Gordon). The *Revolution* editors understood the importance of the press and envisioned their newspaper's role as engaging with controversy to challenge a wide range of gender injustices. To Stanton and Anthony, the Vaughn case symbolized political opportunity more than risk. Infused with moral absolutism, Stanton saw gender oppression as akin to colonialism or slavery. The imperial "He" of the 1848 "Declaration of Sentiments" dominates the colonized or enslaved female: "He has endeavored, in every way that he could to destroy her confidence in her own powers, to lessen her self-respect, and to make her willing to lead a dependent and abject life" ("Declaration"). For Stanton and her colleagues, the Vaughn case provided a perfect opportunity to unmask a brutal system of overpowering and unrelenting male tyranny. On February 5, 1868, a few days before Vaughn gave birth, Stanton published a *Revolution* piece, "Infanticide and Prostitution." For communications scholar Angela Ray, Vaughn's case seemed an ideal way to present "a crystallization of the arguments" in *The Revolution* (2). Indeed, leaders like Stanton and Anthony might have lost credibility if they had failed to adopt her cause. Susan B. Anthony promised: "As soon as we get Hester Vaughn out of prison, we will find someone else to work for. We intend to keep up the excitement" ("Hester Vaughn: Working Women's Meeting").

Representing Hester Vaughn

As in many legal narratives, the defendant Vaughn speaks only occasionally and does not frame her own story politically. Rather, as Angela Ray notes, Vaughn's case is narrated in *The Revolution* and activist speeches primarily through frames created by white middle-class women's rights advocates in contrast to those of her prosecutor, the judge, and the mainstream press. Below is a composite of Vaughn's case constructed from accounts in *The Revolution*, public speeches, the press, and scholarly research; details vary and narrative gaps remain[2]. The 1898 court record of the trial was destroyed in the 1960s. As historian Sarah Barringer Gordon notes: "The most striking feature of the debate over Vaughn is the plasticity of her story" (57). As noted below, women's rights advocates offered varied interpretations of the case in their campaign to save Hester Vaughn. In the mid-1860s, a teenage Hester Vaughn immigrated to the U.S. from Gloucestershire, England, with Welshman John Harris, whom she believed to be her husband. After a short time, Harris left her because he already had a wife; for his bigamy, Harris paid no price. An abandoned Vaughn, with no family or friends in the US, lacked funds to return home. Poorly educated, she found domestic work in different locations in Jenkintown, Pennsylvania, outside Philadelphia. Hester became pregnant in summer 1867. A few months later, her male employer fired her, giving her forty dollars; Hester was also evicted from her boarding house. Some of Vaughn's advocates stated that her pregnancy resulted from rape by her employer or another male in his household; others describe a seduction by a licentious man who preyed on her youth and vulnerability. In court, Hester refused to name the man, as not to disgrace his wife. Later, she filed an affidavit that her child's father was a labourer and that she did not know if he was married.

After being fired, an impoverished— and probably unemployable— Vaughn moved to Philadelphia in November 1867 and rented a sparse unheated attic room, hiding her pregnancy. Vaughn sought no charitable aid but rather took in sewing for her income. Since she was an immigrant and newly arrived in the US, she might have been unaware of charitable networks in Philadelphia. Alternately, a sense of shame or pride may have prevented her from seeking assistance. On February 8 or 9, 1868, Hester Vaughn delivered a child alone in her frigid garret; the newborn was found dead a few days later, an ailing Vaughn beside her. Whether Vaughn killed her infant intentionally—or unintentionally—remains an open question. At trial, Vaughn testified that she asked a female neighbour for a box to bury her child, asking the woman to keep it secret; the neighbour, instead, called police. Hester Vaughn was then arrested, charged with first-degree murder and taken to Moyamensing Prison. Vaughn employed an attorney with her last thirty dollars, yet he only met her the day of trial and presented a hastily prepared defence alleging her temporary insanity. On July 2, 1868, Vaughn was convicted of first-degree murder in Philadelphia's Court of Common Pleas by a male jury and sentenced to hang by Judge Ludlow, who openly characterized Vaughn's punishment as an example to other women contemplating infanticide. Some journalistic accounts of the trial describe Vaughn wearing a black veil to shield her face.

During summer 1868, women's rights activists learned of Vaughn's fate from Philadelphia physician Susan Smith, who had been visiting her in prison. Anthony and Stanton began a petition campaign, sponsored by the WWNA, in November 1868, to save her life. First, they sought a retrial on grounds of "insufficient evidence" and "inadequate defense," and when that demand failed, they petitioned the Pennsylvania governor for a pardon ("Hester Vaughn: Working Women's Meeting"). Their campaign for Vaughn took several forms: organizing public fundraising forums, such as a large meeting on December 1, 1868 at New York's Cooper Union, as well as circulating petitions to the governor and publicizing articles in *The Revolution* to influence their readership as well as the mainstream press (Dubois; S. Gordon). These activists organized events to motivate journalists to portray Vaughn in a positive light; they clearly understood the power of the press to shape debates and influence public opinion. The activists' viewpoints would publicly counter the perspective of Judge Ludlow, who clearly saw Vaughn as a child murderer deserving capital punishment. In contrast, women's rights leaders, advocating for Vaughn in *The Revolution* and in speeches, addressed questions around her guilt in different ways. One feminist framing of the story, laced with melodrama and images of idealized domesticity, portrayed a young loving and grieving mother as unjustly convicted of a terrible crime (Ray).

The stigma surrounding Vaughn as an unwed mother coloured the judgment of a male judge and jury who failed to sympathize with her or recognize the series of crimes against her by men. Stanton, in a November 19, 1868, *Revolution* article, described Vaughn as a "pretty English girl" and "very intelligent for one of her class" ("Hester Vaughn"). In her Cooper Union speech, activist Eleanor Kirk praised Vaughn for decorating her prison cell with "the most exquisite neatness and good taste appealing to the ideals of middle-class domesticity" ("Hester Vaughn: Working Women's Meeting"). Kirk and Stanton encouraged their audiences to view Vaughn not as an immigrant outsider but rather as a daughter or sister who could suffer a similar fate under the wrong circumstances. Stanton pleaded: "In the name of womanhood, we implore the mothers of that state to rescue that defenseless girl from her impending fate. Oh! make her case your own, suppose your young and beautiful daughter had been thus betrayed" (Thomas, "Misappropriating" 14). Feminist spiritualist Lizzie Doten published a poem to inspire "every woman born" to believe that "her cause" stands "side by side" with that of Hester Vaughn. In this framing of the story, Vaughn emerges as a victim who cannot be judged guilty of infanticide because of the multiple crimes against her by men and because she embodies sacred ideals of domesticity and reveres motherhood. In describing Vaughn, activists such as Kirk used language that echoed the ideals of the nineteenth-century "cult of true womanhood," with its emphasis on purity and domesticity (Welter). An alternate frame also presented Vaughn as a stigmatized unwed mother, a noble immigrant but a child herself, who might have killed her newborn in a mad and desperate response to rape, ostracism, degradation, and poverty. An August 6, 1868, *Revolution* editorial states:

> If that poor child of sorrow is hung, it will be deliberate, downright murder. Her death will be a far more horrible infanticide than was the killing of her child.

> She is the child of our society and civilization, begotten and born of it, seduced by it, by the judge who pronounced her sentence,

by the bar and jury, by the legislature that enacted the law (in which, because a woman, she had no vote or voice), by the church and the pulpit that sanctify the law and the deeds.... All these were the joint seducer, and now see if by hanging her, they will also become her murderer. ("Infanticide")

This framework also critiqued the double standard of justice in the US, in which males rarely paid a price for their sexual transgressions and some elite white women committed infanticide with few consequences (S. Gordon).

At her trial, Vaughn maintained her innocence, although a *Herald Tribune* article later stated that she confessed to the murder after her trial (S. Gordon 72). There is no way to know the truth about whether Vaughn felt responsible in any way for her child's death, if her beliefs about her guilt changed over time or whether she confessed to improve her chances for a pardon. The question of whether Vaughn intentionally—or unintentionally—killed her child obviously also rests on interpretation of forensic evidence. Unlike other cases of unexplained newborn death, Vaughn's prosecution cited a report from coroner Dr. Shapleigh of blunt force trauma to the infant's head ("Court of Oyer and Terminer"). After learning Vaughn's fate, activists went to Philadelphia to meet her and asked physicians and women's rights advocates Susan Smith and Clemence Lozier to interview her. Obstetrician Dr. Lozier, hearing the harrowing details of Vaughn's delivery, concluded that her child was likely born a month premature and that after childbirth, a weakened and malnourished Vaughn suffered from delirium, postpartum psychosis, and, possibly, blindness. This altered state might have caused Vaughn to fall upon her fragile infant, causing fatal injury; Smith, a medical practitioner for over fifteen years, concurred. Both physicians also doubted that a premature newborn could survive beyond a few days ("Hester Vaughn: Working Women's Meeting"). Both physicians provided a credible challenge to the prosecution's interpretation of the forensic evidence. In a retrial, they would likely have been expert witnesses.

Drs. Lozier and Smith, pioneering female physicians in the US, played key roles in the Vaughn case. Susan Smith initially brought the case to the attention of women's rights advocates; Lozier also gave an impassioned speech arguing for Vaughn's innocence at the December 1 Cooper Union meeting ("Hester Vaughn: Working Women's

Meeting"). Their medical authority, and especially that of Lozier, founder and dean of the homeopathic New York Medical College for Women, illustrated the importance of opening the field of medicine to women (Perry). Also noteworthy is the fact that Vaughn's trial occurred at a time when male physicians in the US were consolidating power over female midwives, traditional caregivers in childbirth (L. Gordon). On May 8, 1869, Governor John White Geary pardoned Vaughn but required that she return to England. The official report of the pardon acknowledges the medical testimony of Drs. Lozier and Smith: "Grave doubts were entertained as to her having committed the crime or, if she did commit it, it was under an unnatural excitement, if not entire aberration of mind."(*Journal of the Senate Commonwealth of Pennsylvania*). In addition, the report lists these reasons for the pardon, echoing multiple women's rights arguments:

- "she was ... entirely unprotected and without a relative or friend in this country."
- "previous to her conviction she had behaved herself in such a manner as to gain the good will of those who knew her."
- "she was the victim of a seducer." (*Journal of the Senate Commonwealth of Pennsylvania*)

The pardon report also affirmed the need for mercy since, with Hester's "rapidly failing" health, she might "not long survive" (*Journal of the Senate Commonwealth of Pennsylvania*).

Although most accounts describe Vaughn's pardon as a deportation, the Senate record and other sources state that she had always planned to return to England to her father and sister, who were reported to be unaware of her plight. The initial campaign for Vaughn in December 1868 included fundraising for her passage home ("Hester Vaughn: Working Women's Meeting"). The pardon record acknowledges a petition of over five thousand "respectable" Pennsylvania citizens and lists seventy-one individual advocates, sixty men, and eleven women. Among those are Drs. Smith and Lozier (*Journal of the Senate Commonwealth of Pennsylvania*)[3]. While Vaughn's pardon marked a movement victory, her deportation signified her ostracism as a fallen woman and undesirable immigrant. However, returning to England also enabled her to avoid the stigma she would likely have felt in the US after her pardon. Court rulings often prove easier to change than cultural attitudes. Hester Vaughn left, quietly, possibly under a false name, from New York City in June 1869; she did not inform her advocates. A few weeks later, she wrote her supporters, asking for the funds collected; she reported that she was destitute and extremely ill ("Hester Vaughn in England Sick and Destitute"). After that, there is no record of Hester Vaughn's fate in England. By the early 1870s, contrary to Anthony's earlier promise, the movement stepped away from criminal cases, although it did pursue other radical actions, including civil disobedience voting by Anthony and other women's rights advocates in the New Departure strategy during the 1872 presidential election (Dubois).

Hester Vaughn: "Oppressed on All Sides"

Vaughn's case was one among many; infanticide was the most common felony for US women in 1868 (Turner). Her advocates focused less on the question of whether Vaughn caused her child's death but instead called attention to the series of violations by men that led her to that desperate place, giving birth alone, impoverished, and ill in a frigid garret. Her advocates saw this approach as helping not only to save Hester Vaughn but also to transform society so that other women and girls would not experience such an unthinkable situation.

Campaigning to save Vaughn, women's rights advocates reframed a popular conservative cautionary tale of unwed motherhood, which warned young women of urban sexual danger, reminding them of the perils of migration and their responsibility to restrain male licentiousness and seek male protection. For Anthony, Stanton, and colleagues, reframing this story through a feminist lens enabled them to portray the death of Vaughn's child and her criminal conviction as tragic outcomes of a patriarchal society that must change. Fighting for Vaughn's life, advocates focused immediate attention on achieving a new trial or pardon. However, at the same time, activists such as Stanton narrated her story to unmask an oppressive system, viewing such an approach as a corrective to the tendency of some movement leaders to focus narrowly on suffrage. Advocates, such as Ernestine Rose, also saw Vaughn's case as a living challenge to antisuffragists, who claimed that women did not need equal rights, since they already had male family members to support them financially, shelter them from physical and sexual violence, and express their political views for them ("Hester Vaughn: Working Women's Meeting"). In 1868, audiences for advocacy speeches and articles most likely saw Vaughn's case through both narrower and broader lenses. In addition to questioning her conviction and sentence, Vaughn's story raises a number of "what if" questions, prompting consideration of who bears responsibility—in a compounding series of events—for her child's death.

What if Vaughn:

- had not left England with John Harris?
- had opportunities for safer and well-paid employment?
- had been able to defend herself against sexual assault?
- had access to contraception or abortion?
- had not been fired because of pregnancy?
- had been able to secure better housing and health care?
- had been able to afford or obtain legal counsel committed to her defence?
- had been judged by an unbiased judge and a jury that included female peers?

In narrating Vaughn's case, Stanton and others addressed women on the basis of their maternal identities and familial responsibilities. Echoing the language of cultural theorists Stuart Hall and John Fiske, one might see Vaughn's advocates "hailing" women, encouraging them to imagine her as a daughter or sister. Nine out of eleven major organizers (seven women and two men) in the Vaughn case were born between 1810 and 1831; most of Hester's leading female supporters were old enough to be her mother, ranging in age from thirty-seven to fifty-eight. Among the lead organizers, only Anna Dickinson and Charlotte Denman Lozier (Dr. Clemence Lozier's daughter-in-law) were of Vaughn's generation. News reports of the campaign, however, describe many young WWNA members as active fundraisers, with "large numbers of young workingwomen" at the Cooper union meeting ("Hester Vaughn: Working Women's Meeting"). Vaughn's story most likely appealed to readers and listeners through popular nineteenth-century images and narratives of male domination and female victimization drawn from popular fiction, everyday life and antebellum social movements. Her case can be read as an indictment of a patriarchal system, expressed in a series of violations by men and male-dominated institutions that suffered no consequences for their actions.

The first known male betrayal of Vaughn is her abandonment by John Harris. Historian Timothy Gilfoyle describes the bigamist huband as a popular nineteenth-century "cultural metaphor" of masculine deception, seduction, and manipulation. Bigamists "prowled the parlors of respectable households in search of hapless, innocent women whom they looked to conquer and seduce, dupe and destroy" (Gilfoyle 1). Harris's bigamy was particularly odious, since he had deceived young Hester Vaughn into leaving her family and travelling to the US to follow him. The male bigamist mirrored the pimp or seducer of antiprostitution rhetoric, who lured young girls into selling themselves. The second and more serious violation was sexual assault, which likely occurred when Vaughn worked as a domestic servant. Legal scholar Kristi Graunke notes that most domestic workers in the post-Civil War North were white immigrant women who, like Vaughn, became sexual prey: "These workers 'lived-in'... and ... men of the household could take advantage of the proximity to their servants to coerce ... sexual activity. Advocates who worked among poor single mothers in the 19th century noted that many of them had become pregnant by an employer in a domestic work situation" (Graunke 138). The predatory male employer, like the bigamist, the pimp or slave master, became a powerful symbol of the sexual dangers to women, which permeated both the private and public spheres. The final violation occurred in court as Vaughn lacked competent legal representation and was judged by an all-male jury. Vaughn's case epitomized the need of female defendants for quality legal representation and a jury of their peers. As legal scholar Gretchen Ritter notes, for many nineteenth-century women's rights advocates, the right to sit on a jury, linked to suffrage, would enable female citizens to participate meaningfully in public life and draw upon their common experiences and consciousness as women, and especially as mothers, in judging criminal cases. In 1854, Stanton addressed the New York State Legislature:

> Shall an erring woman be dragged before a bar of grim-visaged judges, lawyers, and jurors, there to be grossly questioned in public on subjects which women scarce breathe in secret to one another? Shall the most sacred relations of life be called up and rudely scanned by men who, by their own admission, are... coarse...? And yet shall she find there no woman's face or voice to pity and defend? Shall the frenzied mother who, to save herself

and child from exposure and disgrace, ended the life that had but just begun, be dragged before such a tribunal to answer for her crime? (Stanton, "Address")

1868: Questions Unspoken

Clearly, women's rights advocates in 1868 framed Vaughn's case to ensure their best chance of success; through that framing, they sought to promote certain public conversations and avoid others. For example, articles and speeches supporting Vaughn typically refer to her newborn only as an "infant" or "baby," with no mention of sex. Some accounts of the case describe the child as female; there is also no record of Vaughn naming her child. The omission of the infant's sex and Vaughn's decision not to name her newborn might have served to portray her child as less than human. As Sarah Barringer Gordon notes, the movement did not address the fact that the death in this case was not of a lecherous seducer, but rather a "tiny, defenseless newborn" (76). If that newborn were female, Vaughn's case may have had connections to global female infanticide—a practice clearly opposed by the US women's rights movement.

At the same time that activists avoided focusing on the death of the newborn, they did not want to imply that infanticide was ever justifiable, thus avoiding some difficult but predictable questions. For example, hearing this case, one might wonder if Vaughn killed her child or felt relieved by the baby's natural death because the infant reminded her of her assault or her assailant. Some who heard Vaughn's story might have experienced rape or considered these unspoken questions, especially if they had been abolitionists. Widely circulated in antislavery journals, Elizabeth Barrett Browning's 1848 poem, "The Runaway Slave at Pilgrim's Point," portrays the grim sorrow of a slave raped by her master who murdered her newborn whose white face resembled her assailant. As historian Felicity Turner notes, for some nineteenth-century American women, "Where rape and sexual violence existed, infanticide became not only explicable but also justifiable (106)." Also, Vaughn's advocates did not mention birth control but strongly supported voluntary motherhood. Most historians assume that voluntary motherhood in this era implied abstinence and the commitment to a woman's sovereignty over her own body in marriage (L. Gordon). However, although women's rights activists did not explicitly mention contraception, possibly to avoid controversy and conform to nineteenth-century ideals of sexuality, readers might well have considered these questions. Abortion, for many women's rights advocates in 1868, represented a symptom of the evils of patriarchy rather than a desirable reproductive choice. Stanton prided herself on not taking ads for abortionists in *The Revolution* (Gordon). Although little evidence exists to suggest that these activists supported criminalizing abortion, they did tend to see the prevalence of abortion as yet another symptom of a society that failed to respect women[4]. Of course, readers of *The Revolution* or listeners to a Cooper Union speech may also have interpreted Vaughn's case in their own ways, even "reading against the grain." Texts only assume meaning in reception when they encounter an audience with particular histories (Fiske).

Exploring the Impact of the Vaughn Case in Its Era

Some historians, such as Sarah Barringer Gordon, view the Vaughn campaign as a grave movement error, claiming that "'Hester Vaughnism' tainted the women's movement with an aura of baby killing and irresponsibility;" a virulent backlash appeared in the popular press (75). Ray argues that while movement leaders succeeded in aiding Vaughn, they did so through reinforcing class and racial hierarchies, infantilizing the working-class Vaughn as a pitiful and helpless girl and establishing themselves, through "public mothering" as her noble benefactors (18). This tendency—to portray a poor young woman through a disempowering lens—also had more general implications for first-wave movement building. We do not know and cannot know the story Vaughn would have told herself. Despite its flaws and the inevitable political backlash, however, the Vaughn campaign marks an important moment in the movement's personification of gender oppression through storytelling. Vaughn's narrative reveals the multiple ways that woman could be "oppressed on all sides" (Stanton, "Declaration") and deserving of equality in marriage, the right to control her own body, equity in employment and representation in court. Legal scholar Tracy Thomas views the Vaughn case and other Stanton narratives as a forerunner to modern gender equity legislation, arguing that "Stanton's insight that the law could be challenged by women as a class has become the foundation of modern sex discrimination law" (Thomas, "Elizabeth Cady Stanton" 2).

This case also reveals that motherhood, idealized in prescriptive literature and sentimental fiction, could be a source of deep shame and emotional and physical pain and grief, particularly for young single mothers. Advocating for Vaughn can be seen as fighting to reclaim motherhood as a freely chosen role, supported by society. Perhaps most importantly, however, the Vaughn campaign enabled activists to have the powerful experience of helping to save an individual life through publicizing the case, fundraising, and petitioning. In the words of the Talmud, "Whoever saves one life, it is as if he [or she] has saved the whole world."

Relevance of the Vaughn Case for Contemporary Feminism

Elizabeth Cady Stanton, in her 1893 diary, recounted, "I never forget that we are sowing winter wheat, which other hands than ours will reap" (Stanton, "Diary"). The broader issues of women's disempowerment raised by the Vaughn case represent that "winter wheat" with continuing relevance for contemporary feminism. While the first wave achieved central goals, such as suffrage, other issues—such as sexual violence, poverty, and inadequate reproductive healthcare—remain challenges for the movement today. The unspoken questions of the Vaughn case seem particularly relevant now as second-wave gains, such as abortion rights, risk reversal with an increasingly conservative Supreme Court. The #MeToo movement has also inspired interest in the Vaughn case. As Historian Sally Roesch Wagner notes: "Long before Harvey Weinstein or the #MeToo movement, there was Hester Vaughn, whose case reflected the institutionalization of rape in the United States" (qtd. in Blakemore). In addition, in 2017, a *Congressional Quarterly Researcher* article (O'Malley) and an Indian *Economic Times* piece (Doktor) both highlighted the Vaughn case as an early example of workplace harassment. Also, in the same year, the Pennsylvania Historical Commission approved a commemorative plaque for the site of the trial ("Pennsylvania"), acknowledging its continuing significance.

The Vaughn case has relevance for feminism today because its narrative opens up rich possibilities for thinking about the causes of gender oppression and pathways to gender equality. The right to freely chosen motherhood is at the centre of the Vaughn narrative. Guaranteeing this right for women like Vaughn goes beyond the realm of reproductive healthcare to also include securing equality in education, employment, and housing as well as sexual self-determination, immigrant rights, and legal protection. This first-wave reproductive rights framing can be seen as a forerunner to the intersectional perspective of contemporary feminists of colour, such as Andrea Smith, who transcend a narrower abortion rights frame to define reproductive justice within a broader social and economic context (Smith). Revisiting Vaughn's case, it is important to acknowledge the risks taken by her advocates, the backlash they received, as well as the class, race, and generational lenses through which they viewed Vaughn. Looking backwards, we must recognize the paradoxical position of women's rights advocates who were critiquing a patriarchal system while appealing to that same system to spare Vaughn. We will never know all the facts of this case, how Vaughn might have presented herself in the press, if she felt manipulated by her advocates or whether she supported the goals of the women's movement in the US or in England. However, looking forwards, we can see that the Vaughn case enabled first-wave activists to personify and challenge a patriarchal system in ways that remain compelling and relevant today. For twenty-first-century feminists, Hester Vaughn's narrative remains an open text as they mobilize around issues of sexual assault and harassment, reproductive justice, and immigrant rights at another urgent time in a more inclusive movement. With its stark image of a veiled young immigrant woman sentenced to the gallows in a hostile courtroom, Hester Vaughn's tragic story continues to haunt the present. She will not likely be forgotten soon.

Endnotes

1. First-wave maternalism adapted the nineteenth century "cult of true womanhood" (Welter) for women's rights purposes, rejecting patriarchal elements and expanding on ideas of woman as having a duty to reform not only the home but also the larger society. Many activists, such as Stanton and Anthony, argued that "home" also included the public sphere and that women needed equal rights and

suffrage to fulfill their critical role as social reformers. This maternalist rhetoric was often, though not always, essentialist, defining woman's motherly consciousness as biological in nature, arguing for a distinctly feminine voice in politics. Frequently maternalism included hierarchical elements as well, casting affluent mothers as the benefactors of poor "friendless girls," as in the Vaughn case. This type of benevolent maternalism appeared both in the predominantly white middle-class suffrage movement as well as the Black women's club movement.

2. This narrative of Vaughn's case is drawn from accounts by scholars as well as biographies of her advocates and articles in *The Revolution*, *The New York Times*, *New York World*, and *Philadelphia Telegraph*, as well as the Pennsylvania state report of the pardon. Note that sometimes the spelling Vaughan is used rather than Vaughn.

3. It is interesting to note that Drs. Smith and Lozier are named as "recommenders" of the pardon, together with a list of other individuals assumed to be Pennsylvanians. Since the physicians provided medical testimony challenging Vaughn's conviction and supporting the governor's decision, they would be listed by name. Not surprisingly, the New York women's rights organizers, such as Stanton, Anthony, and Ernestine Rose, are not listed. To justify a pardon, the protocol for the governor was to show the support of citizens of his state rather than advocates from other states. The arguments listed in the pardon, however, testify to the influence of the women's rights campaign. A question remains of whether Governor Geary might have pardoned Vaughn without the women's rights campaign (Gordon).

4. It is important to note that Stanton and Anthony's advocacy of voluntary motherhood, as well as their view that the practice of abortion resulted from the injustices of patriarchy, has been interpreted by some contemporary prolife activists as support for outlawing abortion. It is beyond the scope of this essay to discuss this interpretation at length. See the work of Tracy A. Thomas for a fuller presentation of the argument that substantial evidence does not support the view that these women's rights leaders favoured criminalizing abortion.

Works Cited

"The Administration of Justice: Hester Vaughn's Case." *The New York Times*, 4 Dec., 1868, www.nytimes.com/1868/12/04/archives/the-administration-of-justicehester-vaughans-case.html. Accessed 24 Nov. 2021.

Blakemore, Erin. "The Shocking Infanticide Trial That Exposed Sexual Harassment in 1868." *History*, Jan. 2018, www.history.com/news/the-shocking-infanticide-trial-that-exposed-sexual-harassment-in-1868. Accessed 24 Nov. 2021.

Browning, Elizabeth Barrett. "The Runaway Slave at Pilgrim's Point" in *The Complete Works of Elizabeth Barrett Browning*, edited and with an introduction by Charlotte Porter and Helen A. Clarke. Thomas Crowell and Co., 1900.

"The Case of Hester Vaughan." *The Revolution*, 10 Dec., 1868, digitalcollections.lclark.edu/items/show/9623. Accessed 24 Nov. 2021.

"Court of Oyer and Terminer: Judges Ludlow and Brewster." *Philadelphia Inquirer*, 1 July, 1868, 2, www.newspapers.com/image/167247856. Accessed 24 Nov. 2021.

Doktor, Vikram. "View: A Lot of Ground Still to Be Covered in Sexual Harassment Battle." *Economic Times*, 28 Oct. 2017, economictimes.indiatimes.com/news/politics-and-nation/view-a-lot-of-ground-still-to-be-covered-in-sexual-harassment-battle/articleshow/61280605.cms?from=mdr. Accessed 24 Nov. 2021.

Doten, Lizzie. *Poems of Progress*. Colby and Rich, 1895.

Dubois, Ellen Carol. *Woman Suffrage and Women's Rights*. New York University Press, 1998.

Elbert, Sarah. *A Hunger for Home: Louisa May Alcott*. Temple University Press, 1976.

Farless, Patricia. "Infanticide, Women's Rights and Melodrama." *Florida Conference of Historians Journal*, Spring 2005.

Fiske, John. *Reading the Popular*. Second Edition. Routledge, 1989.

Gilfoyle, Timothy J. "The Hearts of Nineteenth-Century Men: Bigamy and Working-Class Marriage in New York City, 1800–1890." *Prospects*, vol. 19, 1994, www.cambridge.org/core/journals/prospects/article/abs/hearts-of-nineteenthcentury-men-bigamy-

and-workingclass-marriage-in-new-york-city-18001890/46A7F6F019C6F4571E1508C71281F70F#. Accessed 24 Nov. 2021.

Ginzberg, Lori D. *Elizabeth Cady Stanton: An American Life*. Hill and Wang, 2009.

Gordon, Ann, editor. *The Selected Papers of Elizabeth Cady Stanton and Susan B. Anthony: Against an Aristocracy of Sex: 1866-1873*. Rutgers University Press, 2000.

Gordon, Linda. *The Moral Property of Women: A History of Birth Control Politics in America*. University of Illinois Press, 2002.

Gordon, Sarah Barringer. "Law and Everyday Death: Infanticide and the Backlash Against Women's Rights After the Civil War." *Lives in the Law*, edited by Austin Sarat, Lawrence Douglas, and Martha Umfrey. University of Michigan Press, 2002.

Graunke, Kristi L. "'Just Like One of the Family': Domestic Violence Paradigms and Combatting on-the-Job Violence Against Household Workers in the United States." *Michigan Journal of Gender and the Law*, vol. 9, no. 1, 2002, repository.law.umich.edu/mjgl/vol9/iss1/3/. Accessed 25 Nov. 2021.

"Hester Vaughan." *The Revolution*, 6 Aug. 1868, digitalcollections.lclark.edu/items/browse?collection=21. Accessed 24 Nov. 2021.

"Hester Vaughan." *The Revolution*, 17 Sept.1868, digitalcollections.lclark.edu/items/browse?collection=21. Accessed 24 November 2021.

"Hester Vaughn: Her Alleged Infanticide and Sentence of Death—Movement to Secure Her Pardon—Meeting at Cooper Institute—Speeches by Horace Greeley, Susan B. Anthony, Ernestine L. Rose and Others," *The New York Times*, 2 Dec. 1868, www.nytimes.com/1868/12/02/archives/hester-vaughn-her-alleged-infanticide-and-sentence-of-deathmovement.html?searchResultPosition=2, Accessed 24 Nov. 2021.

"The Hester Vaughan Meeting at Cooper Institute." *The Revolution*, 10 Dec. 1868, digitalcollections.lclark.edu/items/browse?collection=21. Accessed 24 Nov. 2021.

"Is Hester Vaughan Guilty?" *The Revolution*, 12 Jan. 1869, digitalcollections.lclark.edu/items/browse?collection=21. Accessed 24 Nov. 2021.

"Hester Vaughan Once More." *The Revolution*, 19 Aug. 1869, digitalcollections.lclark.edu/items/browse?collection=21. Accessed 24 Nov. 2021.

"Hester Vaughn in England Sick and Destitute." *Philadelphia Telegraph*, 23 June 1869, panewsarchive.psu.edu/lccn/sn83025925/1869-06-23/ed-1/seq-1/. Accessed 24 Nov. 2021.

"Hester Vaughn: A Sad Story." *The Public Ledger*, 5 Jan. 1869, news.google.com/newspapers?nid=59&dat=18690105&id=TUI1AAAAIBAJ&sjid=kicDAAAAIBAJ&pg=6158,5829281. Accessed 24 Nov. 2021.

"How Shall Women Be Tried?" *The New York Times*, 10 Dec. 1868, www.nytimes.com/1868/12/10/archives/how-shall-women-be-tried.html. Accessed 24 Nov. 2021.

"Infanticide." *The Revolution*, 6 Aug. 1868, digitalcollections.lclark.edu/items/show/9623. Accessed 24 Nov. 2021.

Jacobs, Harriet Ann. *Incidents in the Life of a Slave Girl: Written by Herself*. Harvard University Press, 2000.

Journal of the Senate Commonwealth of Pennsylvania. B. Gingerly, 1870.

O'Malley, Sharon. "Workplace Sexual Harassment." *CQ Researcher*, CQ Press, 27 Oct. 2017, vol. 27, no. 38, library.cqpress.com/cqresearcher/document.php?id=cqresrre2017102714. Accessed 24 Nov. 2021.

"Pennsylvania State Historical and Museum Commission Approves 18 New Historical Markers." *PA.Gov*, www.media.pa.gov/Pages/PHMC-Details.aspx?newsid=262. Accessed 24 Nov. 2021.

Perry, Marilyn. "Clemence Sophia Lozier." *American National Biography*, 2000, doi.org/10.1093/anb/9780198606697.article.1200552. Accessed 24 November 2021.

Pleck, Elizabeth. "Feminist Reponses to Crimes Against Women, 1868-1896." *Signs*, vol. 8, no. 3, 1983, pp.451-70.

Polletta, Francesca. "'It Was Like a Fever...': Narrative and Identity in Social Protest." *Social Problems*, vol. 45, no. 2, 1998, pp.137-59.

Rambo, Kirsten S. *"Trivial Complaints": The Role of Privacy in Domestic Violence Law and Activism in the U.S.* Columbia University Press, 2009.

Ray, Angela G. "Representing the Working Class in Early U.S. Feminist Media: The Case of Hester Vaughn." *Women's Studies in Communication*, vol. 26, no. 1, 2003, pp. 1-26.

Ritter, Gretchen. "Jury Service and Women's Citizenship before and after the Nineteenth Amendment." *Law and History Review*, vol. 20, no. 3, 2002, pp. 479-515.

Roth, Benita. *Women and Social Movements in the U.S.: 1600-1900*. Alexander Street Press, 2001.

Segrave, Kerry. *Women and Capital Punishment in America: 1840-1899: Death Sentences and Executions in the United States and Canada*. McFarland Publishing, 2008.

Sherr, Lynn. *Failure Is Impossible: Susan B. Anthony in Her Own Words*. Random House, 1996.

Smith, Andrea. "Beyond Pro-Life Versus Pro-Choice: Reproductive Justice and Women of Color." *NWSA Journal*, vol. 17, no. 1, Spring 2005, pp. 119-40.

Snodgrass, Mary Ellen. *Civil Disobedience: An Encyclopedic History of Dissidence in the U.S.* Routledge, 2015.

Stanton, Elizabeth Cady. "Address to the Legislature of New-York." Adopted by the State Woman's Rights Convention, held at Albany, Tuesday and Wednesday, 1854, *NPS*, www.nps.gov/wori/learn/historyculture/address-to-the-new-york-legislature-1854.htm Accessed 24 Nov. 2021.

Stanton, Elizabeth Cady. "The Declaration of Sentiments and Resolutions." *San Jose State University*, 1848, www.sjsu.edu/people/cynthia.rostankowski/courses/HUM2BS14/s0/Womens-Rights.pdf. Accessed 24 Nov. 2021.

Stanton, Elizabeth Cady. "Hester Vaughn." *The Revolution*, 19 Nov. 1868, digitalcollections.lclark.edu/items/browse?collection=21. Accessed 24 Nov. 2021.

Stanton, Elizabeth Cady. "Hester Vaughn." *The Revolution*, 10 Dec. 1868, digitalcollections.lclark.edu/items/browse?collection=21. Accessed 24 Nov. 2021.

Stanton, Elizabeth Cady. "Infanticide and Prostitution." *The Revolution*, 5 Feb. 1868, digitalcollections.lclark.edu/items/browse?collection=21. Accessed 24 Nov. 2021.

Stanton, Elizabeth Cady. *As Revealed in Her Letters, Diary and Reminiscences* in *Women and Social Movements in the United States: 1815-1902*, edited by Harriot Eaton Stanton Blatch and Theodore Weld Stanton, Harper and Row, 1922, https://search.alexanderstreet.com/preview/work/bibliographic_entity%7Cbibliographic_details%7C2525843. Accessed 24 Nov. 2021.

Stanton, Elizabeth Cady. "Our Costume." *The Lily*, 1851.

Stanton, Elizabeth Cady. *Eighty Years and More: Reminiscences, 1815-1897*. 1898. Schocken Books, 1981.

Stanton, Elizabeth Cady. "The Rights of Married Women." *Man Cannot Speak for Her II: Key Text of the Early Feminists*, edited by Karlyn Kors Campbell. Greenwood Press, 1989.

Thomas, Tracy A. "Elizabeth Cady Stanton and the Notion of a Legal Class of Gender." *Feminist Legal History: Essays on Women and Law*, edited by Tracy A. Thomas and Tracey Jean Boisseau. NYU Press, 2011.

Thomas, Tracy A. "Misappropriating Women's History in the Law and Politics of Abortion." *Seattle University Law Review*, 2012, vol. 36, no. 1, pp. 1-68, digitalcommons.law.seattleu.edu/sulr/vol36/iss1/2/. Accessed 24 Nov. 2021.

Turner, Felicity. *Narrating Infanticide: Constructing the Modern Gendered State in Nineteenth Century America*. Dissertation. Department of History, Duke University, 2010.

Wellman, Judith. *The Road to Seneca Falls: Elizabeth Cady Stanton and the First Woman's Rights Convention*. University of Illinois Press, 2004.

Welter, Barbara. "The Cult of True Womanhood: 1820-1860." *American Quarterly*, vol. 18, no. 2, Summer 1966, pp. 151-74.

"The Workingwomen of New York on Behalf of Hester Vaughn Under Sentence of Death in Philadelphia." *The New York Times*, 25 Nov. 1868, www.nytimes.com/1868/11/25/archives/the-workingwomen-of-newyork-in-behalf-of-hester-vaughn-under.html. Accessed 24 Nov. 2021.

Yellin, Jean Fagan and John C. Van Horne, editors. *The Abolitionist Sisterhood: Women's Political Culture in Antebellum America*. Cornell University Press, 1994.

Chapter 9

The Ambivalent Monstrosity: Museum Interpretation of the Infanticidal Mother

Meighen S. Katz

In the nineteenth century, when waxworks, such as London's Madame Tussaud's or the Australian Kreitmayer's, exhibited perpetrators of maternal infanticide, they demonstrated few if any qualms at characterizing the women as monstrous. Modern exhibitions and modern curators have generally avoided this depiction. Nevertheless, the nineteenth-century infanticidal mother continues to create quandaries of display. While the sense of the monstrous has been removed, too often it is not replaced with a substantial interrogation of either the surrounding circumstances or the act itself. The nature of the crime of infanticide precludes its interpretation in broad-reaching general histories aimed at underage visitors. However, so-called dark tourism sites, such as the Old Melbourne Gaol or *The Crime Museum Uncovered*, are more likely to make clear from the outset the confronting nature of their material. Within those sites, inclusion of the interpretation of infanticide and those convicted has the potential to be revelatory. Shani D'Cruze and Louise Jackson have argued that though prostitution is often characterized as the benchmark of desperation, it is infanticide that truly serves as an indicator of the most vulnerable and the most marginalized women (77). Though difficult to broach, discussions of infanticide potentially open up an examination of gender relationships, socioeconomic factors, and the realities of an inability to easily control fertility. The removal of the spectacle surrounding the public history interpretation of infanticide is to be applauded. Yet, in multiple cases, the reworking of the interpretation has simultaneously excised recognition of the women as actors within their own narratives. By removing this sense of women's agency in infanticidal killings, the attendant revelations as to the lives of the women involved also become obscured. Interpretation of this topic will never be an easy inclusion in any exhibition. That said, it need not become a binary choice between ghoulish voyeurism or an oversimplified interpretation that fails to fully convey the complexity of the surrounding circumstances.

This chapter compares the interpretations of infanticidal mothers in nineteenth- and early twentieth-century museums with those in the first two decades of the twenty-first century. It pays particular attention to the cases of Emma Williams and Louise Massett. Williams was hanged in Melbourne, Australia in 1895 for the murder of her son John. Subsequent to her execution, Williams's story has been included in Kreitmayer's Melbourne waxworks (early twentieth century), as part of the *Sideshow Alley* exhibition at Australia's National Portrait Gallery (2015-2016) and in ongoing displays at the National Trust of Australia's Old Melbourne Gaol. Massett was executed for infanticide in 1900 following the death of her son, Manfred. She was included in the Museum of London's *The Crime Museum Uncovered* (2015-2016). All twenty-first-century exhibitions were visited by the author. Discussion of the nineteenth- and early twentieth-century exhibitions is based on primary source material, such as exhibition catalogues/guides to the relevant displays, secondary sources, as well as the interpretation of nineteenth-century displays in *Sideshow Alley, The Crime Museum Uncovered*, and their respective catalogues.

Waxworks and Death Masks: Historical Exhibition of Infanticide

Madame Tussaud's (London)

Neither dark tourism nor true-crime narratives are modern inventions. During the nineteenth century, various museums, entertainments, and travelling exhibitions catered to the public's interest in tales of violent crime and criminality. Of these morbid delights, the most celebrated show was Madame Tussaud's waxworks in London, which first opened in 1835 (McEvoy 53, 59). Although her waxworks included the Chamber of Horrors and gruesome reminders of the French Revolution, the majority of Tussaud's displays were focused on less macabre subjects. The historical exhibitions gave audiences the opportunity to gaze on the visages of a host of famous figures including the sitting monarch, American presidents, and the figures from literature, history, and current events (Tussaud & Sons, 1883 13-14). While there was a degree of consistency in the historical displays, Tussaud's made an effort to keep the nonhistorical exhibits contemporary and relevant (McEvoy 60). A significant draw, both at Tussaud's and other lesser-known establishments, were the tableaux that combined the figures with appropriate sets and props. Cinematic newsreels would eventually supersede the tableaux, but for a time, these elaborate stagings allowed visitors a form of encounter with the celebrities of the day—both those honoured and those feared or despised (Gilmour 111).

Tussaud's Chamber of Horrors room narrowed this approach to a focus on acts of crime and torture. It was in this section of her museum that nineteenth-century Londoners came face to face with the likenesses of women convicted of violent crimes. In the majority of the Tussaud examples, the women were convicted for attacking lovers, husbands, or children. Thus, women's criminality was framed as abominable but nevertheless domestic—simultaneously monstrous and familiar. Emma McEvoy makes the case that the intimate domestic setting of many of the tableaux, such as the replication of a parlour or kitchen, enhanced the disquieting nature of the scenes (70-73). The presentation of Mary-Ann Cotton serves as a case in point. Cotton was suspected in the deaths of up to twenty-one people, many of whom were in her familial circle. Her ultimate conviction and execution in 1873 arose from the murder of her stepson, Charles (Pearman). An 1876 catalogue from Tussaud's captions the wax figure of Cotton in the following way:

> The series of cold-blooded murders for which this wretch was hanged...are crimes against which no punishment in history can atone for. The child that was rocked on her knee today was poisoned tomorrow. Most of her murders were committed for petty gains; and she killed off husbands and children with the unconcern of a farm-girl killing poultry. The story of her crimes is still fresh in the public mind. (Tussaud & Sons, 1876 46)

The waxworks, and similar nineteenth-century institutions of display, presented the behaviour of these women as an inversion of natural maternal instincts. No mention was made of politics or economics or any other factors which might have contributed to violent acts. Despite the absence of context, the display of these acts did not, however, occur in isolation. Margaret L. Arnot has argued that the view of the unnatural mother in the late nineteenth century was a component of a much larger reactionary discourse grounded in concerns regarding gender, class, and empire (273-74, 297). Within this construct, a picture of ideal motherhood was created—one in which women remained only in a domestic sphere and in which motherhood was seen as the ultimate expression of women's natural inclinations. Arnot frames this ideal as being as much an assault on the working classes (who relied on more than one income per family) as on women in general (272, 274). Infanticide trials, and more importantly their reportage within the press, carried the fears regarding loss of the supposedly natural and ordained social order beyond the parliament and the pulpit and out into the street (Arnot 279-80). That these fears should then manifest in waxwork figurines is indicative of the waxworks' commitment to maintain timely exhibitions that were in touch with the general zeitgeist.

The mid-nineteenth through to the early twentieth century was an era in which there were expectations that leisure, particularly the leisure of the middle and lower classes, would be edifying as well as entertaining (Pearce 4; Gilmour, 114). Madame Tussaud's sons certainly asserted that their institution met this requirement, claiming their waxworks were "morally instructive" (McEvoy 61). Although forgoing any outright claims to morality within his introduction to Tussaud's catalogue, George Augustus Sala made a case in 1892 for the instructive nature of the exhibition. He stated that "the whole collection may be considered as an unequalled series of instructive tableaux, truthful, attractive and easily understood" (14). In introducing, and to some extent justifying the Chamber of Horrors, multiple editions of the catalogue introduced these exhibits by reassuring patrons that "so far from the exhibition of likenesses of criminals creating the desire to imitate them, experience teaches them that it has a direct tendency to the contrary" (Tussaud & Sons, 1883 38).

Sohier's/Kreitmayer's (Melbourne)

Waxworks were also a key venue for entertainment in the Australian colonies during the latter half of the nineteenth century. *The Australasian Sketcher with Pen and Pencil* boldly declared in 1876 that "Every large city of the slightest claims to civilization has to support a show, either permanent or travelling, of waxworks" (150). In Melbourne, this need was initially fulfilled by one Madame Lee, who opened a waxworks at the top end of Bourke Street in 1857. A year later, the establishment was acquired by Ellen Williams (no relation to Emma Williams), who expanded the displays to include her partner Philomen Sohier's Phrenological Museum offering the contemplation of skulls and death masks (Gilmour 113). Plaster-cast death masks of executed criminals were a particular tool of nineteenth-century practitioners of the pseudoscience of phrenology. These phrenologists claimed to be able to assess the propensity for antisocial and criminal behaviour through studying the shape and size of the skulls and features of convicted criminals. The masks were displayed during public lectures, showcased within waxworks, and acquisitioned into university collections. In 1863, Max Ludwig Kreitmayer, a maker of anatomical models, joined the Sohiers' commercial ventures (Gilmour 115). Philomen Sohier and Max Kreitmayer were both adherents of phrenology or at the very least benefitted financially from the creation and display of masks and other related artifacts for other true believers. Kreitmayer later cemented his reputation for facial reproduction by making the death mask of Australia's most infamous bushranger, Edward "Ned" Kelly, in the hours after Kelly's execution in 1880 (Gilmour 119). Kreitmayer bought out his partners in 1869 and continued to run the museum until his death in 1906. His widow maintained the displays until the end of the 1910s. (Gilmour 116, 131).

A review of content and programs associated with Kreitmayer and the Sohiers allows for some claim to educational value, at least initially. The museum hosted talks, accompanied by models and displays, for medical students. Kreitmayer's wife hosted female-only talks, which allowed the women of Melbourne some previously unavailable insight into their own anatomies (Gilmour 115-16; Baume and Kreitmeyer iv). While these lectures did provide a valuable side benefit, one must not overstate the intent. The primary emphasis remained on showmanship, spectacle, and entertainment. The majority of the exhibition and the included tableaux depicted famous figures and the noteworthy crimes and criminals of the day. Despite a degree of crossover of display with overseas waxworks, such as Tussaud's in London, the Australian waxworks focused their own chamber of horrors on local content (*Madame Sohiers* 9-20; *Kreitmayer's* 10; Madame Tussaud & Sons, c.1917 66). An early twentieth-century catalogue from the Kreitmayer's features several women convicted of infanticide including Frances Knorr and Emma Williams (discussed in more detail below). Once again, the women are characterized as unambiguously monstrous. Kreitmayer's c.1912 catalogue entry on Williams describes her as "callous-hearted" and an "unnatural mother" who murdered her child because he was an "encumbrance" (8). But there was more to Emma Williams's story.

New Versions and Old Mistakes: Interpreting Infanticide in Twenty-First Century Museums
Emma Williams in The Old Melbourne Gaol

Williams reappears to audiences in two modern museum interpretations. She is featured in the permanent exhibition at the Old Melbourne Gaol, once Melbourne's main institution of incarceration and now a major heritage and tourism site. She also receives attention in *Sideshow Alley* (2015–2016), the Australian National Portrait Gallery's exhibition of nineteenth-century dark tourism, curated by Joanna Gilmour. While neither exhibition disputes Williams's hand in the death of her son, both offer more explanation of the factors leading to the child's death than their nineteenth-century counterparts. The Old Melbourne Gaol's first mention of Emma Williams appears within the general thematic panels on women criminals (National Trust, "Baby Farming"). Significantly departing from the more common public history approach found within former prisons, these thematic panels emphasize the conditions that led to conviction rather than life within the prison itself. They connect the Gaol to the surrounding neighbourhoods and streets, once some of Melbourne's poorest. In doing so, the panels create a picture of the challenges faced by nineteenth-century urban women with low socioeconomic status, whether or not they had a partner. As is made clear, for these women, having a child did not just mean another mouth to feed, although that was certainly one consequence. For them, a causal relationship existed between pregnancy, the potential loss of livelihood and shelter, and a stint within the prison's walls. The Gaol's interpretation brings these realities into sharp focus. In spite of inconsistencies in the characterization of child care/boarding (known colloquially as "baby farming"), the narrative is sympathetic in its depiction of the desperation felt by single mothers, such as Williams (Katz 354-356; National Trust "Baby Farming").

Some of those who were hanged at the Old Melbourne Gaol are also interpreted individually, each within a single cell. These displays follow a formula that repeats along the cellblock, consisting of an interpretive panel, a photograph or drawing if available, and the executed prisoner's death mask. It is in one of these cells that an extended version of Williams's story is told. The loss of her husband to typhoid is explained, as is her unsuccessful attempt to find someone to care for her son, John. Unable to find any other means of support, the panel tells visitors, Williams turned to prostitution. The panel further notes that her pimp William Martin testified against her (National Trust, "Emma Williams"). Martin reportedly told the authorities that it was Williams's customers who viewed the child as a nuisance—a small but significant variation from the tale as told by Kreitmayer's (National Trust, "Emma Williams"). Although the Gaol offers no editorial commentary, the interpretation at least raises a question as to whether it was Williams or the men in her life who sought the child's erasure. While the Gaol itself provides atmospheric interpretation, the sole three-dimensional material culture included in the presentation of Emma Williams's unfortunate life is her death mask.[1] Despite the well-established discreditation of phrenology, the masks live on in a range of museums as a macabre remnant of its practices. These include exhibitions at the Science Museum in London and the Ian Potter Museum of Art at the University of Melbourne as well as a number of crime-related institutions and exhibitions.

Emma Williams in Sideshow Alley

A copy of Williams's death mask is included among an extensive collection of phrenological remnants in an exhibition at Australia's National Portrait Gallery titled *Sideshow Alley*, which was an interpretation of historical interpretation. It explored the fascination with spectacle and death in nineteenth-century Australian exhibitions, entertainments, and displays. Thus, the emphasis of this interpretation of Williams shifted slightly in comparison to that which appears in the Old Melbourne Gaol. The National Portrait Gallery was less concerned with her actual crime. Instead, *Sideshow Alley* focussed more fully on her inclusion in Kreitmayer's displays and the ways in which her crime and subsequent punishment led to her resurrection in the waxworks. Interestingly, while consistent with the Gaol in characterizing Williams as a single mother, *Sideshow Alley* attributes her state of affairs to fleeing an abusive husband rather than being widowed by typhoid. Once again, however, her financial precariousness is paramount, as Williams is quoted as explaining, "I could not get a situation, as any place where they would take me, they would not take the child" (National Portrait Gallery, Exhibition Panel). The interpretation concludes by informing audiences that after her arrest, the authorities were "unsympathetic, painting Williams as a base 'unwomanly' individual" (National Portrait Gallery, Exhibition Panel).

The exhibitions at the Old Melbourne Gaol and the National Portrait Gallery both call into question nineteenth-century characterizations of Emma Williams. They do so, not by challenging her guilt—this variable never arises—but through providing some sense of the broader details of Williams's life and circumstances. These reflect shifts in the overall view of her crime drawing from developments in both psychology and social history. Yet at no time is the actual act of murder interrogated. The bleak realities of Williams's life are told and retold, but this context is not distinguished from that of a broader cohort of desperate women. There is nothing tangible to separate Williams's actions from those of other women who did not resort or were not forced to resort to infanticide. Familiarity with the circumstances of Emma Williams's life does create a more sympathetic picture than she was ever afforded by Kreitmayer. That said, neither modern exhibition attempts to understand infanticide as a specific act. It remains one of a multitude of possible outcomes associated with the combination of economic deprivation and repressive social mores. As a result, while the spectacle and sense of the ghoulish are reduced (though given the presence of the death masks, not entirely removed), the replacement narrative is still not entirely satisfactory. If, as D'Cruze and Jackson have argued, infanticide is the mark of the most significant and pronounced level of vulnerability, marginalization, and desperation then it should not be treated as just one more violent crime. Doing so collapses the possibility of interpreting the full range and extent of what the women in question experienced. To treat it as a unique and extreme crime does not necessitate a return to portraying those women as monstrous. Instead, such an approach provides a means to better understand how very precarious their lives were and just how severe and limited they viewed the options at their disposal.

The Crime Museum Uncovered at the Museum of London

In August 2013, *The Guardian* reported that members of the London Assembly had recommended that the city's Metropolitan Police open its private crime museum, known colloquially as the "Black Museum", to the general public (Gray 12 Aug 2013). The *Guardian* article used this recommendation as the catalyst for a broader discussion on museum ethics in the interpretation of objects associated with violent crimes. Two years later, however, the exhibition came to fruition. For the first time, members of the public were able to see the contents of Scotland Yard's collection at *The Crime Museum Uncovered,* held at the Museum of London from October 2015 to April 2016. The exhibition was curated by Jackie Keily and Julia Hoffbrand and employed multiple interpretive approaches. The initial section was intended to mimic the original nineteenth-century Scotland Yard facility (Keily and Hoffbrand 3). Labels in this section were brief though a free room guide provided visitors with slightly more detailed explanations of the objects and associated narratives. The second section entailed a series of display cases, each detailing the collected evidence pertaining to an individual crime. Finally, there were a series of thematic cases, such as those interpreting weapons, terrorism, and abortion. The catalogue, available for purchase at the end of the exhibition, added another layer, albeit not one seen by every visitor. Much of the publicity was focused on familiar celebrity criminals such as Jack the Ripper, the Kray Brothers and Dr. Crippen, but the exhibition did include several women convicted of infanticide, including Louise Massett.

The Miscarriage of Justice: Louise Massett

Massett, who was hanged in Newgate in 1900, was included in the first section of the exhibition, as were Mary Pearcey, who murdered her lover's eighteen-month-old child in 1890, and Amelia Dyer—a notorious "baby farmer" responsible for the deaths of multiple children—hanged in 1896. Within the exhibition, Louise Massett's story is represented solely by a courtroom illustration by William Hartley. The near identical interpretation in the room guide and the catalogue state the following:

> Louise Massett, 33, was accused of the murder of her 3 year old son, Manfred. She was found guilty and hanged at Newgate in 1900. Manfred was her illegitimate son who had been fostered. Massett removed him from his foster home, saying she was taking him to live with his father. Manfred's body was found in the toilets at Dalston Junction station. He had been beaten and smothered. (Keily and Hoffbrand 50)

That brief paragraph is all that visitors were told about Massett. It implies a straightforward case and a safe conviction, yet there is much to indicate that hers was neither. In her study of women executed in Britain, Annette Ballinger details the dubious nature of Louise Massett's conviction and the social structures that contributed to this outcome. Ballinger argues that Massett was convicted on the flimsiest of circumstantial evidence and suggests that the verdict passed judgement less on Manfred's death than on his mother's approach to life. Massett, as Ballinger characterizes her, enjoyed the social access of work as a private tutor to the wealthy. She was unmarried yet unapologetically sexually active. The combination of access to privilege but rejection of its standards meant that once in the dock, she was characterized as a social deviant for whom child murder was easily within the realm of possibilities, regardless of the lack of any true indicative evidence of her guilt (Ballinger 103-23). The Museum of London exhibition made no mention of the social mores of the time, even though they were arguably central to the conviction. It similarly offered little insight into turn-of-century views on motherhood or the practices of childcare.

As visitors first entered the exhibition, they encountered a panel on which the curators explained one of their key motivations for staging the exhibition:

> The objects also reveal stories about Londoners that are often not told…. These stories are often uncomfortable even disturbing, but they provide a fascinating insight into important aspects of London's History (Museum of London, Exhibition Panel)

The case of Massett as framed by Ballinger does indeed provide an uncomfortable yet revealing view of London, Londoners, and the values they held and enforced. The exhibition is significantly less successful in revealing that narrative or providing insights into these aspects of London's history. It may well be that the curators felt that they were bound within this exhibition section by their own constructions. In trying to preserve a sense of the nineteenth-century interpretation in the original museum, there was little room in the modern iteration to unpack, understand, or challenge the attendant Victorian view of the world. The curators of *Sideshow Alley* potentially faced the same problem in presenting a late nineteenth-century interpretation of Emma Williams in Kreitmayer's wax works. In the Australian case, though, there was a better sense of temporal distance between the original and the modern. As such, the Australian curator was more successful in offering a critique, however subtle, of the manner in which Williams was presented. *The Crime Museum Uncovered* expressed more in intent and presented less on the exhibition floor. However, the Museum of London's exhibition had shortcomings that moved beyond the structural. As the cases of Kathleen Parrott and Ethel Bush, and of Mary Pearcey will indicate, these shortcomings become apparent when considering the overall interpretation of women, whether victim, perpetrator, or investigator.

Crime and Agency: Mary Pearcey

Throughout *The Crime Museum Uncovered*, women's agency with regards to crime was almost entirely absent. At no point were women depicted or understood as actors or decision makers within the narratives. Rather the women in *The Crime Museum Uncovered* are consistently portrayed as passive bodies to which things are done. Any museum exhibition that deals extensively with violent crimes against women runs the risk of reinforcing a paradigm of passivity (Biber 1034-37). Violent crime, rape, assault, and murder are all acts done to women and to women's bodies. However, within this exhibition, that passivity extended to the depictions of those who were not victims of crime but played other, active roles within the interpreted events. The most easily identifiable example of this lack of agency appears in the second section, in the interpretation of two police officers who served undercover to catch a serial sex offender in 1955. WPC Kathleen Parrott and

WPS Ethel Bush were both awarded the George Medal for bravery. However, the object used to interpret their story was not a medal, or a part of their police uniform; it was the piece of wood with which the perpetrator hit WPS Bush. Significantly, the catalogue describes them as "victims" (Keily and Hoffbrand 117). Despite their citation, these officers were interpreted both materially, and in print, as passive participants within the unfolding acts; crime was something done to them rather than something they actively worked to curtail and contain.

Late nineteenth-century murderess Mary Pearcey provides another key example. A comparison between her turn-of-the-century interpretation in Tussaud's and her modern inclusion in the first section of *The Crime Museum Uncovered* highlights the degree to which the Museum of London exhibition places her in a similarly nonactive role to that of the two policewomen. This passivity, this lack of agency, is particularly crucial when considering women's criminality. In brief, Mary Pearcey was responsible for the deaths of two people: Phoebe Hogg, the wife of her lover, and Hogg's eighteen-month-old daughter. She was executed for these murders two days before Christmas in 1890. The interpretation of Pearcey within *The Crime Museum Uncovered* is done indirectly, through a display of hangman's ropes, including the one with which she was hanged. Of her two victims only the adult, Phoebe Hogg is discussed in the exhibition label. Similarly in the room guide, the focus remains on this adult victim. When Hogg's unnamed eighteen-month-old daughter is mentioned, it is in the tone of an addendum (Museum of London, Room Guide 8). Pearcey's actions are not interpreted. The most significant object to be associated with Pearcey within the exhibition is not indicative of her actions. It is, instead, the material culture of actions enacted upon her, her execution, as presented through the rope. And so, much like the infant, Mary Pearcey becomes an addendum to a narrative that would not have occurred save for her actions, her decisions, and her agency. She is the catalyst, yet she remains largely obscured.

Pearcey's interpretation in Tussaud's waxworks is significantly more explicit. At various times, she was interpreted not only by a figure but also by a tableau reconstructing the site of her crimes and by an accompanying object that spoke to active rather than passive criminality. By the twentieth century, Pearcey and others, such as Amelia

Dyer, had replaced earlier child killers, including Mary Ann Cotton in Tussaud's galleries. The labels had by this time become more prosaic and more factual, excising the poetic analogies to farmhands killing poultry. Nevertheless, they were not coy about describing brutality. Amelia Dyer's label describes her young victims as being "strangled and dropped in the Thames … the floating up of the bodies leading to the discovery of the murderess" (Tussaud & Sons, c.1917 70). Mary Pearcey's entry is given an actual title, that of "The Hampstead Tragedy." Her catalogue entry continues:

> Mrs. Pearcey and the actual perambulator. Mary Eleanor Pearcey aka Wheeler, murdered Mrs. Phoebe Hogg and her eighteenth months old daughter at Priory Place, Kentish Town, and conveyed the bodies in the child's perambulator through the public streets, a distance of between one and two miles. She was executed at Newgate, 23 December 1890. (Tussaud & Sons, c.1917 75)

It is not only the acknowledgement of the crime that is notable but also the object included. Tussaud's had scored something of coup by obtaining—just in time for end of the holiday rush—the actual pram Pearcey used to transport the bodies of her victims (McEvoy 71). The pushing of the pram and the lengthy walk through the streets of London are undeniably active. Causing the death of another might be accidental, but rolling the deceased through the crowded streets, concealed in a baby carriage, took thought and action. In *Murder & Its Motives*, F. Tennyson Jesse describes the journey, as witnessed by a neighbour in this way:

> The road inclines upwards under the railway arch and Mrs Pearcey seemed to be having a hard time pushing the perambulator up-hill; her head was drooped right over the handle…her bent figure toiling along behind laden perambulator bent over the white china handle bar which was found stained and broken; so intent she recognized nobody whom she met (174-75).

It is the pram, not its occupants, regular or irregular, that becomes the lightning rod for the fascinations regarding Pearcey. Furthermore, it is not so much the murder which is unfathomable; indeed, Jesse never seems fully convinced that the child was actively murdered, always leaving open the possibility that it succumbed to exposure after being dumped (175). Rather, it is the walk from Kentish town to Hampstead, pushing the bodies of her victims before her, that draws the reader's or visitor's attention to Pearcey.

The lack of display of the pram at the Museum of London is not a cause for censure. Even if the pram had ended up in the collection at New Scotland Yard, there would be a strong case for resisting sensation and the temptation to put it back in front of the public. The exhibition maintains a separation between spectacle and justice, which is in keeping with the ethical concerns of museological display of violent crime. However, it fails to replace that spectacle with anything else. An acknowledgement that Pearcey took actions, that she had agency within these events, remains missing. Recognition that she was violent toward other persons to the extent that she caused their death remains elusive. If the curatorial decision was made to include any narrative about Mary Pearcey, then that aspect needed to be present. It need not be sensationalized and it certainly should not be celebrated, but it must be acknowledged.

Pearcey's story is less revelatory than that of Louise Massett or Emma Williams. The child Pearcey murdered was not one with which she had a relationship, either familial or transactional. Nor does it appear that she set out with a view to murdering the child. Her primary target seems to have been her lover's wife, Phoebe. Most of the re-tellings of Pearcey's story focus on this killing. Remarkably, little seems to be made of the child's death, few sources even mention her name. Perhaps because no one had thought to entrust a child to Mary Pearcey, the murder of the child was less unexpected. Furthermore, despite having killed an eighteen-month-old infant, as Pearcey was not a mother, not even a mother-by-proxy, her crimes were not viewed as besmirching the model of motherhood. That said, the nature of Pearcey's notoriety, and its complete absence in the Museum of London exhibition, is revelatory and useful to this analysis. For if nothing else, Pearcey's walk pushing the perambulator gives some insight into her state of mind in that moment. Without it, visitors to *The Crime Museum Uncovered* were left with an interpretation that made disturbingly little distinction between Pearcey as perpetrator and the Hoggs as victims. All three became simply females, women or girl, to which actions happened resulting in death. Massett, too, was obscured by an interpretive model that failed to engage with women's agency. Ballinger notes that Massett spoke up for herself at the trial, clarifying details and attempting to correct the prosecutor's characterization of her, and her arrangements with her family, with her lover, and with those to whom she maintained that she had entrusted Manfred's care (114, 117-18). Doing so indicates a level of intelligence as well as an ability to articulate her thoughts under pressure. It also, Ballinger speculates, contributed to the misogyny that led to her conviction and execution (117-20).

Women's agency as evidenced by the decisions that they made, or were accused of making, are crucial to understanding these crimes, these convictions, and the societies in which they occurred. It is impossible to fully understand the depths of vulnerability Emma Williams, and women like her, experienced if the severity of her crime is not considered. In the case of Massett, this omission becomes even more pronounced. Both the unconventional aspects of her life and her reactions to the conduct of her trial speak volumes about the nature of the society in which she lived and the expectations placed upon women, particularly women with children. The willingness of both the legal establishment and the media to accept that she had been responsible for the death of her son reflected the prejudice that as she had already put aside acceptable models of motherhood, she was quite capable of further distorting that maternal instinct even unto murder (Ballinger 119-20,123). Yet Massett and even to some extent Williams are interpreted without a robust discussion of their motivations, reactions, and emotions. As a result, the museum visitors are not given access to those aspects and insights that justify the inclusion of the difficult topic of infanticide in the first place.

Still Unspoken: Interpretations of Mental Illness

Changes in public perception with regards to infanticide rendered the old exhibitions obsolete and in need of a new approach even before they fully disappeared from view. A series of law reforms in Great Britain in the 1920s and 1930s demonstrated an increasing concern for the state of the mothers, not as monstrous but as mentally ill.[2] The legal and medical professions continue to refine and reassess their reactions to infanticide and, at a basic level, museums have done the same. The Old

Melbourne Gaol, the National Portrait Gallery, and the Museum of London demonstrate a variety of approaches in providing modern audiences with new interpretations of the crime infanticide. Yet all of these modern exhibitions avoid an in-depth interrogation of the act itself. Though varied, the interpretive models employed by the three institutions each struggle to move beyond a narrative that amounts to "this woman killed this child and was hanged." Brief recognition of some contextual factors, while a marked improvement on what came before, still does little to mitigate the enormous yet unacknowledged silence that surrounds these acts. Granted, through these exhibitions, museum visitors are given insight into the nineteenth- and early twentieth-century fascination with women who committed infanticide. *Sideshow Alley* explores this narrative directly, but it is also transmitted through the collections found in the Old Melbourne Gaol and *The Crime Museum Uncovered* through the death masks, nooses, and courtroom sketches that were collected and preserved. Nevertheless, the lives of the women themselves and the myriad factors influencing their actions remain obscured.

Additionally, not only did these exhibitions fail to present a complete picture of why Williams or Massett or Pearcey might have resorted to infanticide, they also failed to distinguish between them in any meaningful way. Both Williams and Massett were, at the time of their convictions, labelled as "unnatural," a word reflecting the sense that not only had they transgressed criminally but against their own biology (Ballinger 119 quoting *The Daily Telegraph*, 16 December 1899; National Portrait Gallery, Exhibition Label). Beyond that, however, they led very different lives. Emma Williams was a working-class woman in the Australian colonies who had little means of support and appears to have been pressured directly and indirectly to rid herself of her child. Louise Massett was educated, self-supporting, and reportedly enjoyed a doting relationship with her son, for which her lover expressed no resentment (Ballinger 110-11, 113). Williams's guilt is rarely contested; Massett's conviction appears "unsafe" (Ballinger 104). Yet museologically, there is little to separate them and little to encourage the museum visitor to dig deeper and seek out more details.

Engaging with infanticide museologically entails negotiating the challenges associated with dark tourism. Exhibiting topics of trauma and violence opens museums to concerns regarding trivialization of suffering and the commodification of atrocity (Katz 353; Wilson; Witcomb 152-70). The justification for broaching such topics is that while potentially exploitive, they provide the opportunity to discuss difficult topics, particularly difficult histories, and in doing so give voice to the ostracized and the oppressed. The previously quoted opening panel of *The Crime Museum Uncovered* references this interpretive exchange. Yes, the stories are "disturbing" but they provide "insight." However, if those marginalized voices remain silent, then the rationale behind the inclusion is substantially weaker. One of the challenges facing all three modern exhibitions is that increased legal and medical consideration of the mother's mental state necessitates a similar adjustment in museological practice. Unfortunately, museums as a whole do not demonstrate significant prowess in interpreting mental illness. Catharine Coleborne has written on multiple occasions on the interpretation of psychiatry and mental illness in museums. In 2001, when assessing an exhibition at the Medical History Museum at the University of Melbourne, Coleborne noted the repeated tendency for the exhibition publicity to be reduced to a single object, the straight-jacket ("Exhibiting" 114). In 2016, as part of a review article referencing the Wellcome Collection's exhibition on the "Bedlam" Asylum Coleborne observed the following:

> It can be hard to get away from the notion of "Bedlam." This place and symbol overshadow the historical thinking about mental health and illness. The 'puzzles and complexities' of madness before the eighteenth century still present historians with challenges of interpretation ("An End" 423).

Fifteen years, it would seem, have done little to rewrite the points of reference. In a review of the Wellcome Collection exhibition for *The Guardian*, Jonathon Jones laments a lost opportunity. He argues that had the museum focused on the asylum and the debates surrounding it, a moving exhibition might have been achieved. Instead, the stated focus is watered down with additional material resulting in an interpretation that Jones critiques as "confused and complacent" (19 September 2016).

The medium of exhibition, by its nature, necessitates the reduction of narrative to an indicative object. What distinguishes good exhibitions from the mediocre is the curatorial choice that selects objects that challenge both audiences and existing narrative paradigms. Too often, it would seem, museological engagement with mental illness still opts for reduction to the easiest cultural illustrations: the madhouse and the straightjacket. Meanwhile at the time of writing, J-Ward, a tourist attraction in a closed asylum outside of Melbourne, still beckons visitors with the promise on its website that they can "hear stories of murderers, ghosts and the mistreatment of mental illness." Whatever conciliatory gesture is embedded in the wording of the third offering, equating the mentally ill with hauntings and murder does little towards eliminating the stigma associated with psychiatric conditions. Given the greater focus on mental health in the legal and medical discourses surrounding infanticide, it is fair to expect that museum exhibitions will similarly move towards this paradigm. However, if even well-intentioned exhibitions struggle to find a nuanced narrative with regards to infanticide, and museum visitors continue to be conditioned towards a equating the mentally ill with the monstrous and the frightening, it is worth asking how much progress from the waxworks has ultimately been achieved.

Conclusions

None of these modern exhibitions were poorly crafted. Each was well-curated when interpreting aspects other than infanticide. *The Crime Museum Uncovered* broached the normally taboo subject of abortion with care, sensitivity, and balance. The Old Melbourne Gaol does provide insight into the challenges nineteenth-century women faced in Melbourne's inner urban neighbourhoods. *Sideshow Alley* made a strong, well-evidenced case for the long tradition of ghoulish spectacle in the Australian mindset. Yet the inclusion of women executed for infanticide is a weak point for each of them. It is not the intent of this chapter to argue that the model provided by the waxworks is a superior approach for interpreting these women; the level of spectacle and condemnation was far from ideal. What these exhibitions do reveal is that simply removing the aura of spectacle is insufficient, particularly if discussions of agency and of difficult personal history are simultaneously erased. A genuine engagement with the actions and narratives of Williams, Massett, and women in similar circumstances necessitates discussing social-economic conditions but also mental health, misogyny, and societal expectations that were deeply rooted in both gender and class. If museums and/or curators are not in the position to be able to tackle the Pandora's Box of those complex, interwoven themes (and there are professional, institutional, and interpretive environments in which that may well be the case), then they should consider being equally circumspect about including infanticide within their interpretation.

Endnotes

1. For more on the concept of atmospheric interpretation, see Jennifer Turner and Kimberley Peters. "Unlocking carceral atmospheres: designing visual/material encounters at the prison museum." *Visual Communication* vol.14 no.3, 2015, 309-30.
2. For more discussion on the relevant law reforms see Anne-Marie Kilday. *A History of Infanticide in Britain c.1600 to the Present.* Basingstoke, Palgrave Macmillan, 2013, 184-89.

Works Cited

Arnot, Margaret L. "Infant Death, Child Care and the State: The Baby-Farming Scandal and the First Infant Life Protection Legislation of 1872." *Continuity and Change,* vol, 9, no.2, 1994, pp. 271-311.

Ballinger, Annette. *Dead Woman Walking: Executed Women in England and Wales* 1900-1955. Ashgate Publishing, 2000.

Biber, Katherine. "In Crime's Archive: The Cultural Afterlife of Criminal Evidence." *British Journal of Criminology,* vol 53, no. 6, 2013, pp. 1033-49.

Jesse, F. Tennyson. *Murder & Its Motives.* New York, Alfred Knopf & Co, 1924.

Catalogue of Madame Sohiers Waxworks Exhibition. William and McKinnon printers, 1866.

Coleborne, Catharine. "An End to Bedlam? The Enduring Subject of Madness in Social and Cultural History." *Social History,* vol. 42, no. 3, 2017 pp. 420-29

Coleborne, Catharine. "Exhibiting 'Madness': Material Culture and the Asylum." *Health and History,* vol. 3, no. 2, 2001, pp. 104-17.

D'Cruze, Shani, and Louise A. Jackson. *Women, Crime and Justice in England since 1600.* Palgrave Macmillan, 2007.

Gilmour, Joanna. *Sideshow Alley: Infamy, the Macbre, & the Portrait.* The National Portrait Gallery, 2015.

Gray, James. "Jack the Ripper and the Ethics of the (Other) Met Museum." *The Guardian,* 12 Aug, 2013, www.theguardian.com/culture-professionals-network/culture-professionals-blog/2013/aug/12/met-crime-museum-ripper-letter. Accessed 14 Nov. 2021.

Jones, Jonathon. "Bedlam: The Asylum and Beyond Review—Missed Opportunity to Truly Explore Mental Health." *The Guardian,* 19 Sept. 2016, www.theguardian.com/artanddesign/2016/sep/19/bedlam-the-asylum-and-beyond-review-wellcome-collection. Accessed 14 Nov. 2021.

Katz, Meighen. "City of Women: The Old Melbourne Gaol and a Gender-Specific Interpretation of Urban Life." *The Palgrave Handbook of Prison Tourism,* edited by J.Z. Wilson et al., Palgrave Macmillan, 2017, pp. 341-64.

Keily, Jackie, and Julia Hoffbrand. *The Crime Museum Uncovered: Inside Scotland Yard's Special Collections.* I.B.Tauris/Museum of London, 2015.

Kilday, Anne-Marie. *A History of Infanticide in Britain c.1600 to the Present.* Palgrave Macmillan, 2013.

Kreitmayer's Waxworks Exhibition. Melbourne. c.1912.

Lennon, John, and Malcolm Foley. *Dark Tourism.* Continuum, 2000

Madame Tussaud & Sons. *Madame Tussaud & Sons' Exhibition Catalogue: Containing Biographical & Descriptive Sketches of the Distinguished Characters Which Compose Their Exhibition and Historical Gallery.* London, 1876.

Madame Tussaud & Sons. *Madame Tussaud & Sons' Exhibition Catalogue: Containing Biographical & Descriptive Sketches of the Distinguished Characters Which Compose Their Exhibition and Historical Gallery.* London, 1883.

Madame Tussaud & Sons. *Madame Tussaud's Exhibition Guide,* London, c. 1917.

Messers Baume & Kreitmayer. *Catalogue of Messers Baume & Kreitmayer's Grand Anatomical Museum.* Printed by Shaw, Harnett & Co, 1861.

McEvoy, Emma. *Gothic Tourism*. Palgrave Macmillan, 2016.

Museum of London, Exhibition Panels, *The Crime Museum Uncovered*. Visited March 2016.

Museum of London, Room Guide, *The Crime Museum Uncovered*, 2015.

National Portrait Gallery, Exhibition Panels. *Sideshow Alley*. Visited January 2016.

National Trust of Australia (Victoria). Interpretive Panels Old Melbourne Gaol.

Pearce, Susan. *Museums, Objects and Collections: A Cultural Study*. Leicester University Press, 1992.

Pearman, Joanne. "Review of David Wilson: *Mary Ann Cotton:Britain's First Serial Killer*," vol 2, no.3, 2013, *Kent*, journals.kent.ac.uk/index.php/feministsatlaw/article/download/78/211?inline=1. Accessed 14 Nov. 2021.

Sala, George Augustus. "Historic Notes on Madame Tussaud's, April 1892."*Madame Tussaud's Exhibition Guide*, c.1917.

Strange, Carolyn, and Michael Kempa. "Shades of Dark Tourism: Alcatraz and Robben Island." *Annals of Tourism Research*, vol. 30, no. 2, 2003, pp. 386-405.

The Australasian Sketcher with Pen and Pencil, 1876.

Turner, Jennifer, and Kimberley Peters. "Unlocking Carceral Atmospheres: Designing Visual/Material Encounters at the Prison Museum." *Visual Communication*, vol. 14, no. 3, 2015, pp. 309-30.

Wilson, Jacqueline Z. *Prison: Cultural Memory and Dark Tourism*. Peter Lang, 2008.

Witcomb, Andrea. "Using Immersive and Interactive Approaches to Interpreting Traumatic Experiences for Tourists: Potentials and Limitations" *Heritage and Tourism: Place, Encounter, Engagement*, edited by in Russell Staiff et al., Routledge, 2013, pp. 152-70.

Chapter 10

"A Crown of Martyrdom": Infanticide, Insanity, and Capital Punishment in Colonial Victoria

Georgina Rychner

> They took possession of the girl ... determined not to part with her until she had revealed herself to them mentally and physically, to gratify their morbid curiosity.
> —Unknown journalist on the trial of Rosanna Plummer, 1884

Introduction

This chapter examines how different parties conceived of and advanced theories of mental illness as it related to offenders of capital crime tried in the colony of Victoria in the late nineteenth century. It conducts a microanalysis of the trial of Rosanna Plummer (1884), in which doctors, judges, jurors, journalists, and a significant number of lay men and women put forward theories regarding her mental state at the time of committing the crime of infanticide on her infant son. Plummer's case deserves the close scrutiny offered in this chapter because it was one of the first infanticide cases in the colony to see substantial and widespread post-trial activism on the basis of her insanity; indeed, it was the highpoint of this sort of activism. Her story first inspired and then disillusioned the populace, ensuring no other infanticide defendant would receive the same treatment in the state of Victoria. Colonists compared Rosanna to infanticide defendants in subsequent decades, a testimony to the mark she left on the Melbourne legal system (*South Bourke and Mornington Journal*, Mar. 26, 1890, 3). This study comes out of a broader project that examines the 215 capital crime convictions for murder and sexual offences in Victoria between 1880 and 1939. Criminal trial transcripts, medical reports, judges notes, and petitions for commutation are sourced from the capital case files (VPRS, 264) and capital sentences files (VPRS, 1100) located in the Public Record Office of Victoria. These files were passed on to the governor of Victoria and his cabinet, known as the Executive Council, which typically convened two weeks after a convicted capital trial and voted on whether to commute sentence or proceed with execution of the offender. This source base was read alongside contemporary newspaper coverage that had been digitized on the National Library of Australia's database, including the two major newspapers in circulation at the time, *The Argus* and *The Age*, as well as various rural newspapers in print during the period.

Contextualizing Infanticide

Whereas anxieties about infanticide peaked in England during the 1860s, Victoria witnessed its own infanticide panic in the last decades of the century. In England, this panic came about through heightened visibility of children through the more consistent registration of births and deaths, the emergence of more vigilant medical coroners, and an expanding press that seemed to feed off salacious stories of infant murder (Behlmer 407-14). The same changes occurred in Victoria between 1870 and 1900. At the height of Melbourne's industrialization, the city saw an uncomfortable concentration of poverty and a gradual rise in the infant mortality rate, with small corpses appearing in drains, ponds, trains, and rising from the murky depths of the Yarra River (*Australian Year Book* 334-36). Between 1885 and 1914, 614 infants were found dead, the majority discovered in Melbourne. Police records showed an average of twenty-four women charged with infanticide annually (Burton 49-50). However, because infant death could be concealed or attributed to natural causes. identifiable rates of infanticide likely constituted only a fraction of actual incidences (Allen

17). Authorities expressed frustration at the difficulty in locating, apprehending, and prosecuting mothers. The Victorian Vigilance Association, a society devoted to protection of young girls and infant life, claimed to bear witness to numerous cases of infant murder "day to day" during the year 1892 (*Age*, July 4, 1893, 5). In cases where mothers were traced and charged, it was incredibly difficult for inquest juries to distinguish between deaths from exposure, stillbirth, and wilful murder. Insubstantial evidence often saw juries opt for a lesser conviction of abandonment or concealment of birth; the sentence for these minor offences ranged from a fine of forty shillings to eighteen months imprisonment (Swain, "Concealment of Birth" 141-43). Although the press published the number of convicted criminals each year, the "dark figure" of infant murders haunted and troubled colonists and lawmakers from the 1880s onwards (Laster, "Infanticide" 154). Racial anxieties regarding the preservation of culture and population decline prompted legislative reform to improve the policing of infanticide and the protection of infant life. Newspaper coverage portrayed infanticide as a particularly abhorrent crime that reflected poorly on Western nations and overreported on infanticides in China and India (*Argus*, 1884, 4; *Argus*, 1886, 8). A declining population contributed to fears that the settler colony would lose its stronghold on colonized land and eventually die out (Pringle; Murphy). The Victorian government introduced the Infant Life Protection Act in 1890, which granted police power to search any premises under suspicion of neglect or infanticide. Shurlee Swain and Renate Howe identify the pronatalist shift evident in the Infant Life Protection Act in this period: "The problematic illegitimate child transformed into the potential citizen" (111). This shift culminated in the federal 1912 Maternity Allowance Act, which awarded five pounds to every white woman, married or unmarried, who gave birth to a living child.

Through her actions, the infanticidal woman challenged nineteenth-century ideals of femininity and motherhood. The anonymous infanticidal mother drew criticism from the public, with newspapers such as *The Age* and *The Argus* reminding readers what a "fiend of cruelty" a woman could be (*Age*, Oct. 7, 1895, 4). More generally, the press construed infanticide as a chilling, deliberate crime and warned colonists of "a very army of murderesses in our midst" (*Age*, Oct. 7, 1895, 4). However, when a defendant was tried in the Supreme Court and the various details surrounding her past or her circumstances surfaced, colonists could no longer condemn her in the abstract. The women who reached the Supreme Court were certainly in the minority and constitute only the "public face" of infanticide, yet it is through their trials that we can observe how colonists assessed infanticidal mothers who had been found guilty, and all the contradictions they embodied (Burton 22; Swain and Howe 95-96).

Rosanna Plummer as Infanticide Defendant

Rosanna Plummer was the daughter of John and Kate Plummer, respectable farmers who lived at Mokoan, fourteen miles from Glenrowan, in the Northeast of Victoria. In 1884, the family, consisting of five children, had lived in the district for nine years and cultivated close relationships with neighbours. Rosanna was eighteen years old; she performed domestic work within her family household and sewed for local families. She occasionally assisted a neighbouring farmer outdoors for a day or two during harvest. Her neighbours thought her to be an industrious, good-natured young woman. Michael Bergin lived on a neighbouring property. The pair had known each other since they were twelve years old. Many in the area knew them to be sweethearts and thought they would marry. When Plummer realized she was pregnant with Bergin's child, she confided in her mother. The two women travelled by train to Melbourne, where Rosanna was confined at Dr. John Singleton's home for two weeks. She was then transferred to Mrs. Ellen Singleton's home—Dr. Singleton's spouse and a midwife operating in King Street— where she gave birth to a daughter whom she never named (VPRS, 264 P0001/1). Ellen Singleton and a matron named Frances Delaney later testified in court as to Plummer's whereabouts on the day of the alleged murder. Plummer left King Street with a carpet bag and her child wrapped in a red shawl. She headed to Dr. Singleton's office in Collingwood to collect her clothes. From there, the arrangement was to meet her mother at Spencer Street Railway Station to catch the last train home to Benalla. Kate Plummer waited at the station but did not see her daughter there. Unknown to her, Rosanna was pacing up and down a different platform, burdened with heavy deliberations. Rosanna then caught a cab with money provided by her mother that morning back to Dr. Singleton's home in

Collingwood. She had forgotten the address and asked a woman on the street—an iron maker's wife named Lucy Fenn—for directions. Once at Dr. Singleton's, Plummer asked Delaney whether she could stay another night and leave tomorrow instead. Delaney asked where the baby was; Rosanna replied she had given it to her mother, who had already taken the train home. There came a ring at the door. Lucy Fenn had decided to notify Delaney that she had seen a young woman on the street with a dead child. The pair questioned Rosanna, who first said her mother had taken the baby and then denied she had a carpet bag. When the matron discovered the little corpse, Plummer proclaimed: "I know nothing about it. I took the child, it had a little band round its waist excessively tight" (VPRS, 264/P0001/1). By the time a police constable entered the home near four o'clock, Plummer had confessed that she smothered the child at the train station. Her mother—by this time searching for her daughter—would find her in the city lockup the next day, under arrest for murder.

Plucked from the abstraction of the infinite and faceless infanticide offenders purported to roam the metropolis, the Supreme Court trial placed Rosanna Plummer under public scrutiny as an individual with a specific past and circumstances that led to the crime. From the news of her arrest, the press formulated quick judgments and constructed the lens through which the public should view Rosanna. *The Age* described her as the daughter of respectable farmers and reported that it was a young male neighbour who had caused her fall from grace (June 24, 1884, 5). Conversely, *The Argus* described the case as "a most heartless child murder" (June 24, 1884, 7). The most notable addition to the press narrative was Plummer's supposed insanity. Creative reporting told of how Rosanna considered destroying the infant "by placing it on the rails to be killed by some passing train" and had "wandered about with a vague idea of committing suicide herself and thus escaping the true consequence of her crime" but ultimately found herself back in Collingwood, "without knowing how or by what means she got there" (*Age*, June 24, 1884, 5). The press inserted insanity into the narrative before Plummer submitted an insanity defence at trial. Arguably, the reason is the close relationship between notions of late-Victorian femininity and incapacity for violence.

Femininity and Insanity

Sympathy for infanticide defendants has been attributed to a range of cultural factors, with the most overt factor being a visible femininity. The nineteenth century saw the introduction of a new approach to crime and punishment. Previously, criminal law was concerned simply with offense and penalty; however, a new criminological paradigm shifted focus from the crime itself to "the crime, the criminal and the means of repression" (Foucault 2). The criminal needed to be scrutinized, his or her history and motives understood, and a process of confession, self-examination, and self-redemption undertaken to eliminate the danger that they posed to the social body (Foucault 2). The colonial public—in their capacity as journalists and readers as well as jurors and activists—assessed the degree of a criminal's responsibility and the punishment required. These unofficial judgments were informed by social factors, including popular understanding of what a criminal was and how he or she looked and behaved.

Judith Allen's 1990 *Sex and Secrets* demonstrates how crime was a lens through which to examine "the negotiations between the sexes with regard to sexuality and power" (12). Allen has established that gender is pertinent to the study of reproductive crime. Women committed abortion and infanticide largely due to the legislative and social restrictions placed on their freedom to regulate their own reproduction. Jurors, lawmakers, and a vocal public then assessed their culpability in gendered terms. Victorians constructed woman as the morally superior sex based on her gentle nature, instinctive maternalism, and promotion of pacifism in opposition to male violence. A mother who deliberately killed her own child challenged these notions and was often judged by society to be unfeminine and sexless. A mother who presented as appropriately feminine in appearance and demeanour and who nonetheless killed her own child disrupted the feminine-violent binary. In these cases, colonists were reluctant to believe the defendant was responsible for her actions (see *Argus*, Aug. 12, 1884, 4; *Numurkah Leader*, Nov. 7, 1895, 3).Colonists appraised the femininity of female defendants through the glimpses they caught of prisoners in densely crowded courtrooms and, more often, through descriptions in newspapers. Significance was placed on defendants' clothing and conduct in court (Grey). Whereas male infanticide defendants were expected to self-censor emotions in order to demonstrate a masculine self-control, spectators searched female defendants for displays of emotional suffering that revealed grief and shame (Grey 471-72). The youthful appearance of Rosanna Plummer greatly affected the public. This was not a "callous" woman of "ill repute" as the prisoner Emma Williams would be described in 1895 but a domestic servant, the daughter of respectable and well-liked farmers who the press described after the trial as "young and confiding." She was not a convicted criminal but "a poor, deserted victim of man's lust and unfaithfulness" (*Ballarat Star*, July 29, 1884. 2; *Telegraph*, Aug. 2, 1884, 5).

The contradiction posed by a feminine offender with a respectable history was made somewhat more understandable by a narrative of seduction and abandonment by a callous male seducer. Newspapers and individual supporters deplored the anonymous men who courted Rosanna Plummer, as well as other women accused of infanticide—Bella Ferguson and Margaret Heffernan—only to leave them to bear the shame of an illegitimate child alone (*Argus*, June 24, 1884, 7; *Mount Alexander Mail*, Nov. 30, 1889, 3; *Age*, Mar. 14, 1900, 9). In analysing the arbitrariness of the justice system regarding virtuous and promiscuous offenders, Kathy Laster comments that "politics, not law, determined their fate" ("Arbitrary Chivalry" 70-71). If we return to the factors associated with the nineteenth-century criminal—character, confession, and redemption—we can discern the indicators that gained public sympathy for infanticide defendants. The public perceived Rosanna's character through what they knew of her respectable past. Her confession took the form of her emotive display in the courtroom, and her redemption relied on her appearance as an acceptable woman, one who could be restored to her socially ordained role as mother and caregiver in the future. After all, women like Plummer, it was argued, would not have committed infanticide if their male seducers had not driven them, through fear and abandonment, to kill. The gendered politics of respectability that run through infanticide trial narratives are well covered historically, yet less attention has been paid to the factor of insanity that essentially enabled these narratives. This chapter provides a necessary correction to this scholarly vacuum.

Of importance to this analysis is Rosanna Plummer's defence of insanity. On July 16, 1884, the Supreme Court trial commenced before Chief Justice William Stawell and a jury of twelve men. Three doctors testified: The prosecution called a Dr. Stirling who had conducted the postmortem and confirmed death by suffocation, whereas the defence called two doctors on the question of insanity—these being Dr. Stephen Burke, who had attended Rosanna at Portland House during her confinement, and Dr Andrew Shields, who inspected Plummer in prison two days after her arrest. Both confirmed Plummer had been ill with bronchitis, with a fever, at time of birth. Neither of these doctors offered conclusive opinions regarding Plummer's insanity. The defence counsel submitted that Plummer suffered from puerperal mania, a mental illness that attended women in pregnancy and birth (VPRS, 264 P0001/1). Dr. Burke told the jury that puerperal mania generally occurred at the fifteenth day after birth, and the child might be unsafe if left with the mother during this time. Dr. Shields confirmed that a woman suffering from puerperal mania one day might be well a day or two afterwards, establishing the disease as a temporary condition (VPRS, 264 P0001/1). However, due to the subjective nature of the M'Naghtan rules, neither physician could confirm nor deny that Plummer had been suffering from puerperal mania during the crime. In addition, colonial doctors were hesitant to offer concrete diagnoses at trial. Although the doctors believed this to be a possibility, the jury was not persuaded beyond a reasonable doubt resulting in a conviction. The Victorian public were sympathetic to Plummer and were convinced that this was a case of puerperal insanity.

"The Crown of Martyrdom on Her Head"

Plummer's conviction roused the residents of Melbourne into action. Commonly a two-week period, this was the time to make public sympathy known in order to persuade the Executive Council to commute the sentence. "It is seldom that a criminal under sentence of death has so large a claim on public sympathy as the girl Rosanna Plummer," read the *Ballarat Star* a fortnight after the trial (July 29, 1884, 2). Described as having blue eyes and golden hair, the story of this young woman, seduced by a deceitful neighbour and left to shoulder the burden of an illegitimate child alone, captured the imaginations of men and women across the colony. Charitable middle-class women drafted a mass petition for Plummer's mercy and took up posts at Cole's book arcade, the Ladies' Club at 40 Collins Street, the Temperance Hall in Russell Street, and the entrance to Flinders Street railway station, where there they collected signatures from foot traffic. They shared the front page of their petition stating Plummer deserved a commuted sentence, owing to the "insane behaviour" she suffered on the day of the crime (VPRS, 264 P0001/1). It was not any particular aspect of Rosanna's case that ensured the infamy of her trial but the fortuitous timing of the trial amid the awakenings of the first women's rights movement. On May 8, 1884, just two weeks before Plummer admitted herself to Dr. Singleton's Home, Henrietta Dugdale, and Annie Lowe formed the Victorian Women's Suffrage Society in South Yarra (*Ovens and Murray Advertiser*, May 10, 1884, 8). This was the first society dedicated to women's suffrage in the Australian colonies. Although suffrage was the main objective, the society advocated for broader goals, such as women's marital property rights and admission to universities. This budding suffragist movement in Victoria highlighted the structural inequalities placed on women, not only through disenfranchisement and property rights but also through the reproductive burden women carried as a result of divorce laws, lack of maintenance payments, and a dearth of institutions in the city to aid single mothers (*Age*, Sept. 10, 1884, 5). Although Judith Allen has remarked on the relative silence of middle-class suffragists in cases of women convicted for reproductive crimes, the modest participation of Victoria's first suffragists in Plummer's case reveals a passionate attempt to help female prisoners in certain cases. In July 1884, Henriette Dugdale signed her name amid the thousands of signatures pleading for Plummer's commuted sentence (Priestley; Suffrage Collective).

Cases such as Plummer's were widely disseminated as cautionary tales of what could happen to women who fell pregnant with no means or support—a social and financial burden woman often carried alone. Suffragists quickly realized the potential these criminal cases had in highlighting the structural inequalities that governed colonial women's lives. Subsequent high-profile cases, such as the trial of Margaret Heffernan for infanticide in 1900, saw the continued activism on the part of suffragists in this sphere (Rychner). In the volunteer effort that attended the Women's Suffrage Petition in 1891, where women conducted extensive door knocking—talking over fences and trudging through poorer areas of Melbourne to collect signatures—Clare Wright identifies "the first time women came together across class lines" (34). Beyond the question of suffrage, the Women's Suffrage Petition echoed a slightly older tradition of cross-class activism organized around gender. Some of the women who signed their names in 1891 might have recalled the sizable petition for Rosanna Plummer's mercy seven years prior. Plummer's case inspired arguments for greater protections for young mothers, including legal protection against male seducers. There were renewed calls for a maternity charity society, a foundling hospital and mandatory paternal maintenance payments. Journalists and letters to the editor condemned the father of Rosanna's child as "heartless," "deceptive," and "cowardly" (*Ovens and Murray Advertiser*, Aug. 5, 1884, 1; *Telegraph*, Aug. 2, 1884, 5; *Telegraph*, Sept. 27, 1884, 5). The wealthy women of Prahran who had played a large role in organizing the petitions, Mrs. Ball and Mrs. Wilcox, raised money to take legal proceedings against "the betrayer" (*Telegraph*, Aug. 30, 1884, 5). The public vitriol levied at Plummer's seducer helped to recast her as the desperate, frenzied victim of circumstance.

Laster and Douglas write that through the designation of reproductive crime as a capital offence, colonial society placed blame onto the female offender for failing to regulate her own reproduction rather than addressing the structural inequalities that had brought about this failure (152). This is true regarding legal blame; however, in the popular pathologization of distress, public narratives often located the behaviour of a male spouse or sexual partner as the driving force for madness. Just as Rosanna acted in a moment of temporary insanity at her desertion, Sarah Williams's mind was "unhinged at the time through her husband's drunken neglect and abuse" (VPRS, 264 P0001/1; *Mount Alexander Mail*, Dec. 3, 1885, 3). Similarly, the defence for Camelia McCluskey, tried in 1910 for the murder of her three children, successfully convinced jurors that her husband "simply treated her in a way, to use ordinary everyday language, to drive her out of her mind—to drive her crazy" (*Mount Alexander Mail*, Aug. 6, 1884, 2). In these cases, the public viewed insanity as a product of ill treatment from a spouse or a male stranger.

In emphasizing insanity, ordinary people displaced Plummer's responsibility and ultimately championed her case. Middle-class journalists, politicians, and activists attached as much importance to their own unprofessional judgments of Rosanna's state of mind as they did to medical opinion. On July 26, Footscray's *Independent* read: "Dr. Singleton is of the opinion that the poor girl Rosanna Plummer ... is not of sound mind. We have thought so from the first" (2). Similarly, the *Geelong Advertiser* commented on the "strong and widespread feeling that the fearful deed was due to mental aberration ... which opinion is held by medical men as well as laymen" July 31, 1884, 3). A week after trial, an MP raised Rosanna's case in Parliament, asking the solicitor-general whether further investigation could be made into her mental health (*Geelong Advertiser*, July 25, 1884, 3). The politician explained that though he found Rosanna to be perfectly sane on meeting her in prison, he believed she had been insane at the time of the crime (*Argus*, July 25, 1884, 7; *Colac Herald*, July 25, 1884, 3). Where medical estimations of madness assessed a set of symptoms before reaching a diagnosis, popular conceptions accepted Plummer's distress as prima facie evidence of madness. Most telling is the phrasing Mrs. Ball used in a letter to *The Telegraph*: "It was quite impossible for her to commit a crime in her right mind. Her open innocent face forbade the thought at once" (Aug. 23, 1884, 5). Abandoned by the father of the child, she was "left to face her shame and battle with the world as best she might ... her desperation and despair affected her intellect to such an extent as to render her scarcely accountable for her acts" (*Ballarat Star*, July 29, 1884, 2). This "feeling of utter desperation and despair" was believed to "oftentimes overtake youthful victims ... unhinge their minds [and] impel" them to take the lives of their infants (*Gippsland Times*, Aug. 1, 1884, 3; *Independent*, Aug. 9, 1884, 2; *Age*, Aug. 12, 1884, 4). Here, the eagerness of the public to ascribe insanity originated in their own conviction regarding her innocence rather than any medical opinion.

At the height of this public activism, an extraordinary amount of evidence emerged. Thirteen men and women stepped forward announcing that they had seen Rosanna on the day she had murdered her infant and signed statements for the Executive Council to that effect. These witnesses had not appeared at trial. There was the cab driver who had taken Rosanna from Portland House to Fitzroy; two men who had happened to share a cab with Rosanna from Fitzroy to Bourke Street; a police constable and a male bystander who had noticed her on the platform at Spencer Street Station; a husband and wife who had seen her close to their business in King Street, two female lodgers at Portland house; a boarder at Dr. Singleton's Home; and a woman who had seen Rosanna walk past her house in Collingwood (VPRS, 264 P0001/1). The witness assessments of Rosanna's insanity were vague, with no specific reference to words or actions. Many simply stated, "she had the appearance of not being in her right mind" or "she seemed excited." Only George Wilkinson, a man who had allegedly seen Rosanna on the train platform elaborated: "She looked wild.... I thought she had broken out of a lunatic asylum—her eyes were rolling and glazed" (VPRS, 264 P0001/1).

These witnesses undoubtedly came forward as Melbourne buzzed with speculation over Rosanna's insanity; the newspapers largely peddled a consensus that Rosanna had been mad. Their descriptions were not elaborate; there were no references to childbirth or puerperal mania. There was no public debate regarding symptoms, medical theories, or the effects of pregnancy. Female madness was distress, excitement, and the occasional glazed eye—all of which were ostensibly clear and apparent to the everyday person. Public, rather than medical, determinations of insanity had influenced the decision of the Executive Council. The combined efforts of individual MPs, such as Mr. Hall, the benevolent ladies of Prahran, the thousands of colonists who stopped at train stations to sign their names for Rosanna's cause, and the witnesses who stepped forward in the weeks after her trial and the advice of Chief Justice Stawell all played a part in informing the Executive Council's decision. Towards the end of the fortnight, the Executive Council decided to "reserve their decision until further enquiries had been made with reference to the state of the prisoner's mind" (*Mount Alexander Mail*, Aug. 12, 1884, 3). On 12 August 12, 1884, in the wake of several mass petitions and two weeks of feverish news coverage across Melbourne, the Council granted Rosanna a free pardon "on the ground of her insanity at the time of putting her child to death" (*Leader*, Aug. 9, 1884, 28).

The decision to grant Plummer a free pardon, with no gaol time or good behaviour bond, shocked the city of Melbourne. Initial elation expressed by bourgeois women in the press gave way to an atmosphere of disillusionment, as colonists realized a woman that had killed her child was to escape any form of punishment at all. The *Geelong Advertiser* was scathing of Rosanna's multitude of supporters, deploring the way in which they "took possession of the girl ... determined not to part with her until she had revealed herself to them mentally and physically, to gratify their morbid curiosity" (Aug. 19, 1884, 2). The journalist went on to sarcastically suggest her figure be placed in the Waxworks—the

Melbourne equivalent of Madame Tussauds in London. The fervent interest in maternal insanity began and peaked with Rosanna Plummer in a case where colonists, in their pursuit of justice, felt they had shown too little restraint. No other female infanticide defendant in the period would receive so many pages of press coverage or so many signatures on petitions. In an ironic twist of events, the public reconciled with the penalty-free outcome by placing blame on doctors' failure to present sufficient medical evidence at trial. In the Victorian Parliament, one MP asked his fellow members how a woman could be pardoned on the ground of insanity when no evidence was brought forward to that effect at her trial, rendering Plummer's case "a standing outrage upon the administration of justice" (*Geelong Advertiser*, Sept. 12, 1884, 3). The press argued that the failure of doctors had left the public with no choice but to act: "It was left to popular clamour to determine that she should go forth free into the world again with the crown of martyrdom on her head" (*Geelong Advertiser*, Aug. 19, 1884, 2). Several MPs defended the Crown and the chief justice, laying the blame on the woman's defence counsel, yet no one addressed the uncomfortable question of why the substantial evidence of Rosanna's insanity only surfaced after her trial (*Geelong Advertiser*, Sept. 12, 1884, 3). No one suggested that Rosanna's insanity was largely determined, not so much by the doctors who attended her during her confinement but by thousands of citizens only once they saw a young, respectable woman sentenced to death in the criminal dock and read of how she had been left to bear the shame of an unwanted child alone.

During the public circus of impassioned activism followed by cynical blame, Plummer herself kept quiet. Beyond signing her name to the petition defending her, Plummer largely declined to speak to the various parties who visited her prison cell, and kept a distance from the efforts taking place beyond the prison walls (*Argus*, July 28, 1884, 5). On her release, she politely declined to accept pecuniary assistance from the benevolent ladies eager to raise funds for her and did not pursue action against the man who had allegedly seduced her (*Colac Herald*, Aug. 15, 1884). The only words Plummer communicated directly to the public after her trial were written in a tactful letter published in the *Herald*. In her letter, she thanked the women who devoted time and energy into drawing up the large petitions for her cause and the MP who raised her case in Parliament. Plummer signed off her final goodbye to the public with a reference to the mental state that she, through the goodwill of charitable strangers and her return to the family home, had overcome: "God bless and reward all those who have exerted themselves toward me when everything looked dark and blank" (Aug. 16, 1884, 4). Rosanna Plummer remains obscured by the myriad of discourses that sought to inscribe meaning onto her actions, but some of her own words do survive, and they exhibit all the grace, peacefulness, and modesty that was expected of her.

Beyond Plummer

The young women convicted of infanticide after 1884—the year of Plummer's case—did not receive such lenient sentences, despite each case in the period raising some claim of insanity. Although the death sentences were commuted, the Executive Council opted for long prison sentences that communicated a firm stance against the crime. However, this stance was ostensibly only for the sake of public appearance and deterrence. Defendants convicted in the 1880s, such as Mary Kempton and Bella Ferguson, were sentenced to ten years' imprisonment with hard labour only to be released quietly after serving two years. On occasion, these women were released into the supervision of religious or benevolent women. Although Melbourne societies and journalists continued to petition and write on behalf of infanticide defendants, the groundswell of support that originated in Plummer's case was lost. It was replaced by a cynicism regarding the role of ordinary people in the administration of justice. A lengthy letter to *The Argus* editor dissected the "tendency to explain away crime as an act of temporary insanity" (Apr. 10 1890, 4). An agitation to change the law or remove infanticide as a capital offence would be understandable, the anonymous correspondent wrote: "But it is a different thing to ask that the decision of court and law be set aside on merely sentimental grounds" (4). If this were to keep occurring, "we might as well dispense with the jury and take the verdict of the class of petition signers" (4). The extreme outcome of Plummer's case meant that greater prudence was commanded in public activism.

Legislative amendments would change the course of infanticide prosecution into the twentieth century. The Crimes Act of 1946 created a new offence of infanticide as distinct from murder, taking the definition of the English 1938 Act with the one exception of expanding the amount of time between birth and killing to twelve months. The sentence for this offence was equal to manslaughter. The 1946 legislation effectively defined infanticide as a crime that resulted from mental disturbance. Lucia Zedner characterized this change in England as "a remarkable victory" for the medical profession that "effectively replaced a traditional legal discourse with that of psychiatry" (90). Others, such as Ania Wilczynski and Tony Ward, submit an explanation that might be more fruitful for the Australian context. Ward suggests that medical categories continue to be "reconstructed" or "stretched" to arrive at results which conform to psychiatrists', lawyers', and laypersons' shared understandings of what is reasonable (176). Rather than the law of infanticide existing as a purely legal or purely medical construction, the various infanticide laws redefined the crime in accordance with the myriad of social, legal, and medical views that had dominated trial proceedings since the late nineteenth century. In mandating mental disturbance as an attendant factor to the commission of the crime, the Victorian 1946 legislation legitimized the insanity defences that had been recurring since Plummer's trial. A woman who killed her child was now assumed to be insane unless the prosecution was able to disrupt this presumption.

Plummer's case is a useful introduction to the dynamics of knowledge that operated between medical witnesses, jurors, and public voices, from journalists to society women to members of Parliament. The rigid test of the M'Naghtan rules constrained medical testimony at trial, weakening the position of physicians like Dr. Burke and Dr. Shields. A confident lay public pointed to puerperal insanity as an explanation and turned on the medical profession for failing to note this frailty in the first place. The Executive Council granted Plummer a free pardon on the grounds of her insanity based on assessments by laypersons rather than doctors. As this chapter showed, a politics of activism, protesting the death penalty and the penalties paid by women rather than men, drove this diagnosis. Madness was the language through which this activism was legitimized. Plummer's case demonstrates how insanity was not merely a factor that cropped up in certain infanticide cases, as past studies have characterised it. Insanity was central to the way society grappled with guilt and responsibility in these cases and crucial to sentencing outcomes. The 1880s was the decade in which a vocal public realized the legal power that the claim of "temporary insanity" held and ushered in an era of activism and contestation over which defendants were less responsible than others. In 1946, Victoria's Crimes Act incorporated mental disturbance in the very definition of infanticide when a woman was charged, reflecting an association that had endured in the state's trials from the 1880s. Rosanna Plummer faded into obscurity and was gradually erased from public memory. The last archival glimpse of her comes from a newspaper article in 1890, a brief mention that she was now "a respectable married woman" (*South Bourke*, Mar. 26, 1890, 3).

Works Cited

Legislation

Infanticide Act (1922) (UK).

Infanticide Act (1938) Second Reading, House of Lords Hansard, 22 March 1938.

Crimes Act (1949) Vic.

Primary

Capital Case files. Public Record Office of Victoria (PROV), VPRS 264 P0000/9—P0001/11.

Plummer petitions, parts 1, 2 & 3, PROV VPRS 264 P0001/1.

Register of Female Prisoners, PROV VPRS 516 vol.12-13.

Trial transcript, *R v Plummer* (1884) PROV VPRS 264 P0001/1.

Unknown author. "Mortality of Male and Female Infants, 1871-1890", *Australian Year Book 1890-1*. Melbourne: Government printer, 334-336.

Unknown author. *Statistical Register of the Colony of Victoria for the Year 1890*. Melbourne: Government printer, 1891.

Secondary

Ainsley, Jill. "'Some Mysterious Agency': Women, Violent Crime and the Insanity Acquittal in the Victorian Courtroom." *Canadian Journal of History*, vol. 35, no. 1, 2000, pp. 37-55.

Allen, Judith. *Sex and Secrets: Crimes Involving Australian Women Since 1880*. Oxford University Press, 1990.

Arnot, Margaret. "Perceptions of Parental Child Homicide in English Popular Visual Culture, 1800-1850." *Law, Crime and History*, vol. 7, no. 1, 2017, pp. 16-74.

Behlmer, George. "Deadly Motherhood: Infanticide and Medical Opinion in Mid-Victorian England". *Journal of the History of Medicine and Allied Sciences*, vol. 34, no. 4, 1979, pp. 403-27.

Burton, Barbara. *"Bad" Mothers? Infant Killing in Victoria, 1885-1914*. 1986. University of Melbourne, Honours thesis.

Coleborne, Catharine. *Reading "Madness: Gender and Difference in the Colonial Asylum in Victoria, Australia, 1848–1888*. Network Books, 2007.

Dawson, Maree. *National Fitness or Failure? Heredity, Vice and Racial Decline in New Zealand Psychiatry: A Case Study of the Auckland Mental Hospital, 1868–99*. 2013. University of Waikato, Dissertation.

Douglas, Roger, and Kathy Laster. "A matter of life and death: The Victorian executive and the decision to execute, 1842-1967". *Australian and New Zealand Journal of Criminology*, vol. 24, no. 2, 1991, pp. 144-60.

Foucault, Michel. "About the Concept of the 'Dangerous Individual' in Nineteenth-Century Legal Psychiatry." *International Journal of Law and Psychiatry*, vol. 1, no. 1, 1978, pp. 1-18.

Gammon, Jan. *Melbourne's Magdalenes: Crimes of Reproduction, 1895–1902*. 1991. Monash University, Honours thesis.

Garton, Stephen. *Medicine and Madness: A Social History of Insanity in New South Wales, 1880-1940*. UNSW Press, 1988.

Grey, Daniel. "Agonised Weeping: Representing Femininity, Emotion and Infanticide in Edwardian Newspapers." *Media History*, vol. 21, no. 4, 2015, pp. 468-80.

Jones, Ann. "Equal Opportunity Criminals?" *The Women's Review of Books*, vol. 11, no. 12, 1994, p. 12.

Krueger, Christine. "Literary Defences and Medical Prosecutions: Representing Infanticide in Nineteenth-Century Britain." *Victorian Studies*, vol. 40, no. 2, 1997, pp. 271-94.

Laster, Kathy. "Infanticide: A Litmus Test for Feminist Criminological Theory." *Australian and New Zealand Journal of Criminology*, vol. 22, no. 3, 1989, pp. 151-66.

Laster, Kathy. "Arbitrary Chivalry: Women and Capital Punishment in Victoria, Australia, 1842-1967." *Women & Criminal Justice*, vol. 6, no. 1, 1994, pp. 67-95.

MacNally, M. "Domestic Servants and Infanticide in Victoria, 1910-1914." 1982. La Trobe University, Honours thesis.

Marland, Hilary. *Dangerous Motherhood: Insanity and Childbirth in Victorian Britain*. Palgrave Macmillan, 2004.

Murphy, Kate. "'Very Decidedly Decadent': Elite Responses to Modernity in the Royal Commission on the Decline of the Birth Rate in New South Wales, 1903-04." *Australian Historical Studies*, vol. 126, 2005, pp. 217-33.

Priestley, Susan. *Henrietta Augusta Dugdale: Activist 1827-1918*. Melbourne Books, 2011.

Pringle, Rosemary. "Octavius Beale and the Ideology of the Birthrate: The Royal Commissions of 1904 and 1905." *Refractory Girl*, vol. 3, 1973, pp. 19-27.

Robinson, Dana. "Bodies of Evidence, States of Mind: Infanticide, Emotion and Sensibility in Eighteenth-Century England." In Mark Jackson, ed. *Infanticide: Historical Perspectives of Child Murder and Concealment, 1550-2000*, edited by Mark Jackson, Ashgate, 2002, pp. 73-92.

Rychner, Georgina. "Murderess or Madwoman? Margaret Heffernan, Infanticide and Insanity in Colonial Victoria." *Lilith: A Feminist History Journal*, vol. 23, 2017, pp. 91-104.

Saunders, Kay. *Deadly Australian Women: Stories of Women Who Broke Society's Greatest Taboo*. HarperCollins, 2013.

Smith, Roger. *Trial by Medicine: Insanity and Responsibility in Victorian Trials*. Edinburgh University Press, 1981.

Suffrage Collective. *They Are But Women: The Road to Female Suffrage in Victoria*. University of Melbourne, 2007.

Swain, Shurlee. "Maids and Mothers: Domestic Servants and Illegitimacy in Nineteenth-Century Australia." *History of the Family*, vol. 10, no. 4, 2005, pp. 461-71.

Swain, Shurlee. "The Concealment of Birth in Nineteenth-Century Victoria". *Lilith: A Feminist History Journal*, vol. 5, 1988, pp. 139-47.

Swain, Shurlee, and Renate Howe. *Single Mothers and their Children: Disposal, Punishment and Survival in Australia.* Cambridge University Press, 1995.

Swain, Shurlee. "Maids and Mothers: Domestic Servants and Illegitimacy in Nineteenth-Century Australia." *History of the Family*, vol. 10, no. 4, 2005, pp. 461-71.

Ward, Tony. "The Sad Subject of Infanticide: Law, Medicine and Child Murder, 1860–1938." *Social and Legal Studies*, vol. 8, no. 2, 1999, pp. 163-80.

Watts, Alison. "Maternal Insanity in Victoria, Australia: 1920–1973". PhD thesis, Southern Cross University, 2015.

Wiczynski, Ania. "Mad or Bad? Child Killers, Gender and the Courts". *British Journal of Criminology,* 37, 3 (1997): 419-436.

Wright, Clare. *You Daughters of Freedom: The Australians who won the vote and inspired the world.* Melbourne: Text Publishing, 2018.

Zedner, Lucia. *Women, Crime and Custody in Victorian England.* London: Clarendon Press, 1991.

Part III
Global Literary and Cultural Narratives

Chapter 11

"She Cut Her Hair and Changed Her Name, from Fair Elinor to Sweet William": Constructions and Reconstructions of Female Identity in Early Modern Infanticide Ballads

Chrissie Andrea Maroulli

In 1624, the notoriously harsh Act to Prevent the Destroying and Murdering of Bastard Children was established in England as a measure against fornication and illegitimacy. The statute deemed both concealment of pregnancy and infanticide criminal and punishable by hanging. Under this act, the unmarried mother of a dead infant was automatically guilty of infanticide unless she proved that the child was stillborn. Her murder motive was considered to be the avoidance of shame. Therefore, the legal principle of innocence presumption did not apply to unwed mothers. The law, however, was substantially different for the married infanticidal mother. Married women were most often acquitted on the grounds of temporary insanity; the crime itself was the supporting evidence of the woman's lunacy. There is no way to know exactly how many children were victims of infanticide in early modern England, but Keith Wrightson's research shows that the rate was only around four per ten thousand births or two per one hundred illegitimate births. Even though infanticide was rather uncommon, the subject matter was recurrently featured in sermons, plays, pamphlets, and ballads. Based on the murder ballads extant, it seems fair to presume that the Elizabethans had an exceptionally strong inclination for gore and were fascinated by sinister tales. The canon of infanticide balladry typically includes fictional narratives of impregnated single women who give birth, eliminate their offspring, and die. Most often, these women are victims of posing suitors who eventually desert them.

Infanticide ballads are not esteemed for accounting real events; even if a ballad had been inspired by an actual crime, the events would have suffered manipulation for aesthetic judgment or purpose, as in the case of the abundant versions of *Mary Hamilton* (Child 173). This chapter employs close examination of infanticide balladry to demonstrate constructions of certain ideologies, for even though balladry served for popular amusement, it was also a back door into the folk's cognition. Masquerading as entertainment, these songs became a vehicle to moralize wives, daughters, and sisters as well as to enforce the preservation of the patriarchal life events sequence. At the same time, they verbalized apprehension about the female biological prerogative of motherhood by presenting it to be dangerous unless regulated by male authority. The early modern maiden had a clear vision of her reproductive life path; the traditional sequence was courting, betrothal, marriage, consummation, pregnancy, and childbirth. Infanticide narratives typically employ a different timeline; thus, they interrupt social expectations. The tales demonstrate how the fall of womanhood from chastity to nonvirginity can cause a sweeping upheaval to the status quo. From then on, a series of chain reactions that irreversibly disturb the social order bring the woman face to face with death. Order can be restored only by the intervention of male agency, and in its absence, the female and her offspring die.

This chapter ventures to demonstrate that early modern infanticide ballads surface fundamental anxieties about womanhood by equating the disturbance of social order to inevitable tragedy.[1] As Susan Staub notes: "The murdering mother embodies both her society's expectations and its anxieties about motherhood to be at once empowering and destructive" (Staub 345). By analysing the subtext of these once popular texts, I reveal hidden patriarchal agendas; these are significant, for they show how the creators of the infanticide ballads attempted to moralize the unsuspected female, using one of the most tender subjects—eliminating her own offspring.

"She Shall Be Called Woman, Because She Was Taken Out of Man" (Gen. 2:23)

The Bible presents womanhood to be secondary, for the chronology of Eve's creation is only after Adam. Her body is constructed by reshaping a piece from his rib cage—a symbol for the inauthenticity of female matter—and her incapability to be independent. Her character is flawed and naïve; she does not know better, so she commits the original sin and achieves expulsion from Paradise. God puts her under her husband's close surveillance: "Your desire shall be for your husband, and he shall rule over you" (Gen. 3:16). Similarly, the early modern woman belongs to a male agent, as Eve is defined by being Adam's wife. Balladry tends to introduce women largely based on their relationship to men; women are presented to be bakers' daughters, goldsmiths' wives, or mistresses of amorous gallants. In several instances, even from the title itself, the (often nameless) woman is described in terms of her surrounding males, for example, *The King's Dochter Lady Jean, The Farmer's Curst Wife, Willie's Lady, The Wanton Widow's Pleasant Mistake* and so on. (Child 278; Child 6; EBBA 21322) The status of her virginity is sometimes employed to indicate if the protagonist of the ballad is a proper specimen of womanhood, as in *The Ruined Virgin* and *The Maiden Triumph* (EBBA 36771; EBBA 36725). Occasionally physical beauty traits accompany the woman's name, such as *The Seamans Adieu To His Pritty Betty, Bonny Barbara Allen,* and *Fair Janet* (EBBA 37430; Child 84; Child 64) This motif shows that a woman was largely thought of in terms of her relationship to men or what appertains to her usefulness to men, that is, her physical beauty and sexuality. Ballads with male protagonists are often entitled by his name as in *Geordie*, his class as in *Lord Thomas and Fair Annette,* his nobleness as in *The Knight and the Shepherd's Daughter* or his profession as in *A Dialogue Between a Baker and His Wife* (Child 209; Child 73; Child 110; EBBA 21811). The self-possessed male is rarely described as someone's son or husband, whereas a woman is almost always a daughter, a wife, a mother, or a widow. This modelling of socially constructed identity aimed at manipulating the female's own sense of self, a concept Stephan Greenblatt has called "self-fashioning." Self-fashioning of womanhood chiefly promoted chastity and dependence on men. In other words, balladry constructs a female identity that can only coexist with the male agents of her environment. The ballad, preliterate in in origin, was the perfect self-fashioning vehicle; it allowed for effortless and rapid circulation throughout all classes. What's more, its rhyming and repetitive nature made it easy to remember and gave it the capacity to creep into one's ear even if no memorizing process was involved. Afterlives of a ballad kept its purposes alive long after its performance was over. According to Deborah Symonds, the majority of the known early modern ballad singers were women, and David Buchan notes that women sang and vastly outnumbered men as sources of ballads; these texts lived and flourished in the female mouth and mind.

"The Token of Virginity" (Sharpe 43)

The infanticide ballad's heroine is a weak version of her kind because she has been sexually active or performed "the act of Generation" (Sharpe 33) out of wedlock. She is by definition the exact opposite of the ideal maiden fashioned by society, descriptions of whom revolve around modesty and self-restraint. As Laura Gowing argues, "Female chastity was a public matter because it was manifestly central to early modern patriarchy ... elite culture, visual, oral, dramatic and written, worked hard to differentiate virgins and whores" (*Common Bodies* 30). The contrasting qualities of the infanticidal mother to the virtuous virgin enhance and enforce the patriarchal expectations of womanhood by demonstrating examples for avoidance. The infanticidal narrative's horrifying aura is not merely owed to the murder itself; the moralizing begins with the woman's very first wrong move, which is the untimely loss of her virginity. "Unchastity, in the sense of sexual relations before or outside marriage, is for a man, if an offense, none the less a mild and pardonable one, but for a woman a matter of the utmost gravity," notes Keith Thomas (210). Early modern society applied a double standard to virginity, for even though it takes two to make a child, the ballads make a villain out of the female based on the fact that she did not practice her authority to reject premarital loving. In *A Lamentable Ballad of the Lady's Fall* (EBBA 31270) the narrator informs the crowds that "Too soon, alas! she gave consent to yield unto his will." Based on this common denominator shared by the ballads of the canon, it seems that these narratives are more concerned with premarital sex rather than murder. The giving away of female virginity triggers a series of inevitable events that happen consecutively and beyond the woman's control, almost as if the loss of chastity was equal to the loss of power. "Let a woman have chastity, she has all. Let her lack chastity and she has nothing," notes Ruth Kelso (24). Based on the close connection of sexual promiscuity and murder presented in the texts, it is reasonable to propose an equivalence of the female loss of virginity and death. In the case of the imprisoned murderess in *The Norfolk Tragedy* (Bodl 9053),[2] the woman is sitting in her cell waiting to be hanged, when she cries:

> Alas! Alas! What shall I do,
> what has one sinful moment brought me to?

She is referring to premarital sexual intercourse, murdering her child or both, since in this context, they seem interlinked and interchangeable.

"Alas, My Sweet Janet, I Fear Ye Gae With Child" (Child 39)

In the early modern era, there was no definite way to recognize pregnancy due to the lack of medical expertise. It was normal for women's menstrual cycles to be irregular because of malnutrition; therefore, it was impossible to reach conclusions solely based on the absence of menstruation. The best way to validate pregnancy was the growing belly combined with quickening—the movement of the fetus in utero that starts somewhere between the fourth and sixth month of gestation. Contrary to the married woman, the unmarried one was not aiming to conceive and was possibly oblivious to the signs. Moreover, maidens, being excluded from married women's circles, probably had limited knowledge on reproduction and signs of pregnancy. By the time she realized she was pregnant (if she ever did), she might have already been close to her due date. Other than rough estimates based on her sexual activity, she had no way of knowing when labour was going to start, which can be particularly troublesome in a concealed pregnancy. In the ballad *Tam Lin* (Child 39), Janet is not aware that she is pregnant, but her father recognizes the signs and tells her, "Alas, my sweet Janet, I fear ye gae with child." Not only does this show how an inexperienced youth could fail to identify a pregnancy, but it also demonstrates patriarchal authority over womanhood, in the image of a man knowing the body of a woman better than she does, even in the most sensitive of situations. In some instances, when women realized they were pregnant, they sought abortifacients in an attempt to overturn the situation. Accounts of women dying from such remedies are actually in existence, like the case of Hannah Stocks in 1774 (Thorn 48). In *Tam Lin,* Janet attempts to pick a particular rose as a way "to kill the bonie babe." She is more fortunate than the average infanticidal heroine because the father of the baby, who sees what she is about to do, intervenes, and prevents her from doing so.

The infanticidal heroine's pregnancy posed a danger to her own livelihood but also burdened the community financially; the parishes disapproved of these pregnancies not only because of their immoral nature but mostly because they wanted to avoid having to support children and single mothers: "Pregnant single women, like the rest of the poor, had to negotiate a place in the parish economy; but, with their bodies providing visible evidence of their sins, and their histories well-known, no amount of pleading or petitioning could prove them worthy recipients of poor relief" (Gowing, *Common Bodies* 118). The heroine is ashamed and keeps her pregnancy secret. Concealment of pregnancy was a common practice associated with the infanticide cases in early modern England, as in the 1762 case of Agnes Walker, who was found "guilty of having brought forth a child without discovering her pregnancy or calling assistance during her labor" (Howell et al. 245). There are plenty of examples to show attempted pregnancy concealment in ballad literature as well. In *The Norfolk Tragedy*, we learn that "she being big with child, it was not known to any of her friends, but she alone." In *A Lamentable Ballad of the Lady's Fall*, the woman keeps her pregnancy from her father and the world "and so put on a silken gown, none might her swelling see." In *No Naturall Mother But a Monster* (EBBA 36049) there is an entire quatrain on the pregnancy's concealment:

> How I my fault might hide,
> still I mus'd, still I mus'd,
> That I might not be spide,
> nor yet suspected.

These women attempted to hide their sensitive state from the world, perhaps to gain some time to figure out what to do or because they had already planned to eliminate their child.

"And There She Had Two Pritty Babes Born" (EBBA 22221)

In early modern England, labour was a private but also social affair. Although "male intrusion into the birthing chamber were disorderly, lewd and uncivilized," (Gowing, *Common Bodies* 151), some female friends and neighbours called "gossips" came to offer advice, support, or even criticize; more often than not, at least one (typically female) midwife was also present. It was important that births had honest matrons as witnesses because if a woman gave birth alone, she would have had no proof in case of stillbirth, whereas an attendee could testify so that the mother would not be condemned for infanticide. There is no way of knowing exactly who was welcome to attend because of a lack of accounts; indeed, there seems to be no existing document that describes the complete ritual of labour. Based on the fragmentary evidence, we can be sure of the absence of men and the sense of sisterhood; the birth room was an all-female world. As Adreian Wilson has noted, "Before childbirth belonged to medicine, it belonged to women" (qtd. in Pollock 288). The more experienced women offered advice, emotional support, and functioned as honest observers of the midwife's skills. Moreover, they provided much needed material necessities for the birth and newborn. Not all expectant mothers could afford childbed linen and baby clothes, so they had to borrow such items from female friends and family. This conventional portrayal of sisterhood united is probably how a maiden of any class envisioned her own future births. Since the infanticidal heroine keeps her pregnancy concealed, she is also deprived of the traditional childbirth ritual, and she cannot borrow any items for her newborn. Anxiety over lack of necessities does occasionally surface in balladry, as in *The Cruel Mother* (Child 20 G) in which a woman who just has just given birth to twins has "nothing to lap them in, But a white apprun, and that was thin."

Linda Pollock aptly points out that those "who failed to comply with accepted standards and customs encountered little support ... aid was predicated upon a set of assumptions about how women should behave in order to receive and retain support, and it was governed by a set of norms over what was appropriate" (287). This fear of seclusion was an essential aspect of the moralizing ballads, for young women absorbed that if they found themselves in such a situation, then they would deliver their babies helpless and alone. In the numerous versions of *The Cruel Mother* appear refrains that revolve around the feeling of loneliness, for example, "All alone and alone ee"; "Sing hey alone, and alonie O"; "All alone, alone O'" "All in a lone and a lonie O'" "All a lee and aloney O" (Child 20 D, E, G, H, M); and so on. One must keep in mind that refrains were the part of the ballad that was repeated with each new verse, so the particular lines were heard over and over again, which helped in the process of engraving information in the listeners' minds. The virgin would learn the lesson well: Be patient or end up utterly alone with a baby in your arms. As Gowing argues: "For legitimate mothers labor was a period to be planned for and managed in the semi-public female world of neighborly support. For illegitimate mothers, it was exactly the opposite: a time to hide and afterwards deny" ("Secret Births" 99). A single woman is automatically deprived of and excluded from the traditions of the birth room. The undisclosed pregnancy of the infanticide ballad evolves into a solitary labour, and the heroine delivers her baby alone, outside the safety of the home and usually into the open air. Like the sexual openness of her body, her private sphere is invaded.

> Into the yard I ran,
> Where sudden pangs began,
> There was no woman than,
>   neere to assist me,

says the posthumous voice of Besse in *No Naturall Mother But a Monster*.

Childbirth is a notoriously painful procedure even when the circumstances are ideal, but to make things much worse, the environment in which the infanticidal heroine gives birth is inappropriate and hostile; there is dirt and soil, thorns are pricking her feet, and the lack of a midwife induces further agony. She is usually in the woods among hostile elements of nature, often leaning against a tree or rock, which is, at that moment, her only companion. In the ballad, *The Duke's Daughter's Cruelty* (EBBA 22221), Elinor "went into the wide Wilderness," "leant her back against an Oak," and "she set her foot against a Thorne" when delivering her twins. In the numerous versions of *The Cruel Mother,* the woman "set her foot to a stone" or "leaned her back against the stile" and in its Scottish version "she sat down below a thorn" to deliver her baby. In one vivid description, the elements of nature blend in with the birthing woman and fluctuate with the labour pains:

> She's set her back untill an oak,
> First it bowed and then it broke.
> She's set her back untill a tree,
> Bonny were the twa boys she did bear. (Child 20 H, Q, B, D)

The nature references establish the lack of human contact and an involuntary relapse to precivilization, which would have sounded terrifying to the virgin receiver of the ballad. They also clash with the unnaturalness of the woman's character, since the natural maternal instincts are absent, as we can see, for instance, in the very title of *No Naturall Mother But a Monster.* Nature references mostly concern the ballad but are occasionally true of the real-life infanticidal mother as well, as in the 1756 case of Mary Thomas, who went into a barley field to give birth all alone "for decency sake" (Sharpe 44).

Another dimension of childbirth was its duration and intensity; the belief was that the longer and more painful labour was, the better for the woman's reputation. Women accepted and understood the pains of childbirth as punishment for the original sin and a test of their relationship to God: "To the woman he said: 'I will surely multiply your pain in childbearing; in pain you shall bring forth children'" (Gen: 3:16). In some prayer books, the ordeal of labour was practically glorified as a chance for suffering and exemplification of female piety. Slow and painful labours marked a virtuous, civilized woman, and quick, effortless labours indicated whoredom and social inferiority. Infanticidal Martha Scrambler in the 1614 pamphlet *Deeds against Nature* notably delivered her child very easily because of "her lusty body, strong nature, and feare of shame." *The Death of Queen Jane* (Child 170) describes the events of Queen Jane Seymour's childbirth of Edward VI in 1537, in which the queen's labour is described as highly challenging or even impossible. Some versions start with the line "Queen Jane was in travail for six weeks or more," therefore highlighting her virtuousness from the onset and establishing that what is to follow concerns a respectable woman. At the end of the narrative, the queen nobly dies after giving birth to the heir.[3] The infanticide ballad, in contrast, typically makes no indication of labour duration, which gives reason to believe that the labours were brief. In *No Naturall Mother But a Monster*, Besse informs us:

> "With little paine or smart,
> strange to think, strange to think,
> I with my child did part."

That goes to show that the nonvirgin, unmarried woman does not deserve to have an esteemed labour; her condition is inherently immoral, and her labour is insignificant. The unmarried mother becomes stereotyped as a person of loose morals and sin, who ultimately becomes a murderess of her own child.

"Come Then, You Masculine-Women, For You Are My Subject"—Anonymous

As described in the 1620 pamphlet *Hic Mulier*, a female adopting masculine qualities was considered unnatural and blasphemous; a woman's effort to resemble the opposite sex was read as a usurpation of masculine authority and sexual freedom. The infanticidal heroine occasionally departs from the characteristics of her sex and ventures to become a man in order to control the dangerous situation she is in. The picture is clearly painted: a Man creates her problem, so she becomes a man to solve it.

Literary poetics of long hair are traditionally associated with femininity; the shortening of female locks in balladry is one of the images employed to show the heroine's conversion. As the anonymous writer of *Hic Mulier* notes with poise, "the long hayre of a woman is the ornament of her sexe." In *The Duke's Daughter's Cruelty*, Elinor takes a hairpiece or ribbon off her hair and ties the babies "hand and leg"; therefore, when she buries the infants, she also buries a part of her female identity in the "coldest Earth" along with her children. Having laid her womanhood to rest, we learn that she "cut her hair and changed her Name, From Fair Elinor to Sweet William." The deliberate acquisition of physically masculine attributes like short hair and the identity transformation evident in the name change contribute to constructions of patriarchal anxiety over potential female authority. Through the heroine's attempts to envision and reconstruct herself as male, the ballad demonstrates not only the powerlessness of female nature but also her prospect of usurping power. Ultimately, the narrative presents a woman's inability to handle crises, making the "man as savior" necessary; in his absence, the woman is forced to become him, but she fails.

Elinor's weapon of choice is "a Penknife long and sharp" and similarly in *The Cruel Mother*, "She took a knife both long and sharp." From a psychoanalytic perspective, the phallic-shaped knife resembles and represents the "yard,"[4] which when used to penetrate the flesh shows the deathly power of patriarchy. The sharp stabbing reverberates Elinor's nonvirginal state by reconstructing the invasion of her own body by the forceful penis. Elinor did not just stab her babies in random places; she purposely "stuck them to the heart." The fact that she chose to use a phallic penknife to pierce the twins' hearts shows that her own heart was figuratively damaged as a consequence of the untimely access permission she granted to her lover. She also "dug a Grave, it was long and deep, And there she laid them into sleep." The depth of the grave shows how she wanted to bury her sins deeply into the earth, where they would lay safe and undiscovered. Elinor is projecting her personal trauma onto the elimination of her twins by constructing their death and burial as a reflection of her own experiences. In a different reading, the phallic connotations of the knife might show that the murderer is not truly Elinor. The double murder is the inevitable result of a man's actions, and he is metaphorically holding her hand while she kills.

"And the Hottest Place in Hell Is Reserved for Thee" (Child 20 N2)

In early modern diary logs, one notices the common motif of prayer and trusting in God's will for a healthy infant and surviving mother. Oftentimes the birthing woman believed that divine power equipped her with the virtue to endure the pains of childbirth, as in the case of Alice Thornton: "I was upon the rack in bearing my child with such exquisite torment, as if each limb were divided from other, for the space of two hours, when at length, being speechless and breathless, I was by the infinite providence of God in great mercy delivered ... The Lord God had great pity upon my distress" (Thornton and Jackson 40). Other times, as in a log by Samuel Woodforde, a man is praying for his wife to have a smooth pregnancy and healthy child: "Bless my poor wife I beseech thee. I continually pray for her and the fruit in her womb that it may have right form and shape ... Oh my God stand by thy poor handmaid and put under thine everlasting arms ... command the loins to give up and the womb not to forbear" (qtd. in Houlbrooke 124).

But the infanticidal mother should not be entitled to divine assistance. Her merciless sin is twofold: She allows for a man to prematurely "lay her down" and then kills the offspring. Her relationship with God at this point is troubled, and her prayer is theoretically weakened by the inherent impiety of her condition. She is terrified of going to hell, and her fear is justified. A substantial aspect of self-fashioning motherhood was based on this frightful possibility of eternal doom. In fact, the terror of descending into hell resounds repeatedly in infanticide balladry; its monstrous context provides fertile ground for voicing anxieties about the afterlife, as in *The Cruel Mother*, in which the doomed heroine voices her concern by asking the babies' ghosts. "Dear children, can you tell, where shall I go? To heav'n or hell?" Her inquiry shows her agony about a fate she knows can be nothing but sinister. In *The Duke's Daughter's Cruelty*, the twin infants' ghosts haunt the mother and inform her of her grim future:

> O, Mother, O Mother for your sin,
> Heaven-gate you shall not enter in
> O, Mother, O Mother for your sin,
> Hell-gates stand open to let you in.

Another reference to hell can be found in *The Maid and the Palmer* (Child 21), in which a woman asks a pilgrim for penance for the murder of her nine children, but he refuses and proceeds to punish her by transforming her into a stepping stone, a bell clapper, and an ape in hell for seven years each, after which she can "come a mayden home." This is a unique representation of a potential restoration of chastity that is typically unredeemable but only after numerous years of unendurable suffering in the dungeons of hell.

Some ballads, for example, *No Naturall Mother But a Monster* present an ungodly woman that is more animalistic than a "savage" snake, an image that reverberates the Garden of Eden. References of this kind establish a connection between an immoral Eve and womanhood as a whole and stereotype the corruption or lack of judgment in female nature as universal features that women need to be working against constantly. In this case, the murderess clearly states that the devil assisted her:

> To this bad thought of mine,
> the Devil did incline,
> To any ill designe,
> he lends assistance.
>
> ...
>
> All those that God doe feare,
> Are frightened when they heare,
> That you more cruell are
> Than Savage creatures.

In *Catherine Skelly, for the Drowning of her Child* (Bod 11465), the protagonist says that she plunged into "mortal sin" by drowning her child. This ballad uniquely employs an entire stanza blaming the devil for the infanticidal woman's condition, painting a picture of her being distanced from God and possessed by the evil spirit:

> It was cursed Satan led me astray,
> It was Satan tempted me on that day,
> It was Satan tempted my guilty mind,
> To drown my infant both meek and mild.

Devil references draw attention away from the trigger of the crime, which is typically the woman's deception and abandonment by a man. In this way, infanticide balladry presents Satan and man to be interchangeable. Early modern anatomist William Hunter insisted that unmarried pregnant women are weak, credulous and deluded, therefore less guilty than the world perceives, and that the true blame lies with the fathers, whose actions are criminal. Also, Jane Anger in her second epistle characteristically writes: "Fie on the falsehood of men! ... if a woman trust unto a man, it shall fare as well with her as if she had a weight of a thousand pounds tied about her neck and then cast into the bottomless seas" (qtd. in Henderson and McManus 22). In the ballad *Wandering Girl* (Bod 17298), a man deserts the heroine and her baby for another "fair girl," and she warns:

> Come ye pretty fair maids wherever ye be
> Never trust a young man in any degree,
> They'll kiss you, and court you, and swear they'll be true
> And the very next moment they'll bid you adieu.

In *Catherine Skelly, for the Drowning of her Child*, Catherine says, "A false young man he courted me, and promised that we would married be"; in *No Naturall Mother But a Monster*, Besse says, "The father on't was fled, and all my hopes were dead". In *The Norfolk Tragedy*, the man "betray'd this lady fine" and in *A Lamentable Ballad of the Lady's Fall* the lady cries:

> O false, forsworn, and faithless wretch
> Disloyal to thy love;
> Hast thou forgot thy promise made?
> And wilt thou prejurd prove?
> And hast thou now forsaken me,
> In this my sad distress?
> To end my days in open shame,
> Which thou mightst well redress.

Albeit in the ample examples mentioned above the villain is clearly the man, infanticide ballads almost always intend to moralize women. This is unequivocal, based on the fact that the majority of the texts specifically address females. Therefore, the sin of untimely loss of virginity is presented to be much worse than paternal neglect or refuted betrothal on behalf of a man, leaning once again on the weakness of the female sex.

"No Husband to Cover Her Act of Shame" (Anonymous)

The infanticide ballad heroine is powerless over her own body and future. If she chooses to keep the baby, she and her baby are going to be branded with the shame of bastardy. Moreover, she will have to be supported by the parish and be a financial burden to her community, thus acquiring poverty humiliation as well. But there is one way for the tables to turn. Ballad infanticide is always the direct result of a man's deed, and death is inevitable—that is, unless he intervenes, as a saviour. In *The Maid Freed From the Gallows* (Child 95 B, J), a young unmarried maiden is about to be hanged, but her "sweet-heart," and father of her child, comes and saves her:

> Oh yes, I've got some gold for thee.
> Some money for to pay thee free;
> I'll save thy body from the cold clay ground,
> And thy neck from the gallows-tree

But things are not always as simple; a man's saving hand does not always appear deus ex machina. Often, the heroine is challenged to win her man over. An example can be seen in *Tam Lin*. Even though the ballad starts with the premarital loss of Janet's virginity and pregnancy, which is a perfect set up for an infanticidal ending, order is restored by the timely intervention of male agency. In this case, Tam Lin is willing to marry the pregnant woman and lovingly calls himself "father of your child" (Child 39 D). But in order for that to happen, Janet needs to rescue him from the Queen of Fairies. He instructs her to fearlessly hold him tight in her arms while he transforms through a number of different anomalous phases, such as being a lion or a bear. When she succeeds, he is reborn as a mortal man. Janet gets a husband, a father for her child, and instead of a bloody murder ballad, *Tam Lin* is celebrated as a tale of true love.

Child Waters (Child 63) is another ballad in which the father of the child steps up and assumes responsibility, but once more, the woman needs to earn her rescue. "'If the child be mine Fair Ellen,' said he, 'Be mine as you doe sware'" and offers land to support the baby. However, he instructs her to eradicate her feminine features like cut her yellow locks "above your eye," so he can sneak her into his castle as his footpage. He warns her that until he is ready to marry her she has to work hard serving him as a true footpage and that he will treat her worse than he would his horse:

> O my horse sal eat the good white meal,
> An ye sal eat the corn;
> Then will ye curse the heavy hour
> That ever your love was born
>
> ...
>
> My horse shall drink the gude red wine,
> And you the water wan
> And then you'll sigh, and say, alas!
> That eer our loves began. (Child 63 B, J)

In some versions, she has to give birth to her son in a barn, among the horses' feet, resembling the circumstances of the infanticide ballad. But, ultimately, the woman endures the tribulations and gets rewarded by marriage. The subliminal message is that the sinful nonvirgin has to suffer in order to obtain salvation.

"You Youthful Charming Ladies Fair, I Pray Now Give Attention" (EBBA 31476)

In case the lady listeners of the ballads did not pick up on their apparent didactic tone, the writers would add lines at the beginning, the end, or both to state their intentions clearly. The didactic lines or stanzas usually explicitly addressed maidens, a detail that clearly shows the attempt at self-fashioning the female identity. A typical example can be seen in *The Duke's Daughter's Cruelty,* which ends with: "Young Ladies all of beauty bright, Take warning by her last good-night." Another concluding moralizing verse can be seen in *Rachel Bradley's Downfall*:

> Let this be a warning to all sister females
> Pray govern your conduct as well as you can
> Beware how temptation may prove your downfall
> You see what I'm come to by loving a man. (Bod4025)

At times, moralizing lines appear in the body of the ballad as well, as a reminder of social expectations, as in *No Naturall Mother But a Monster*, which demonstrates the highest number of moralizing lines in the canon. It is also unique in that it provides advice to the women who might have made the mistake already:

> Sweet Maidens all take heed,
> Heedfully, heedfully,
> Adde not unto the deed
> Of fornication
> Murder, which of all things,
> The soule and conscience stings
>
> ...
>
> If you begot with childe,
> Through lawlesse sporting,
> Be griev'd for your offence,
> And with true penitence,
> Strive to make recompence,
> for former vice.

It would be wrong, however, to think that men escaped the jaws of self-fashioning. Greenblatt has showed how texts like Castiglione's *The Book of the Courtier* instructed noblemen how to dress, speak, compose, and educate themselves in order to represent their sex and rank in society properly. Although the vast majority of infanticide ballads targeted maidens, there is one ballad that actually addresses both sexes. *The Norfolk Tragedy* opens with the line: "Young men and maidens all, I pray draw near" and closes with:

> Let this a warning be to each young maid,
> and to all young men,
> I'd have them be true,
> And be constant in love whatever they do.

This one of a kind infanticide ballad represents a bifold self-fashioning attempt that simultaneously shows the disastrous results of the loss of virginity to target females and breach of betrothal to target males. In this tale, a squire dramatically threatens to kill himself if the lady refuses to marry him, but when she eventually agrees "for pity's sake," she finds herself pregnant and deserted, stifles the baby, and ends up in prison, where the regretful man sneaks in and gallantly cries, "I'll die for thee." With a gesture that shows the recognition of his sex's power over womanhood, he proposes they exchange identities; his idea is for her to wear his men's clothes to break out of prison and for him to wear hers so that they hang him instead. The woman refuses to repudiate her sex and wishes to face the consequences of her sins. She dies in his arms, he kills himself, and they poetically expire together. In this case, male intervention did not save the infant or the woman from death because the initiative was taken too late, and it was weakened by the disagreeable behaviour of the man whose conduct was unacceptable in the community.

"Come Little Boy and Rock Asleep; I Can Do Nought Else But Weep" (EBBA 36255)

A rare portrayal of a single mother with a living infant is presented in the ballad *A Lullaby*. Deserted by her lover, whose "sugared lips" betrayed her, she is singing to her baby boy while rocking him to sleep. She calls him "his Fathers shame & Mothers grief." The woman is lamenting her situation in which the child's "Father false is fled away" and refers to keeping the baby by "doles," possibly meaning reception of some kind of charity. Statements like "I myself am all alone" and "I that can doe nought else but weep" paint vivid images of abandonment and distress, feelings identical to the ones of the infanticidal ballad heroine. In a stretch of imagination, this loving lullaby can be described as a prequel to the infanticide ballad or a way of soliloquizing the thoughts of an infanticidal mother. The concept of "putting to sleep," which is the theme of the ballad, is itself a metaphorical term for murder. There is no proof in the text that the baby survives. Based on the social and personal circumstances of the mother, it would be reasonable to assume that she was at a serious risk of becoming infanticidal. This could have happened while she was singing the song or even afterwards. Therefore, it is possible that this ballad, which poses as a lullaby, is in fact, an infanticide ballad. This suggestion does not seem farfetched if one considers that there are real accounts of mothers who sang while killing their children, like Rachel Henry, who smothered her three children in Phoenix in January 2020 (McCloskey).

The world is a cruel place for the infanticide ballad heroine. No matter which decision she takes, she has to live with unbearable humiliation. Her crime is essentially the once preventable loss of her virginity, but in its turn, it triggers inevitable tragedies. The ballads promote the male agent as necessary and irreplaceable but more importantly they present the contradictions of sisterhood. The sinfulness of the heroine's condition causes her to be shunned by her own sex, which is supportive only selectively, to the ones who respect patriarchy; this is an oxymoron in itself. The self-fashioned woman whose life has already been structured by patriarchal traditions continues the work by dragging other members of her kind into their dance and presenting them with the prospect of exclusion in case of departure from the plan. Therefore, the shamed maiden—deserted by men and unable to seek refuge with her own sex—inexorably becomes the infanticidal ballad heroine.

Endnotes

1. This chapter is concerned exclusively with representations of infanticide in early modern ballads. Infanticide is represented differently in other forms of popular press like pamphlets, analysis of which is beyond the compass of this chapter. Balladry is typically concerned with the unmarried woman, but in pamphlets, one also finds narratives that are based on true trials or tales of married women who kill their children for reasons like lust, poverty, religion, diabolic temptation, or domestic power struggles.
2. Where ballads from the Bodleian Libraries Database are cited, they are identified with their unique catalogue number (BodXXX).
3. Queen Jane died after giving birth to Edward, but the exact circumstances of her death are a mystery to this day. There is an ongoing debate on whether she had a caesarean operation or if she gave birth naturally and died of complications or puerperal fever. The matter is a complicated one, for there was no survival rate after

caesareans at the time, and they were only performed on mothers who had died in order to save the infant. King Henry VIII is suspected of authorizing a surgeon to cut an alive Jane open disregarding her life in a desperate attempt to secure the crown. This was never confirmed and the accounts extant vary greatly. Please see: DeMolen; Lipscomb; Vannan.

4. Early modern term for the male genitals.

Works Cited

Anonymous. *Deeds Against Nature, and Monsters by Kinde Tryed at the Gaole Deliverie of Newgate.* 1614.

Anonymous. *Hic Mulier: or, the Man-Woman and Haec-Vir: or, the Womanish-Man.* 1620. *Internet Archive*, the Rota at the University of Exeter, 1 Jan. 1973, archive.org/details/hicmulierormanwo00exe tuoft/page/18/mode/2up/search/ha. Accessed 17 Nov. 2021.

Botelho, Keith M. "Maternal Memory and Murder in Early-Seventeenth-Century England." *SEL Studies in English Literature 1500-1900*, vol. 48, no. 1, 2007, pp. 111-30.

"Broadside Ballads Online." *Ballads Online*, ballads.bodleian.ox.ac.uk/. Accessed 17 Nov. 2021.

Buchan, David. *The Ballad and the Folk (RLE Folklore)*. Routledge, 2015.

Child, Frances James. *The English and Scottish Popular Ballads*. Edited by Robert Graves, Macmillan, 1957.

Coffin, Tristram P. "'Mary Hamilton' and the Anglo-American Ballad as an Art Form." *The Journal of American Folklore*, vol. 70, no. 277, 1957, p. 208.

Crawford, Nicholas. "Language, Duality, and Bastardy in English Renaissance Drama." *English Literary Renaissance*, vol. 34, no. 2, 2004, pp. 243-62.

Dolan, Frances. *Dangerous Familiars: Representations of Domestic Crime in England, 1550-1700*. Cornell University Press, 1994.

Donath, Orna. "Regretting Motherhood: A Sociopolitical Analysis." *Signs: Journal of Women in Culture and Society*, vol. 40, no. 2, 2015, pp. 343-367.

English Broadside Ballad Archive. University of California, ebba.english.ucsb.edu. Accessed 17 Nov. 2021.

Fildes, Valerie. *Women as Mothers in Pre-Industrial England*. Routledge, 2014.

Gowing, Laura. "Secret Births and Infanticide In Seventeenth-Century England." *Past & Present*, vol. 156, no. 1, Jan. 1997, pp. 87–115.

Gowing, Laura. *Common Bodies: Women, Sex, and Reproduction in Seventeenth Century England*. Yale University Press, 2003.

Greenblatt, Stephen. *Renaissance Self-Fashioning: From More to Shakespeare*. The University of Chicago Press, 2013.

Heavey, Katherine. *The Early Modern Medea in English Literature, 1558-1688*. Palgrave Macmillan, 2015.

Henderson, Katherine U., and Barbara F. McManus. *Half Humankind: Contexts and Texts of the Controversy about Women in England: 1540-1640*. University of Illinois Press, 1985.

Higginbotham, Jennifer. "Female Infants and the Engendering of Humanity."

Higginbotham, Jennifer. *The Girlhood of Shakespeare's Sisters: Gender, Transgression, Adolescence*. Edinburgh University Press, 2013.

Houlbrooke, Ralph A. *English Family Life, 1576-1716: An Anthology from Diaries*. B. Blackwell, 1989.

Howell, Thomas Bayly, et al. *A Complete Collection of State Trials and Proceedings: from the Earliest Period to the Year 1783 and Continued from the Year 1783 to the Present Time*. XIX, Printed by T.C. Hansard, 1816.

Hunter, William. *On the Uncertainty of the Signs of Murder in the Case of Bastard Children*. Callow, 1818.

Jackson, Mark. *Infanticide: Historical Perspectives on Child Murder and Concealment, 1550-2000*. Ashgate, 2005.

Josselin, Ralph. *The Diary of the Rev. Ralph Josselin 1616-1683*. Edited by E. Hockliffe, XV, Offices of the Society, 1908.

Kelso, Ruth. *Doctrine for the Lady of the Renaissance*. University of Illinois Press, 1996.

Krappe, A. H. "The Maid Freed from the Gallows." *Speculum*, vol. 16, no. 2, 1941, pp. 236-41.

Lezra, Jacqes. "The Pleasures of Infanticide." *Qui Parle*, vol. 19, no. 1, 2010, p. 153.

Loughnan, A. "The Strange Case of the Infanticide Doctrine." *Oxford Journal of Legal Studies*, vol. 32, no. 4, 2012, pp. 685-711.

McCloskey, Jimmy. "Boy Tried to Stop Mom Murdering Sister, 1, Then Clawed at Her as She Killed Him." *Metro*, 22 Jan. 2020, metro.co.uk/2020/01/22/mother-sang-lullabies-two-toddlers-baby-sat-smothered-12104545/. Accessed 17 Nov. 2021.

Miller, Naomi J., and Naomi Yavneh. *Maternal Measures: Figuring Caregiving in the Early Modern Period*. Routledge, 2000.

Paster, Gail Kern. *The Body Embarrassed: Drama and the Disciplines of Shame in Early Modern England*. Cornell University Press, 1993.

Peck, Linda Levy. *Women of Fortune: Money, Marriage, and Murder in Early Modern England*. Cambridge University Press, 2018.

Pollock, Linda A. "Childbearing and Female Bonding in Early Modern England." *Social History*, vol. 22, no. 3, Oct. 1997, pp. 286-306.

Raber, Karen L. "Murderous Mothers and The Family/State Analogy in Classical and Renaissance Drama." *Comparative Literature Studies*, vol. 37, no. 3, 2000, pp. 298-20.

Sharpe, Jane. *The Midwives Book: or the Whole Art of Midwifry Discovered. Directing Childbearing Women How to Behave Themselves in Their Conception, Breeding and Nursing of Children, Etc.* 1671. Women Writers in English. Oxford University Press, 1999.

Sharpe, Jim. "Infanticide in Court: Chester, 1650-1800." *Infanticide: Historical Perspectives on Child Murder and Concealment, 1550-2000*, edited by Mark Jackson, Ashgate, 2002, pp. 35-51.

Spoto, Stephanie Irene. "Jacobean Witchcraft and Feminine Power." *Pacific Coast Philology*, vol. 45, 2010, pp. 53-70.

Staub, Susan C. *Nature's Cruel Stepdames: Murderous Women in the Street Literature of Seventeenth Century England*. Duquesne University Press, 2005.

Symonds, Deborah A. *Weep Not for Me: Women, Ballads, and Infanticide in Early Modern Scotland*. Pennsylvania State University Press, 1997.

Thomas, Keith. "The Double Standard." *Journal of the History of Ideas*, vol. 20, no. 2, 1959, pp. 195-216.

Thomas, S. S. "Early Modern Midwifery: Splitting the Profession, Connecting the History." *Journal of Social History*, vol. 43, no. 1, Jan. 2009, pp. 115-138.

Thorn, Jennifer. *Writing British Infanticide: Child-Murder, Gender, and Print, 1722-1859*. University of Delaware Press, 2003.

Thornton, Alice, and Charles Jackson. *The Autobiography of Mrs. Alice Thornton, of East Newton, Co. York*. P. for the Society by Andrews and Co., 1875.

Tolman, Albert H. "Mary Hamilton; The Group Authorship of Ballads." *PMLA*, vol. 42, no. 2, 1927, p. 422.

Travitsky, Betty, and Anne Lake Prescott, editors. *The Early Modern Englishwoman: A Facsimile Library of Essential Works*, vol. 7, part 1, Ashgate Pub. Co., 2006.

Travitsky, Betty S. "Child Murder in English Renaissance and Drama." *Medieval and Renaissance Drama in England*, vol. 6, 1993, pp. 63-84.

Urcia, Ingeborg. "The Gallows and the Golden Ball: An Analysis of 'The Maid Freed from the Gallows' (Child 95)." *The Journal of American Folklore*, vol. 79, no. 313, 1966, p. 463.

Wrightson, Keith. "Infanticide in Earlier Seventeenth Century England." *Local Population Studies*, vol. 15, 1975, pp. 10–22.

Chapter 12

The Wicked Stepmother in the Age of Maternalist Politics

Sace Elder

This chapter considers the tradition of the wicked stepmother in late nineteenth and early twentieth-century Europe. It is grounded in several observations. First, the tradition of the wicked stepmother, most famously articulated in the Grimm fairy tales, informed assumptions about stepmothers and their relationships with dependent children. Second, these assumptions about stepmothers were in evidence at a moment when high maternal mortality (later replaced by increased divorce rates) and illegitimacy led to increased reliance on stepmothers to restabilize the normative bourgeois nuclear family. Third, in the latter nineteenth century, relational feminists' commitment to the idea that one need not be a mother to be motherly pushed against the persistent belief in the naturalness of motherly love and that biological motherhood protected women from psychopathology and violent behaviour. These two propositions pointed in opposite directions: Either all women could be successful mothers, or stepmothers would always be a potential source of danger. Like the infanticidal mother, the stepmother was an "unnatural mother," whose violence arose from a lack of biologically determined maternal feeling.[1] Unlike the infanticidal mother, her unnaturalness was not the thing to be narratively or juridically explained. In other words, it was not her rejection of motherhood but her pretention to it that made her suspect.

These three observations suggest that the stepmother's presumptive wickedness contained anxieties about the agency of mothers within the nuclear family and the relationship between motherhood and violence. The wicked stepmother, as this chapter will demonstrate, had a history, one that was bound to Western normative understandings of biological motherhood. She emerged in the modern period as the dark side of the maternal ideal and the epitome of female irrationality. Over the course of the nineteenth century, as the cult of domesticity evolved and women began to claim for themselves a feminine role in society outside the home, stepmothers became rather more sympathetic figures. Yet by the beginning of the twentieth century, she once again emerged as a problem woman. In what follows, I will be focusing on German-speaking Europe, the home of the Grimm Brothers and their famous published fairy tales. Germany also had a highly developed professional legal culture. As mothers by marriage, stepmothers' relationships to their children were governed by civil law and their transgressions of parental responsibility were punished under criminal law. The values, beliefs, and attitudes of jurists, courts, and legal scholars regarding stepmotherhood thus framed stepmothers' experiences and the attitudes of the broader culture. This specific national context should not, however, allow us to overlook the stepmother's transnational existence within the context of the Atlantic world.

I start with the figure of the stepmother in popular culture, where folk songs and popular wisdom held that stepmothers are nearly always up to no good. The lyrics of a folk song from the area of Bückelburg, captured in 1843 under the title "Stiefmutter" ("Stepmother"), serves as a useful example.[2] The lyrics describe a child returning from the home of its stepmother's sister. The child is asked what the stepaunt had given the child to eat, and the child replies, "ein Brei mit Pfeffer / wie weh ist mir!" ("a broth with pepper, / oh, woe is me!"). The child then reveals that the aunt has poisoned the dog and the cat with this same concoction and that the child expects they, too, have been poisoned. At the close of the song, the child is asked about its father, and the child replies that the father should have a seat in heaven. And when asked what the mother should have, the child replies, "Ein Stuhl in der Hühle / wie Weh ist mir!" ("A chair in hell / oh, woe is me!"). The stepmother in the song is thus a conspirator in the child's murder (Kühn 12). Alongside the various versions of this and other songs that could be found in mid-nineteenth-century Germany were myriad sayings about the dangers of being a stepchild. In them, stepmothers were unloving, jealous, vengeful, and mean, withholding of food and resources: "Stiefmutter haben harte Händ" ("Stepmothers have hard hands"); "Stiefkinder und Spitalsuppen sind selten Fett" ("Stepchildren and hospital soup are seldom fat"); and "Das Stiefmutter Kind bekommt doppelte Bissen" ("The child of a stepmother gets bitten twice") (Kühn 9). A dictionary of German adages published in 1876 counted twenty-eight such sayings involving stepmothers found in the German tongue, some originating from neighbouring countries and others originating from the German-speaking lands. By contrast, the volume listed only five involving stepfathers (Wander 852-54). Such aphorisms carried with them not only the belief that stepmothers were unloving but also the notion that the hateful stepmother was a potential filicide who may poison a child or allow them to suffer and die through neglect. The stepmother was, in many ways, an early criminal type who was deeply engrained in popular culture and language. Her motivations to cruelty, murder, and negligence were selfishness, jealousy, envy, or greed.

It would be a mistake to understand this model of the stepmother as the atavistic remnant of a premodern sensibility. To be sure, the evil stepmother had been a presence in European popular culture for centuries.[3] But recent research on eighteenth- and nineteenth-century stepfamilies on both sides of the Atlantic suggests that while stepmothers might have been recurring characters in cultural productions, the reasons for their wickedness and the problems their wickedness illuminated changed significantly during this transitional period. Nathalie Blaha-Peillex notes that no fewer than fourteen Grimm fairy tales involved cruel stepmothers, who seek either to make the stepchild suffer or to eliminate the stepchildren altogether. The evil queen in *Snow White* is perhaps the most memorable of the would-be filicidal stepmothers; in the story, her envy of Snow White's youth and beauty drives her to poison her stepdaughter. In *Hansel and Gretel*, the siblings' stepmother suggests to the father that they should abandon the children in the woods, where they would surely starve. In fact, after 1819, Wilhelm Grimm, who continually revised the collected tales, replaced evil mothers with evil stepmothers in his new edition of the *Kinder- und Hausmärchen*. Blaha-Peillex explains that Grimm's revisions brought the stories in line with the norms of domesticity, which expected mothers to be kind and loving to their own children. In the revised stories, the stepmothers (those that had biological children) were compassionate and tender with their birth children but treated their husband's children with nothing but antipathy. A common theme in the stories was stepmothers' fear that their own children would not enjoy the benefit of inheritance from the new husband (79–80). In other words, Blaha-Peillex concludes, "unnatural mothers" were not "denaturalized mothers" (181). That is to say, their treatment of their own children was consistent with the expectations of biological motherhood of the day, whereas their cruelty and even murderous violence as a stepmother also affirmed the cultural commitment to the ideal of biological maternity in bourgeois domesticity.

Writing of the wicked stepmother in England, Marilyn Francus agrees that eighteenth- and nineteenth-century stories of monstrous mothers were indeed tales about domesticity. But Francus goes further to suggest that the wicked stepmother provided a vehicle through which to explore the tensions and contradictions of domesticity, such as in the Earl of Carlisle's play *The Stepmother* (1800). By dominating her husband, the wicked stepmother exposed the limitations of patriarchy. She drew attention to the inadequacy of companionate marriage in providing a foundation for good parenting. Narratives about stepmothers also exposed the silence surrounding the absence of the dead mother. "The wicked stepmother," Francus writes, "enters a preexisting domestic narrative and destroys it from within" (126).

Lisa Wilson finds similar tensions within the North American ideal of domesticity in her study of stepfamilies of the early republic. Where the early modern stepmother had been seen as corrupting, malicious, and cruel because of her womanhood, the stepmother who entered the nineteenth century had become "the opposite of idealized mothers. Stepmothers had become both wicked women and wicked mothers" (Wilson 57). Leslie Lindenauer adds to these analyses the imperatives of republican motherhood, whether in the form of breastfeeding or in the nurturing of natural emotional bonds between child and birth mother. Stepmothers could never achieve this biological standard of maternalism, yet the period's high maternal death rate necessitated second marriages to perpetuate the ideal nuclear family. Stories of wicked stepmothers in popular literature explored the dangers of unnatural mothers. Sophia Johnson's 1841 purportedly autobiographical *The Friendless Orphan* tells the story of a young woman driven from her family home by an evil stepmother who offered a poor substitute for her saintly departed mother. Similarly, in Caroline Rush's 1850 romance novel, *Robert Morton, or the Step Mother*, the eponymous character returns home after the death of his mother to find his father remarried to a much younger woman who has not married for love, as his mother had, but rather for convenience (18–25).

Across both sides of the Atlantic in the early nineteenth century, wicked stepmothers represented the inherent threats to the bourgeois domestic ideal, constructed as it was around the nuclear family and natural maternity. Just as courts and legal systems came to understand the violence of infanticide as an act of desperation by natural (and usually unmarried) mothers brought on by adverse social conditions[4]— narratives of the wicked stepmother interrogated the potential violence of the selfish and self-serving unnatural mother. But as the cult of domesticity gave way to new forms of women's maternalism in the latter half of the nineteenth century, the stepmother proved herself a protean character. In the American case, Lindenauer has found that by mid-century, the American stepmother had been rehabilitated in popular songs and fiction and now increasingly appeared as a figure of youth and virtue as well as of love and compassion. By the latter decades of the century, motherhood came to be seen as a profession that could be learned and practiced by even nonbiological mothers. The expansion of social reform and professionalization of welfare work relied upon this trope of nonbiological maternalism. Stepmothers also served the important purpose of reinforcing the white, middle-class patriarchal family, at least in white society (59-88).

In Germany, maternalist politics similarly created a space for women to mother other people's children. As Ann Taylor Allen has shown, feminists at the turn of the century rejected the notion that motherly duty "should be reserved for one's own children" (233). Allen demonstrates that activists—such as Frieda Duensing, Adele Schreiber, and Alice Salomon (all active in the movement against cruelty to children)—pushed against the trends in developmental psychology and evolution that conspired to reduce the significance of the mother's pedagogical role in childrearing by elevating her genetic and biological roles. Duensing, for example, in her 1903 legal dissertation on the violation of custodial authority over children, took pains to demonstrate that children had more to fear from married fathers than from stepmothers or single mothers (93). Indeed, child protectionists knew very well that biological maternity was no guarantee against cruelty and mistreatment of one's children. The chairman of Vienna's Pestalozzi Association for the Advancement of Child Protection and Youth Welfare, Lydia Wolfrig, noted in her 1907 address to the first Austrian Children's Congress, that maternal love and hate were two sides of the same coin. The modern woman, she argued, experiences a "Skala" ("spectrum") of feelings and emotions that cannot be reduced to a natural instinct; thus, hate, resentment, and rejection are also possible feelings for mothers in civilized society, especially in cases in which children are inconvenient or unwanted. Yet the assumption of motherly love forms the basis of jurisprudence, justice, and the law (31-33). The best possible conditions for the development of motherly love, Wolfring asserted, had nothing to do with natural instincts and everything to do with peaceful domestic lives in which mothers could practice self-care as well as care for the household. It was the external conditions of childrearing, not biology, that were the key to the development of motherly love (34).

Although she was not writing specifically of stepmothers, Wolfring's characterization of maternal feeling as an emotion shaped by experience and environment ran counter to the criminological assumptions expressed by Cesare Lombroso and William Ferrero, who have argued that maternity offered "a moral prophylactic against crime and evil" (254). Karsten Uhl has analyzed German criminological theories about the relationship between motherhood, sexuality, and criminality in the late nineteenth and twentieth centuries. Uhl finds that criminological scholarship asserted an inverse relationship between motherly love and criminal behaviour among women. Criminologists associated the lower participation of women in the crime rate with women's attachment to children and home. Similarly, they attributed increases in criminality to emancipatory social changes that ran counter to women's putative natural motherly proclivities. These explanations, Uhl argues, were remarkably resilient, persisting right up into the 1960s (48-62).

Criminal psychologists located stepmothers' putative criminality within the void that should have been occupied by motherly love. Most obvious was the belief that the lack of a physical bond between stepmother and stepchild prevented genuine love and compassion from developing. The German translation of Italian jurist Lino Ferriani's 1897 *Entartete Mütter* (*Degenerate Mothers*) noted that the stepmother's love arose not from blood but from the law (*Gesetz*)—to which the translator added, "Wohl mehr durch das Mitleid und die Gerechtigkeit" ("possibly more through compassion and fairness") than through the law (122). Ferriani expressed some empathy for the role of the stepmothers, who in his view deserved special consideration under criminal law because of the difficult task set before them, raising another's children. Yet Ferriani continued to note that in the cases he had reviewed, the mistreatments perpetrated by stepparents were particularly monstrous in nature (123). Related to this lack of natural feeling was the presumptive rivalry between the stepmother and her predecessor's children. Echoing the old fairy tales, Ferriani posited that the stepmother alienated the father's affections from his children. Ferriani gave considerable space to the putative penchant of the father for his second wife that was stronger than the attraction to the first. The robbing of the father's affections is what made the cruel stepmother every bit the "degenerate mother" (123). Thus, the older stereotypes of wicked stepmothers found new expression in criminological theories of degeneration.

Like Ferriani, prison cleric Reinhold Stade imbued some of the women convicts he had interviewed as prison cleric with the stereotype of the wicked stepmother.[5] His 1903 book, *Frauentypen aus dem Gefängnisleben* (*Types of Women in Prison Life*), clearly written for a popular audience, detailed numerous cases of murderous and violent women, including that of a "heartless" stepmother who had killed her two-year-old stepchild through cruel and brutal mistreatment. According to Stade, even in prison, the woman spoke of her stepchild in the harshest of terms, expressing "empörenden Roheit" ("shocking brutality") and "absoluten Unempfindlichkeit auch für die geringeste wärmere mutterliche Liebe" ("insensibility to even the slightest warmer motherly love") (230). She embodied, in other words, "both inside and out, the classic picture of stepmother in its worst sense" (231). Where Stade resisted generalizing about all stepmothers, others were less circumspect in their characterizations. In his 1908 study *Familienmord durch Geisteskranke* (*Family Murder by the Mentally Ill*), psychiatrist and respected criminologist Paul Näcke noted that illegitimate children were particularly abused by stepmothers and became a "bone of contention" ("Zankapfel") within the family, especially under the conditions of privation and poverty and if the child was poorly behaved. Citing Ferriani, Näcke wrote that such harsh conditions caused parental love to contract, leading to abuse that ended "nicht selten mit tödlichem Ausgange" ("frequently with deadly outcome") (11).

After the turn of the century, the stepmother was also believed to introduce psychosexual tensions into the nuclear family, according to the literature of the day. Psychologists began to write of the "stepmother complex," which referred to adolescent boys' sexual desire for the stepmother or authority figure, which could be satisfied through corporal punishment.[6] Criminological writings also emphasized psychosexual tensions within stepmother families. In his 1910 essay "Das Kriminelle in deutschen Volksmärchen" ("The Criminal in German Folk Tales"), which appeared in one of the foremost criminological journals of the period, Erich Wulffen attributed the wicked stepmother's behaviour to sexual pathology. In *Aschenbrödel* (*Cinderella*), he found the stepmother's humiliation of the protagonist "sadistic," in that she derived pleasure from making the young girl suffer (352). In such tales, the stepmother's hatred for the stepdaughter is "sexuell gefärbt" ("sexually tinged") (353). Later, in his 1923 *Das Weib als Sexualverbrecherin* (*Woman as Sexual Criminal*), Wulffen would echo Ferriani by claiming the stepchild reminds the stepmother of the love the husband had for the previous wife and that the stepmother feels an inevitable sexual jealousy. The stepdaughter in particular reminds the woman of her dead rival, or she suffers from the motherly "egoism" on behalf of her own biological children (267).

The popular and criminological insistence on the inherent cruelty of stepmothers seemed particularly out of step with German law and jurisprudence. Stepmothers occupied a liminal space in the law when it came to their relationship with their stepchildren. Under the German Civil Code (Bürgerliches Gesetzbuch, BGB, promulgated in 1900) fathers possessed "the right and duty" to educate children through "appropriate means of discipline," by which the dominant jurisprudence interpreted as physical punishment (§1631). The mother had "next to the father" the same "right and duty" to educate the child but only for the duration of the marriage (§1634). Stepmothers were entirely absent from the BGB, but jurisprudence held that fathers implicitly granted stepmothers the authority to use physical discipline as part of the marriage agreement (Bitter and Lehmann 656). Under the same logic, the abuse of that right would also be grounds for divorce under §1568 BGB, specified as legal standing "serious injury to marital duties." Stepmothers were expected to support the wellbeing, both physical and moral, of their husbands' children, and could lose custody in their husband's absence if, as in one 1915 case, she provided the child "ehrlosen und unsittlichen Lebenswandel" ("dishonorable immoral living conditions") (Anonymous 166). Such wartime court cases reflected contemporary concerns about the perfidy of war wives in the absence of the male heads of household.[7]

German law thus gave the stepmother considerable legal responsibility with few legal rights. The distance between the professional legal culture of jurists (Wulffen notwithstanding) and popular legal culture is well illustrated by a 1907 Berlin trial of a woman for grievous bodily harm against her fourteen-year-old stepdaughter. Coverage of the trial echoed the culturally available narratives about wicked stepmothers, including the stepmother's accusation that the stepdaughter had ruined her marriage. Witnesses attested to beating, heavy chores inappropriate given the child's physical size and ability, the withholding of food, as well as psychological torment. The *Berliner Morgenpost* made a direct comparison between the stepdaughter and the fairy tale protagonist Cinderella. The child's wan and frail appearance contrasted with the stepmother's good looks, fine clothing, and haughty attitude. In her defense, the stepmother claimed that her stepdaughter was a difficult child who had required the legally-prescribed 'reasonable and appropriate' discipline. Just a few years later, Erich Wulffen gave five pages to the case in his *Psychologie des Verbrechers* (*Psychology of the Criminal*) as an example of antipathetic emotion in criminal behavior. Wulffen reproduced in detail witnesses' descriptions of the myriad injustices the girl had suffered under the control of her wicked stepmother (156-60). Given the vivid descriptions of the defendant's alleged cruelty, observers were stunned by the light sentence the Berlin Criminal Court II handed down: 300RM and time served. The *Berliner Morgenpost* reported on February 16 the following year that court had considered the defense's allegations of the stepdaughter's incorrigibility and the stepmother's inexperience as a new parent. If protectionists, the public, and (several years later) Erich

Wulffen were convinced that she was indeed a wicked stepmother, the court, it seemed, was not. It was also telling that the defendant's husband, was not considered an accomplice in the case, and that the state attorney as well as the court left aside the question of his failure to protect his child from mistreatment when he was legally responsible for her welfare.

Narratives of the wicked stepmother proved persistent and continued to find their appeal in the coming decades. Researchers investigated the correlation between step-mothers and waywardness among youth, an interest that continued after the war.[8] In 1918, Gertrud Alexander-Katz of the Görlitz chapter of the Deutsche Verband-Kinderschutz warned her fellow protectionists of the plight of "mutterlose Waisen" ("motherless orphans"), whose fathers were in the field and whose mothers were either dead or feckless. The children left alone with stepmothers are to be most pitied, according to Alexander-Katz. "Denn wir alle, die wir in der Kinder-schutzarbeit stehen,' she wrote, "haben nur zu oft Gelegenheit, uns davon zu überzeugen, daß 'die böse Stiefmutter' nicht allein der Märchenliteratur angehört, sondern leider auch in der realen Welt des öfteren existiert." ("For all of us engaged in child protection work have only too often had the opportunity to be convinced that the 'wicked stepmother' belongs not only in fairy tales, but rather unfortunately also in the real world") (14). Other critics and commentators wrote more generously of the stepmother. The growing literature on parenting advice assumed that parenting was a realm of expertise that must be acquired, preferably under the guidance of experts.[9] In the logic of this literature, biological maternity did not necessarily lead to effective mothering. Stepmothers, too, could learn to become good mothers. In 1920, Ruth von Kleist-Retzkow published an article in *Eltern und Kind* (*Parents and Child*) titled "Mutterliebe und Stiefmutter." Here, she argued that adoptive parents, though lacking the 'natural bond' with their children, could nonetheless learn to care for their children as biological parents do. Although one must simply be aware of the challenges, she insisted, the negative image of the stepmother from the Grimm fairy tales bore no relation to the reality (69-72).

Developmental psychologists also began offering rather more complex analyses of the so-called stepmother problem. The best example of this kind of analysis was Hanna Kühn's 1929 study published in William Stern's series on youth and social psychology. Kühn's methodology made use of census data collected by the city of Hamburg, questionnaires, and interviews with young people in compulsory educational institutions, juvenile court records, and literary sources. In all, she examined around five hundred cases of stepmother families. She found that 18.3 per cent of wayward girls in the study attributed their misbehaviour to difficult relationships with their stepmothers, whereas the number of girls who actually had stepmothers was only 2 to 3 per cent of the overall population. Where Wulffen had attributed to stepmothers a natural tendency towards jealousy and callousness towards another woman's children, Kühn argued that the cultural representations of step-motherhood found in popular culture, particularly folk tales, shaped children's perceptions of the stranger women who cared for them. Kühn hypothesized that adults influenced the perception of step-children regarding their stepmothers by posing leading questions, such as "How does your stepmother treat you?" or "Your stepmother isn't as nice as your real mother, is she?" (89-98). Fear of the second mother could arise from the fact that many women died of tuberculosis, leaving behind sick children who were too weak to deal with the emotional loss of their parent (106). To be sure, stepmothers sometimes mistreated their stepchildren. But this often happened, she claimed, when children with behavioural problems or intellectual disabilities tested the abilities of inexperienced mothers (86-87).

Kühn did not stop there, however; she went on to locate the source of the stepmother problem in the individualism of modern society. Starting with literary scholar Hermann Ploss's observation that the wicked stepmother was a figure found among so-called civilized cultures,[10] Kühn argued that that the conflicts and tensions she described between stepmothers and stepchildren arose from increasing individualism in modern societies. Alfred Vierkandt had warned several years earlier of a shift towards individualism that threatened the foundations of society. Divorce played a particularly important role in this shift and signalled a new emotional regime in which earlier "überperönliche" ("extra-personal") emotional bonds and subordinations were now purely and specifically interpersonal and private.[11] Vierkandt's diagnosis of contemporary society, Kühn wrote, would explain Ploss's observations some two decades earlier as to why wicked stepmothers appeared only in the popular and literary cultures of "Kulturvölker" ("civilized" peoples) (72–73).

By way of conclusion, Kühn wrote,

> Wir haben demnach im Stiefmutterproblem eine endlose Kette von Wechselwirkungen zwischen den Objectivationen der Volksmeinung über die Stiefmutter und den tatsächlich empirisch gegebenen Verhältnissen in der Stiefmutterfamilie vor uns.
>
> (We have therefore in the stepmother problem an endless chain of interactions between the objectivations of popular opinion over the stepmother and the actual, empirically existing relations in the stepmother family.) (152)

Kühn's expansive perspective and multifaceted analysis located found the problem not with the stepmothers but with the sociocultural context in which women became stepmothers.

Given the power of the stepmother as a criminal type, it is interesting to observe what happened when Kühn's work came to the attention of criminal psychologist Hans von Hentig. Reviewing Kühn's book for *Monatsschrift für Kriminologie und Strafrechtreform* (*Monthly for Criminology and Criminal Law Reform*) in 1930, von Hentig praised the study for drawing attention to the stepmother problem. But von Hentig disagreed fundamentally with Kühn's cultural etiology of the problem. Echoing Wulffen's characterization of stepmother-child relations, he placed responsibility for conflict within the stepmother family firmly on the shoulders of stepmothers. Disregarding Kühn's careful critique of cultural narratives that presumed the stepmother was the source of conflict in stepmother families, von Hentig asserted that second wives jealously guarded their husband's attentions and undermined the affections between children and fathers. Fathers regularly sided with the stepmother against the children, and often such conflicts eventually ended with the child pushed out of parental heart and house. Such alienation of parental affections, according to von Hentig, had become even more pronounced with the increase in divorce rates, as the first wife is a constant threat to the second wife. Stepmothers, he concluded, posed a real if latent threat of neglect to nervous and psychopathic children and, thus, also posed a criminological threat. Although he found Kühn's work unsatisfying, von Hentig believed it would open new discussions about the criminal stepmother and would provoke academic criminologists to finally take up an issue that they had encountered in their own experiences. Hopefully, von Hentig wrote, new questions would be asked, such as, what kind of woman marries a widower? (62). Thus, as if determined to make Kühn's point for her, Hentig relocated the stepmother problem firmly in the character of the woman.[12]

Hentig's response to Kühn certainly illustrates the imperviousness of the male-dominated field of criminal psychology to feminist perspectives and to the persistence of the old tropes regarding the dangers of stepmother families. But the image of the cruel stepmother who threatened her stepchildren with physical and psychological violence was giving way to another kind of stereotype. Kühn's work coincided with a marked increase in publications about stepchild-stepparent relations, most of which dealt with the psychology of the stepchild.[13] Psychoanalytic explanations based on sexual competition between stepparents and stepchildren rendered the stepmother the object rather than the subject of narratives about the family and crime.[14] The new research undermined the figure of the wicked stepmother, whose motivations were easily explicable and predictable. Yet it must also be pointed out that the wicked stepmother also had a kind of agency, however blameworthy, that the new stepmother did not enjoy.

This trajectory of the wicked stepmother suggests that she had a history. In the Grimm version of the fairy tales, the stepmother's cruelty to her stepchildren contrasted with the care and love she rendered her birth children. Like Marilyn Francus's "rebellious" infanticides of the eighteenth century who defended their actions to the courts (115-120), the wicked stepmother possessed a kind of agency that challenged conventional notions of feminine docility and maternal self-sacrifice. In the latter nineteenth century, as motherliness became an attribute of all women, new possibilities for the stepmother emerged. The wicked stepmother, however, remained a powerful figure in popular legal culture. Limited evidence suggests that jurists appeared to be more circumspect than the public in their adjudication of cases involving abusive stepmothers, especially when taking into consideration the behaviour of the stepchild. As waywardness and delinquency became an increasing concern, criminologists, psychologists, and social welfare experts gave the stepmother renewed attention as a possible source of the problem. By now, however, her role was largely passive, as the object of or obstacle to a child's sexual desire (as in the stepmother complex). The wicked stepmother, far from an atavistic artifact from a bygone primitive culture, accommodated new models of the family structure, motherhood, and female sexuality.

Endnotes

1. For an example of this usage, see "Eine unnatürliche Mutter."
2. All translations in this chapter from original German texts are mine.
3. On stepmothers in Greek and Roman antiquity, for example, see Watson, especially chapters III and IV; Noy 345-48.
4. On judicial and popular leniency on infanticide, see Francus 109-115; Higginbotham 323; Schulte 92-98. For a sociological consideration of infanticide in imperial Germany, see Richter.
5. On Stade's work, see Wetzell 87, 92.
6. For an example, see Ansaourow 254. For a contemporary analysis of the stepmother theme in Western literature, see Rank 119-64. On the stepmother complex in the United States, see Lindenauer 89-95. Lindenauer notes that this complex first emerged in popular culture in the 1920s.
7. On concerns about the morality of women on the home front during the First World War, see Daniel chapter 4; Todd 75-99.
8. See Gruhle 92; Kühn 1-2. A Prussian Ministry of the Interior report of 1901 report indicated that 10.4 per cent had stepfathers and 8.3 per cent had stepmothers. According to the report, "die Zahelen lassen erkennen, welch unheilvollen Einfluß die Zerrütung des Elternhauses durch den Tod der Eltern an die Kinder hat. Auch die Ergänzung des Elternhauses durch eine zweite Heirat bringt für die Kinder oft mehr Verderben als Segen." ("The numbers suggest that the breakdown of the parental household through the death of a parent has a negative effect on the children. Also the supplementing of the parental household through a second marriage often brings the child more corruption than blessing."). Prussian Ministry of the Interior, xviii.

9. On advice literature of the period, see Gebhardt chapter 1; Kay 105-21.
10. See Ploss 580.
11. See Vierkandt 301.
12. An American reviewer of the book found that Kühn's formulation of the problem and the methodology belonged to the last decade of the nineteenth century but, unlike von Hentig, praised Kühn for identifying the influence of popular beliefs in influencing family conflicts. See Finner 205.
13. For further examples, see Hoenig 188-331; Neumann 348-67; and Stern 144-57.
14. As an example, see Aichhorn 124-27. Werner Lincke, in contrast, insisted that fairy tales are best understood as a "social motif" that had its roots in primitive society, rather than as expressions of transhistorical psychological phenomena (25-26).

Works Cited

Allen, Ann Taylor. *Feminism and Motherhood in Germany, 1800–1914*. Rutgers University Press, 1991.

Anonymous. "Eine unnatürliche Mutter." *Mitteilungen des Vereins zum Schutz der Kinder vor Ausnutzung u. Mißhandlung* vol. 6, 1904, pp. 5-6.

Anonymous. "Deutschlands oberstrichterlichen Rechtsprechung." *Das Recht*, vol. 19, no. 4, 1915, p. 166.

Asnaourow, Felix. "Über strenge Erziehung." *Heilen und Bilden. Arztlich-Padagogische Arbeiten des Vereins für Individualpsychologie*, edited by Alfred Adler and Carl Fürtmüller, Ernst Reinhardt, 1914, pp. 252-61.

Blaha-Peillex, Nathalie. *Mütter und Anti-Mütter in Den Märchen Der Brüder Grimm*. Tübinger Vereinigung für Volkskunde, 2008.

Daniel, Ute. *The War from Within: German Working-Class Women in the First World War*. Berg, 1997.

Duensing, Frieda. *Verletzung der fürsorgepflicht gegenüber Minderjährigen: Ein Versuch zu ihrer strafgesetzlichen Behandlung*. Schweitzer, 1903.

Ferriani, Lino. *Entartete Mütter: Eine Psychisch-Juridische Abhandlung*. Translated by Alfred Ruhemann, Siegfried Cronbach, 1897.

Finner, P. F. "Review of Psychologische Untersuchungen über das Stiefmutterproblem: Die Konfliktsmöglichkeiten in der Stiefmutterfamilie und ihre Bedeuting für die Verwahrlosung des Stiefkindes, Hanna Kühn." *The American Journal of Psychology*, vol. 44, no. 1, 1932, p. 205.

Francus, Marilyn. *Monstrous Motherhood : Eighteenth-Century Culture and the Ideology of Domesticity.* Johns Hopkins University Press, 2013.

Gebhardt, Miriam. *Die Angst vor dem kindlichen Tyrannen. Eine Geschichte der Erziehung im 20. Jahrhundert.* Deutsche Verlags-Anstalt, 2009.

Gruhle, Hans Walter. *Die Ursachen der jugendlichen Verwahrlosung und Kriminalität.* Julius Springer, 1912.

Hentig, Hans von. "Review of Hanna Kühn, Psychologische Untersuchungen über das Stiefmutterproblem. Die Konflichtsmöglichkeiten in der Stiefmutterfamilie und ihre Bedeutung für die Verwahrlosung des Stiefkindes. Abrg. Barth, 1929." *Monatsschrift für Kriminalpsychologie und Strafrechtsreform*, vol. 21, 1930, p. 62.

Kay, Carolyn. "How Should We Raise Our Son Benjamin? Advice Literature for Mothers in Early Twentieth-Century Germany." *Raising Citizens in the "Century of the Child:" The United States and German Central Europe in Comparative Perspective*, edited by Dirk Schumann, Berghahn, 2010, pp. 105-21.

Kühn, Hanna. *Psychologische Untersuchungen über das Stiefmutterproblem. Die Konfliktsmöglichkeiten in der Stiefmutterfamilie und ihre Bedeutung für die Verwahrlosung des Stiefkindes.* Johann Ambr. Barth, 1929.

Lindenauer, Leslie J. *I Could Not Call Her Mother: The Stepmother in American Popular Culture, 1750-1960.* Lexington Books, 2014.

Lombroso, Cesare, and William Ferrero. *The Female Offender.* D. Appleton, 1909, hdl.handle.net/2027/ucl.$b268722. Accessed 17 Nov. 2021.

Näcke, Paul. *Über Familienmord durch Geisteskranke.* Carl Marhold, 1908, hdl.handle.net/2027/chi.087054844. Accessed 17 Nov. 2021.

Ploss, Hermann Heinrich. *Das Weib in der Natur- Und Völkerkunde: Anthropologische Studien.* Th. Grieben's Verlag, 1897.

Prussian Ministry of the Interior. "Vorbemerkungen." *Statistik über die Fürsorgeerziehung Minderjähriger ... und über die Zwangserziehung Jugendlicher für das Jahr 1901*, 1903, pp. v–xxv.

Rank, Otto. *Das Inzest Motiv in Dichtung und Sage. Grundzüge einer Psychologie des dictherischen Schaffens*. Franz Deuticke, 1912, babel. hathitrust.org/cgi/pt?id=hvd.32044011255072&view=1up&seq=8. Accessed 17 Nov. 2021.

Richter, Jeffrey S. "Infanticide, Child Abandonment, and Abortion in Imperial Germany." *Journal of Interdisciplinary History*, vol. 28, no. 4, 1998, pp. 511-52.

Schulte, Regina. "Infanticide in Rural Bavaria in the Nineteenth Century." *Interest and Emotion: Essays on the Study of Family and Kinship*, edited by Hans Medick and David Warren Sabean, Cambridge, 1984, pp. 77-102.

Stade, Reinhold. *Frauentypen aus dem Gefängnisleben: Beiträge zu einer Psychologie der Verbrecherin*. Dörffling & Franke, 1903, hdl.handle.net/2027/hvd.32044103229670. Accessed 17 Nov. 2021.

Todd, Lisa M. *Sexual Treason in Germany during the First World War*. Palgrave Macmillan, 2017.

Uhl, Karsten. "Mutterliebe Und Verbrechen–Mutterschaft und Sexualität im kriminologischen Diskurs 1880-1980." *Tel Aviver Jahrbuch für deutsche Geschichte*, vol. 36, 2008, pp. 48-62.

Vierkandt, Alfred. *Gesellschaftslehre. Hauptprobleme der philosophischen Soziologie*. Ferdinand Encke, 1923, hdl.handle.net/2027/mdp.39015052543983. Accessed 17 Nov. 2021.

Wander, Karl Friedrich Wilhelm. *Deutsches Sprichwörter-Lexikon. Ein Hausschatz für das deutsche Volk.*, vol. 4, Leipzig, 1876, hdl.handle.net/2027/pst.000031822190. Accessed 17 Nov. 2021.

Watson, Patricia A. *Ancient Stepmothers: Myth, Misogyny, and Reality*. E. J. Brill, 1995.

Wetzell, Richard. *Inventing the Criminal: A History of German Criminology*. University of North Carolina Press, 2000.

Wilson, Lisa. *A History of Stepfamilies in Early America*. University of North Carolina Press, 2014.

Wolfring, Lydia von. *Die Kindermisshandlung, Ihre Ursachen und die Mittel zu ihrer Abhilfe*. K.K. Hof- und Staatsdruckerei, 1907.

Wulffen, Erich. "Das Kriminelle Im Deutschen Volksmärchen." *Archiv Fur Kriminal-Anthropologie Und Kriminalistik*, vol. 38, 1910, pp. 340–70.

Wulffen, Erich. *Der Sexualverbrecher: Ein Handbuch für Juristen, Verwaltungsbeamte und Ärtze.* Langenscheidt, 1910.

Wulffen, Erich. *Das Weib als Sexualverbrecherin. Ein Handbuch für Juristen, Verwaltungsbeamte und Ärzte mit kriminalistischen Originalaufnahmen.* Translated by David Berger, P. Langenscheidt, 1923.

Wulffen, Erich. *Psychologie des Verbrechers. Ein Handbuch für Juristen, Arzte, Pädogogen und Gebildete aller Stände,* vol. 2, Langenscheidt, 1910, hdl.handle.net/2027/ucl.d0004168746. Accessed 17 Nov. 2021.

Chapter 13

Assia Djebar's *La Soif*: Abortion and Crime

Anna Rocca

> As a feminist and a Catholic,
> I believe a woman's freedom to abort a fetus
> is a monstrous, a tyrannous,
> but a necessary freedom in a fallen world.
> —Judith Wilt xii

Assia Djebar's earliest literary work *La Soif* (1957) was written during a period of hostilities between Algeria and France. Historians have defined the years from 1956 to 1958 as the three bloodiest years of the Algerian War of Independence (Orlando, "La Soif" 142).[1] In *La Soif*, the female protagonist, Nadia, who is half-Algerian and half-French, lives a modern and liberated life that mirrors that of French women living in urban areas. The more traditional female character, Jedla, a Muslim who is married to Ali, is reserved, discrete, and perceives all forms of French influence on her society as despicable contamination. Jedla would love to have a child with her husband but because she questions his fidelity, once pregnant, she decides to have an abortion and later dies as a result of the operation. Jedla acts without consulting Ali and despite Nadia's insistence that killing an unborn baby is a "crime" (148). In deciding to terminate her pregnancy, Jedla formally commits multiple crimes at once: She defies the state, her religion, her husband, her future offspring, traditions, and herself. Abortion is indeed the most transgressive and final act, and it lies at the heart of the novel. When Djebar published *La Soif*, in France and in all French colonies, both abortion and all methods of contraception were illegal.

From a historical perspective, in the twentieth century, there was an unsurprising consistency throughout the majority of the nation-state's regulations: Abortion became a state affair in times of war and military politics (Collectif IVP 16). In France, the Vichy government considered abortion a crime against the state, which was punished in 1942 by means of decapitation.[2] Whereas the death penalty was abolished under the Act of 9 October 1981,[3] from 1945 to 1961, the French political, medical, and religious powers unanimously allied against women's control on fecundity (Collectif IVP 17). Two fundamental moral issues are generally involved in the question of abortion: a woman's right to decide what happens to her body and a fetus's right to life. As a consequence, abortion has been consistently discussed in its interconnections with infanticide. Therefore, the analysis of its value within *La Soif* is central to the topic of this book collection. In his 1972 milestone essay titled "Abortion and Infanticide," Michael Tooley states, "It seems very difficult to formulate a completely satisfactory liberal position on abortion without coming to grips with the infanticide issue" (37-38). Forty-seven years have passed since that article was published, yet the abortion debate and its implications regarding infanticide have in many respects intensified.

While discussions about both abortion and infanticide's moral issue are beyond the scope of this article, I argue that Djebar's inclusion of Jedla's abortion and the manner in which the author treats the complex subject of conflicting nationalisms should be regarded as exceptionally politically subversive. Although on the surface *La Soif* seems to exclusively deal with the futile and narcissistic introspection of the young bourgeois Nadia, abortion is crucial to the understanding of the author's intrinsic political overtones that disrupt Algerian nationalist associations between womanhood and motherhood. Furthermore, by means of the character Nadia—who is morally opposed to abortion while serving as an incarnation of the caricatured stereotype of the emancipated French woman—Djebar underscores the glaring contradictions that are inherent to modernity as envisioned by colonialism for Algerian women. Therefore, abortion reveals the hypocrisy of both the Algerian nationalist agenda and the French notion of female emancipation. It also shows the profound alienation that women in particular have faced in both traditional and modern worlds. Nationalist and colonialist systems imposed conflicting, irreconcilable, and undesirable affiliations for women's identity in which both modern or traditional women were doomed to be miserable and to suffer. Indeed, despite their different choices, Nadia and Jedla share a common condition: They both succumb to societal rules. They both repress their inner yearnings and thirst for life simply because there is no room for those aspirations in their society, not for an emancipated woman or for a traditional mother and wife.

Advertised in Paris by Juilliard as "Le premier roman d'une jeune musulmane" ("The first novel of a young Muslim woman"), French critics recognized *La Soif* as a product of the imperial French 'mission civilisatrice' and welcomed Djebar as the new Westernized Algerian woman (qtd. in Lançon 119).[4] On the Algerian front, critics were outraged and found the main character Nadia's "exclusive preoccupation with sexual problems indecent at a time when Algeria was subject to a merciless war" (Marx-Scouras 172). The unfavourable critical reception of *La Soif* stands as an exemplary case of what literary critic Clarisse Zimra defines as an "ideological battle" ("In Her Own Write" 207). Underlining the young Djebar's political manipulation from both fronts, French and Algerian, Zimra affirms that this battle may have been the impetus for Djebar's ten-year silence and withdrawal from the literary world that preceded the publication of *Femmes d'Alger dans leur appartement*. About the critics' reaction, Zimra stresses: "To the revolution, these self-indulgent 'bourgeois' stories that did nothing to advance the cause of national liberation proved an embarrassment. Djebar was criticized in vitriolic attacks ad hominem" ("Writing Woman" 68). In reaction to these attacks, Djebar initially spoke about *La Soif* as a naive "exercise of style,"[5] but then she politically contextualized the novel, more than forty years later, in *Ces Voix qui m'assiègent*.[6] The following section aims to offer an overview of women and motherhood's representations during and in the aftermath of the Algerian War of Independence.

Patriotic Motherhood and the Algerian War of Independence

War, particularly during the time of anticolonial struggles, Natalya Vince contends, is "a moment of identity consolidation, reformulation, and ... of invention and transformation," within which women's representations are used as both the "signifiers of a new identity" and the "guarantors of an immutable national 'essence'" (448). Indeed, during the Algerian War of Independence, both French and Algerian governments appropriated the image of Algerian women to create their own nationalist narrative. On the French side, as Vince stresses the following: "A number of contrasting constructions of French Algerian Muslim womanhood came to prominence. Supporters of *l'Algérie française* paraded the figures of the *evoluée* and the yet to-be-saved submissive 'Fatma'" (458). On the Algerian side, the Front for National Liberation (FLN) fabricated and promoted the image of "the unveiled bomber and the mother hiding weapons under her *hayk*" (458). According to Neil MacMaster, in the final years of the War, the French government "was highly ambiguous and Janus-faced" towards Algerian women (91). On the one hand, it was extremely violent and repressive and did not spare them from rape and torture; on the other, it was progressive, "particularly in regard to the reform of the *statut personnel*, the laws on marriage and the family governing Muslims, in 1959" (92).

In Algeria, the FLN encouraged women to support the national struggle through what is commonly characterized as "patriotic motherhood"; women were defined according to their ability to be good mothers, homemakers, and good wives, who would teach their sons religious behaviours based on "traditional moral standards" (Helie-Lucas 108). In a similar vein, MacMaster stresses how Algerian women as "mothers and educators" were viewed in the private sphere of the family as a "bastion in which core values were transmitted from one generation to the next" (105). Winifred Woodhull goes further and remarks that during the Algerian War, women were the "guarantors of national identity, no longer simply as guardians of traditional values but *as symbols that successfully contain the conflicts of the new historical situation*" (11). In fact, the FLN's radicalization of mothers' roles within the family stood as a political counterpoint against the 1957–1959 French government emancipation campaign. Strategically launched in the final years of the war, the campaign would have ensured "equality of rights between Algerian Muslim women and women in metropolitan France in relation to voting, education, professional training, employment opportunities, health care and welfare rights" (MacMaster 92). This operation, which also included campaigning for Algerian women's unveiling, was aimed to disrupt "the private sphere of the Muslim family" and "to transform Algerian women into westernized beings that would share all the cultural features of bourgeois French women, in relation to everything from dress style to consumerism and an idealized model of the couple bound by mutual affection" (MacMaster 92). Marnia Lazreg interprets the French strategy to win the war as one based on a gender prejudice that sees women as representing the nation: "Therefore, taking them [and] appropriating them [signify] the taking and appropriation of their nation" (Torture 150).

It comes as no surprise then that Algerian nationalists during the war "demanded that the feminist struggle be subsumed under the revolutionary struggle" (Cooke, *Women* 123). While recognizing that the FLN found itself in a "delicate position," Lazreg also stresses how their view of women as "'passive' and in need of protection" was in strident contrast with women's participation in the War, which stands as a clear "challenge to their countrymen's conceptions of women as fragile" ("Gender" 766, 769). For Lazreg, by willingly joining the war, women "acted as contestants of men's monopoly over nationalist militancy," which she understands as "a radical break in gender relations" ("Gender" 767). MacMaster describes Algerian men returning from the war as "deeply anxious and insecure in relation to such change" and maintains as well that by attacking the 1959 law, the FLN "reinforced, the conservative topos of the immutable family as a bastion of identity, a form of religious nationalism that bound women into the status quo" (110, 106). The FLN position towards women also created the beginning of a "long-term, post-independence mental association between almost any form of progressive agenda on women or 'emancipation,' and the idea of an alien, western invasion and subversion of Algerian culture and society"—an association that persists to this day (MacMaster 106-07). MacMaster concludes that on the Algerian side, the "'traditional' family ... went hand-in-hand with a vigorous reinforcement of the patrilineal ideology that maintained women in their 'natural' role of mothers and daughters claustrated within the home" (110). Both the traditional family and the figure of the patriarch were crucial to the postwar reconstruction of the country, a nation that has been described as a society of "women without men" (qtd. in MacMaster 109).[7]

The dissolution of the Algerian household is clearly illustrated in the literary works of the period in that it is presented as "a nation devoid of both familial and political structure," where the mother figure is idealized, and the father figure is absent (Knight-Santos 82). By comparing novels written in French by Algerian female and male writers during and after the war, Miriam Cooke notices gendered nuances concerning the idealized mother, woman, and nation. In works written by female authors, Cooke maintains, the war as a topic is rather absent or not understood as liberating for women. Female writers are more worried about prioritizing topics forging equality between men and women. Conversely, Algerian male writers like Kateb Yacine, Mohamed Dib, and Malek Haddad "filled their works with ideal types" of women (*Women* 129). Sometimes women represent the land, the nation, the lost mother, the lost mother tongue, or they are represented as bearers of authentic values and traditions: "The hope of Algeria, Yacine tells the reader, lies in the women.... Again and again Dib evokes the sea/mother/woman who prepares the men for the fight they would not otherwise be able to undertake" (Cooke, "Deconstructing" 8, 9). The association between water and mother, Lucie Knight-Santos affirms, "highlights women's role as a genealogical source ... as the guarantors of regeneration ... as fertile providers of the future Algeria" (84). According to Cooke, Algerian male authors write "not so much out of admiration as of dread." (*Women* 129) She continues: "The reader senses the fear that women are gaining control and that the danger they pose to the social order, their *fitna* (an Arabic word that means both women's physical attraction and political unrest), is about to be unleashed" (*Women* 129).

Men's fear of a new woman also stands for male writers' deepest fear of losing the maternal figure. As Cooke states: "Already in 1962, Dib was warning Algerians that the mother, the most honored role for women within Algerian society, was going to be forgotten" (*Women* 135). The mother figure symbolizes the origin, affirms Héli Abdel-Jaouad, and the "Maghrebian authenticity" untouched by French modernity, the latter perceived "as the source of the son's alienation"

(24). Ahlam Mostaghanemi adds further nuances and sees how in some writings of Rachid Boudjedra, Mohamed Dib, Mouloud Feraoun, and Mouloud Mammeri, love, longing, and respect for the mother figure replace feelings of affection, esteem, and regard towards the wife. The admiration and adoration of the mother also constitute a way for Mostaghanemi to compensate for the lack of a paternal figure: "la mère se présente toujours comme le seul refuge contre l'hostilité du monde paternel de l'enfance et contre les 'déceptions' conjugales du monde adulte" ("the mother is always presented as the only refuge from both the hostility of the paternal world during childhood and the conjugal 'deceptions' of the adult world") (47).[8] Abdel-Jaouad additionally stresses that the father is perceived by the son-writer as the "anti-mother par excellence" and the "utopian kingdoms of mothers, as conceived by the son-writers, is founded essentially on the ruins of castrating Maghrebian patriarchy" (18, 15).

In sum, in relegating women back to their domestic role, the patriotic motherhood trope functions as a means to regaining control over women for both the Algerian nationalist and religious systems. This trope also serves to restore the family's structure ravaged by the war and also to reaffirm the role of women as reproducers of Algerian offspring. While historically the figure of the patriotic mother strengthens the patriarchal authority, the mother's representations in male literary accounts seem to challenge that authority. However, Abdel-Jaouad suggests that in the son literary accounts, the nostalgic love-bond construct between mothers and sons against the father eventually creates a "neopatriarchy" (16). As Abdel-Jaouad maintains:

> "Writing, whether it be on, about, or in the name of the mother, becomes for the son a mode of self-empowerment, which potentially becomes a will to power over others…. For many writers, the maternal serves mainly as a pretext for the psycho-analytical exploration of repressed sexuality" (17).

Abortion: Life or Death?

Reproduction and motherhood have long been central to nationalist, patriarchal, colonial, imperialist, and religious agendas. These subjects have, and continue to, stir up tensions and to fuel discord among women in general as well. Cooke links reproduction to motherhood and patrilineage: "*La soif* deals with the need for progeny, particularly male progeny. Jedla has a miscarriage and she is wrought with anxiety: will her husband divorce her?" ("Deconstructing" 4). Perhaps related to her feelings of inadequacy as child bearer, anxiety brings Jedla to attempt suicide. In Maghrebian society, Camille Lacoste-Dujardin asserts that women's fear of being unable to reproduce lies next to their fear of being unable to be a male producer. Both inabilities, she remarks, are punished in a similar way, repudiation: "une femme n'ayant eu que des filles peut être répudiée tout comme une femme stérile" ("a woman who had only daughters can be repudiated just like a sterile woman") (58). Lacoste-Dujardin shows how at the core of the patrilinear and patriarchal reproduction there is the Maghrebian mother of sons who eventually becomes the often bitter mother-in law, the antagonist of the son's wife. By taking pride only in male progeny, the son-reproducer unwittingly perpetuates a system in which she and her daughter are the primal victims. Lacoste-Dujardin remarks: "Pour une Maghrébine, être femme ce n'est pas vivre avec un homme, c'est posséder un fils" ("For a Maghrebian woman, to be a woman is not to live with a man, it is to possess a son") (144).

Abortion occupies a more contentious domain by standing at the intersection of women's sexuality, motherhood, and infanticide. Abortion, bell hooks affirms, "directly challenged the notion that a woman's reason for existence was to bear children. It called the nation's attention to the female body as no other issue could have done" (27). Historically, similarly to France, Austria, Belgium, Italy, Spain, Netherlands, Great Britain, Ireland, Canada, and the US entered "the twentieth century with laws that made abortion a crime with few exceptions.... It was not until the 1960s that the veil of public policymakers' ignorance of the status and effects of these inherited nineteenth century criminal codes was lifted" (McBride Stetson 271). In Algeria, in 1966, the Criminal Code sanctioned the prohibition of abortion with the only exception being of those performed as an indispensable measure to save the mother's life.[9] From a literary perspective, although in the twentieth century abortion became "a more established literary *topos*," there were few works written in French during this period that dared broach the subject (Jensen 160). Fewer still were the examples in which the experience was narrated from the point of view of a woman undergoing abortion. This silence, Jessica Jensen maintains, does not come as a surprise, "considering the social stigma and legal repression around the topic" (161). Louise Weiss's *Délivrance* (1936) and José-André Lacour's *Confession interdite* (1955) are two unique examples of abortion narratives "recounted from the woman's perspective" (Jensen 163). Often, Jensen remarks, abortion appears as only one of a series of misfortunes faced by the female character. This is what happens in *La Soif*: Jedla first endures a miscarriage, survives a suicide attempt, then decides to end her pregnancy, and eventually dies. According to Jensen, the direct use of the word "abortion" was also uncommon; metaphors, euphemisms, or paraphrases were used in its place in order to circumvent criticism and somewhat to deny its existence. In *La Soif*, Nadia defines this word as a horrible term, and she also confesses that every time she pronounces the word "abortion," she really feels an insurmountable disgust, as if Jedla is orchestrating an inconceivable and despicable act (148).

Indeed, Jedla is described as a traditional and proud Algerian woman with strong moral principles, who despises mundane life and appearances. She seems to incarnate the uncompromised rigour of a disappearing world, that is, a world based on religious and traditional values. Yet, between life and death, Jedla chooses death—first for herself when she attempts suicide and then for her offspring. In so doing, she opens a gendered breach in the facade of unquestioned national belonging. Jedla's abortion also questions the association between traditional women and maternity, and it challenges, to use Cooke's words, "the archetypes of the Mater Dolorosa, the Patriotic Mother, the Spartan Mother, or the Amazon" (*Women* 5). Djebar's radical criticism of Algerian patriarchy coming from within was too ahead of its time and too bold to be accurately read in 1957, in the midst of the war. Abdelkébir Khatibi was one of the first writers to underline in 1968 that Nadia's most crucial revolution was the exploration of her body (62). However, critics mostly focused on Nadia's excessive foreign and extravagant customs and on the futility of her life and sentimental issues. As a result, the character of Jedla was significantly overshadowed and the significance of the abortion, until recently, predominantly overlooked.

At the time of publication, three literary critics mentioned the abortion in their reviews of *La Soif*, only to include it along with other irreverent, audacious, and modern understandings of life. Catholic priest Jean Déjeux asserts: "Jalousie, adultère, désir de suicide et avortement, il faut tout dire parce-que c'est rentable" ("Jealousy, adultery, desire of suicide and abortion, everything needs to be said in order to turn a profit") (cited in Lançon 122). In 1967, François Raymond stated: "Il fallait avoir une certaine audace pour presenter ces portraits de jeunes filles parlant d'avortement, de jalousies et de rivalités amoureuses dans un monde où, dans ce domaine, rien n'avait encore changé" ("One had to be particularly audacious to present portraits of young women talking about abortion, jealousy and love rivalries in a world within which, in this field, nothing had really yet changed") (Lançon 136). Zimra notices that "*La Soif* had everything: beautiful females, well-off males, fast cars, lazy days at the beach, and, to top it off, a botched abortion resulting in death" ("Writing Woman" 68). Besides the differences in tone, perspective, and moral judgment, in the three quotes, abortion seems to be understood as an (extreme) manifestation of women's modern, adventurous, and unbridled sexual life, a life that, only for Zimra, comes with certain risks: death. However, the implied association between abortion, modernity, and Western societies is misleading and should not be interpreted as the author's opinion or personal stance on the matter. Historically, as Rasha Dabash and Farzaheh Roudi-Fahimi confirm: "Abortion is one of the oldest medical practices, evidence of which dates back to ancient Egypt, Greece, and Rome. Abortion techniques used by Egyptian pharaohs were documented in the ancient Ebers Papyrus (1550 B.C.)" (1). *La Soif* indirectly endorses the use of abortion in that it presents it as a rather common practice: abortion appears to be apprehended as an intervention that transcends religious, class, age, and other kinds of cultural boundaries. Nadia's half-sister Leila, for example—who married at a young age, according to traditional Muslim rituals, and is depicted as a rural woman who wears heavy and unsophisticated djellabas—is also the point of reference for women who want to terminate their pregnancies. Leila helps Jedla by referring her to a clinic in Algiers.

In the novel, abortion also seems to be one of the preferred subjects of women's gossip. Women's sexuality and sexual transgressions are prime fodder for women's gossip, and abortion seems to be viewed as the most common way of resolving the problems of both the unwanted children and possibly that of a lifetime of social stigma and ridicule. Because Nadia likes to shock Jedla and to draw attention to herself and to her sexual freedom, before Jedla learns that she is pregnant for the second time, Nadia intentionally tells her some scandalous and salacious stories that result in abortion. Nadia also likes to feed Jedla's hostility towards Western habits and to pretend that she supports Jedla's belief that immorality (i.e., pre- or extramarital sexuality) can only occur among women brought up with French values. To nurture Jedla's aversion, Nadia recounts the story of her female cousin, who decided to run away with a young man, a foreigner, "oui, un Européen!" (129) "yes, a European!" (*The Mischief* 88). To protect their social respectability, her cousin's parents would tell people that their daughter had gone on a retreat abroad. While Nadia takes pleasure in reinforcing Jedla's beliefs, the story is also intended to demonstrate the fissures of desire breaking the monolithic separation between national fronts. Nadia's sarcastic and superficial tone in the following passage is intended, this time, to mock the bigotry of domestic patriarchy. The protagonist is her religious aunt. Described as a pure and naïve woman who is always pregnant, after five pregnancies and five daughters, on the occasion of her sixth, her husband forces her to abort. Leila arranges everything for her in Algiers, but after the abortion, Nadia cynically comments: "il se trouva que, cette fois-là, l'enfant aurait été un garçon" (130) "as it turned out, the child, if it had lived, would have been a boy" (*The Mischief* 88).

Ruse, sarcasm, and a certain dose of Nadia's declared cruelty towards the envied and teased Jedla also invite the reader to look beyond the typical view of abortion as being associated with women's sexual freedom. Djebar's decision to have Jedla, the reserved Muslim woman, and not Nadia, the transgressive urban character, experience an abortion is a clear indicator that abortion, in this context, is meant to serve as more than a simple comment on the liberated sexual life of Westernized Algerian young women like Nadia. Why did Djebar choose the character of Jedla for such a controversial and radical act? As we learned, Jedla is morally austere and abhors French habits as well as the negative influence that its education had on Algerian women and men's mores. If abortion is not meant be interpreted as a result of Western influence or as an expression of female sexual freedom, then what is its significance within the novel? What does it mean, in 1957, for an Algerian woman writer to include abortion in her novel? These questions are paramount if we think about the different perception that readers could have according to the character's choice. Had the Westernized Nadia made the decision to interrupt her pregnancy, her act would coherently fit the characteristics attributed to her personality. Abortion would be interpreted as one among the many other narcissistic, irresponsible, and provocative actions and attitudes that Nadia carries out and embodies in order to mimic and to ridicule French manners.[10]

By selecting Jedla, who by extension represents Algeria in its traditions, ethics, and, above all, in its firm rejection of French colonialism, Djebar takes on a wider range of political issues. Consequently, this relatively minor event, which within the novel takes up only a few pages, now acquires a more prominent role, and it invites readers to transcend conventional associations such as French/modern/unethical vs. Algeria/tradition/values. Furthermore, as Judith Wilt remarks, for a woman, "the abortion decision is often about something other than abortion" (18). First of all, abortion symbolizes Jedla's deferred dream of believing in a future with her husband Ali. Lacoste-Dujardin thus understands the gendered collusion between the patriarchal system and the mothers' expectations:

> "dans l'idéologie de couple, une femme désire un enfant d'un homme, un enfant qui soit une création à deux, une œuvre qui consacre et prolonge le couple, dans l'idéologie patriarcale une femme attend ... un garçon qui appartiendra socialement à un homme, certes, mais qu'elle possédera affectivement" ("in the couple's ideology, a woman desires a child from a man, a child who is a creation of two, a piece of work that sanctions and extends the couple, in the patriarchal ideology, a woman expects ... a boy who will socially belong to a man, of course, but that she will possess emotionally") (144).

Abortion thus stands for both Jedla's unappropriated fertility within an unprepared (male) humanity and the impossible trust between women and men. By aborting, Jedla refuses Ali as a husband and a father and refuses the limited societal roles assigned to women like her. Nadia provocatively anticipates to Jedla what the future holds for traditional women like her, once they become integrated wives and mothers:

Pourvu qu'elles aient leur foyer, qu'elles puissent servir, obéir à leur époux, c'est tout ce qu'elles demandent...L'homme peut avoir quelque aventure au dehors, elles, elles sont respectées, cela leur suffit. Elles savent aussi qu'une fois vieilles, il prendra peut-être une autre épouse, une jeune vierge; elles ne sont pas jalouses. Elles sont calmes, sage, soumises. C'est peut-être elles qui ont raison. (145-46)

As long as women have a home of their own where they can serve and obey their husbands, they need ask nothing more. What if their husbands do have affairs on the outside? As long as their wifely position is respected, what does it matter? Of course they know that as they grow old, other and younger wives may take their place. But they're not jealous; they remain calm and submissive, and who's to say they haven't the right idea? (*The Mischief* 100)

Unexpectedly, Jedla's resolution to abort deeply changes Nadia who experiences for the first time a sense of ethical responsibility. In this sense, her friend's abortion also stands for Nadia's awareness of being a woman in a man's world—a sphere in which the seeds of misogyny are sown even among women. Describing herself, and often perceived by others, as a volatile, indolent, frivolous, uninhibited, and superficial young woman, after she learns that Jedla wants to interrupt her pregnancy, Nadia behaves as if she feels that abortion is intrinsically wrong. Before the abortion, she experiences a strong need to dissuade Jedla and says: "—As-tu pensé, dis-je d'une voix innocente, qu'un avortement est un crime? Tuer ainsi son enfant... " —Tu aurais peut-être mieux fait d'attendre Ali, de le voir...—Tu sais, c'est grave... Tu devrais encore réfléchir. Tu peux le regretter ensuite!" (148, 149). ("'Has it occurred to you,' I now asked with false ingenuousness, 'that abortion is a crime? To kill an unborn baby' ... 'Perhaps you should have waited to talk with Ali' ... 'it's a serious matter, you know. You ought to think it over. Someday you may be sorry'") (*The Mischief* 102). Then, the reader witnesses Nadia's increasingly judgmental tone regarding Jedla's choice. Once she and Jedla get to the clinic, Nadia feels disgust "à la pensée de la suivre là, pour cette besogne" (151) ["at the idea of following her there, for this need"].[11] The word "besogne" implies a moral judgment: It evokes the idea of individuality vs.

collectivity and also the tension between personal need and societal values. The word "need" belittles both women's inner and social struggles and the risks involved in abortion and suggests the association between abortion and selfishness. Finally, the word "need" echoes Simone de Beauvoir's 1949 essay *Le deuxième sexe* and some of her ethical battles concerning abortion and contraception. Although Beauvoir dedicates twelve pages to its discussion and advocates "for both legal abortion and freely available contraception, which would 'permit woman to freely assume her Maternities' (II:343)," she also emphasizes "the deep emotional and bodily wounds that having an abortion can inflict on women" (cited in Stone 123).[12]

The description of the clinic in which the abortion takes place allows Djebar to confront colonialism and modern French perceptions of aesthetic ideals—instituted in order to critique women's imperfections and perhaps illustrating what Orlando defines as "colonial capitalism" (*The Algerian New Novel* 89). In this kingdom of beauty salons and clinics, ruled by women with sharply calculating eyes, abortion is just one of the many procedures offered in which, "tout se réglait à coups de cisailles, d'éther. On n'y connaissait ni la tendresse, ni la haine, ni même le caprice, ou la faute—seulement des cas, des complexes et des remèdes décisifs: un avortement" (152) ("Tools were knives and scissors and anesthetics. They knew neither love nor hate, neither caprice nor sin. To them everything was a case or a client, calling for some drastic remedy—such as an abortion") (*The Mischief* 104). Once entering the modern aseptic institute, the unexpressive, impersonalized, and unemotional woman with makeup, who welcomes Nadia and Jedla is juxtaposed with Nadia's imagined old, toothless, dirty, and quasi-witch woman belonging to the old world. This image is not necessarily a nostalgic evocation of the good old days but rather a critique of French modernity as a constructed spectacle of flawless perfection that causes alienation and confusion about what is real and what is artificial, what is critical and what is futile. In so doing, the author also anticipates one of the most debated aspects of modernity, which is the advent of society as spectacle that Guy Debord would develop ten years later, in 1967, in the essay *La société du spectacle*. By contrasting the sterilized atmosphere of the allegedly recognized safe clinic with Jedla's agony after an imperfect abortion, Djebar links Jedla's death to the dysfunction of a French institution and accuses it of a crime.

Abortion, here, also speaks to women's alienation from themselves and to their existential need for (new) ethics and honesty. The idea of abortion as an impulsive solution that originates from self-hatred and self-punishment largely anticipates Adrienne Rich's association between violence and abortion. For Rich, abortion is, "a deep, desperate violence inflicted by a woman upon, first of all, herself" and violence done to women by society is the source of infanticidal, ultimately suicidal, rage (274). Furthermore, in *La Soif*, Nadia and Jedla's need for new ethics is stressed by their common thirst for truth. Expressed in the narrative by means of scrutiny, reflection, and internal monologues, the idea of discernment and cognition are at the core of the novel's structure. Beïda Chikhi interprets this novel as the starting point of Djebar's female character's intrusion into physical and above all mental spaces traditionally attributed to men. Orlando further speculates on the female articulation and expression of a psychological space and compares *La Soif* with Nathalie Sarraute's *Portrait d'un inconnu*. In both novels, Orlando comments, the protagonists "confront the torment of modern realities, living in a world that is unstable, temporal, and driven by fear of the other's influence on the authenticity of the Self"; the protagonists also share "an exploration of emotions and confrontations with others (*tropisms*) that contribute to the quest for knowledge of the Self" (*The Algerian New Novel* 85).

Nadia remembers, in the first person, the emotional tumult of that summer when she was twenty years old. Her internal analepsis takes the reader back to events that have already taken place but that the character is reflecting upon again. The internal focalization also brings the readers into Nadia's thoughts and grants them access to her internal monologues, at times ironic, that conflict with her external facade. At present, she revisits the intensity of those capricious desires, feelings, and actions from the distant calm of a supposedly happily integrated married woman, whose life conforms to societal expectations. While reconsidering the passionate turbulences of that summer, Nadia reexamines both her own emotions and those of the people around her, their secret motives, and their public behaviors. Nadia also scrutinizes how much Jedla manipulated her and her own role in the events leading up to Jedla's death. Nadia's analepsis thus exposes the gap between people's inner intentions and outer actions, the societal mask, as well as the entire range of exploitations and compromises that occur in relationships.

Jedla's self-examination happens in the background of the story and is explored through the lens of the omniscient Nadia. More fiercely than the protagonist, Jedla wants to know the truth and is willing to discern and to engage with a world ruled by fakeness, ruses, and power plays. This state of mind will tragically bring her to some sort of consciousness and self-awareness. Jedla will choose abortion after a period of honest, painful, and conflictual introspective reasoning that starts from her first encounter with Nadia, in the presence of Ali. Through the eyes of Nadia, the reader witnesses Jedla's physical deterioration that parallels her extenuating need to know the truth about her husband's moral integrity. When she gets pregnant, for a brief period she is propelled into a fantasy world of delusions in which her child will restore harmony and bring the couple back together. For Jedla, pregnancy is neither about becoming a mother nor about having a child; it is about having the chance to believe again in Ali's honesty. Her initial joy is quickly replaced by a self-destructive lucidity, an obsessive desire to know the truth: "je veux savoir. A cela seul je tiens" (147) ("I want to know what was due to happen without it. That's my only concern") (*The Mischief* 101).

It is only at the end of the story that Nadia's internal focalization gives readers a deep understanding of her dilemma and the opportunity, for the first time, to develop empathy for her and her situation. In the middle of the night, in her bed, while her husband sleeps, Nadia resumes reflecting upon Jedla and her death and trying to make sense of her present existential disillusionment and disquiet as a wife. At first, she feels guilty for having taken part in Jedla's demise, then, using discernment, Nadia progressively distinguishes her own remorse from what really troubles her: Jedla's self-deception, avoidance, escape, and flight from life for being unable to love herself and to escape societal oppression. Ultimately, Nadia discerns that what she is projecting onto her friend is her own self-deception and avoidance— that is, the fact that she has lied to herself in order to conform to society.[13] Some critics have been puzzled by the ending of the novel and have interpreted Nadia's final state of quietness and distance as a sign of submission and integration into the system. As Cooke argues: "Men have come between these two friends; they have destroyed not only their friendship but also their lives" (4). I argue that Nadia and Jedla's paths are processes of not only life disenchantment but also of lucidity and discernment that bring about and magnify women's solitude, disconnection, and alienation as partners, mothers, wives, and members of a community. Regardless of their conformity or opposition to the patriarchal system(s), as women, wives, and mothers who are looking for alternative spaces of expression, they confront an unresponsive male world that crushes their life's hopes and desires. Djebar seems to indicate that on both political sides, not only do firm patriarchal social restrictions isolate the female domestic world from politics, but also they suppress any form of affectionate bonds within the family and between parents and their progeny. Jedla's abortion thus emphasizes the reality of women's isolation and the failure of the concept of Algerian women's national assimilation. It breaches the nexus between womanhood and motherhood and consequently questions the possibility of a future nation built on distrust and self-hatred.

Endnotes

1. The year 1957, Christiane Chaulet Achour notices, is the year of the paras, General Massu, and the Battle of Algiers.
2. In France, Marie-Louise Giraud, a "faiseuse d'anges" ("angel maker") who helped women to abort, is decapitated in 1943 (Collectif IVP 17).
3. See https://www.diplomatie.gouv.fr/en/french-foreign-policy/human-rights/abolition-of-the-death-penalty/france-and-the-death-penalty/.
4. Between 1947 and 1980, Daniel Lançon reminds us that Algerian literature could count only four female authors, Taos Amrouche, Djamila Debèche, Assia Djebar, and Aïcha Lemsine. Amrouche's *Jacinthe noire* (1947) was the first female novel written in French (119).
5. Djebar's affirmation of *La Soif* as an "exercice de style" appears in Jean Déjeux 218 (qtd. in Orlando's *The Algerian New Novel* 91).
6. See *Ces voix* 87, 224.
7. The expression comes from Willy Jansen's study *Women Without Men: Gender and Marginality in an Algerian Town*.
8. Unless otherwise indicated, all translations are mine.
9. In 1976, the Public Health Code added to the exceptions the case of

abortion performed before fetal viability as an essential therapeutic measure to save the mother's life or to safeguard her seriously endangered health. In 1985, the Law on the Protection and Promotion of Public Health included an additional exception by also permitting abortion to be performed as an essential measure to preserve a woman's mental equilibrium when it is seriously jeopardized (Amnesty International). In all other circumstances, abortion "remains criminalized, with punishment of up to five years for doctors and two years for women and girls" (Amnesty International). Amnesty continues: "As a result, women and girls often resort to unsafe clandestine abortions, and are therefore at high risk of death and grave injury. Furthermore, the requirement of spousal consent for abortions creates barriers to accessing health services for all women and girls, and effectively denies access to safe abortion services for unmarried women and girls" (Amnesty International). Some exceptions had been made in Algeria during the 1990s' civil war for raped women, concessions that did not pass unobserved: "In April 1998, Algeria's Islamic Supreme Council was said to have issued a *fatwa* that shocked many in the Arab and Muslim world. The Council stated that abortions would be allowed for women raped during attacks by Islamic extremists, who used sexual assault as a weapon of war" (World Bank 14).

10. In 1958, during an interview, Djebar states: "j'ai effectivement voulu presenter la caricature de la jeune fille algerienne occidentalisée et qui s'identifie dans tout son comportement à la jeune fille française" ("I really wanted to present the caricature of the westernized Algerian young woman whose behavior completely identifies with the French young woman") (qtd. in Lançon 122).

11. My translation since Frenaye's version does not contain the word "besogne."

12. Jensen links de Beauvoir's work with the first national debates during the 1950s over the use of contraceptives, "leading to the formation of groups like 'La Maternité Heureuse' (which would later become the Mouvement français pour le Planning familial [MFPF]), providing the bodies in question with a voice and prompting additional open discussion on abortion" (44). Jansen continues: "Throughout this controversy, the woman's perspective which had been all too often silenced during these debates, emerged" (44).

13. This theme, the need for fidelity to the self before reaching out to the other, is at the core of Djebar's poetic, and it will find its most dramatic expression in her last work, *Nulle part dans la maison de mon père.*

Works Cited

Abdel-Jaouad, Hédi. "'Too Much in the Sun': Sons, Mothers, and Impossible Alliances in Francophone Maghrebian Writing." *Research in African Literatures*, vol. 27, no. 3, 1996, pp. 15-33.

Amnesty International Public Statement. "Algeria: Revise Draft Law On Health." *Amnesty International*, 2 June 2017, www.amnesty.org/en/documents/mde28/6390/2017/en/. Accessed Nov. 10 2021.

Beauvoir, Simone de. *Le Deuxième sexe.* Vol. 2, Folio, 1949.

Chaulet Achour, Christiane. "L'entrée En Écriture D'assia Djebar En 1957." *Diacritik*, 1 Dec. 2017, diacritik.com/2017/12/01/lentree-en-ecriture-dassia-djebar-en-1957/. Accessed Nov. 10 2021.

Chikhi, Beïda. *Assia Djebar: Histoires et fantaisies.* PUPS, 2007.

Collectif IVP. *Avorter: Histoires des luttes et des conditions d'avortement des années 1960 à aujourd'hui.* Tahin Party, 2008.

Cooke, Miriam. *Women and the War Story.* University of California Press, 1996.

Cooke, Miriam. "Deconstructing War Discourse: Women's Participation in the Algerian Revolution." Working Paper #187, *Women in International Development*, Michigan State University, East Lansing, MI, June 1989.

Dabash, Rasha and Farzaheh Roudi-Fahimi. "Abortion in the Middle East and North Africa." *Population Reference Bureau.* Sept. 2008, www.prb.org/resources/abortion-in-the-middle-east-and-north-africa/. Accessed Nov. 10 2021.

Debord, Guy. *La société du spectacle.* 3e ed, Gallimard, 1992.

Déjeux, Jean. *La Littérature Maghrébine.* Vol. 2., Centre culturel français, 1970.

Djebar, Assia. *Ces Voix qui m'assiègent...en marge de ma francophonie.* PUM, 1999.

Djebar, Assia. *Femmes d'Alger dans leur appartement.* Des femmes, 1980.

Djebar, Assia. *Nulle part dans la maison de mon père*. Paris: Fayard, 2007.

Djebar, Assia. *The Mischief*. Translated by Frances Frenaye, Simon & Schuster, 1958.

Djebar, Assia. *La Soif*. 1957. Barzakh, 2017.

France Diplomacy. "France and the Death Penalty. Abolition of the Death Penalty in France." 2 October 2018, www.diplomatie.gouv.fr/en/french-foreign-policy/human-rights/abolition-of-the-death-penalty/france-and-the-death-penalty/. Accessed Nov. 14 2021.

Helie-Lucas, Marie-Aimée. "Women, Nationalism, and Religion in the Algerian Liberation Struggle." *Opening the Gates: An Anthology of Arab Feminist Writing*, edited by Margot Badran and Miriam Cooke, Indiana University Press, 2004, pp. 105-114.

hooks, bell. *Feminism is for Everybody: Passionate Politics*. South End Press, 2000.

Jensen, Jessica R. *Hysterographies: Writings on Women's Reproductive Body Image in Contemporary French Fiction*. 2010. University of Pennsylvania, PhD Dissertation, repository.upenn.edu/edissertations/108/. Accessed 10 Nov. 2021.

Jansen, Willy. *Women Without Men: Gender and Marginality in an Algerian Town*. E.J. Brill, 1987.

Khatibi, Abdelkébir. *Le Roman maghrébin*. Maspéro, 1968.

Lacoste-Dujardin, Camille. *Des mères contre les femmes. Maternité et patriarcat au Maghreb*. La Découverte, 1985.

Laghouati, Sofiane. "Assia Djebar: Quand l'écriture est une route à ouvrir, un territoire entre les langues... Prolégomènes pour une 'diglossie littéraire.'" *Assia Djebar: Littérature et Transmission*, edited by Wolfgang Asholt, Mireille Calle-Gruber, and Dominique Combé, Presses Sorbonne Nouvelle, 2010, pp. 97-118.

Lançon, Daniel. "L'invention de l'auteur. Assia Djebar entre 1957 et 1969 ou l'Orient second en français." *Assia Djebar: Littérature et Transmission*, edited by Wolfgang Asholt, Mireille Calle-Gruber, and Dominique Combé, Presses Sorbonne Nouvelle, 2010, pp. 119-39.

Lazreg, Marnia. *Torture and the Twilight of Empire. From Algiers to Baghdad*. Princeton University Press, 2007.

Lazreg, Marnia. "Gender and Politics in Algeria: Unraveling the Religious Paradigm." *Signs*, vol. 15, no. 4, 1990, pp. 755-80.

MacMaster, Neil. "The Colonial 'Emancipation' of Algerian Women: The Marriage Law of 1959 and the Failure of Legislation on Women's Rights in the Post-Independence Era." *Stichproben: Wiener Zeitschrift für kritische Afrikastudien*, vol. 12, no. 7, 2007, pp. 61-90.

Marx-Scouras, Danielle. "Muffled Screams/Stifled Voices." *Yale French Studies*, vol. 82, 1993, pp. 172-82.

McBride Stetson, Dorothy, ed. *Abortion Politics, Women's Movements, and the Democratic State. A Comparative Study of State Feminism*. Oxford/New York: Oxford U P, 2001.

Mostaghanemi, Ahlam. *Algérie: femme et écritures*. L'Harmattan, 1985.

Orlando, Valérie. *The Algerian New Novel: The Poetics of a Modern Nation, 1950-1979*. The University of Virginia Press, 2017.

Orlando, Valérie. "*La Soif* d'Assia Djebar: pour un nouveau roman maghrébin." *El-Khitab*, vol. 16, 2013, pp. 137-46.

Rich, Adrienne. *Of Woman Born: Motherhood as Experience and Institution*. W.W. Norton Co., 1976.

Stone, Alison. "Beauvoir and the Ambiguities of Motherhood." *A Companion to Simone de Beauvoir*, edited by Laura Hengehold and Nancy Bauer, John Wiley & Sons, 2017, pp. 122-33.

Tooley, Michael. "Abortion and Infanticide." *Philosophy and Public Affairs*, vol. 2, no. 1, 1972, pp. 37-65.

Vince, Natalya. "Transgressing Boundaries: Gender, Race, Religion, and 'Françaises Musulmanes' during the Algerian War of Independence." *French Historical Studies*, vol. 33, no. 3, 2010, pp. 445-74.

Wilt, Judith. *Abortion, Choice, and Contemporary Fiction. The Armageddon of the Maternal Instinct*. The University of Chicago Press, 1990.

World Bank Report. "Fertility Decline in Algeria 1980–2006. A Case Study." *The World Bank*, May 2010, https://openknowledge.worldbank.org/bitstream/handle/10986/27492/630730WP0P10870geria0pub08023010web.pdf?sequence=1&isAllowed=y. Accessed Mar. 2018.

Woodhull, Winifred. *Transfigurations of the Maghreb: Feminism, Decolonization, and Literatures*. University of Minnesota Press, 1993.

Zimra, Clarisse. "Writing Woman: The Novels of Assia Djebar." *SubStance*, vol. 21, no. 3, 1992, pp. 68-84.

Zimra, Clarisse. "In Her Own Write: The Circular Structures of Linguistic Alienation in Assia Djebar's Early Novels." *Research in African Literatures*, vol. 11, no. 2, 1980, pp. 206-223.

Chapter 14

Image Shatterer: Delores Phillips's *The Darkest Child*

Trudier Harris

This chapter focuses on *The Darkest Child*, a novel that Delores Phillips published in 2004. Phillips lived until 2014, but she never published another book after that first novel. It is unclear why the novel disappeared rather quickly into the cracks of literary scholarly commentary, but more than a decade after its publication, there was still not a single scholarly article on it. Although I had received an "advance reader's copy" of the novel in March of 2003, I shelved it without reading it, and it languished in its assigned space for more than a decade. Then, during my summer reading in 2017, I pulled it off the shelf and finally read it. The profound impact it had upon me in its depiction of an African American mother and her relationship to her children led me to consider writing on the book. I therefore eagerly put forth a proposal for a chapter on it for *Mothers Who Kill*.[1] I also presented a paper on *The Darkest Child* at the Lost Southern Voices conference hosted at Georgia State University in March of 2018, and I have continued to explore what is a striking aberration in African American literary portrayal—that is, a mother who acts aggressively and violently against her own children.[2] Since these actions coincided so perfectly with the intent of *Mothers Who Kill*, I wanted to explore how an African American mother, in the deep South in the mid-twentieth century, turns her energy towards destroying her children emotionally, psychologically and then actually killing one of them. A close reading of this mother's actions in bas relief against a tradition of portrayals of mothers in African American literature could broaden conceptions of what we expect to see represented in certain literary texts. This unique portrayal, therefore, enriches scholarly commentary about a tradition of portrayal, a tradition of reading, and expectations when encountering both.

African American literature can be read as a primer of sorts for the mothers who make sacrifices for their children. From Harriet Jacobs's stowing away for seven years in her grandmother's attic in part to keep track of her children in *Incidents in the Life of a Slave Girl* (1861), to Zora Neale Hurston's Lucy Potts in *Jonah's Gourd Vine* (1934) "taking low" in order to protect her children, and to Lizzie's debasing herself in Dolen Perkins-Valdez's *Wench* (2010) to try to improve the lots of her enslaved son and daughter—African American literary mothers are mostly icons of self-sacrifice and models of workers who tolerate almost any kind of abuse for their children, whether that abuse comes from husbands and boyfriends or from their employers. Rare is the occasion that a literary mother puts her own interests above those of her children. Drug addiction can be one such occasion, as Sonia Sanchez depicts in her "Poem for Some Women"; a Black mother gives her seven-year-old daughter to a drug dealer to be sexually violated for a week in exchange for crack. Another occasion might showcase a mother who kills an offspring to prevent others from doing so, as Suzan-Lori Parks depicts a mother in *Fuckin' A* (2001), who kills her son to prevent his torture and mutilation by a mob that is chasing him. Arguably, temporary insanity might combine with a desire to save a child, as Toni Morrison's Sethe is under extreme duress when she kills her baby daughter in *Beloved* (1987).[3] It is fairly safe to posit, therefore, that the vast majority of African American literature is absent of mothers who willfully, intentionally, and without extenuating circumstances kill their children. Phillips's *The Darkest Child* offers a striking exception to that almost perfect generality.

Rozelle "Rosie" Quinn, the mother in *The Darkest Child*, is an aberration by whatever standard of measurement we use. African American women have historically and literarily used their incredible physical and moral strength for the benefit of their offspring. To portray a mother in African American literature who is impressively strong but who uses that strength against her own children is an abomination in the tradition. Phillips's characterization of Rosie is therefore not only shocking but remarkably distinct. This aberration may account, in part, for the lack of critical attention to the novel. Given the fact that, historically, the literature has been almost too straightforwardly connected to life, writing about Rosie Quinn might have seemed to confirm some of the sociological and pathological accusations that have been hurled at Black communities, especially that involving children born out of wedlock. In many ways, Rosie borders on the domineering, welfare-dependent, hypersexual Black female that has given so many pages to sociological rhetoric about dysfunctional Black families. My response to such possibilities is that the quality of writing and the power of the narrative outweigh its being cast aside for subject matter or character development that might seem stereotypical.

The lack of scholarship on the novel is especially surprising in light of the fact that it contains several components that usually command attention in African American literary studies. In other words, aside from its portrayal of Rosie, it fits into several expected categories of African American literary portraiture. First, to begin its potentially attractive features to scholars, it is set in the South, in Georgia, and it deals with a struggling mother and her children. Second, it reiterates the poverty that undergirds so many African American literary texts. Third, it deals with the rape of a Black woman by a group of Southern white men. Fourth, it highlights the sharp and intense segregation of Blacks and whites on Southern soil in the 1950s and 1960s. Fifth, it deals, in the tradition of Ernest J. Gaines's Jimmy in *The Autobiography of Miss Jane Pittman* (1971), with the struggle of a young Black man to get Black people registered to vote in the South. These very familiar factors pale, however, in comparison to the unexpected features of the text. It deals with a mother who segregates her own children according to their skin colour and values them accordingly, with the lighter ones, such as her favourite son, Sam, getting the most attention from her. Of the ten children she has borne out of wedlock, Rosie classifies them as "white," "Indian," and "Negro," depending on their pigmentation. Tangy Mae, the narrator of the novel, comments that Rosie "took pleasure in categorizing her children by race. Mushy, Harvey, Sam [who can literally pass for white], and Martha Jean were her white children. Tarabelle, Wallace, and Laura were Indians—Cherokee, no less. Edna and I were Negroes" (16).[4] Tangy Mae is the "darkest child"; her father is nicknamed "Crow" because of the darkness of his skin.

Set in a small town in Georgia between 1958 and 1961, the novel chronicles Rosie's interactions with and abusive domination of her children; Tangy Mae's desire to get an education instead of being forced to prostitute herself for decades (the novel moves from her ninth grade year through her graduation from high school); conflicts between local Blacks and whites; and local civil rights activity. The Quinn family is unique in its isolation from its neighbours, in its poverty, and in the "queendom" that Rosie has carved out for herself; Tangy Mae notes that Rosie, in one instance, "swept through the doorway of her castle and plopped down on her throne—the only bed in the house" (9). Their house stands "alone on a hill off Penyon Road, about half a mile outside the city limits. It was old, crippled, and diseased—an emblem of poverty and neglect" (7). Light that filters in through the walls of the house is their "only source of illumination until dusk, when [Tangy Mae and her siblings] were allowed to light the kerosene lamps" (9). The absence of electricity and cracks in the walls are punctuated with a leaky roof through which rainwater falls onto Rosie's offspring as they sleep on pallets throughout the dilapidated house. Cooking involves heating a wood stove; food is often a repetition of grits, and taking baths means heating water on that stove. (Baths are a luxury that Rosie orders her children to prepare for her on several occasions.) The recipient of largesse from church members and Goodwill, Rosie nonetheless resists any designation that she is poor, even as she simultaneously lambasts other Blacks who are judged to be poor: "The one thang we ain't is po', and the one thang we ain't never gon' be is niggers" (78), she asserts in response to her friend Pearl's comment that instead of repairing the leaky roof, the landlord will "just rinse y'all out and rent to the next po' niggers come along" (78). The mixture of acute poverty, combined with parental abuse and domination, does not portend well for the Quinn family. There is an aura of sanction that surrounds Rosie, from her friend Pearl's explicit negative commentary on her actions as a mother, to her children's recognition that they are at war with their own mother, to the neighbours gossiping about Rosie, and to Rosie's having a child by Miss Pearl's husband and then giving that child to the father. There is no applause or approval, from anyone, of her actions as a mother.

This background provides context, but certainly not excuse, when Rosie willingly, knowingly, calmly, and consciably kills her five-month-old daughter by dropping her off the back porch of that hill-perched house and down into the rocky gully behind it. There is no legitimate extenuating circumstance for Rosie's action. This is not a morally inspired Sethe who kills Beloved because she wants to prevent her from enduring a life of slavery. This is a mother who kills her daughter because the child's crying annoys her. Once the child is born, Rosie shows no interest in it; in fact, she turns it over to Martha Jean, her mute daughter, to whom she refers as "the dummy," to raise, a situation that consistently disturbs Tarabelle, who comments that it is not natural for a mother never to touch or interact with her child: "Martha Jean shouldn't have to take care of her. Mama ain't doing nothing all day 'cept laying up on her ass" (121). On the occasion of the infanticide, when Martha Jean is outside playing jump rope with Tangy Mae and their younger sister Edna, and the baby starts to cry, Rosie simply drops it into the gully to stifle the noise. The moral imperative that usually guides so many African American women and female characters is totally absent in Rosie Quinn. Her primary motivation is self-satisfaction and the money that temporarily brings bliss, so she will do anything for her pleasure (including killing an annoying, crying child) and to get the financial resources that she needs, including prostituting herself and her adolescent daughters. Her infanticide, therefore, must be placed in the context of the thoroughgoing unusualness in Rosie's character. Rosie's personality begins with an absence of caring, an uninterrupted self-centeredness. Rosie's own needs and desires always come first. When Rosie arrives from work, or just when she demands it, her daughters must heat water and fill the portable tub in which she takes leisurely baths. They must do the cooking. They must do the caretaking for their younger siblings. Tangy Mae asserts that Rosie wages war against her own children, but they cannot wage war in return. After Rosie attacks one of her children, Tangy Mae comments as she and her siblings help the injured child: "We work as a silent, defeated army, beaten down by our mother, tending our wounded. We do not retaliate, for our victory is inconceivable" (15).

    The infanticide must also be read against the backdrop of the physical violence that Rosie perpetrates constantly against her children, which represents a lack of caring that probably shocks most readers. Rosie uses violence to convey lessons to her children. The monstrosity of what she does is almost belied by the casualness with which she accomplishes her purposes. To ensure that her children will not touch things that belong to her, especially a metal box into which she secrets items, she gathers them around her to illustrate the point. When the mute Martha Jean reaches for the box that her mother holds out to her, Rosie responds in this manner:

> *She seizes Martha Jean's wrist with one hand, but her other hand is wrapped into a fist of thunder that flashes a spike of lightning through the flickering shadows. The ice pick pierces the flesh of my sister's hand and stands there, the handle sways back and forth as if it might fall, but we can all see that it is not going to fall. It is embedded in Martha Jean's hand.*
>
> *Mama grips the handle, and deliberately rips flesh as she wrenches the ice pick from the tiny, trembling hand that rises with the motion. A dark crimson oozes from the wound and begins to spread across the skin and down onto the paper bouquet that has fallen to the floor....*

In less than five minutes, our mother had taught us to never touch her metal box, and the true meaning of fear. (14, 15—italics in original)

The seven-year-old Martha Jean gets helping attention from her siblings as Rosie very casually exits the room. Tangy Mae is the recipient of an equally memorable lesson. When she runs from a group of bullying girls calling her "tar baby," Rosie allows Tarabelle and Martha Jean to rescue Tangy Mae, then she teaches her not to run.

> "You a Quinn, baby," she says softly. "We don't run from nobody. Nobody! Do you understand that?" ... "I'm gon make sho' you understand it," she says, loosening her grip on my thighs. "Hand me that poker and hold her feet, Tarabelle."
>
> *Tarabelle clamps down on my feet, immobilizing me. There is no time to cry out as my mother brings the searing fire iron down onto my leg. I swoon from the pain, and my mother's voice trails me as I enter into darkness that is death and float deeper still into Hell.* "I done branded you a Quinn, girl. Don't you ever run from nobody else long as you live." (52)

Unapologetic about her abuse, Rose only comments the next day that it would not have hurt so badly if Tangy Mae had kept still during that branding. Any expectation that readers may have that Rosie would be verbally apologetic comes to naught. Her belief in the absolute rightness of the stances she takes is in sharp contrast to any possible reader disapproval of her violence or any possible reader hope that she will digress from her destructive path and begin to show some signs of caring for her children. She fails to do so as she forces her young daughters into prostitution and beats them with whatever objects might be handy, from belts to ironing cords. Her blatant cruelty may also lead readers to wonder how the text could possibly come to any healthy resolution. Although these actions may suggest that Rosie is somewhat crazed and is perhaps capable of almost anything, it is nonetheless shocking when she turns her very casual ire against Judy, her five-month-old daughter and the last of the children she will be able to bear. The shock comes in part from what readers bring to the text. If they are readers of African American literature, then they are aware of the tradition that mothers help their children more than they harm them. If they are other readers, then they might be shocked not only by a mother's killing a child but also by the frivolous motivation for such an action as well as by the great gap between violence and the serenity with which the violence is carried out.

The fateful occasion of Judy's death brings together Rosie's violent tendencies, her trickster-lying ability, her lack of remorse, and her manipulation of her children as well as the authorities in her small town. The incident occurs about halfway through the text. As Martha Jean and Tangy Mae are twirling rope for their sister Edna to jump, Martha Jean senses disaster. Tangy Mae records:

> I saw her head lift and tilt slightly as if she'd heard something, then the rope flew from her hand and she cut loose the most bloodcurdling wail. She began to run for the house. My gaze followed her. She had seen Judy, whimpering in our mother's grip.
>
> Mama stood at the edge of the porch dangling our baby sister over the side by one arm. As Martha Jean rushed toward them, Mama swung out once, twice ...
>
> With my hands to my throat, I waited for a third swing that never came. Mama, staring blankly into space, opened her hand and

> released Judy. I saw my baby sister sail through the air, flipping and jerking, as she began a descent that took her over the rocky incline and down into the gully.
>
> If there was a sound of impact, I did not hear it over Martha Jean's wails. She teetered for a moment between the bottom step and the yard, then she ran beneath the porch, between the poles that supported the house. Her feet left the ground and she dived down the incline as she raced against death to be the first to reach her baby.
>
> I tried to move, but I could not. I stood there staring at the space where my sisters had disappeared until finally Martha Jean's head came into view. She crawled out of the gully with Judy's lifeless form cradled in one arm, then she sat on the bank and began to rock back and forth. There was no wailing now, only the rustle of leaves as the wind sang through the trees behind the house, a soft mournful hymn.
>
> Mama peered down from the porch. At some point she had lit a cigarette, and smoke, barely visible, rose toward the porch ceiling and seemed to settle as a halo above her head. (ellipses in original 175-76)

What is most striking in this description is the calm and detached way in which Rosie kills her baby daughter, highlighted even more so by her lighting of a cigarette (the halo from which provides an almost ironic angelic glow). There is no remorse here, which accentuates again the amorality that governs Rosie's character. She certainly exhibits emotion after Judy's death, but whether she has a conscience is highly debatable. Her actions make clear yet again how her character undermines any expectations readers may have for good mothering. In that blunting of expectations, Rosie is a criminal who gets away with killing her child and succeeds not only in getting authorities to believe that Judy's murder was an accident but in leading Tangy Mae to almost question what she has seen with her own eyes.

Rosie shows no remorse for the remainder of the text; instead, emotional detachment reigns, which leads readers again to witness a mother whose crimes against her children are all the more outrageous because the indiscretions she believes the children have committed are so small. Judy's cries had annoyed Rosie, and Martha Jean had not been a few steps away to protect the child that had been forced upon her. So Rosie kills, deliberately and detachedly. And she moves from that murderous act to lying about and making excuses for what she has done. She tells Pearl's husband Frank that "the baby fell off the porch" (176). She tells the sheriff that she does not "really know" (178) what happened and that she was playing with the baby "and she musta kicked or something 'cause the next thing I knew she was falling. Wadn't nothing I could do" (178). Rosie's lies carry the day, as neither Martha Jean nor Tangy Mae is strong enough to contradict Rosie's version of the story—although both of them were eyewitnesses to the sequence of events. Once Martha Jean can be convinced to release her dead sister's body, which she has held for hours, Velman takes Martha Jean away from Rosie's house (which will result in violence later when an unrepentant Rosie insists that Martha Jean return home; fortunately, that return is only temporary). Even more egregious in Rosie's behaviour is that there is absolutely no sign of mourning and that she refuses to allow Judy's name to be spoken in the house following the infanticide. Such calculated responses scream loudly that Judy's death was not remotely the accident that Rosie tries to convince the sheriff that it is. Indeed, Rosie continues cunningly on her domineering, dehumanizing ways. For example, in anticipation of her daughter Laura's first school day, Rosie sends Tangy Mae to town to steal a dress for Laura to wear: "She told me to go into town and slip a nice dress from a rack for Laura's first day of school" (187-88). She forces Tarabelle to go on a "run" with her (to the "the farmhouse") on her seventeenth birthday, and she solicits Pearl to induce abortions on two separate occasions when Tarabelle gets pregnant from some of her many sexual encounters (223-24, 256). It is also revealed that at an earlier point in their lives, Rosie beat Mushy for a week and tied her to a rail when she ran away from home (290). Rosie tries to put out a cigarette on Tangy Mae's thigh (295), and she and Tarabelle get into a horrible fight when Tarabelle refuses to be beaten yet again (298-99). When Rosie is unwilling to dirty her hands in beatings, she allows one of her costumers to do so. Although Tangy Mae resists going to "the farmhouse," she is eventually forced there, which leads Rosie to report to one of her regular customers, the racist white Chadlow, how Tangy Mae has been "giving her a rough time," is "lazy," "won't help her out at the house," is being "disrespectful, backtalking," and that she does not want Chadlow to touch her. Chadlow, whose only interest in Black people is to keep them oppressed, resolves to "straighten ... out" Tangy Mae. He attempts to do so in a brutally vicious way. Forcing her facedown into a mattress, he beats her mercilessly.

> It was pure rawhide that cut into my backside, and Chadlow brandished the weapon with expertise. Someone downstairs must have heard the whirr, hiss, crack of the strap as it struck my defenseless body, but if they heard, no one came to investigate. I closed my eyes, twitched and moaned with each excruciating blow, dug my toes into the mattress, and tried to fade away. An inferno roared through my arms, legs, buttocks and back.
>
> After what seemed an eternity, Chadlow ended the beating. (332)

What mother, any sane reader would ask, would initiate and sanction such behaviour towards her teenage daughter?

It would be easy, with its numerous deviations from a tradition in the portrayal of Rosie, to claim that the novel represents a character suffering from mental illness. I resist that interpretation. Nevertheless, it does occur to Tangy Mae. She thinks there must be something "terribly wrong" (15) with Rosie when she stabs Martha Jean with the ice pick, and after Judy's death, Tangy Mae reports several times that Rosie is picking at invisible bugs around her face and indeed sometimes claws blood. We also learn late in the novel that the metal box for which Martha Jean had to receive such a horrible injury contains locks of hair from all of Rosie's children; Rosie saves the hair as a "magical" way of keeping her children tied to and owing loyalty exclusively to her. And there is one memorable occasion on which Rosie asserts that Satan has come into the house through Judy and must be exorcized (71-72). These aberrations in behaviour seem to be the norm for Rosie; indeed, there is only one occasion in the text during which readers see a slightly different Rosie. Tangy Mae remembers an occasion when Rosie was tender with her during an illness.

> Once, when I was very young, I had a high fever and a chest that was tight with congestion. My mother had lifted me from the

floor and carried me to her bed. For the duration of my infirmity, her delicate hands had dampened my fevered brow with a cool cloth, stroked my lips with ice chips, and wet my palate with the delicious juice of a peppermint-flavored orange. She had curled on her bed beside me, attentive to my every stir and groan. She had warmed me in the mingled scents of camphor and talcum power, then holding my small hand in hers, she had said "You gon be awright, baby. Mama's here."

That was the mother that faded in and out of my memory as I reeled in and out of consciousness. The more I tried to hold onto her, the more my head throbbed. Finally, I had to let her go. (249)

 This memory of Rosie occurs while Tangy Mae is recovering from a beating that Rosie gave her by slashing her about the head with a belt. This sweet image of a once attentive Rosie, however, is one that none of Tangy Mae's siblings corroborates.
 Even when Rosie ends up at the close of the narrative in a seemingly legitimately diagnosed mental debilitation, that is long after the actions that she carries out during most of the text. It is also a direct result of the trouble that her "white" son Sam gets into and her exceptional maternal concern about him as well as because she was on the scene when the murderous Chadlow was killed and believes a "ghost" killed him (really it was Crow—as payback to Chadlow's beating Tangy Mae). To label Rosie insane earlier on would simply be to excuse her actions, and excuse will not suffice to explain her character. Instead, the text requires a long hard look at what is possible in the creation of a character who does not adhere to any preconceived or tradition-bound expectations. As Toni Morrison argues about creating characters who go beyond what some readers consider possible, life is large enough to accommodate those deviant or unusual characters. So too with Rosie Quinn. Phillips challenges readers to face the fact that not all mothers in African American life and literature are models of respectability, religious fervour, or personal or Christian-based codes of ethics. Rosie is out for herself, and she will step on anyone who stands in her way, especially those to whom she gave birth. The only sad part about her actions is that the stakes for her cruelty are so small. Ordering her daughter to steal a dress is not a life-threatening event. Paying her rent

is small in comparison to prostituting her daughters and forcing them to have abortions when those encounters result in pregnancies. Selling her mute daughter for a beaten-up old car is not the equivalent of winning a million-dollar lottery. Choices Rosie makes concerning her children are more about control and her ability to use them as chess pieces than they are about the value of some of the exchanges (although certainly getting rent money is important). Bartering with Velman for Martha Jean is to show Velman that although Martha Jean might be old enough to court and get married, she can do so only if Rosie assents. Rosie might refrain from taking the mute Martha Jean to the farm for prostitution, but she beats her without mercy and controls her fate just as assuredly as she controls that of her other children.

The only time Rosie seems to regret an action—and the one that could possibly have contributed to her destabilization at the end of the text—is her joining the unrelentingly racist Chadlow in the events surrounding the lynching of Junior, a civil rights crusader. Junior is lynched about a third of the way through the text. Much, much later, Rosie confesses her involvement in that event to Pearl.

"Rosie, how you know Chadlow killed Junior?" Miss Pearl asked.

Mama seemed barely able to get the words out. "I was wit' him when he done it," she whispered. "He beat Junior wit' a crowbar 'til Junior was all broke up in pieces on the ground, but he wadn't dead. Chadlow coulda stopped. He coulda stopped, Pearl, but he wouldn't. He made me help him hang Junior from that tree. I didn't wanna do it, I swear I didn't. Junior was begging me to help him. 'Help me, Miss Rosie. Please, Miss Rosie, don't let him kill me.' But Chadlow had done made up his mind, and wadn't nothing I could do." (354)

Rosie claims innocence and ineffectualness here, just as she did with Judy. Still, the trauma with Junior and Chadlow is noteworthily outside of Rosie's immediate family. Not a single member of Rosie's family is able to inspire change in Rosie. Her feeble claims that she treats them harshly in order to keep them with her backfires constantly; her oldest daughter, Mushy, leaves, her son Harvey gets married to escape his mother, her youngest son Wallace chooses to live with his grandmother, and Tangy Mae finally escapes with one of the younger children at the end of the narrative. Rosie's style of mothering is a formula for disaster, but it is nonetheless one that broadens—in significant ways—our perceptions of who African American literary mothers are and what they should or can be.

A question lingers in the consideration of sanity—or lack thereof—in Rosie's treatment of her children. In what ways does Rosie benefit from killing Judy? Immediately and most superficially, she stops the baby's annoying crying, which relaxes her, as is evidenced by her smoking a cigarette moments afterwards. She also benefits by being recentred in her community as well as within her family. Earlier, Rosie has been the subject of community gossip, as one of her friends reports to Tangy Mae: "My mama say half the men in Triacy County pay yo' mama's rent. She say Miss Rosie do nasty, filthy animal things wit' men, and they give her money to do it" (115). Now, those same folks as Tangy Mae's friend Mattie's mother can feel sympathetic towards a mother who has not only lost a child but a baby. From this perspective, killing Judy thus becomes another one of Rosie's trickster moves—one that gains her social currency among her neighbours as well as among the men, including Chadlow and the sheriff, whose opinions she values. Equally important, the infanticide solidifies her unassailable control of her family, as the two of her children—Tangy Mae and Martha Jean—who witnessed the killing are too intimidated to say anything. As Tangy Mae has used war imagery earlier, so it is relevant here. Rosie has won a significant battle for continuing psychological control and all indications at this point are that she will win the war.

A master manipulator, Rosie uses tears to gain the social currency mentioned above, which also adds to her role as trickster. Just as Brer Rabbit cries out to be thrown into the briar patch because he knows that will bring his release from captivity from the other animals from whom he has stolen water, so Rosie cries because she anticipates the response it will bring from those around her. Most cultural norms suggest that a mother is expected to cry upon the death of a child, so Rosie cries, and the boon of sympathy from her neighbours envelops her. Having witnessed her various manipulations throughout the text, however, including when she pretends to be dying at the beginning, and when she cons church members into supplying food for her family, readers know that Rosie's displays of emotion cannot be trusted. They are only surface deep, for Rosie can switch them on and off like the proverbial faucet. Tears in this instance thus become another layering of benefit in that they enrich the effort to gain sympathy and excuse for the brutal act Rosie has just committed against her own daughter. By claiming that she has swung all her children, as she did Judy, and never dropped one before and by collapsing into a ball of tears, Rosie evokes this response from the sheriff: "Softening in the face of my mother's assumed anguish, the sheriff said, 'These things happen sometimes and only God knows why'" (179). Rosie watches the crowd surrounding Martha Jean and Judy and gives "a short cry, swoon[s], and [falls] into the sheriff's arms" (179). Performance. It is a good one from Rosie, whom Tangy Mae judges to be "convincing" and who describes her mother's condition as "assumed anguish." Having dealt with Rosie for years and apparently not having proven to be astute judges of her character, the persons who count in this scenario—the sheriff and Chadlow—have little defense against Rosie's tears and fainting spell. Rosie succeeds in not being charged with a crime, indeed in not even going to jail. She has tricked, wiggled, cried, and fainted herself into a position where she literally gets away with murder.

We might also view killing Judy as a calculated act of revenge against the body that has caused Rosie not to be able to produce more little bodies. Although she might misuse her children, there is apparently some kind of perverse pleasure—or power—for Rosie in actually giving birth to them. Judy's birth leaves her barren: "It broke something inside me they can't fix. Had to take it out. Took everything out, said I couldn't have no mo', and all I got was a darkie" (72). Rosie therefore harbours an anger from two sources: her inability to have more children and her disappointment that the last one, the last memory she will ever have of children issuing from her womb, is "a darkie," as dark as Tangy Mae, she tells her daughter Mushy. Innocent little Judy is thus surrounded by a perfect storm of emotions—one that causes her mother to reject her and pass her on to Martha Jean and one that is shrouded in the colourphobia issues that define Rosie and her relationships to her children. A pigmentocracy reigns throughout the text, and Judy ends up being on the lower scale of value in that hierarchy. To get a sense of how much colour matters to Rosie, consider Crow's account of his proposal to and rejection by Rosie: "She said, 'Crow, I can't marry a man dark as you. I just can't do it.' That's all the reason she ever gave…. She kinda stuck on that color thang, you know? I was willing to take them babies she had and give 'em a home, but all yo' mama could see was color" (164). Her aversion to darker skin tones, combined with the loss of her womb, could easily combine to lead Rosie to kill Judy. However, Rosie's action would still not fit into a morally inflected infanticide comparable to that of Sethe Suggs's killing Beloved.

By creating Rosie, Delores Phillips shatters one of the most lingering taboos inherent in African American literature. For centuries, African American writers kept Black mothers to a prescribed script. Just as lesbianism and homosexuality were mostly taboo in early versions of the literature, so were Black women who were out of the church and not committed to their children. Think of how James Baldwin depicts Esther in *Go Tell It on the Mountain* (1953). She is the unmarried, sexually active, and always available scarlet woman who tempts Gabriel, the reformed, married preacher. Out of the church and out of the sanctity of marriage, Esther is an expendable female character, one for whom few other characters—except perhaps Gabriel's wife, Deborah—and few readers would feel a great deal of sympathy. In contrast, church-bound Elizabeth, wife of Gabriel and mother to his children, provides the model of longsuffering that stays comfortably within the parameters of the sacred presentation of African American female characters, especially mothers. Return as well to such depictions as Mama Lena Younger in Lorraine Hansberry's *A Raisin in the Sun* or Baby Suggs in Toni Morrison's *Beloved* (1987) or even Lizzie in Dolen Perkins-Valdez's *Wench* (2010). An enslaved woman, Lizzie endures all for her children and for the possibility that her lover/master will set them free. Lizzie and the other literary mothers sacrifice for their children; they do not sacrifice their children. And nor in the case of Judy, it might be argued, does Rosie sacrifice her baby daughter. She simply kills her.

To ensure reader sympathy for self-sacrificing literary mothers, authors usually portray these Black women as less than beautiful. Even Lizzie wonders why her master Drayle has selected her from among the enslaved women, given the fact that she is dark skinned and has an unsightly mole near her nose. Hansberry paints Mama Lena as matriarchal and longsuffering, certainly not a woman to inspire romance. Similarly, Baby Suggs is longsuffering, aged, disabled, and not considered the least bit beautiful. The beauty of all these women is in their actions, not in their bodies. By sharp contrast, Rosie Quinn is gorgeous. The product of her mother's rape by several white men, she has the physical features of the despised race that are nonetheless valued in her own community. Equally noteworthy, she, unlike the Mama Lenas of African American literature, is a sexual being. The lack of sexuality in the portrayals of African American female mothers for the majority of the literature's history might have led readers to wonder how the women came to be mothers. Prevailing ideas about representation mostly precluded allusions to or representations of sexual activity. Rosie shatters that stereotype. Her body plays a crucial role in everything she does. Indeed, it is arguably her primary asset. This combination of beauty and sexuality in a woman whose actions consistently shatter expectations moves the portrayal of African American female character into a different realm of imagination.

Since Phillips's book was published in 2004, and since it clearly has not earned an impressive readership, we cannot measure its impact upon any particular African American writer. Nor is there evidence of any African American writer following a parallel path in shattering expectations about Black female representation. Nonetheless, I believe that this earth-shattering portrayal of a Black female character and mother will eventually inspire other writers to consider stepping outside expectations in fiction and doing what playwright Katori Hall did in drama with her presentation of Martin Luther King Jr., in *The Mountaintop* (2011). Hall refused to be bound by the history, the mythology, or the heroic legacy surrounding King. Instead, she waded into unchartered waters and painted a flawed King, one who is vain, flirtatious, a liar, self-serving, egotistical, and as concerned about the sizes of crowds attending his speeches as about the messages he delivers. The sky did not fall because Katori Hall viewed King in this light. Neither will it fall when readership of *The Darkest Child* increases and when writers accept the text as the prototype for something that could transform future literary representations of African American mothers.

Endnotes

1. Since that time, novelist Tayari Jones provided an introduction to the 2017 republication of the novel.
2. Lost Southern Voices is an annual conference hosted by Georgia State University that is designed specifically to re-situate into literary conversations writers who have not received significant critical attention.
3. See Sonia Sanchez, "Poem for Some Women," in *Wounded in the House of a Friend* (New York: Boston: Beacon, 1995), pp. 71-74, Suzan-Lori Parks, *The Red Letter Plays* (Theatre Communications Group, 2001), and Toni Morrison, *Beloved* (Knopf, 1987).
4. Delores Phillips, *The Darkest Child* (2004; Rpt. Soho, 2017), p. 16. Introduction by Tayari Jones. I will indicate additional references to this source in parentheses in the text.

Works Cited

Angelou, Maya. *I Know Why the Caged Bird Sings*. Random House, 1969.

Baldwin, James. *Go Tell It on the Mountain*. Dell, 1953.

Gaines, Ernest J. *The Autobiography of Miss Jane Pittman*. Dial, 1971.

Hall, Katori. *The Mountaintop*. Methuen Drama, 2011.

Hansberry, Lorraine. *A Raisin in the Sun*. Random House, 1959.

Hughes, Langston, and Arna Bontemps, eds. *The Book of Negro Folklore*. Dodd, Mead & Company, 1958.

Hurston, Zora Neale. *Jonah's Gourd Vine*. J. B. Lippincott, 1934.

Jacobs, Harriet. *Incidents in the Life of a Slave Girl*. 1861; Rpt. Harvard University Press, 1987.

Morrison, Toni. *Beloved*. Knopf, 1987.

Parks, Suzan-Lori. *The Red Letter Plays*. Theatre Communications Group, 2001.

Perkins-Valdez, Dolen. *Wench*. HarperCollins, 2010.

Phillips, Delores. *The Darkest Child*. 2004; Rpt. Soho, 2017.

Sanchez, Sonia. *Wounded in the House of a Friend*. Boston: Beacon, 1995.

Wright, Richard. *Black Boy*. Harper and Row, 1945.

Wright, Sarah E. *This Child's Gonna Live*. Dell, 1969.

Chapter 15

Smother Love: Maternal Filicide in Veronique Olmi's *Beside the Sea*

Amy B. Hagenrater-Gooding

Introduction

In "Mythical Mothers and Dichotomies of Good and Evil," Deborah Connolly observes that women's mothering is often depicted in polarized ways. Specifically, she states that images "of the virtuous caring mother and the evil, neglectful one are carefully maintained in the public imagination and in public policies" (265). Depictions of maternal roles, be it through literature or news stories, further reinforce how these social scripts are dominant in creating the "good mother" or "bad mother" that prevails in our socially constructed understanding of mothering. Fictional narratives are often a good (relatively safe) place to explore this dichotomization because they do not evoke the outrage prompted by real cases. French author Veronique Olmi's 2001 work *Beside the Sea* examines the script of what a mother should do against what a mother actually does, including issues related to agency and maternal impotence. Although fictional narratives give us this space for hypothetical contemplation, Olmi found inspiration from real life— "by four lines I read in the newspaper: a mother killed both her children after taking them to the fair and buying them some chips" (qtd. in Bidisha). The novel tells, essentially, this story. It is one woman's attempt to create a happy memory before she ushers her children to their death. Our understanding of her comes through snippets of events, reflections of memories, and questions juxtaposed within the actual happening of the narrative: the trip to the sea. Tackling issues of anger, depression, and alienation, Olmi uses the protagonist in her work as a way to dissect the multilayered complexity of a mother who kills and of a woman who is rarely just one thing—be it a mother, an individual, or, more pointedly, even a murderer. These murderous mothers are often labelled monstrous, yet in Olmi's work, the protagonist attempts to exert agency and control in her life, and the lives of her children, even if it comes at the cost of subverting those very same lives she, as mother, is charged with protecting.

Because of the uncomfortable nature of the narrative, Adrianne Hunter, the translator for the novel, endured rejections for four years after she finished the translation she completed on her own initiative, solely because of her passion for the story. She notes: "It apportions no blame. It gets right inside the head of someone who does the unthinkable, and you come out of it sympathising with her, rather than hating her. It may not be an evil act; it may be an act of desperation or a misguided act of love" (qtd. in Bidisha). It was only after linking up with Meike Ziervogel of Peirene Press that the book was given an English-speaking audience, nine years after its original French release. Of the text, Ziervogel says, "The book had given me the right to contemplate an aspect of motherhood that society wishes to ignore. The mother in the book is not a monster, nor are her children. She kills them out of love, because she is incapable of realising that her children's reality is a different one from her own. Our society assumes that maternal love is wholly positive, that as long as a mother loves her children, she will do them no harm" (qtd. in Bidisha). This story, rooted in truth, is one that needs to be told. In Olmi's work, readers are introduced to a single mother who has the laudable intention to create a perfect day for her two boys. Hearkening back to her own childhood memories, albeit the few memories that stand out as pleasant, she sets out to give to her children a sliver of happiness. As the novel progresses, readers see her history unfold. Her present—the day-to-day concern with keeping the children fed, dividing up money to feed and shelter them, and managing their endless wants and requests—is more telling. This chapter explores several tensions in the work and asks the following questions. Which aspect of her experience is more damning and more determinative of her destructive choices? Is it the experiences she has endured that she cannot surmount, or is it the relentless and repetitive demand to provide for her children? Ultimately, the mother makes a tragic choice in keeping with the theme of infanticide that this chapter works to analyze.

Background

Stories about actual maternal filicide are posited in fragments as headline grabs and rehashed on shows like *Nancy Grace*—a salacious news show that tries newsworthy, current cases with former prosecutor and conservative thinker, Nancy Grace, serving as the prosecutor and judge. Neglectful and murderous mothers are Grace's specialty; promoting the script of the evil mother is foundational to her success. The understanding of these women as people is secondary; first and foremost, they are evaluated as failed mothers. Fundamental to the beliefs and scripts about motherhood is the equation child > self, which means placing the child's interests before the mother's. What happens, however, when the equation is reversed, when self > child, when the mother seems to prioritize her own needs? In the United States, the mothers in three well-publicized cases of child murder—namely Susan Smith, Andrea Yates, and Casey Anthony—hold triumvirate status as the penultimate monstrous mothers or maternal bogeywomen, perpetuating the bad mother archetype. Susan Smith claimed her vehicle was carjacked, yet she later confessed to standing by as her car rolled into a lake, killing her two sons. It appears irrelevant that Smith might have been struggling with past abuse or lack of familial/spousal support. Andrea Yates was advised by her doctor not to have more children and ultimately drowned her five children in the bathtub of her family home. In mainstream news reports, it seems immaterial that Yates was experiencing depression and psychosis. Casey Anthony was tried legally and publicly ("the social trial of the century" according to *Time* in 2011) for the death of two-year-old Caylee Anthony. It seems inconsequential for the many who villainized her that Anthony was found not guilty. Seemingly, no reason justifies exoneration or understanding. As Ayelet Waldman notes in regard to one case, "Even if we sympathize with Andrea Yates's postpartum depression ... we condemn Yates for having succumbed to her despair. She valued her own misery more than her children's lives" (14). Once a woman becomes a mother, she is often cast as a new entity that loses her personhood and becomes caregiver and mother with her identity as individual sidelined for the sake of the child.

In the 2005 memoir, *Down Came the Rain* (an interesting echo of an external referent to her interior status), actress Brooke Shields explores her bout with postpartum depression. Although her struggle does not exactly parallel the narrator's struggle in the novel under review in this chapter, much like Shield's, there is a conflict between imagined motherhood (presented through social narratives, external evaluators) and the very real motherhood she faced. Shields writes, "Once I was a mother, the different parts of my world would all converge, and I would experience life as I'd envisioned it and in turn would know what I was meant to be" (69-70). For Shields, and many mothers, what is sold to them and what is experienced are two disparate things. She acknowledges this as she notes the day to day is a struggle: "I'd always had this idea that women should be able to mother their children without help, but this was probably just another one of my idealized notions of motherhood" (101). The imagined ideal and the experienced reality feed in to the either/or mentality that maintains that there is only one way to mother. This chapter ponders: Could these societal scripts be damning women to a role that is impossible to play, thereby fuelling destructive choices? An investigation into the lives of these women seems to foster understanding, even while not attempting to justify child murder. In "Anger and Tenderness," Adrienne Rich suggests that women's discomfort with mothering is common. She describes an evening she spent with several women discussing "the case of a local woman, the mother of eight, who had been in a severe depression since the birth of her third child, and who had recently murdered and decapitated her two youngest, on her suburban front lawn" (13) and how those women could identify with her. Rich asserts: "We spoke of the wells of anger that her story cleft open in us. We spoke of our own moments of murderous anger at our children, because there was no one and nothing else on which to discharge anger" (13). Based on this example, we might ask: What role does anger hold within the pantheon of hallowed motherhood? If anger is a contentious emotion for a woman to display, how much more magnified is that selfsame anger for a mother?

Veronique Olmi's 2001 Work *Beside the Sea*: The Environment as Interior Register

The protagonist of Olmi's novel is nameless, seemingly representative of every woman/mother who feels maternal invisibility and conflict; in the narrative, she is simply "MOMY" to her two boys: Kevin, five, and Stan, nine. From the onset of the novel, readers sense disquietude and uncertainty, especially through the portrayal of the external environment. The novel begins with the line, "We took the bus, the last bus of the evening, so no one would see us" (5). The sense of covert behaviour is implied here, along with operating under the cloak of darkness. This theme becomes predominant in the narrative as reflected in the environment and atmosphere that is often described as hidden or obscured. When the family of three arrives at the hotel by the sea, it is dark, and they must make their way through the town where it has seemingly been raining for a long time. This rain persists during the entirety of their visit and even becomes almost like another character. We read: "The rain was spattering against our window, poison released from above, the rain was at war with us," and "The rain was hurling its gobs of saliva against the window" (78, 80). The rain is presented as a victor—as "the rain always wins in the end" (94)—and the imagery of battle is a powerful juxtaposition with our main character's own struggles. Even on their visit to the carnival, another vain attempt to try and eke out some joy from their trip as described later in chapter four, they traipse through the night through the mud and rain. Their "wet jackets" never dry; "they were sponges, just putting them on was like going out into the cold" (85). As they walk from the hotel, they slip "on tire tracks and other people's footprints as if [they] were all trampling on each other, never in sync" (85). The characters soak up the effects of their environment; symbolically, they never seem to gain traction. Throughout their entire stay, the freezing room and cold persist as an external reflection of the character's inner state. We are told: "It was still raining outside, the same icy monotonous rain, this town had no imagination, it could only do rain" (59). In much the same way as the town and the environment of the narrative are plagued by darkness, wet, misery and cold, so, too, is our protagonist. This inner, emotive state and outer, physical manifestation come to parallel our character's mind-body divide. At first, this state is presented through the mirroring of the physical environment to our character's inner conflict.

The Sea as a Mirror of Internal Conflict

The sea is another place where the external mirrors the interiority of our primary character, and it, too, also functions almost as a unique and multivaried symbol in the novel. The external environment seems to be attacking and deriding the mother, and as is displayed here through the pelting rain, churning sea, and entrapping mud, it becomes a pervasive reminder of the weight of the environment on her interior status. When they venture to the sea, our protagonist is dismayed to see that the sea "had lost all its color" (41). She tries to tell her boys about the blue of the sea, how it appears in summer, and she reflects on past experiences "sit[ting] on the sand eating ice cream and it melts on your fingers in the heat" (50). Although Kevin believes her, we are given clues that Stan is dubious. Olmi's protagonist reflects: "I would have liked Stan to believe it, too, to ask me questions, but I didn't know what the little smile he gave me meant, did he think my story was nice, did he think I was managing it well and that I was full of wonderful memories" (50-51). This disbelief is central to one of the conflicts in the narrative: the juxtaposition between the innocence of childhood and the knowledge of the adult world. Before I move on to this theme, it is important to recognize how the sea is aspirational for the mother here, too. While it disappoints, as mentioned above, it also serves to be a point of hope—a direction in which she can steer her family to alleviate the suffering they are experiencing from the outside world and the inner turmoil the mother is, and by extension her children are, facing. Though plagued by "chilling black thoughts" that she is fearful of "swimming in" and "drowning" (33), the sea is a source of power and comforting memories for the mother. She laments that all her memories are lost, yet she does seem to find peace through small reflections, most notably of her own childhood and the water-based songs that she recalls. Although her mother is not mentioned, her father would sing to her. The tune "Brave Sailor Back from the War" and the love song about a river in the middle of the bed continue to evoke that elusive peace she seeks through her journey to the sea (34). We are even told her one wish is "for the sea to come to the foot of my bed" (34). For her, it represents something she cannot be, simply by the role given to her as mother; "I ... wanted to be like it, self-contained, not giving a damn about anything and taking up as much space as I liked" (42). Her world, as readers work through the narrative, is fraught with an uncertainty regarding her purpose, of a feeling she needs to adhere to the cliché of not rocking the boat—not creating a disturbance. This seems to be confirmed by the fact that she can only act at night. Furthermore, she attempts to follow the social scripts presented to her by those whose presence she feels, those seemingly in power of regulating maternal behaviour.

The Human Forces That Plague Her

The triad of the family unit is the focus of the novel but the powerful external forces sitting in judgment weigh on the mother and on the narrative. The first reference to an external evaluator comes early on when we are told that she does not share the diagnosis given at the health centre that she is "paralyzed" by her anxieties (17), even though she reveals that she does not sleep well because "it's like something's been lowered onto me ... like someone sitting on me" (9). The reader may question: Is she plagued by anxiety and a victim of panic attacks? We are told she does not "have the strength to get up to go to school" in the morning and that Stan takes Kevin to school (8) and that "everything brings me down" (25). Sleep seems to be her only refuge, causing the reader to wonder: Is she depressed? Moreover, her thoughts are policed: "I'm not allowed to start thinking like that, the psychiatrist at the health center said, there are some ideas that take you straight to the bottom of the pit" (22). The mental health presence reveals more about her interiority, as we are told that "the talking started all on its own in my head" (24). Is she schizophrenic? At the end of the first section, we learn that she has not taken her medicine, although she recognizes the benefit of chemical assistance to enhance her mood: "I'm just missing a few chemicals, yes, that's what I tell myself when I swallow my pills ... maybe it's that simple" (73). Yet is it? This medicated state reveals less about who she is than the admonitions given by the medical professional. The mother, we learn, has been told by the psychiatrist to "avoid breaking down in front of the children" (70). In many ways, the reader sits in evaluation of the mother as well.

This judgment, as it were, is reinforced by the presence of a social worker who makes a shadowy appearance early on. The mother asserts the very real challenges of being a [perfect] mother when she observes "we can't be good at everything, we can't know how to do everything, all of it, that's what I tell the social worker 'til I'm blue in the face" (35). The implicit message is she should be good at everything. Despite all of the watchful persecution, for that is what she feels, we see the mother champion some of her own decisions. One instance comes when she reflects on "Kevin's wall"—a white wall solely given over to his artwork of "little men with no arms and red aliens"—but the social worker experiences horror, making a written record of such behavior in her book. This diction suggests that there is a lengthy record of misgivings she holds about the protagonist and her limited maternal capabilities. While scrutinized, the mother derives a small victory in placating Kevin's worry that he is missing school and promises him that they will take his favourite teacher, Marie-Helene, a seashell. The mother notes: "I was proud of myself, I know how to handle my kids.... I just need to be left to get on with it, would a social worker have thought of that?" (19). Even so, professionals, such as Kevin's beloved Marie-Helene, are also a source of anxiety to the maternal protagonist, who feels judged by the teacher. When the mother is called in to speak with the teacher, she laments that she is never praised but rather bombarded with questions. Even with Kevin's teachers, she is judged: "Why hasn't he got his sneakers for gym? What time does he go to bed because he is falling asleep in lessons?" (26). As readers, we are invited to be implicit in this judgment. Through these narrative clues, we, too, begin to wonder if the missing shoes were just forgetfulness or neglect, if the fatigue is lack of care or perhaps a growth spurt.

Combined, we are later forced to join with the men in the café, who judge the threesome and their economic worth as they scrape to find coins with which to pay for their Cokes, hot chocolate, and coffee on their first full day in the town and after their dismal visit to the sea. We silently join the inquisition levelled at the mother, twice, by one of the men regarding the boys being in a café rather than in school. The critical observers of her maternal behaviour are everywhere, even bystanders and occupants of the hotel in which they stay. The mother in Olmi's novel thinks to herself: "Everyone's always waiting for you to put a foot wrong, for you to fall, it's like walking on soap, yes, our lives are full of soap, that's what I think" (32). It is the mother's emotional state that has us positioned as jury in the narrative, and the facts are presented with clarity. Yet, even so, it is her emotional state and interiority that help to move us from dismissal and disdain to empathy and understanding.

The mother, despite the mental health issues alluded to, is presented as an everywoman, a single all-mother. She is apathetic: "Sometimes I sit in the kitchen for hours and I couldn't give a damn about anything" (6). She is twice alone in her parenting, the boys having different fathers: "I'm abandoned. Dumped" (33). And she feels a farce in her abilities: "I decided to ... act like I knew what I was doing. What matters is looking like you know" (39). Her fantasy life gives way to opportunities to rest: "Didn't I used to long to be knocked down by a car and break my leg so I'd finally have a good enough reason to be left in peace?" (73). This fantasy is not unique to this novel; it can be seen in other works of fiction with the character of Susan, "the Wife," in Leni Zumas's *Red Clocks* or with the character of Amelia Lamkin in Mary E. Wilkins Freeman's "The Selfishness of Amelia Lamkin." Our protagonist adopts what Susan Maushart calls "the mask of motherhood" or the "repertoire of socially constructed representations that have crossed that line [between self-control and self-delusion]" (460-61). It is expected that the mother look competent and in control and that much of her actions revolve around completing simple tasks (cleaning up the boys, feeding them, and putting them to sleep) that are inordinately difficult for her. As readers, we learn that she perseveres because it is important to look the part of competent, in-control mother, especially under the watchful gaze of the hotel clerk, the men in the restaurant, and the occupants of the town. This mask, our narrator assumes, renders her hidden but at the same time serves a purpose. Drawing from Maushart, we come to understand that "the mask keeps us quiet about what we know, to the point that we forget that we know anything at all...or anything worth telling." Maushart further explains: "At the same time, the mask of motherhood is a useful coping mechanism.... When the coping mechanism becomes a way of life, we divest ourselves of authenticity and integrity.... [W]e no longer make a life—we fake a life" (16). Here, her mask that she assumes for the men in the café, for the hotel clerk, and for the shopkeeper where she buys chocolate cookies for the boys preserves the life of her children and enables her to fake a semblance of stable maternity. She puts on the competent mother mask yet notes of these strangers that "People can come into your life like that, from one moment to the next, even if you don't want them to. You should be able to screen them" (71). There are, however, judges everywhere and the mask is wily. The slippage of the mask—through revelations of unmentionable aspects of mothering, including maternal anger, maternal ambivalence, and maternal rejection, to name a few— is both a breakthrough for her personhood but a break in the mental (albeit faked) stability she has thus displayed so far. She observes: "Me, I couldn't wait to get inside, had enough of exposing my face to the air" (72). She is too tired to maintain the role any longer, and as the narrative goes on, readers see her maternal mask slip until it is completely eradicated by her actions.

Physicality and Violence: Trauma's Response

In addition to the emotional fatigue she experiences, her body is marked by trauma. She identifies with her youngest and his "three missing teeth ... the two of us, with the gaps in our gums" (11) and what might be a simple note about her physical appearance is soon followed by the revelation that "ever since I broke my collarbone I've had trouble carrying stuff" (12). It is this brokenness of her body that is telling, symbolically, but registers more. Although she says her son, Stan is the only boy who treats her so nicely, he is, in this instance, a boy. The precarious dance between boyhood and manhood that she recognizes is imminent is ultimately one of the factors that causes her pause and reconsideration in regard to her final action. It is this violence seen echoed through her son that is, partly, the catalyst for her decision to end the lives of her children. Even though she has been the object of violence, we see that she is prone to violence, or violent thoughts at the very least. Of the dog whose bark sounds like "spiteful laughter," she says: "I could have crushed that one with my hand" (14). But it is in her frustration at trying to capture her eldest son's attention on the beach, his active ignoring of her calls, that she sees in her mind the man he would become. She grabs the hood of his coat and he "raised his hand and hit my arm.... He'd never ever done anything like that to me. There's the future, I thought, misery goes on forever" (43). Although we are not told much about her previous relationships, we know she has been left alone and that she has been abused. As the mother of two sons, is it a justifiable fear to recognize in her child the presence of the absent parent? We read: "I wondered how long a child could go on being his *mother's* son, exactly when he became unrecognizable, I mean: just like the others" (my emphasis, 49). Stan, though older, is not the only one who elicits her worry: "What frightened me was this violence they'd kept in check and couldn't hold back anymore ... incredible how you can go from love to hate, there's never any warning" (60). And while this seems like a reasonable fear in light of her circumstances, what this taps into more than anything is her own anger and rage at being a victim: of circumstance, of biology, of others' demands. She continues: "There's like an irritation, a fury that builds up..., sometimes I wish I could scream, to find who it is I've got it in for" (60). At her core, the novel seems to make it clear that she is angry.

Even as her frustration mounts, our protagonist is rendered mute. The reader is once again thrust into this meta-position, whereby they must overhear through the text what is ultimately a confession. Authentic words fail the protagonist and the words that do occupy her space as a mother are rote: "Be careful when you cross the road, Don't talk to strangers, Keep an eye on your brother.... They're sacred, compulsory" (65). Just like she acts like a mother, as noted above, here she talks like a mother would, following a script of sorts. She notes her love of the saying "many a mother," as it aligns her with a group and makes her part of a collective with similar understanding (25). Even so, she is adrift in her aloneness. When she tries to rationalize that many people feel panicked, she notes the health worker tells her "You've got to reason with yourself," which she hears as "you forgot to" reason with yourself (66). Even well-intentioned advice is misheard and misinterpreted as accusatory and demonstrative of something she lacked or forgot to do. When she deviates from the maternal script of behaviour, she faces accusations. After all, what is the meaning of "you forgot to" apart from an accusation that she is failing when measured against the "sacred, compulsory" duty of motherhood?

Despite the precariousness of her being, we see a seemingly rational motivation for the action she takes at the end of the novel, one that has, no doubt, been fomenting since the undertaking of the journey. Quite lucidly, she pronounces, "That's the problem: we bring babies into the world and the world adopts them. We're the incubators" (80). For the protagonist, her childhood seems to be the only point of refuge. Based on her own adult experiences, she fears, as most parents do, the lot that will be given over to the child once they cross into adult experience. At nine, Stan stands on the cusp of maturity, a place his mother dreads. We see him take on adult roles when he tells his mother that it is time for them to go home from the carnival, something that she should be doing as the parent. We are informed that Stan writes his own notes excusing himself from school, only asking from his mother that she sign them. When they go into town to get Cokes and hot chocolate, he listens to the men at the bar talk about women with lasciviousness and, as the mother notes, "Stan knew loads of things already. Far too much" (105). In some respects, Stan is just a precocious child reacting to the environment of which he is a part, yet for the mother, she draws a stark line between childhood (which she deems acceptable) and adulthood. or as she puts it, "the whole hostile world" (105). She queries, "Had Stan already finished his childhood? I really hoped not" (105). Clearly, the mother wants to preserve the innocence of her son, yet she does so because she recognizes all she has lost. At the carnival, she looks at the girls and boys laughing and cavorting and observes, "I never was their age" (87). In contrast, her boys were "wide-eyed and impressed" (88). She gives to them this moment she never had as a means of exerting control over their lives, their happiness. For her, the lights, noise, and rain all become too much, and she escapes by centring her gaze on a ride where "people hung in the air for a moment then they were brought back down very fast—like in life. A breath of air and then you fall" (92). The loss of herself is momentary, as even the sparkling lights and cacophonous fun of the carnival are shattered. When she remerges from her fuguelike state, she hears Stan telling her that Kevin is sick. How to preserve a perfect moment void of heartbreak and trial? It seems impossible, adding to the mother's frustration and disconnection.

It is on their way back to the hotel where the "nightwatchman still didn't give a damn," where they climb six flights of stairs which are "a punishment," that she feels that anger and maternal rage and the impotency she has in protecting them. She is no longer their incubator as they are "sad, tired, and struggling, it was the law, that's what I thought, These stairs are the law. Fuck this life where stairs are the law" (97). Her anger gives her the momentum to act as before her she sees how their lives will be spent. The mother notes: "We walked like old men, the ones who don't talk anymore because they've got the message, so they just keep their heads down. Yes, we'd grown old. Let's hope it's not too late, I thought ... my boys were walking in exhausted old shoes, why should they carry on if even their shoes couldn't follow?" (97-98). She cannot protect them, and although she asserts, "I'll never let that happen again, never, I swear to you" (100)—the cost for such a promise is one she does not yet realize. Here, our protagonist realizes that she is what Alta Gerrey terms "the final mother," for she is "the one it all comes back to" (7). She realizes the finality of her maternal imperative and that she is the one who must answer for the kinds of adults her children will become. For a single mother, like the protagonist, this is doubly true. Ultimately, it is the mother who must bear the responsibility, burden, and duty to usher these children into the adult world already fraught with so much coldness and hate. She has seen the disappointment she generates in her children: "You're never what they want you to be. You irritate them, disgust them. The whole world's disappointed by its neighbors....The rest of the human race is all mistrust and hate, what I mean is love's nowhere as common as hate" (53). To prevent that inevitable deterioration of expectation, the mother decides to render her children frozen, smothering them both in their sleep.

As readers approach the last chapter of the novel, we learn that the room is "freezing" and that our protagonist feels the cold; she notes the moon, at first, as a "beautiful round" whole, as she might imagine it, and then quickly as it is, "nearly a half, a rough drawn shape" (99). The fractured external half-light and cold must be tamped down. She is fearful of the cold (external, internal) and knows "we had to fight it" (102). The mother now welcomes the half-light and welcomes the night as "there's a sort of preparation, like before a journey" (102). Almost like the loved ones preparing the dead for their journey, she prepares her children. She notes: "Kevin wanted to go to straight to bed. I didn't want him to. I wanted him to be clean. To have the face of a five-year-old, with no black stains from his tears and the rain, no snot or salt from his fries, no reminders of that day" (100). She encourages Stan to "have a wash," and thus water is imparted again (but not through the disappointment of the sea) to cleanse and renew her boys. The fractured, half-life she has lived is soothed through the reflections of Kevin and Stan together in this room, cleaned (purified), and ready for slumber, captured in a childlike innocent state (ready for bed). Although we were previously told that her memories were gone—that "everything that's happened is lost" (96)—she remembers Kevin as an infant grasping Stan's hair and saying his first word: Stan. She recollects Stan's assertion that Kevin wasn't his half-brother but his whole brother (109). By uniting the two boys in death, she can prevent any repetition of her own discontent that might stir in the adult men they seem destined to become.

The most poignant reflection on the mother's interior state comes as she reflects on the speed with which children grow up. There is a sadness and loss in her interior monologue, but also a worry and fear from remembering the damage one can do even in infancy. She reflects:

> Kids grow up fast, they stick out in every direction, they're heavy...you don't know how to go about it.... It isn't any better with babies. You're frightened you'll drop them, or make them sick, everyone says, Careful with his head! you have to hold the head, it's fragile, it's heavy ... it's dangerous holding a baby in your arms, it doesn't matter how often they show you how to in the hospital, it's not reassuring...And when the head does stay put all on its own, the baby's not a baby anymore and cuddles hurt. Maybe the only real cuddle is in your tummy, when you've still got the baby in your tummy, I mean. No one to tell you what to do, to say you're pampering too much or not enough or not at the right time. (101)

The vestiges of admonitions still echo for the mother; we gain further clues that her mind has mentally equated a sense of stasis with safety. For her, the child is safest when it is unseen, cloistered, and trapped. For infants, she finds that to be in the womb, but after birth, we see her grappling with recreating a sense of safety and with keeping her promise to the boys to replicate a sense of serenity and warmth. As mentioned earlier, she fears that it is already too late. She notes that she let Stan grow up because of Kevin and that he needed an older brother. The bottom line, however, is her assertion that "I shouldn't have let Stan get so big" (114). She must stop time.

Returning to her physicality though, we see how she is disappearing, as she begins to take steps in acting on the ruminations within her mind. She laments: "If I'd had any voice I'd have sung a song to Kevin" (103). She is silenced both literally and figuratively, muted in part. The idea of capture is even called on in reference to herself, as she considers "maybe I'm the one I can't capture anymore because I wasn't really there" (115). In a very real sense, she has left the room and is floating above it. In this state, she is unmoored. Right before she places the pillow over Stan's face, she remembers how he told her: "We stand on the ground instead of falling over or flying away; it's because the earth pulls us toward it" (117). But this pull is not enough. Instead, she is pulled by the half-moon, a personified "proud" entity" that is "badly drawn ... that couldn't make up its mind to be a proper one ... that wasn't generous and dazzling" or "on [her] side" (118, 116). She may be fractured and half-there, but she does exert agency against a brutal world, declaring "I had to take care of Stan" (116). Here, pillow in hand, she is partly removed from herself, succumbing to an intrinsic desire to protect her children: "Maybe it's an animal thing; it's stronger than us" (15). Conversely, it is more than that for when she questions who will give her strength, she summons her own strength, finding victory that the children will "never [be] cold again ... never cold or ashamed again" (118). It is a dark solution, but one that preserves her boys in a static, peaceful rest, a rest that eludes our exhausted mother. The delusion, however, does not hold. It is not just stasis that she tries to achieve but also the image of serenity, perfection, and peace by replicating a clean, warm space and trapping them there. This image is rendered unviable when she realizes Kevin's face, in death, is turned to the wall and Stan's faces the window. Her desire to trap them together has worked, yet they are facing away from one another. They are fractured, not whole brothers but halves lost in death. It is the realization of the loss she has suffered—the concept of her boys not joined in death, but rather lost there—that shocks her. The novel ends as she finds her voice and realizes the horror she has enacted rather than the image she tried to preserve. "And I screamed"—Olmi's final three words of the narrative again make us participants in the horror and reflective of the multiple causalities in the novel.

Conclusion

Veronique Olmi's *Beside the Sea* is much more comfortable than the real stories of women who suffer with their maternity. However, it is when we examine the intersection of real and fictional mothers that we come to better understand the power of the image of the ideal mother. In this analysis of Olmi's novel, we have seen that the protagonist is helpless; she is not incapable, but she is literally bereft of any help or meaningful support. She faces judgment through those imbued with the authority to hear her and to see her without the mask she attempts to don to satisfy idealized notions of motherhood. We read: "Deep down I knew everything had given up on me" (116). At the close of the novel, we seem to be placed in a position that requires us to ask ourselves: How are we complicit in this judgment? How do we evaluate, try, and convict her despite her struggles? How does her troubled maternity negate hers and our humanity? As readers, we may be able to empathize with her desire to protect her children, even if we concede her methods are flawed. The ambiguity in the narrative about her story is representative of the ambiguity present in all stories. What is omitted? What is shared? As Ruth Cain has posited: "In a time of increasingly harsh and reflexive moral judgments and shrill public blaming, of which 'imperfect' and particularly poor or lone mothers receive a disproportionate share, attention to the context of the crime and the story of the perpetrator is not simply fair but politically necessary" (qtd. in McCloskey). As readers, as witnesses, to this story, we must take in the whole narrative and process the entirety of her story. Being a mother does not render one less than, nor does it create the superhuman, but it results in a whole person, fallible, conflicted, and responsible—responsible for a future we should all care enough to improve and rectify instead of merely judging those seen as problems. The protagonist in *Beside the Sea*'s exercise of agency might have been misplaced, yet the novel invites us into the inner world of the mother. By reading fictional narratives like the one written by Olmi and by applying a greater understanding to the applicable nonfiction ones, we can, in some way, control and recreate the narrative crafted around motherhood and the narrowly written script that can be determinant in how mothering is enacted.

Works Cited

Bidisha. "'It Unlocks You From the Inside': Staging Veronique Olmi's Infanticide Novel." *The Guardian*, 17 Feb. 2012, www.theguardian.com/books/2012/feb/18/beside-the-sea-veronique-olmi-monologue. Accessed 18 Nov. 2021.

Connolly, Deborah. "Mythical Mothers and the Dichotomies of Good and Evil." *Ideologies and Technologies of Motherhood*, edited by Helena Ragone and France Winddance Twine, Routledge, 2000, pp. 263-94.

Gerrey, Alma. *Momma: A Start on All the Untold Stories*. Times Change, 1974.

Maushart, Susan. "Faking Motherhood: The Mask Revealed." *Maternal Theory: Essential Readings*, edited by Andrea O'Reilly, Demeter, 2007, pp. 460-81.

McCloskey, Nanci. "Mother or Monster: Veronique Olmi's *Beside the Sea*: An Interview with Ruth Cain." *Tin House*, McCormick Publications, 26 Oct. 2012, tinhouse.com/mother-or-monster-veronique-olmis-beside-the-sea-2/. Accessed 18 Nov. 2021.

Nancy Grace. HLN. 2005–2016. Television.

Olmi, Veronique. *Beside the Sea*. Tin House Books, 2001.

Rich, Adrienne. "Anger and Tenderness." *Maternal Theory: Essential Readings*, edited by Andrea O'Reilly, 2007, pp. 11-26.

Shields, Brooke. *Down Came the Rain*. Hyperion, 2005.

Chapter 16

From Murderous Monster to Loving Mother: Reconsidering and Rewriting the Legend of La Llorona in Children's Literature and Film

Anne McGee

In his 1950 book-length essay, *The Labyrinth of Solitude*, Nobel laureate Octavio Paz describes the folktale of La Llorona (the Weeping or Wailing Woman),[1] as one of the most important "Mexican representations of Maternity" (75). Yet this figure of Mexican and Chicana motherhood is traditionally represented in Mexican and Chicano folklore and cultural productions as a mother who kills her own children. Although there are numerous variations of the legend, La Llorona is typically described as a single, Indigenous mother who drowns her children out of grief, lunacy, or a desire for revenge after being abandoned by her lover. She dies from guilt and is condemned to eternally roam the shores of rivers and lakes, wailing and searching for her lost children. Although patriarchal society interprets La Llorona's eery wail as the repentant cry of an *ánima en pena* (soul in torment), and thus as a cautionary warning to all women, she is simultaneously cast as a murderous monster or bogeywoman whose siren call lures men and children to their deaths. In fact, the story persists in Mexican and Chicano oral tradition as a story used by parents to warn children of a variety of dangers. In this chapter, I will examine two contemporary rewritings of La Llorona—Gloria Anzaldúa's bilingual work of children's literature, *Prietita and the Ghost Woman / Prietita y la Llorona* (1995) and Alberto Rodriguez's 2011 Mexican animated film *La Leyenda de la Llorona* (Legend of La Llorona)—which question and subvert the traditional tale. Using Domino Renee Perez's classification of Llorona cultural productions, as outlined in *There Was a Woman: La Llorona from Folklore to Popular Culture* (2008), I will place these works as resistant narratives, which return La Llorona to her positive Indigenous origins. Moreover, I will demonstrate how these works, which are primarily produced for children, are a part of a larger movement to rewrite and supplant traditional folk and fairy tales from a feminist perspective.

There are various alternative Llorona narratives throughout Mexican and Chicano folklore. In the 1980s, Chicana feminist theorists and writers, such as Gloria Anzaldúa in *Borderlands/La Frontera: The New Mestiza*, called on Mexican and Chicana writers and artists to reconsider and rewrite Mexican icons of womanhood, such as La Llorona. As a result, Chicana writers began to feature La Llorona and Llorona narratives in their work, including poetry, drama, and short stories. These contemporary revisions question the details of the traditional story, especially the infanticide at its centre, often revealing the oppressive forces at work in the legend. This questioning and rewriting of La Llorona is especially significant, as for nearly five hundred years, conventional Llorona narratives have been used by patriarchal society to reinforce traditional gender roles and social norms. La Llorona is a transgressive figure—a single mother who takes a lover above her social class and is severely punished for her actions. In life, she becomes an outcast, a social pariah, and is driven to infanticide. When she ultimately violates her maternal role, her soul is condemned for all eternity. More than a simple bogeywoman, her story is meant to literally frighten young girls into conformity. Thus, rewritings that question this tale challenge the misogynistic values upon which it is based. Not surprisingly, some texts go far beyond a simple revision of the tale, subverting the conventional story and recasting La Llorona as a figure of maternal resistance while others explore the life of La Llorona before the loss of her children.

Although a number of critics, such as Cordelia Candelaria, Tey Diana Rebolledo, and Ana Maria Carbonell, have focused on these revisionary and resistant literary works, perhaps the most subversive and least studied rewritings of La Llorona are those that appear in children's literature and film. Unlike texts produced for an adult reader, Llorona narratives directed towards children have the potential to supplant traditional versions of the legend and change its retelling in Mexican and Chicano oral tradition. Such is the case with literary fairy tales, such as those written by Charles Perrault and the Brothers Grimm. Although these authors originally gathered oral material in the creation of their tales, their literary versions eventually crossed back over into oral tradition, irrevocably altering the original folktales. Not surprisingly, in most works produced for children, La Llorona is no longer a mother who kills. In Gloria Anzaldúa's *Prietita and the Ghost Woman / Prietita y la Llorona*, the murderous bogeywoman meant to frighten children is transformed into a beautiful spirit guide who aids and protects the female child protagonist in her mission to find a folk cure for her mother's illness. Conversely, in *La Leyenda de la Llorona*, La Llorona initially appears as a monstrous spectre in colonial Mexico, who is kidnapping children in the town Xochimilco. However, the child protagonists who come to investigate the abductions soon discover the true story behind the legend and reunite La Llorona with her children. Through a close reading of these works, I will examine how these rewritings transform the traditional legend, which is based on the taboo of a mother killing her children, into empowering tales that call on children to be critical readers. In both works, the children protagonists confront a Llorona figure that does not conform to the stories adults have told them. Thus, they must construct new meanings based on their firsthand experiences. This is important, as through these rewritings of La Llorona, child readers learn to read critically and, in this way, to question the gender roles and social norms upon which most children's stories are based.

Although the trauma of infanticide is central to the legend of La Llorona, it is important to note that the complex origins of the story are not rooted in the violent act of a murderous mother. In fact, the antecedents of La Llorona are found among the female deities of pre-Columbian Aztec mythology, which often combine both life-giving and destructive powers. In *Borderlands*, Gloria Anzaldúa associates La

Llorona with the Serpent Woman, the Aztec goddess of both war and birth, Cihuacoatl, who like La Llorona "howls and weeps in the night," often predicting impending events (57-58). Anzaldúa also relates La Llorona's wailing to that once performed in mourning rites by Aztec women as they sent their male family members off to war (55). In her book-length study of La Llorona, Domino Perez similarly argues that the legend predates the Conquest, as the appearance of a woman crying for her lost children was one of eight omens that foretold the arrival of the Spanish in 1519 (17).[2] According to Perez, Indigenous portrayals of La Llorona as a powerful prophetic figure were later rewritten by the Spanish, who assimilated European motifs into the pre-Columbian legend (17-18). Perez's emphasis on the legend's Indigenous origins contradicts the work of early folklorists, such as Robert Barakat and Bacil Kirtley, who contend that it is principally of European origin. Although La Llorona has clear Indigenous roots, traditional versions reflect a combination of both Indigenous and European elements. Recognizing this mixed origin is vital, as La Llorona's pre-Columbian antecedents were powerful, and largely positive figures who were rewritten during the Conquest and colonial period in Mexico in order to control the Indigenous populations. Thus, rewriting La Llorona was part of a larger colonial project to restrict the role and power of native peoples, and women in particular. José E. Limón describes La Llorona as "a distinct relative of the Medea story and now a syncretism of European and indigenous cultural forms" (400). Rebolledo similarly characterizes La Llorona as a "syncretic image," which links Euripides's Medea, medieval Spanish beliefs in *ánimas en pena*, and pre-Columbian Aztec mythology (63). Interestingly, Limón identifies the "revengeful infanticide," committed by a betrayed mother as a European addition to the legend (408). Additionally, in popular culture La Llorona is often mistakenly associated with another important figure of Mexican and Chicana womanhood, La Malinche, the Indigenous woman who facilitated the Conquest of the Aztecs as Hernán Cortés's interpreter and mistress. Although there are many parallels between the stories of La Llorona and La Malinche, they are distinct figures. According to Rebolledo, even though both are important to Chicana writers, they "are never confused nor united" in their works (63). Perez also rejects the conflation of La Llorona and La Malinche and argues that the association detracts from their individual power and "minimizes the potential of both as symbols of resistance" (32). Given its complex origins, rooted in both Indigenous and European traditions, it is not surprising that the legend of La Llorona has been continually rewritten. This is part of a long tradition, as at the time of the Conquest, figures from Indigenous mythology and cosmology were rewritten and appropriated as a part of the colonial project—namely, the subjugation and evangelization of native peoples. Thus, contemporary reimaginings that rewrite La Llorona and attempt to return her to her Indigenous roots are significant, as they challenge both traditional gender roles and centuries of oppression.

Although the origin of La Llorona is a matter of academic debate, most scholars (Barakat, Hartley, Kirtley, Limón, Pérez) agree on the remarkable dynamism and persistence of the legend, which has survived in both oral tradition and cultural production for nearly five centuries. This endurance is due in large part to the act of infanticide. By disrupting the expectations of patriarchy and taking the lives of her children, La Llorona ensures that her "voice and narrative endure in the folklore and lives of the men, women and children of the borderland" (Harvey 184). Committing the act of infanticide essentially immortalizes La Llorona. However, the tenacity of the legend is not merely due to the inherent violence of infanticide but to the act's multiple, ever-changing meanings. While in some versions of the tale the infanticide is portrayed as a desperate act of lunacy by a hysterical, abandoned woman, in others, it is defined as a vengeful crime committed by a calculating, jealous woman, whose partner married a woman of greater social standing. In some retellings, the race of the lovers is meaningful, as the infanticide becomes an act of resistance by an Indigenous mother who kills her children rather than see them taken by their Spanish father, thus making it an act of Indigenous resistance to colonial rule. In versions that conflate the stories of La Llorona with La Malinche, the infanticide is framed as an act of revenge for the Conquest, as a Llorona/Malinche figure murders Cortes's son; and in others, the murdered children represent the native peoples killed as a result of La Llorona/Malinche's treachery. Cordelia Candelaria argues that the legend persists in folklore precisely because the act of infanticide has various alternative significations and interpretations, which emerge as the legend is continually retold and reshaped (114). Moreover, she explains that these various meanings have the potential to uncover the injustices inherent in the traditional story (114). What drives La Llorona to infanticide is not consistent across different versions of the legend, and despite her wails, she rarely tells her side of the story. In many ways, the absence of words in her cries opens her story up to continual reinterpretation. Perez argues that this flexibility contributes to the dynamism of the legend, which allows for both traditional versions of the story and new retellings that "reflect the changing concerns of Mexican Americans and Chicanas" (13). Perez describes La Llorona as "an avatar of social and cultural conflict," who transcends the limited role of murderous mother (13). However, traditional versions of the legend continue to demonize La Llorona while casting the power of women as "frightening and seemingly destructive" (Hartley 138). Cordelia Candelaria explains that in Mexican and Chicano oral tradition La Llorona is used as an "effective disciplinary instrument" (112-13) that goes well beyond warning children of the danger of strangers:

> On its face it teaches that girls get punished for conduct for which men are rewarded; that pleasure, especially sexual gratification, is sinful; that female independence and personal agency create monsters capable of destroying even their offspring; that children are handy pawns in the revenge chess of female jealousy; and other lessons of scapegoat morality. (113)

In this way, despite its alternative meanings, the legend of La Llorona still serves primarily as a cautionary tale meant to teach children, especially girls, the consequences of not conforming to traditional gender roles and appropriate standards of behaviour.

With the development of both the feminist and Chicano movements throughout the 1970s, it is not surprising that in the 1980s Chicana writers began to reexamine traditional female models and archetypes, such as La Llorona. In *Borderlands*, Gloria Anzaldúa presents the Virgin of Guadalupe, La Malinche, and La Llorona as the symbolic mothers of Chicanas. She argues that the Indigenous roots and true identities of these female figures were rewritten by men in order to reinforce the virgin-whore dichotomy, thereby restricting the roles of women in society. These figures, and specifically their rewriting, became central to Chicana feminist thought. As conventional female myths and archetypes failed to provide "active, energetic, and positive figures," women writers began to invent new role models or to radically transform traditional ones (Rebolledo 49). They were particularly fascinated with "symbols of female marginality," such as La Llorona and La Malinche, as their stories allow for a questioning of the misogynist aspects of Mexican and Chicano culture (Fernández 82). Long used as a convenient "scapegoat and a crucible" by Mexican and Chicano culture, La Llorona was particularly overdue for a transformation. As Candelaria explains:

> Yes, I think it's past time for her to cut her hair, put on her Nikes and tie-dyed T-shirt, and get a life—at least, that's how I would re-image her. So transformed, she would learn a new walk to replace the head-down, bent-over crouch she's been doing for 400 years ... she would lead the radicals in organizing the quincentennial protests marking *La Conquista de Mejico* [The Conquest of Mexico] in 2021. (113)

Despite such calls to reinvent her for a new millennium, La Llorona was the last of the three major Mexican/Chicana feminine cultural symbols to be recuperated by writers, largely due to the maternal infanticide that is central to the tale (Perez 44). Yet La Llorona was eventually taken up and reimagined by Mexican and Chicana/o cultural producers in a wide array of literary and artistic productions. For example, in the story "Cariboo Café" from Helena María Viramontes's *The Moths and Other Stories* (1985), La Llorona is rewritten as a Central American refugee who comes to the US after her son is murdered by her government's military regime. In Cherríe Moraga's play *The Hungry Woman: A Mexican Medea* (2001), the main character combines elements of Medea and La Llorona. In this case, La Llorona figure is not abandoned but rather leaves her husband for her lesbian lover, ultimately killing her son in an act of resistance.

In the first interdisciplinary book-length study of La Llorona, *There Was a Woman: La Llorona from Folklore to Popular Culture* (2008), Domino Renee Perez considers over two hundred representations of La Llorona from a variety of sources, placing them into four useful categories.[3] First, she uses the terms "conventional" or "traditional" to describe works that remain faithful to the lore. In these cultural productions, the infanticide is portrayed as La Llorona's response to her abandonment by her lover (16). Whereas she is characterized as selfish, vengeful, and even whorish, the behaviour of the man is overlooked or accepted, as conventional narratives neither critique nor question the story (23). The representation of La Llorona as a monstrous and "threatening figure" is central to these traditional renderings (Perez 23). Next, Perez considers revisionist productions that maintain some elements of the lore but which revise others in an effort to question and challenge conventional views on La Llorona. Although the infanticide is problematic to any revisionist effort, Perez explains that it is central in many revisions. By changing the context or circumstances surrounding the murderous act, revisions can reveal the "mitigating or hidden factors that contributed to the infanticide" and offer a more sympathetic portrayal of La Llorona (42). Revisions raise a number of critical questions regarding the oppressive forces at work in the legend, yet they do little to overturn, resist, or subvert them. In her third category, Perez includes works that move beyond simply revising the conventional portrayal of La Llorona by recasting her as a resistant figure "that resists oppression directly or inspires others to do the same" (72). In resistance narratives, La Llorona is no longer a cultural villain. In order to achieve this repositioning, the infanticide may be eliminated from the story entirely or the outcome may be altered. The infanticide can even be transformed into a "radical act of resistance" (76) or a "revolutionary act of salvation" (81). These narratives subvert the traditional meanings of conventional versions of the legend and reinterpret La Llorona's story; however, they continue to define La Llorona in reference to the confines of the traditional lore (107). Finally, Perez uses the term "re-turnings" to refer to cultural productions that move La Llorona beyond the limits of the traditional folktale "by re-turning her to the past and toward new cultural possibilities" (107). These re-turnings or recuperations may include the infanticide, but they also explore La Llorona's life before her tragedy by recuperating elements not included in the traditional lore (111). Re-turnings often give her a name and a voice, or they may reconnect her to her antecedents in Aztec mythology (130). By revealing the preinfanticide life of La Llorona, re-turnings ask the reader to consider the story that lies behind conventional versions of the legend and to question how these previously excluded parts of her life may change our views (111). Re-turnings require the reader to recognize the woman behind the legend. Although Perez's four categories are helpful when approaching works that rewrite the figure of La Llorona, it is important to note that they are not mutually exclusive, as Llorona narratives can exhibit characteristics from more than one category. Perez views them not as strict categories but rather as a model that allows the cultural reader to better understand "the complexity and scope of portrayals of La Llorona as a person, spirit, and/or story" (7). For my analysis, I will utilize Perez's model and focus primarily on resistance narratives and re-turnings.

In her study, Perez includes a brief final chapter, which surveys cultural productions that are geared specifically towards children in order to examine if and how the legend of La Llorona will be passed on to the next generation. Perez finds that contemporary children's literature uses La Llorona folklore to teach children about cultural identity and history (179). She further explains that such works encourage children to be critical readers and to become involved in the process of storytelling by inviting them to create new versions of La Llorona's story (184). Although I agree with Perez's insights, she fails to sufficiently appreciate the subversive potential of children's literature. After all, La Llorona has existed as a folktale primarily aimed at children for centuries. Whereas most of the works analyzed in Perez's study reimagine and reconfigure La Llorona for an adult audience already familiar with the lore, rewritings aimed at children are distinct, as they seek to interrupt the transmission of conventional versions of the legend to the next generation. Rather than simply revise the lore, they seek to replace it. Resistant narratives and re-turnings written for children have the potential to displace the traditional lore, not simply exist alongside it. Perez also fails to consider how these productions are a part of a larger movement to rewrite traditional folk and fairy tales, which reinforce the values of patriarchal society.

It is a common misconception that folk and fairy tales are somehow "timeless and unchanging," when in reality, most have been continually reconfigured by storytellers for centuries (Taxel 108). Such tales play a key role in the socialization of children, as they represent and reinforce traditional cultural norms and values. Leslee Farish Kuykendal and Brian W. Sturm describe fairy tales as "powerful cultural agents," which can be particularly influential in the development of gender identity in children (38-39). Not surprisingly, as writers of literary fairy tales, such as Charles Perrault, the Brothers Grimm, and Hans Christian Andersen, produced their versions of folktales, others began rewriting them. Contemporary women writers have published countless collections that reimagine traditional fairy tales. From works from the 1970s, such as Anne Sexton's *Transformations* (1971) and Angela Carter's *The Bloody Chamber* (1979), to more recent texts, such as Emma Donoghue's *Kissing the Witch: Old Tales in New Skins* (1997) and Nikita Gill's *Fierce Fairytales: Poems & Stories to Stir Your Soul* (2018), traditional fairy tales are constantly recast. In fact, there is a three-hundred-year-old tradition of women writing and rewriting fairy tales in order to challenge this literary form that was "institutionalized and aligned very quickly with the values and perspectives of patriarchy" (Haase, "Feminist" 19).[4] In seventeenth- and eighteenth-century France, women writers of literary fairy tales challenged traditional constructions of gender, whereas in eighteenth- and nineteenth-century Germany, women authors deconstructed traditional collections like those written by the Brothers Grimm (Haase, Preface viii). Donald Haase explains that these writers inspired twentieth-century women writers "who (re)wrote fairy tales in order to interrogate gender" ("Feminist" 19). This was especially the case following the 1970s, when modern fairy tale studies and feminist scholarship developed.[5] In the 1980s and 1990s, a number of feminist fairy tale collections were published, many of which focused on cultural diversity (Haase, "Feminist" 8). Chicana and Mexicana writers who rework La Llorona in children's stories are a part of this larger movement.

Recognizing the subversive potential of children's literature from a Chicana perspective, Gloria Anzaldúa produced two illustrated bilingual children's books *Friends from the Other Side/Amigos del otro lado* (1993) and *Prietita and the Ghost Woman/Prietita y la Llorona* (1995), which feature a young, dark-skinned Chicana protagonist, Prietita, who lives in South Texas.[6] Though better known for her theoretical texts, Anzaldúa inscribes her theories and writings regarding "personal, gender, and political liberation" into Prietita's experiences, making them accessible to young readers (Vásquez 64). Anzaldúa's children's books put her theories into praxis. In *Prietita*, she transforms La Llorona into a positive figure that aids the protagonist in her mission to find a plant in the woods of the King Ranch, which will cure her mother's illness. In the process, Prietita learns to question the stories of others, especially those regarding La Llorona, and takes an important step towards womanhood. Following Perez's model, *Prietita* is a resistant narrative, as La Llorona empowers and enables Prietita to overcome and question her fears. In this way, Anzaldúa presents children with a counternarrative to conventional versions of the legend. Such counternarratives of La Llorona are significant, as they give the next generation of Mexicana and Chicana women alternatives to traditional models of womanhood. Moreover, through writing these narratives Mexicana and Chicana writers such as Anzaldúa take over the power of defining and forming such role models, a power long held by patriarchy.

In the traditional lore, children play limited roles, as they are either portrayed as La Llorona's offspring, the nameless, passive victims of her original act of infanticide, or as her later victims. Although infanticide is central to the legend, its victims rarely play an active part in the tale. Conversely, in *Prietita*, Anzaldúa casts the child in the story as its hero. This is significant, as Prietita is a dark-skinned Chicana female and not the heroic prince who typically saves the day in children's stories. When the curandera (female folk healer) Doña Lola tells Prietita that she needs rue, a common herb, in order to cure her mother's illness, Prietita does not hesitate to cross the barbed wire fence of the King Ranch to find it, despite Doña Lola's warning that "it is not safe for a little girl" and that "they shoot trespassers." This border crossing is notable, as the King Ranch, whose territory was once a part of an original Mexican land grant, has been in the hands of Anglo Texans since 1853. Violating the limits of this Anglo-controlled territory is a transgressive act. Clearly, Prietita is not the passive victim of traditional Llorona narratives, as she courageously puts herself in danger in order to heal her mother. This is an inversion of the mother-child relationship in the traditional legend, as here the child saves the mother. Healing, as opposed to death and suffering, is central to the story. The form this healing takes is also significant, as Prietita assists a curandera, a female folk healer, in gathering her ingredients. In modern patriarchal society, folk healing, especially that performed by curanderas who practice traditional Indigenous forms of healing, is largely dismissed as superstition. This is particularly true in Western culture, where historically women healers were long accused of witchcraft. Here, the curandera, Doña Lola, is not the evil witch of traditional fairy tales, but a woman whose knowledge of herbal remedies, as well as other Indigenous practices, gives her the power to heal. This rewriting of the traditional figure of the witch recalls the positive indigenous origins of La Llorona. What is more, Prietita serves as the curandera's apprentice, as she states in the opening of the story: "Doña Lola can cure almost any sickness. She knows lots of remedies. She's teaching me all about them." Whereas in traditional Llorona narratives Prietita would be cast as a nameless victim, here she is the tale's hero. Moreover, she is placed as a future curandera, who will inherit Doña Lola's power and knowledge.

Despite this inversion, like other resistance narratives, *Prietita* incorporates elements of conventional versions of the legend. For example, when she first hears a crying sound in the woods of the King Ranch, Prietita instantly thinks of her grandmother's cautionary stories about a ghost woman dressed in white: "Her grandmother said that *la Llorona* appeared at night by rivers or lagoons, crying for her lost children and looking for other children to steal. Prietita shivered." In this way, the legend of La Llorona has been passed down in the protagonist's family, and she is the next link in this familial oral tradition. Yet in this reference the violence of the infanticide is minimized, as La Llorona lost her children and now searches for others to steal. While readers familiar with the lore would understand the meaning of these ambiguous terms, others would not. This partial erasure of the infanticide is not surprising given the intended audience of the work. Taxel explains that as early folk tales were recorded and children became their primary audience, most went through a "process of sanitization" that eliminated or downplayed violence and sexuality (108). However, this ambiguity is also due to the text's questioning of conventional versions of the legend. In both the English and Spanish text, the story goes back and forth between referring to Prietita's guide as "La Llorona" and "the ghost woman." This questioning is similarly reflected in Prietita's actions. Although she shivers upon recalling her grandmother's stories, she does not run away in fear and continues on her quest, helped along by a number of animal guides. When she finally encounters La Llorona, who is dressed in white and floating above a lagoon, she politely asks for her assistance: "Please, *Señora*, can you help me find some rue?" By using the title "Señora," Prietita demonstrates a respect for, not a fear of, La Llorona. Through her actions, Prietita rejects the traditional version of the legend reflected in her grandmother's stories. This rejection is significant, as Prietita no longer fears La Llorona but views her as a positive, helpful figure, thus overturning the characterization of La Llorona as a mother who kills.

The representation of La Llorona in *Prietita* bears little resemblance to the monstrous figure of Mexican and Chicano folklore. In an interview with Debbie Blake and Carmen Abrego, Anzaldúa explains that in *Prietita*, she is "rewriting her in a different light" in direct contrast to the horrific murderous mother featured in the stories her grandmother told her as a child ("Doing" 229). Anzaldúa explains that despite her family's stories, for her La Llorona became an important cultural figure that "empowered" her "to scream out, to speak out, to break out of silence" (229). In *Prietita*, La Llorona is similarly characterized as a powerful figure who aids the protagonist. In fact, she first appears in the story in the form of various animals that guide Prietita through the woods (Hartley 139). George Hartley argues that these animal guides have "sacred significance to Mesoamerican peoples" and can be read as naguals, or manifestations, of La Llorona (139). In Mesoamerican folklore, a "nagual" refers to a guardian or protective spirit that resides in certain animals or other beings that can shapeshift into different animal forms. In this way, Anzaldúa imbues La Llorona with supernatural powers and casts her as a protective force. When Prietita finally encounters La Llorona in human form, she is a beautiful woman with long flowing hair, dressed in white and surrounded by golden rays of light.[7] Rather than kidnapping or killing Prietita, La Llorona guides her out of the forest. In this way, she is a healing force in the story. She also allows Prietita to successfully complete a task that was deemed too dangerous for a little girl. Although she does not speak, this ghost woman's actions are inconsistent with the vengeful Llorona of traditional lore and cast doubt on its veracity. This representation not only undoes the negative portrayal of La Llorona but leads to a questioning of the values of patriarchal society and other models of Chicana and Mexicana womanhood.

This questioning of the legend and its importance is made clear in the final scenes of the book. When Prietita emerges from the woods and comes upon her family and friends that have been looking for her, she tells them that "a ghost woman in white" was her guide. The only male voice in the work, Prietita's cousin Teté,[8] identifies this woman as La Llorona, as he replies in disbelief: "*La Llorona!* ... But everyone knows she takes children away. She doesn't bring them back." Teté's declaration, like the stories of Prietita's grandmother, reflects the prevalence of the traditional portrayal of La Llorona as a bad mother and bogeywoman. According to Hartley, these stories reflect the "lie of patriarchy" that labels La Llorona as an evil and dangerous figure (139). In this way, Prietita and her family members have grown up listening to stories that are a part of what Hartley calls "the transborder Mexican cultural practice of denigrating female figures" (138). However, Doña Lola interrupts this practice as she responds: "Perhaps she is not what others think she is." With this statement, the curandera opens the legend to alternate interpretations and calls on the children to question the stories they hear. More importantly, it interrupts and complicates the transmission of the legend of La Llorona to the next generation, as Prietita will tell a much different Llorona story to her future children. Prietita's experiences have the potential to displace her grandmother's stories. In this same way, Anzaldúa's text seeks to subvert and replace traditional versions of the legend of La Llorona, thus transforming its meaning and future retellings. By taking the form of a children's story, *Prietita* moves well beyond the limits of most resistant Llorona narratives. Rather than simply rewriting or questioning a traditional folktale that denigrates women for an adult audience, *Prietita* interrupts the transmission of negative Llorona narratives and replaces them with a positive one.

While *Prietita* falls into the category of a resistant narrative, the 2011 Mexican animated film *La Leyenda de la Llorona* corresponds to Perez's conception of a re-turning, in that it reveals the life of La Llorona before the death of her children. In considering rewritings geared towards children, it is important to look beyond literary publications. Donald Haase explains that contemporary versions of folk and fairy tales can take on a variety of forms, as electronic and visual media are "primary sites for the performance and transmission" of such tales ("Feminist" 31). The impact of film in the dissemination of folk and fairy tales often far exceeds that of published materials, and animated adaptations often become the new standard of centuries old stories. For example, the 1950 Walt Disney animated version of the folktale Cinderella takes precedence in popular culture over earlier literary versions upon which it is based. Thus, the subversive potential of Alberto Rodríguez's *La Leyenda de la Llorona* is perhaps even greater than printed rewritings, such as Anzaldúa's *Prietita*. Produced by Ánima Estudios, the film is the second in the *Leyendas* series of Spanish language horror-comedy animated features, which star a male adolescent named Leo San Juan and a motley band of friendly spirits and fantastic creatures that together embark upon adventures in colonial Mexico, where they uncover mysteries and challenge various monsters from traditional Mexican legends.[9] In *La Leyenda de la Llorona*, Leo and his friends travel to the colonial city of Xochimilco, where La Llorona has been terrorizing the community and kidnapping its children.[10] However, they soon discover that La Llorona is not the monster of legend but rather the traumatized spirit of a single mother whose children died in a tragic accident.

Unlike *Prietita*, which portrays La Llorona in a largely positive manner, in the opening scene of *La Leyenda de la Llorona*, it seems that the film will present a conventional version of the legend. It begins on the eerily deserted and foggy streets of Xochimilco, where Kika, a young Indigenous girl, is trick or treating with her older brother, Beto. At one point, Beto is separated from his sister, and he hears the cries of La Llorona: "¡Ay! ¡Mis hijos!" ("Oh! My children!").[11] Beto tries to flee, but at the banks of a canal, he is kidnapped by La Llorona, who appears as a floating shadowy figure with red-glowing eyes. This frightening scene introduces La Llorona to the audience as the conventional monstrous mother. However, in the next scene, the film questions this representation. As they arrive in Xochimilco, Leo and his friends discuss the story of La Llorona. Don Andrés, the Quixote-like spirit of a Spanish conquistador, explains that there are many versions of La Llorona: "Muchas son las historias que narran la tragedia de la mujer que vivió la muerte de sus propios hijos" ("Many are the stories that tell the tragedy of the woman who experienced the death of her own children"). Don Andrés confirms that there are various versions of the legend. Moreover, he identifies La Llorona not as a murderer but rather as a victim who suffered the loss of her children. When Leo asks why she kidnaps others, Don Andrés explains that she is an *ánima en pena* who cannot find peace. He asks Leo to imagine the pain and anger La Llorona must suffer from, as her love for her children was cut short and turned into madness and resentment. An orphan himself, Leo understands this pain. Don Andrés concludes by stating that there is no treasure greater than a mother's love. In this way, Don Andrés casts La Llorona as a sympathetic figure, as frustrated love is the source of her current monstrous acts.

As a re-turning, the film moves beyond simply explaining La Llorona's actions, as it returns to her past, revealing the woman behind the legend. When Leo meets Kika's mother, Señora Rosa, she tells him (and the audience) the story of La Llorona. The monster currently terrorizing her community is the spirit of an Indigenous woman named Yoltzin, a single mother who arrived in Xochimilco with her two small children, Ollin and Tonatiuh, years earlier.[12] Yoltzin supported her children by growing and selling flowers from her modest chinampa and became known for her generosity and kindness. This narrative is notable, as it contradicts traditional versions of the legend. First, it names both La Llorona and her children and describes their life as a family. Moreover, there is no mention of Yoltzin's lover or husband and her supposed abandonment. Yoltzin arrived in Xochimilco and through hard work built a life for her family. In this version, the death of Ollin and Tonatiuh is the result of a tragic accident and not infanticide. When returning home in their small boat one night, Yoltzin discovered her home ablaze. As she battled the flames, the boat drifted off with her children, whose bodies were found days later. Here, La Llorona is not a vengeful murderer but a loving single mother who loses her children, as she tries to save their home. According to Señora Rosa, Yoltzin was driven mad with pain and grief and refused to accept the death of her children. She died of a broken heart, and now her restless spirit wails in regret and steals the children of others. In this way, the film presents La Llorona as a victim. Traumatized by the loss of her children, Yoltzin is unable to mourn their passing. Her melancholia leads to her own death and transforms her into the monster known as La Llorona. As in traditional Llorona narratives, Yoltzin is an *ánima en pena* in that her suffering soul continues to wander the earth. However, in this case, she is a victim like her children and not a guilt-ridden murderous mother condemned by her sinful acts.

As in *Prietita*, the child protagonists of *La Leyenda de la Llorona*, Leo San Juan and Kika, are heroic figures and not the nameless victims of La Llorona. In fact, Leo and his friends save both the children of Xochimilco and La Llorona as well. The key to this salvation is the tomb of Ollin and Tonatiuh, as Leo discovers that La Llorona must see the truth and accept the death of her children in order to find peace. Despite her appearance, Leo understands that she is not a monster but a tortured soul who needs to be saved. In fact, in a sunken church, he discovers the missing children have been well cared for by La Llorona. At the end of the film, close to death, Leo calls out to La Llorona: "Yoltzin tienes que ver" ("Yoltzin you have to see"). Recognizing her real name, La Llorona turns and finally sees her children's tomb and realizes the truth. At this moment, she is transformed into a beautiful Indigenous woman. The monstrous Llorona disappears, as Yoltzin returns and is reunited with the spirits of Ollin and Tonatiuh. Speaking in an Indigenous language, she thanks Leo for his help and walks into the afterlife with her children. Leo also sees the spirit of his mother who explains that a mother's love protects her children in both this life and the next. This transformation is significant, as it goes well beyond simply revising the story of La Llorona or portraying her in a sympathetic manner. In the end, the film returns La Llorona to her former identity and her role as a loving mother. Both Yoltzin and the audience see the truth—that La Llorona is not a monster who killed her children but rather a positive maternal figure. This narrative directly challenges and subverts conventional versions of the legend. In fact, the central theme of *La Leyenda de la Llorona* is the boundless power of a mother's love and not infanticide. In many ways, the film returns to La Llorona's pre-Columbian roots in which female deities combined both life-giving and life-taking powers, as both are a part of motherhood and creation. Grossing 3.9 million USD in Mexico and 2.9 million in foreign markets, *La Leyenda de la Llorona* was a box office success for a Mexican animated feature and was seen by nearly 1.4 million viewers in that country. With such distribution, this returning of the legend of La Llorona has the potential to displace conventional versions and ultimately alter its retelling in Mexican and Chicano oral tradition. This displacement is significant, since for nearly five hundred years La Llorona has been a negative figure in Mexican folklore—used as both a pariah and bogeywoman to inspire fear and social conformity in children. *La Leyenda de La Llorona* effectively returns La Llorona to her positive pre-Columbian depiction as a protective maternal figure, thus undoing the original legend's rewriting by patriarchal Spanish society.

Clearly, La Llorona is a complex figure of Mexican and Chicana motherhood that is open to rewriting and reconfiguration. Whereas academics have dedicated a number of studies to literature and other cultural productions that present alternative readings of La Llorona, children's literature and film have received relatively little attention. This is unfortunate, since works geared towards the next generation are perhaps the most subversive of these rewritings, as they have the potential to alter and even replace conventional versions of the legend in oral tradition. Moreover, they are a part of a larger tradition of feminist rewritings of folk and fairy tales. In *Prietita and the Ghost Woman/Prietita y la Llorona*, Gloria Anzaldúa transforms La Llorona into a beautiful and powerful spirit guide who empowers the young Chicana protagonist to overcome her fears and heal her mother's illness. Rather than killing or kidnapping children, in this resistant narrative the ghost woman gives Prietita agency and challenges her to question the stories she is told. In a similar manner, Leo San Juan, the child protagonist of *La Leyenda de la Llorona*, uncovers the truth of La Llorona's story, as he recognizes the apparently monstrous Llorona as a victim, a loving mother traumatized by the loss of her children. Leo is La Llorona's saviour, as he returns her to the past so she may once again become Yoltzin and be reunited with her children. Ultimately, the film reveals not a mother who kills but rather the extreme power of a mother's love, which transcends even death. In the end, these narratives disrupt and subvert conventional versions of the legend, which are based upon the taboo of infanticide, and empower children to critically question such tales. Moreover, such disruptions and subversions are culturally significant, as they challenge the five-hundred-year-old-lie of patriarchy that La Llorona is an evil force to be feared and, as a consequence, that the power of women is frightening and destructive. Reimagining La Llorona as a loving mother or helpful spirit and returning her to her Indigenous origins is a transgressive and, in many ways, decolonizing act.

Endnotes

1. Unless indicated, all translations are my own.
2. Perez contends that the first published account of the legend appears in book twelve of Fray Bernardino de Sahagún's *Historia general de las cosas de la Nueva España* (1578), also known as the Florentine Codex.
3. It is important to note that Perez's study excludes works from Mexico and elsewhere, as it focuses on cultural productions from the US.

4. For a review of the history of women writers and fairy tales, see Harries, *Twice Upon a Time*.
5. For a review of the development and principal trends in feminist fairy tale scholarship from the 1970s to 2000, see Haase, "Feminist Fairy-Tale Scholarship."
6. In Spanish, Prietita is a nickname meaning "little dark girl."
7. The golden rays, which emanate from La Llorona in the story's illustrations, are reminiscent of those in the venerated image of the Virgin of Guadalupe, the idealized role model for Mexican and Chicana motherhood.
8. Although in the English text Teté's sex is not indicated, in the Spanish text, it uses the masculine "primo" (cousin) to identify him.
9. There are five films in the *Leyendas* series, and Ánima Estudios also produced a thirteen-episode Netflix series (2017) called *Legend Quest* featuring the same characters.
10. Xochimilco is a borough of Mexico City, which is well known for its extensive system of canals and artificial islands called chinampas.
11. All Spanish transcriptions from the film and English translations are my own.
12. Yoltzin means "little heart" in Nahuatl, the language of the Aztecs. Ollin means "to act with all your heart," and Tonatiuh is the name of the Aztec sun god as depicted in the centre of the Aztec calendar.

Works Cited

Anzaldúa, Gloria. *Borderlands/La Frontera: The New Mestiza*. 4th ed., Aunt Lute Books, 2012.

Anzaldúa, Gloria. *Friends from the Other Side/Amigos del otro lado*. Illustrated by Consuelo Méndez. Children's Book Press, 1993.

Anzaldúa, Gloria. "Doing Gigs: Speaking, Writing, and Change." *Interviews/Entrevistas*, edited by AnaLouise Keating, Routledge, 2000, pp. 211-34.

Anzaldúa, Gloria. *Prietita and the Ghost Woman/Prietita y la Llorona*. Illustrated by Maya Christina Gonzalez. Children's Book Press, 1995.

Barakat, Robert A. "Aztec Motifs in 'La Llorona.'" *Southern Folklore Quarterly*, vol. 29, no. 4, 1965, pp. 288-96.

Candelaria, Cordelia. "Letting La Llorona Go or Re/reading History's Tender Mercies." *Heresies*, vol. 7, no. 27, 1993, pp. 111-15.

Carbonell, Ana María. "From Llorona to Gritona: Coatlique in Feminist Tales by Viramontes and Cisneros." *Melus*, vol. 24, no. 2, 1999, pp. 53-74.

Carter, Angela. *The Bloody Chamber*. Harper & Row, 1979.

Donoghue, Emma. *Kissing the Witch: Old Tales in New Skins*. HarperCollins, 1997.

Fernández, Roberta. "'The Cariboo Café': Helena Maria Viramontes Discourses with her Social and Cultural Contexts." *Women's Studies*, vol. 17, 1989, pp. 71-85.

Gill, Nikita. *Fierce Fairytales: Poems & Stories to Stir Your Soul*. Hachette, 2018.

Haase, Donald. "Feminist Fairy-Tale Scholarship." *Fairy Tales and Feminism: New Approaches*, edited by Donald Haase, Wayne State University Press, 2004, pp. 1-36.

Haase, Donald. Preface. *Fairy Tales and Feminism: New Approaches*, edited by Donald Haase, Wayne State University Press, 2004, pp. vii-xiv.

Harries, Elizabeth Wanning. *Twice Upon a Time: Women Writers and the History of the Fairy Tale*. Princeton University Press, 2003.

Hartley, George. "The Curandera of Conquest: Gloria Anzaldúa's Decolonial Remedy." *Aztlán: A Journal of Chicano Studies*, vol. 35, no. 1, 2010, pp. 135-61.

Harvey, Brandy A. "The Cries of *La Llorona*: Maternal Agency in 'Woman Hollering Creek.'" *Sandra Cisneros's Woman Hollering Creek*, edited by Cecilia Donohue, Editions Rodopi, 2010, pp. 169-88.

Kirtley, Bacil F. "'La Llorona' and Related Themes." *Western Folklore*, vol. 19, no. 3, 1960, pp. 155-68.

Kuykendal, Leslee Farish and Brian W. Sturm. "We Said Feminist Fairy Tales, Not Fractured Fairy Tales!" *Children and Libraries: The Journal for the Association for Library Service to Children*, vol. 5, no. 3, 2007, pp. 38-41.

La leyenda de la Llorona. Directed by Alberto Rodríguez. Ánima Estudios, 2011.

Limón, José E. "La Llorona, The Third Legend of Greater Mexico: Cultural Symbols, Women, and the Political Unconscious." *Between Borders: Essays on Mexicana/Chicana History*, edited by Adelaida R. Del Castillo, Floricanto Press, 2003, pp. 399-432.

Moraga, Cherríe. *The Hungry Woman: A Mexican Medea*. West End Press, 2001.

Paz, Octavio. *The Labyrinth of Solitude and Other Writings*. Grove Press, 1985.

Perez, Domino Renee. *There Was a Woman: La Llorona from Folklore to Popular Culture*. University of Texas Press, 2008.

Rebolledo, Tey Diana. *Women Singing in the Snow: A Cultural Analysis of Chicana Literature*. University of Arizona Press, 1995.

Sexton, Anne. *Transformations*. Houghton Mifflin, 1971.

Taxel, Joel. "Reading Multicultural Children's Literature: Response, Resistance, and Reflection." *Transformations: The Journal of Inclusive Scholarship & Pedagogy*, vol. 17, no. 2, Fall 2006/Winter 2007, pp. 106-16.

Vásquez, Edith M. "La Gloriosa Travesura de la Musa Que Cruza/The Misbehaving Glory(a) of the Border-Crossing Muse: Transgression in Anzaldúa's Children's Stories." *Entre mundos/Among Worlds: New Perspectives on Gloria E. Anzaldúa*, edited by AnaLouise Keating, Palgrave Macmillan, 2005, pp. 63-75.

Viramontes, Helena María. *The Moths and Other Stories*. Arte Público, 1985.

Chapter 17

"I Never Made Those Marks on My Girl": Challenging Cultural Narratives about Mothers Who Kill in Sara Paretsky's Crime Novel *Brush Back*

Charlotte Beyer

Introduction: Feminism and Maternal Crime

Sara Paretsky's powerful detective novels featuring female Private Investigator V.I. Warshawski have rightly gained widespread admiration and praise for their hard-hitting feminist reimagining of the masculinist hard-boiled crime writing tradition.[1] Through her twenty detective novels featuring Warshawski, Paretsky is credited with transforming the genre with her unapologetically feminist perspectives and focus on social justice issues. As Natalie Kaufman and Carollee Kaufman-Hevener argue in their discussion of Paretsky's work, "Popular culture can offer alternative strategies for reading the map of a patriarchal society" (19), and this is precisely what Paretsky's novel does. The crime fiction genre specifically foregrounds and investigates crime and its representation. This work includes challenging gendered stereotypes, as Nicoletta Di Ciolla and Anna Pasolini argue.

They suggest that "narrative fiction, with its mass reach, can contribute to the deconstruction of the fixed paradigms that continue to be in place in the categorization and evaluation of female behaviour and, through its contribution, can support positive cultural and social changes" (Di Ciolla and Pasolini 138). Feminist crime fiction interrogates the patriarchally driven causes of crime, including the gender-political aspects of its representation. For motherhood scholars, these preoccupations are investigated through focusing explicitly on mothers and their representation within the genre.

In her novel *Brush Back* (2015), Paretsky explores the controversial theme of filicide, portraying a mother who stands accused of having murdered her daughter. This chapter argues that Paretsky uses the crime genre's conventions to investigate the complex theme of mothers who kill and to explore maternal histories and landscapes. The crime fiction genre enables this important revisionist feminist work through its focus on criminality and its structural drive to restore order and achieve justice for victims (Beyer, "Crime Fiction and Migration"). The theme of criminality is foregrounded through crime fiction's textual functions, thereby interrogating the role of cultural narratives and the gender- and textual politics of portraying maternal filicide. In her doctoral thesis, *Monsters in Our Minds: The Myth of Infanticide and the Murderous Mother in the Cultural Psyche*, Melissa Scher argues that "The telling of the story of maternal child-murder is, however, a site of profound anxiety" (23). Scher is emphasizing a point that is central to our book—namely, that maternal filicide is a profound and pervasive source of cultural silence and unease that requires more research. My argument focuses on how Paretsky's *Brush Back* redraws the crime fiction narrative about mothers who kill in order to investigate representations of crime and the mother-daughter relationship from a feminist point of view. Paretsky's novels frequently feature plots focused on mothers, mothers and children, and furthermore the mother-daughter relationship is a recurring feature in her writing. Reimagining the hard-boiled mode and the female detective importantly also includes attending to those features, thus assessing the significance of thematic content important to women readers and to feminist politics presented in crime fiction.

In the patriarchal working-class families portrayed in *Brush Back*, mothers are as likely to be seen as the perpetrators of domestic violence and held to blame for it, as they are to be on the receiving end of it as victims. This reassessment of the American home and family as a crime scene—a place where a crime is committed and where the detective hunts for evidence (Lexico)—rather than an idyllic private shelter is central to Paretsky's representation of mothers. In *Brush Back*, Warshawski returns to her childhood streets when she is asked by an old boyfriend to investigate a case involving his mother, Stella Guzzo. Stella was convicted of beating her teenage daughter Annie to death during a violent argument twenty-five years previously but has always maintained her innocence. On her release from prison, Stella seeks exoneration, insisting that someone entered her house on the night of the murder and killed Annie. During the course of her investigation, Warshawski discovers that Stella was innocent and that her conviction was a miscarriage of justice. Annie was in fact murdered in her own family home as part of a coverup of white-collar crime involving prominent politicians and the local mob and street gangs. Criminals murdered Annie because she had been gathering incriminating evidence and was about to expose them, instead framing Stella for the killing (Beyer "Chicago Crime"). Warshawski unravels the case, coming to terms with her own unresolved grief over her mother's death and achieving justice for Annie and Stella. However, thus far critics have paid insufficient attention to the complex and class- and gender-based analysis of maternal filicide that Paretsky's novel offers.

My analysis of *Brush Back*'s representation of filicide focuses on gender and other social factors, such as ethnicity and class, as significant and persistent barriers preventing women's progress, requiring mothers to raise their daughters to be submissive (Kaufman and Hevener 19). Drawing on crime fiction criticism, I employ textual analysis from a feminist perspective as my methodology in order to investigate the novel's literary allusions and its interrogation of patriarchal constructions of mothers. These critical discourses provide the vocabulary and concepts to enable my focus on mother-daughter relations and ambivalences, including psychoanalytic perspectives. Such blended critical perspectives furthermore demonstrate how feminist criticism can be used to interrogate and challenge one-dimensional representations of mothers as victims and/or perpetrators of crime, specifically in cases of murdering their own children. I argue that Paretsky uses the crime genre's conventions to produce a complex representation of mothers and of intersecting modes of oppression, thereby challenging prevailing stereotypes of mothers who kill. By investigating social class and ethnic marginalization and its impact on women's employment and educational opportunities, Paretsky's novel provides a nuanced context for the representation of maternal violence and murder. Paretsky's novel challenges the masculinist focus of hardboiled crime fiction by drawing on literary and cultural allusions to evoke and represent the complexities of the mother-daughter relationship and further contributing to the feminist reassessment of genre through her female detective Warshawski and her memories of her own mother-daughter relationship, which take an important aspect in *Brush Back*. The novel provides an important revisionary narrative in several respects. First, the reader gains further insight into Warshawski's youth, and thus a better understanding of the emotional devastation she felt at her mother's death and the experiences that made her into such a tough detective. Second, the novel's revisionary detective process challenges a false verdict which was based on patriarchy's propensity to blame the mother, as identified by Andrea O'Reilly.

Crime Fiction Criticism on Mothers Who Kill their Children

Examining the theme of mothers who kill in crime fiction requires a multifaceted examination of the crime genre's mechanisms and representations as well as an engagement with prior scholarship providing critical assessments of the theme. Crime fiction as a genre centres on investigating and solving crime, restoring order and achieving justice for the victims of crime (Beyer, "Crime Fiction and Migration", 380). Problematically, the genre predominantly features stereotypical representation of mothers. Mothers rarely occupy the position of narrator and/or detective in crime fiction, with their mothering activities playing a vital role in the crime narrative. Mothering activities and identities, then, are regularly marginalized from and invisible in crime fiction, as the staple roles of femme fatale, sexual temptress, or victim so frequently seen in the masculinist maledominated hardboiled crime genre leave little to no room for alternative depictions. In the case of portraying mothers who kill, this focus produces a particularly complex and ambiguous sort of crime text. In crime fiction, mothers who kill their children tend to appear in plots revolving around infanticide. When mothers are depicted murdering their offspring in crime narratives, the plot often centres on babies and the emotional pull this trope creates rather than older or grown-up children. To illustrate, Diane Jeffrey's crime novel *The Guilty Mother* (2019) portrays a mother accused of killing her baby and disguising it as cot death. The novel places the mother on trial, explicitly and symbolically. Consequently, the role of both the detective and reader is to find out the truth by challenging their own preconceptions and unconscious bias. Even in crime fiction, a genre that centres on violence and transgression, the theme of maternal filicide is controversial. As Jennifer L. Kunst suggests: "Perhaps one of the reasons that people recoil from attempts to develop an understanding of this crime is it is commonly believed that filicide is the result of severe child abuse and thus associated with the mother's selfishness, anger, or revenge" (20). Such representations are at the heart of the crime narratives depicting maternal filicide and mothers accused of killing their children. Currently, a limited number of scholarly assessments exists of crime fiction texts specifically focusing on the theme of mothers who kill their children. This absence may be connected to a general critical tendency to minimize or marginalize mothers and research about mothers and also with the taboo which maternal infanticide and filicide represent. According to Lizzie Seal, "The mother who kills can be represented as a figure of feminine evil, echoing the myth of Medea, who murdered her sons after being abandoned by her lover, Jason" (2). As Seal argues, the powerful taboo associated with violent maternal transgression means that the theme of maternal infanticide and/or filicide has given rise to cultural, mythical and literary stereotypes that run through literature, including crime fiction. In *Brush Back*, Stella is repeatedly referred to as Medea by other characters in the novel, including police and prosecutors, thus evoking this mythological figure who killed her children but also challenging the reader to think beyond the stereotypes associated with maternal filicide.

In her study "Women, Murder and Femininity: Gender Representations of Women Who Kill," Seal uses a feminist framework to examine narratives of women who kill, drawing on legal discourses and popular gender stereotypes in order interrogate popular cultural texts producing and reproducing representations of gender and violent transgression. In her 2018 article, "Murderous Motherhood: Munchausen Syndrome by Proxy in 1990s Crime Fiction," Victoria Bates specifies 1990s crime fiction and popular culture as the site for the emergent trope and medical preoccupation: the mother who kills her child through Munchausen by proxy. Using a medical humanities approach that emphasizes the clinical aspects of the crime and its literary representation, Bates analyses a range of crime texts that feature this plot device, identifying this particular historical moment as the point of the manifestation of a new type of maternal murderer and establishing the importance of popular culture in communicating this new knowledge (Bates 1128). In their chapter, "The Violent Mother in Fact and Fiction," Nicoletta Di Ciolla and Anna Pasolini analyze representations of the violent mother in fact and fiction in order to investigate representations of crime and maternity in domestic noir crime texts. Drawing on positivist criminology and ideas of intersectionality to scrutinize and interrogate constructions of maternal identity and normativity, Di Ciolla and Paolini apply these issues specifically to crime fiction's representations of mothers in the domestic sphere and the depiction of mothers transgressing norms for maternal behaviour and thought. In their 1999 article "Mères Fatales: Maternal Guilt in the Noir Crime Novel," Katharine and Lee Horsley investigate the depiction of mothers and motherhood in noir crime fiction: "Women's noir very often challenges assumptions about female identity and, through the sympathetic representation of 'transgressive' female desire and insecure, fragmented female identities, subverts the idealized cultural possibilities of stereotypical femininity" (374). Their attention to the topic of motherhood and the depiction of mothers in crime fiction plots opens up a new area of critical investigation in which investigation of specific themes is married to analysis of form and style in order to examine the gender politics of representation, an area of study that this chapter further extends. Importantly, Carolyn Beasley has researched maternal filicide focusing on the killing of adult children. She employs a creative writing lens in her study of crime fiction and its portrayal of filicide. Exploring the character of a mother who kills her adult children within the context of crime fiction, Beasley's research has important intersections with my own, although her methodology and lens differ from mine.

In my own research into the textual politics of representing mothers who kill their children or are accused of killing their children, I have used feminist narratology and textual analysis to examine how a focus on mothers and maternal crime challenges and reframes the conventional crime fiction plot. My 2011 article, "Mediatization and Mothers Accused of Murder in Sophie Hannah's Crime Novel *A Room Swept White*," investigates the representation of mothers accused of infanticide disguised as cot death. I examined how Hannah's novel explored the role of mediatization in depicting maternal crime and made it part of its crime plot, interrogating popular cultural discourses which trivialize, fictionalize, and/or sensationalize these complex issues. My examination of Hannah's novel focused on the use of flawed science in contributing to popular cultural narratives that can potentially falsely frame mothers for the murder of their children. I furthermore commented on the disjointed and multifocalizer mode of the novel, concluding that Hannah's text draws attention to the ways in which stereotyped and one-dimensional media accounts serve to condemn mothers accused of murdering their children. I furthermore examined Joyce Carol Oates's short story 'Dear Husband' (2009), an experimental story written by a mentally ill wife who has murdered her five children and now explains to her husband why; it is based on the story of Andrea Yates, a mentally ill woman who killed her children. My analysis focuses on Oates's use of a confessional perspective to explore the private domestic sphere as a crime scene which systematically victimizes and traumatizes women. Crime accounts such as that featuring Yates play an important role in popular culture and the media; however, these narratives offer a limited and one-dimensional construction of mothers as mad and dangerous, or else depressed and suicidal, stuck in suburban hellholes of domestic violence, religious fundamentalism, and never-ending domestic drudgery (Beyer, "She Decided"). Such one-dimensional representations fail to recognize that maternal filicide is a more complex and wide-ranging crime than these tropes imply. Horsley and Horsley discuss the importance of recuperating the mother's perspective in crime fiction, moving away from earlier tendencies to blame the mother, focusing instead on the ways in which patriarchy pathologizes and punishes what it defines as maternal transgression. Important new research on monstrous mothers and transgression is emerging, enabling representations such as Paretsky's and Oates's to be seen in a new light (O'Reilly and Palko). Furthermore, Horsley and Horsley show how critics neglect to pay sufficient attention to issues surrounding race/ethnicity, sexuality, and class in their examination of mothers who kill. It is evident from this research, then, that the topic of mothers who kill requires research and representation that acknowledges its complexity and, as such, is in urgent need of further research. Paretsky explicitly focuses on these issues in *Brush Back* as we shall see in my analysis of the novel's reclamation of the mother accused of filicide.

Mothers and motherhood are central recurring themes in Paretsky's crime novels, with *Brush Back* exploring the politics of reevaluating and reimagining mothers in crime plots. These themes are part of Paretsky's overall preoccupation with challenging the gender politics of crime fiction and the stereotypical roles female characters are often cast in. With Warshawski, Paretsky wanted to create a female detective and a take on the hard-boiled crime mode which showed women as problem solvers (Murray). The traditional hard-boiled model is masculinist and male identified; it represents female figures as either victims or femme fatales who use their sexuality to gain power but never as problem solvers. Paretsky and other second-wave feminist authors reimagined the genre's conventions by creating female detective figures who reflected hard-boiled sensibilities without emulating the male identification of the traditional masculinist form. Paretsky articulates a feminist critique of gender roles and the oppression of women—including mothers, using Warshawski's mother, Gabriella, and a range of other characters who are mothers and/or play maternal functions—to investigate class-, race- and gender-related oppressions of mothers within a changing patriarchal American society (Kaufman and Hevener 19). In *Brush Back*, Warshawski explores the maternal landscapes of her childhood and youth through the filicide case she is investigating. Through this confrontation with her past and the people in it, she is also forced to reassess what motherhood is and what it means. The maternal figures of her past are complex and do not reflect patriarchal requirements of women to be demure, selfless, gentle, or fulfilled by marriage and motherhood. Instead, the deprived multicultural working-class environment of Warshawski's youth shows her that both motherhood and crime are circumscribed by patriarchal domination. Furthermore, apportioning guilt and establishing responsibility for the crimes of the past and present means looking to systemic inequalities and oppressions supported by politicians and men in power rather than blaming individual mothers.

Paretsky's critique of society's preference for submissive women is directed at the patriarchal idea of the Angel in the House and its enduring effect on women, especially mothers (Paretsky, *Writing*). This literary construction of domestic femininity has governed women's lives since the nineteenth century and still holds much symbolic sway. "The Angel in the House" is an 1854 long poem written by British author Coventry Patmore to his wife, praising and admiring her submissive, gentle, and self-effacing nature. In her memoirs, *Writing in an Age of Silence*, Paretsky discusses the impact of the Angel in the House on her personally as a woman writer (Paretsky, *Writing* 14; Beyer, "Life of Crime"). The Angel in the House furthermore affected representations of female characters, including mothers, in crime fiction, as Paretsky shows: "Women could be vamps, or virgins, or, very often, victims, but they couldn't be effective problem solvers. In short, women could be Coventry Patmore's 'Angel in the House,' or they could be monsters, but they couldn't be human" (Paretsky, *Writing* 60).

In *Brush Back*, Warshawski's investigation of a mother accused of murdering her daughter serves to expose the psychologically damaging and emotionally destructive effects of the domestic Angel in the House stereotype, revealing instead the complex, violent, and ambivalent relationships between mothers and daughters, which the figure of the angel glosses over and erases. Instead, Paretsky often implicitly draws on the Demeter-Persephone myth to depict mother-daughter relations and to offer a counter-representation to toxic masculinist narratives about mothers. Feminist critics have singled out this particular myth for its enduring thematic significance in women's writing (Yu; Hansen; Hirsch). According to Marianne Hirsch, the Demeter-Persephone myth is central in much women's writing because it "reverse[s] heterosexual plots of disconnection in favour of a model of female connection" (36). The traumatic plot traced in the Demeter-Persephone myth furthermore provides an opportunity to explore dimensions of the effect evoked through representation to impact readers and audiences. Cultural intertexts such as myth may inform and shape the ways we think, both about mothers and about crime. *Brush Back* features a plot in which the mother found guilty of killing her teenage daughter is part of a more general critique of gender inequality, social and class deprivation, and their effect on family dynamics in an immigrant family. The victim is not the expected cute, vulnerable baby but a grown daughter with a complex and wilful strong personality who challenges her mother and has her own ideas about life—a different and more complex mother-daughter relationship as context for the alleged crime. As Paretsky shows in *Brush Back*, in poverty-stricken working-class families negotiating complex diasporic identities and experiences, mothers often strive to teach their daughters to compromise their social and educational ambitions and accept their lowly place in a world governed by traditional values, which are promoted by the church and the patriarchal family.

Challenging Stereotypes and Rewriting Narratives of Blame

In *Brush Back*, Paretsky uses the crime genre's conventions to investigate stereotypes of mothers who kill, placing intersecting categories of oppression at the centre of its investigation. Exposing the stigma leading to scapegoating of mothers, the novel explores the systemic oppression of mothers that leads to crime. However, no scholarly and critical readings to date have really focused on the vital importance of Paretsky's novel seeking justice for victims by making the crime genre interrogate mother-blame and reexamine representations of mothers who kill. This chapter is the first to take on these themes. The crime plot in *Brush Back* highlights how setting, class, and religion act as barriers for women's progress and require mothers to train their daughters in patriarchal subordination. At the same time, the novel uncovers how, under patriarchy, mothers are framed and made to take the blame for crime, including murder. By portraying Stella not from her own point of view but through the detective's perspective, Paretsky generates ambiguity and contradiction in the reader's perception of Stella—is she a murderer or a victim? This nuanced treatment of maternal filicide—an otherwise frequently sensationalized subject—enables Paretsky to challenge mother-blaming narratives, uncovering instead far-reaching white-collar crime and corruption involving the higher political echelons of

American patriarchy (Beyer "Chicago Crime").

Brush Back is set in an ethnically diverse working-class community in South Chicago. Paretsky thus takes the image of the mother who murders out of the culturally privileged spheres to examine how multiple intersecting oppressions affect the crime narrative and the reader's engagement with the characters—victim, perpetrator, and detective. In *Brush Back*, the female characters are shown to be circumscribed by a polluted and run-down cityscape—which places severe limitations on working-class women's educational and employment opportunities—and corrupt white-collar male criminals whose grasp on power prevents not only change but also actively seeks to eliminate anyone challenging it or seeking to change it. Only Warshawski has the agency to move freely through the city's different class and social strata, defying gender roles and expectations through her detective activity (Kinsman). The novel's dilapidated and deprived multicultural working-class South Chicago setting is dominated by family loyalties, neighbourhood rivalries and hostilities, and the Catholic Church, which controls women's lives and maintains patriarchal oppression (Imani and Ramin 13, 18). Through this portrayal of the social crime scene, Paretsky problematizes the nature and definition of maternal crime and instructs the reader to look further than the obvious scapegoat, the struggling mother. In *Brush Back*, the tough South Chicago neighbourhood where the murder took place highlights the seeming inevitability of domestic and/or maternal violence in financially deprived neighbourhoods and families. Setting the novel in Warshawski's childhood area of Chicago provides Paretsky with the opportunity to explore the maternal landscapes of her detective and hard-boiled feminist crime fiction. Paretsky explores ways that class and cultural marginalization bear on the lives of mothers and families, as in the case of Stella—the mother falsely convicted of beating her teenage daughter, Annie, to death during an argument. The implication is that this neighbourhood is teeming with domestic abuse and familial violence. Other characters in *Brush Back* suggest that the deprived living conditions and lack of opportunity relate the inevitability of the way this abusive relationship ends: "Oh, these South Side Irish families, with their outsized voices and quarrels squeezed into tiny houses, they're tinderboxes. I know them well—I grew up in one of those families" (81). This representation reflects Cheryl L. Meyer's point that class is a determining factor in how abusive mothers are perceived: "Women who abuse their children have received scant research attention. In part, this may be due to definitional issues. For example, a fine line often distinguishes abuse from neglect. In addition, there are clear ethnic and cultural variations regarding what constitutes acceptable disciplinary practices and what is abusive" (126). In *Brush Back*, harsh physical disciplining carried out by mothers of their children is seen as normalized in certain ethnic and class groups—a fact that contributes to the authorities framing Stella as guilty and hampers Warshawski's search for the truth about Annie's death.

The representation of Stella, the mother accused of killing her teenage daughter Annie, is central to *Brush Back*'s investigation of maternal crime. The description of female characters, particularly villains, is crucial to crime fiction specifically and in cultural texts generally. Stella is described as athletic but not conventionally pretty, feminine, or maternal: "She'd kept her height even after all the years of bad diet and poor exercise. Her hair had gone that iron shade of gray that makes the face beneath it look hard—or harder, in her case—but her eyes were still a bright blue ... and her arm muscles remained firm. She must have been attractive when she was young, in an athletic kind of way. In a different era, she might have become a sports star herself" (20). Avoiding female stereotypes, such as the sexualized femme fatale of traditional hard-boiled crime fiction, Paretsky focuses instead on the context of deprivation and struggle, which has shaped and hardened Stella. The Judge Grigsby's memories of Stella from the trial reveal the prejudice and bias she faced based on her class and ethnicity: "She was a difficult client, unsympathetic. I knew dozens like her from growing up at Forty-seventh and Ashland—rock-hard women who had to fight for every piece of bread their children ate. My own mother, God rest her soul, was one of them" (143). Stella is thus presented as herself a victim of a harsh and violent patriarchal society; the novel states that she "had grown up in a hardscrabble house herself and shouting and hitting were her main modes of functioning" (5). The unsparing punishment meted out by the state to the mother who kills—no ameliorating circumstances—punishes the immigrant older mother with full prison time. Stella has been judged and condemned already by the time she steps into the court room, based on her abrasive personality and offensive language use. Even Warshawski buys into the narrative of maternal culpability to begin with, based on her personal knowledge of Stella, and is reluctant to consider the possibility of a miscarriage of justice. She reflects how "I believe she wants to rewrite the story of her life ... she has to change the past so she's the martyr, not the villain" (6). In contrast, Stella insists on her innocence, although she admits to having a difficult relationship with Annie, which resulted in violent confrontations: "I didn't kill my girl.... It was an intruder. When I left the house to go to the bingo, Annie was alive. Everyone thought she was so sweet, they should have heard what she was saying. If she died with those words in her mouth, she's been burning in hell for it" (22). The representation of Stella as both victim and aggressor invites consideration of the politics of representing maternal crime and justice for victims as central themes in *Brush Back*. Paretsky's novel uses the crime theme to expose the prejudices mothers are subjected to and the double standards and hypocrisies evident in the assessment of their guilt.

Crime novels by women writers often draw on intertextual allusions and cultural subtexts, both in their representation of patriarchal crime against women and in representing mothers. As critics have shown, *Brush Back* draws on literary intertexts to support its interrogation of and challenge to constructions of mothers and the mother-daughter relationship (Ramin; Hevener Kaufman and Kaufman Hevener). Such textual strategies reflect the literary and cultural range of crime fiction, with the genre drawing on textual allusions and echoes to bridge the gap between popular culture and high art. Thus, we see characters in *Brush Back* explicitly allude to cultural texts and myths to describe Stella, which underlines the significance attributed to the mother who kills. These allusions also include cultural texts about the mother-daughter relationship. According to Susan Koppelman: "Women who write fiction write stories about mothers and daughters ... return to the literary contemplation and portrayal of mothers and daughters again and again throughout their careers. Women of every race, ethnicity, religion, region, and historical period write stories about mothers and daughters" (Koppelman, xv).

In *Brush Back*, Paretsky draws on central tropes and myths that illustrate the mother and the mother-daughter relationship respectively: the Angel in the House (Scher 32) and the Demeter-Persephone myth (Amani and Ramin). In her aggression, Stella fails to adhere to the patriarchal construction of submissive femininity embodied by the figure of the Angel in the House. Her violent behaviour puts her at odds with the submissive and self-sacrificing femininity of the Angel. Stella's assumed guilt, her court case, and her imprisonment—all based on assumptions about her behaviour—reflect Scher's point about patriarchy, "chastising women who fail to conform to preconceived notions of 'appropriate' and 'acceptable' female behaviour" (32). Paretsky's preoccupation with these ideas in her crime fiction not only reflects feminist criticism but demonstrates a constructive dialogue with feminist debates. Maryam Imani and Zohreh Ramin refer to Stella as a "disintegrated shadow of Demeter" (3) to illustrate the way in which society has diminished and fragmented her and compromised the mother-daughter relationship, never giving it a chance to flourish on its own terms. On several occasions, Warshawski's partner, Jake, refers to Stella as "Medea" during discussions, referencing the Greek play about the mother who killed her children: "This woman—what's her name? Medea?—she doesn't even merit a phone call," Jake protested (11). He continues: "'She is Medea, isn't she? You think it's a myth, and then you meet it in real life. Euripides knew something about human nature.' 'Medea gets off scot-free at the end,' I said, 'she rides off in Apollo's chariot. I guess that's what Stella's trying to do.' 'In Cherubini's version, she's burned up in the temple with the children she murdered,' Jake said. 'I like that one better'" (45-46). With her volcanic temper and violent behaviour, Stella lives up to all the stereotypes of the bad mother. Her gratuitously vicious badmouthing of Warshawski's dead mother and cousin highlights the difficulty of evoking empathy for the mother accused of filicide. Stella's case foregrounds issues of justice and fairness, and Warshawski's role is thus to serve as the mediator between the scapegoated mother and society and to deliver justice for both Stella and Annie.

Brush Back focuses on the invisibility and marginalization of mothers and the ambivalent feelings associated with the mother-daughter relationship and its portrayal in mainstream patriarchal literature. Paretsky uses the detective genre's conventions of justice seeking and truth finding to investigate complicated and painful mother-daughter relationships and the ambivalence of those relations—themes and concerns that are common to the works of many contemporary women writers (Palmer 112). Maternal ambivalence is "'the crime that dare not speak its name" in the 21st century," as Barbara Almond calls it. Andrea E. Willson et al. further comment on ambivalence and the way in which it is used to describe complicated family relationships: "The concept of ambivalence has been used to refer to contradictions in relationships between parents and offspring that arise from social structure in the form of norms linked to statuses and roles, and from the subjective level as cognitions and emotions" (236)[2]. Paretsky challenges and revises the narrative of maternal filicide by questioning the idea and construction of truth in the crime narrative and re-imagining the role of the detective (Scher 619). Warshawski's family history with Stella and Annie complicates matters further, resulting in her approaching the case with preconceived ideas. Warshawski's mother, Gabriella, was harassed and bullied by Stella, who was envious of Gabriella's friendship with Annie and her giving the girl piano lessons, but also resented Gabriella's standing in the local community. The built-up antagonism between the Warshawskis and the Guzzos is unravelled in the novel. Warshawski remembers how Stella resented Gabriella's friendship with Annie, as she encouraged Annie to break away from her mother's traditional working-class woman's domestic life and instead better herself and her prospects by pursuing her academic ambitions. Stella's jealousy and resentment led her to spread malicious gossip about Gabriella and be physically violent towards her daughter, Annie. These old grievances come out in the open when Warshawski visits Stella, resulting in a fight between the two women. The novel thus portrays ambivalence in the mother-daughter relationship by splitting the maternal figure into a nurturing mother (Gabriella) versus a violent mother (Stella). Stella explains to Warshawski that she disciplined her daughter to enable her to fit in and conform to patriarchal expectations of femininity; she went through Annie's things and discovered her concealed contraceptive pills and saved-up money. Stella perceives these as her daughter rejecting the traditional South Chicago Catholic working-class woman's life of marriage and multiple babies, which she herself endured. Amani and Zuhren argue that Stella's experience of hardship and bitterness has made her a violent bully. They suggest that Stella sees her daughter's submissiveness and conformity to expectations of traditional working-class life for women as a measure of her own success as a mother (Amani and Zuhren 5). However, Annie refuses to conform and rejects her mother's life and everything she represents. Paretsky's novel thus contains a highly significant feminist and political critique of women's rights and contraception; it shows how motherhood is a political issue for women and at the forefront of feminist preoccupation with patriarchal crimes against women. *Brush Back* demonstrates that these issues can become a subject of contention and conflict between mothers and daughters, leading to antagonism and violence, and that rather than allowing patriarchy to divide them, mothers and daughters need to join forces and fight those issues together.

The volatile and violent relationship between Stella and Annie resembles that between Paretsky and her own mother, as narrated in her memoirs, *Writing in an Age of Silence*. She writes the following:

> My mother was bitter over opportunities lost or denied and took a savage delight in the failures of other women. Such failures proved to her that she had been defeated by the System, not by her own fears or withdrawals from life. Accepted into medical school in 1941, when that door was closed to many women, she chose not to take the bus from her home town to the University of Illinois on the day she needed to report to class.... If I brought home any achievement from school, she was almost savage in her bitterness. I quickly learned to keep success to myself. (3)

This description bears many similarities to the antagonistic and violent relationship between Stella and Annie in *Brush Back*—the daughter wanting independence and education but the mother expecting her daughter to conform to class- and gender expectations. Stella explains how she was trying to get Annie to understand the facts of life: "She was getting those big ideas, way above herself. She didn't think she needed to vacuum or do the laundry because she was going to school, but she needed to remember she was part of a family. Everyone has to carry their weight in a family" (4). These intergenerational mother-daughter conflicts form an important part of *Brush Back*'s crime plot, reflecting the complex emotional dynamics produced through patriarchal inequity. In its nuanced and unsparing depiction of the mother-daughter relationship and the mother accused of filicide, *Brush Back* demonstrates Paretsky's creative risk taking and innovation of the genre. She tackles this most transgressive and taboo laden of all crimes, revealing the patriarchal family as a crime scene and the domestic sphere to be a deadly dangerous place for women, not a safe haven or shelter. The novel does not whitewash the volatile mother-daughter relationship, or Stella's violent behaviour, but insists on justice for victims. In *Brush Back*, a teenage girl is murdered, and her mother is framed and made to carry the punishment. Warshawski sees it as her mission to put this injustice right by challenging false narratives about maternal filicide and uncovering the truth about Annie's death. While working as a clerk in a lawyers' office, Annie uncovered a scandal involving political corruption and misuse of funds and paid for this with her life. By identifying who murdered Annie and why, Warshawski places the responsibility for that murder firmly back with the patriarchal judicial system and the corrupt powerful criminals who had Annie killed.

Conclusion: Feminism and Justice for Victims in Paretsky's *Brush Back*

In the end, it turns out Stella beat her daughter, but she was not the one who killed her—Annie was murdered by unscrupulous influential men because of what she knew. Paretsky's exploration of maternal contexts in *Brush Back* has the important outcome of exonerating Stella of killing her daughter, a heavy burden that had hung over her and her family for twenty-five years. Through this important revisionary investigation, Paretsky urges the reader to reconsider popular cultural stereotypes and mythical constructions of mothers who kill their children. She demonstrates how, in Stella's case, presumptions and prejudices linked to gender, class, ethnicity, and religion influenced the processes of justice in order to find her guilty and achieve a conviction. Warshawski's determined and skillful detective work reveals that these prejudices were the primary reason behind Stella's conviction rather than incontrovertible evidence. Through the reassessment of the mother who kills her child and the cultural baggage that accompanies this figure, Paretsky's novel makes a vital contribution to ongoing feminist debates and discussions around motherhood, violence, transgression, and taboo. The mother who kills her child is often portrayed in a sensationalist manner in popular cultural texts, typically depicting infanticide masqueraded as cot death and Munchausen by proxy in an emotive and lurid way. In contrast, Paretsky focuses on a highly complex scenario, which draws on the complicated and ambivalent emotional context of the mother-daughter relationship, ethnicity, religion, and social class. To Paretsky's credit, she resists taking a sensationalist angle to the controversial subject of maternal filicide. Instead, she stays true to her social realist and feminist vision in *Brush Back*. The novel's references to Medea indicate the preordained crime narrative that serves to incriminate Stella—the culturally sanctioned script about the mother who murders her child. Because of this powerful narrative, the framing of Stella is straightforward for Annie's real killers, as class- and gender-based stereotypes of the bad mother serve to cement her guilt.

As we have seen in *Brush Back*'s treatment of the theme of the mother who kills her child, Paretsky uses the crime novel's conventions to interrogate the construction of maternal guilt and uses the genre's focus on criminality and its structural drive to restore order to achieve justice for victims. In this case, achieving justice for the victims means not only identifying Annie's true killer but also exonerating her mother, whose imprisonment was a miscarriage of justice. This does not mean exonerating Stella for her violent behaviour towards Annie but exposing the social, class, and financial inequalities that lead to conflicts between females within families and the ways these inequalities were exploited to incriminate Stella. Paretsky uses the theme of maternal filicide to generate the narrative's emotional pull and capture the reader's fascination, but then intelligently uncovers the complexity of the crime. Behind the superficially sensationalist story of the murdering mother and the seemingly straightforward judgments it commands hides a complex reality in which large companies, speculators, and corrupt politicians are in charge and routinely kill people and frame others to evade discovery. This vital revelation serves as a powerful reminder that mothers in patriarchy are circumscribed by multiple oppressive structures and that blaming the mother is a product of a kneejerk response and a simplistic narrative. Stella's phrase "I never made those marks on my girl" becomes a rallying cry for the novel's refutation of the prevailing stereotypes of mothers who kill, presenting instead a nuanced hinterland for the representation of maternal violence and murder.

Brush Back urges the reader to reassess Stella, and to recognize that Stella's seemingly irrational and excessive rage is a reaction to her daughter's death and being made to take the blame for it. Likewise,

Stella's staying physically fit in prison can be seen as an indication of her rejection of guilt and her determination to seek justice for her daughter and for herself. Paretsky's novel challenges the masculinist focus of hard-boiled crime fiction by drawing on literary and cultural allusions to evoke and represent the complexities of the mother-daughter relationship. The novel further contributes to the feminist reassessment of the genre through her female detective Warshawski and her memories of her own mother-daughter relationship, which play an important role in *Brush Back*'s plot. Paretsky's exploration of the maternal context of crime and her detective's family history form the compelling background for *Brush Back*'s investigation of that most taboo of crimes: mothers who kill. In this case, however, Stella, the mother under investigation, did not make those "marks on her girl," although she had to serve many years in prison for her daughter's murder. Paretsky's *Brush Back* exposes this injustice by challenging false cultural narratives about mothers who kill and replacing them with more complicated stories that expose class inequality and challenge patriarchal oppression and injustice.

Endnotes

1. The title quotation is taken from Sara Paretsky, *Brush Back*, Penguin, 2015, p.4.
2. Willson et al. reference Kurt Lüscher and Karl Pillemer. "Intergenerational ambivalence: A new approach to the study of parent-child relations in later life." *Journal of Marriage and the Family* (1998): 413-425.

Works Cited

Almond, Barbara, "Maternal Ambivalence: The Dilemma of Modern Parenting." *Psychology Today*, 16 Sept. 2010, www.psychologytoday.com/gb/blog/maternal-ambivalence/201009/maternal-ambivalence. Accessed 20 Nov. 2021.

Bates, Victoria. "Murderous Motherhood: Munchausen Syndrome by Proxy in 1990s Crime Fiction." *The Journal of Popular Culture*, vol. 51, no. 5, 2018, pp. 1113-32.

Beasley, Carolyn. "Writing a murderous mother: a case study on the critical applications of creative writing research to crime fiction." *TEXT* 20. Special 37, 2016, pp. 1-11.

Beyer, Charlotte. "Life of Crime: Feminist Crime/Life Writing in Sara Paretsky, *Writing in an Age of Silence*, PD James, *Time to Be in Earnest: A Fragment of Autobiography*, and Val McDermid, *A Suitable Job for a Woman: Inside the World of Women Private Eyes*." *Constructing Crime*, edited by Christiana Gregoriou, Palgrave Macmillan, 2012, pp. 209-23.

Beyer, Charlotte. "'This Really Isn't a Job For a Girl to Take on Alone': Reappraising Feminism and Genre Fiction in Sara Paretsky's Crime Novel *Indemnity Only*." *This Book Is an Action: Feminist Print Culture and Activist Aesthetics*, edited by Jaime Harker and Cecilia Konchar Farr, University of Illinois Press, 2015, pp. 226-44.

Beyer, Charlotte. "Mediatization and Mothers Accused of Murder in Sophie Hannah's Crime Novel *A Room Swept White*." *Northern Lights: Film & Media Studies Yearbook*, vol. 9, no. 1, 2011, pp. 79-93.

Beyer, Charlotte. "'She Decided to Kill Her Husband': Housewives in Contemporary American Fictions of Crime." *Violence in American Popular Culture*, edited by David Schmid, Praeger Press, 2015, pp. 71-94.

Beyer, Charlotte. "Crime Fiction and Migration." *Routledge Companion to Crime Fiction*, edited by Janice Allan, Jesper Gulddal, Stewart King, and Andrew Pepper. Routledge, 2020, pp. 379-387.

Beyer, Charlotte. "Chicago Crime, Blue Collar and White: Sara Paretsky's V. I. Warshawski Novels." *Chicago: A Literary History*. Cambridge University Press, edited by Frederik Byrn Køhlert, Cambridge University Press, 2021, pp. 356-369.

Horsley, Lee, and Katharine Horsley. "Mères Fatales: Maternal Guilt in the Noir Crime Novel." *MFS Modern Fiction Studies*, vol. 45, no. 2, 1999, pp. 369-402.

Imani, Maryam, and Zohreh Ramin, "A Study of Irigaray's Mother-Daughter Genealogy in Sara Paretsky's *Brush Back*." *Dilemas Contemporáneos: Educación, Política y Valores*, vol. 7, 2019, pp. 1-21.

Kaufman, Natalie Hevener, and Carrollee Kaufman Hevener. "Mythical Musical Connections: The Mother-Daughter Bond in the Work of Sara Paretsky." *Clues*, vol. 25, no. 2, 2007, pp. 19-28.

Kinsman, Margaret. *Sara Paretsky: A Companion to the Mystery Fiction.* McFarland, 2016.

Koppelman, Susan, editor. *Between Mothers and Daughters: Stories across a Generation.* Feminist Press at CUNY, 1987.

Kunst, Jennifer L. "Fraught with the Utmost Danger: The Object Relations of Mothers Who Kill Their Children." *Bulletin of the Menninger Clinic*, vol. 66, no. 1, 2002, pp. 19-38.

Murray, Jenni. "Woman's Hour." *BBC Sounds*, 15 July 2015, www.bbc.co.uk/sounds/play/b062kqzq. Accessed 20 Nov. 2021.

Palmer, Paulina. *Contemporary Women's Fiction: Narrative Practice and Feminist Theory.* Harvester Wheatsheaf, 1989.

Paretsky, Sara. *Brush Back.* Penguin, 2015.

Paretsky, Sara. *Writing in an Age of Silence.* Verso Books, 2009.

Scher, Ingrid. *Monsters in Our Minds: The Myth of Infanticide and the Murderous Mother in the Cultural Psyche.* University of New South Wales, 2005.

Seal, Lizzie. *Women, Murder and Femininity: Gender Representations of Women Who Kill.* Springer, 2010.

Willson, Andrea E., et al. "Ambivalence in Mother-Adult Child Relations: A Dyadic Analysis." *Social Psychology Quarterly*, vol. 69, no. 3, 2006, pp. 235-52.

Yi-Lin Yu. *Mother, She Wrote: Matrilineal Narratives in Contemporary Women's Writing.* Peter Lang, 2005.

Notes on Contributors

Caitlin Adams is a PhD candidate and member of the Cambridge Group for the History of Population and Social Structure at the University of Cambridge. She is interested in histories of poverty, transportation, and the labouring family. Her doctoral thesis maps how plebeian language travelled within the British Empire during the late eighteenth and early nineteenth centuries. This project extends and develops her findings from her master of research, which she completed at Macquarie University, Sydney. Her master's research interrogated poor mothers' relationships with their children in New South Wales and the county of Gloucestershire during the early nineteenth century.

Charlotte Beyer, SFHEA, is senior lecturer in English Studies at the University of Gloucestershire, UK. She is author of *Murder in a Few Words* (McFarland, 2020) and *Contemporary Children's and Young Adult Literature* (Cambridge Scholars Publishing, 2021) and has published widely on crime fiction and contemporary literature. She is the author and editor of *Teaching Crime Fiction* (Palgrave, 2018), *Mothers without Their Children* (editor with Andrea Robertson; Demeter 2019), and *Travellin' Mama: Mothers, Mothering, and Travel* (edited with Janet MacLennan, Dorsia Smith Silva, and Marjorie Tesser; Demeter, 2019).

Judith Broome is Associate Professor of British literature and culture at William Paterson University, Wayne, New Jersey. She is the author of *Fictive Domains: Body, Landscape, and Nostalgia, 1717–1770* (Bucknell University Press, 2007). Her research interests include trauma theory and the representation of violence and women in literature.

Sace Elder is professor and chair of history at Eastern Illinois University, where she is also affiliate faculty in women's, gender, and sexuality studies. A specialist in modern German history, she is the author of *Murder Scenes: Normality, Deviance, and Criminal Violence in Weimar Berlin* (University of Michigan Press, 2010). Her recent work focuses on violence against children, adult authority, and the movement against child abuse in early twentieth-century Germany.

Rachel Franks is the coordinator, Scholarship at the State Library of New South Wales and a Conjoint Fellow at The University of Newcastle, Australia. A qualified educator and librarian, Rachel holds a PhD in Australian crime fiction (CQU) and a PhD in true crime narratives (Sydney). Her research on crime fiction, true crime, popular culture, and information science has been presented at numerous conferences. An award-winning writer, her work can be found in a wide variety of books, journals, and magazines as well as on social and in traditional media.

Amy B. Hagenrater-Gooding is an associate professor at the University of Maryland Eastern Shore where she has taught for ten years. Her research interests deal with women's studies and gender issues as seen in her publications "The Impossibility of Male/Female Relationships in Willa Cather's *My Antonia*" in *CEA-Mag* and "Pink Is the New Green: Raising Little Shoppers From Birth," featured in a collection from North Georgia University Press. Motherwork is her primary interest; she has a forthcoming publication with Lehigh University Press dealing with mothering concerns in the Josh Mallerman novel *Bird Box*.

Trudier Harris, formerly J. Carlyle Sitterson Distinguished Professor of English at UNC Chapel Hill, is university distinguished research professor, English, University of Alabama. Her books include *Fiction and Folklore: The Novels of Toni Morrison*, *The Scary Mason-Dixon Line: African American Writers and the South*; and *Martin Luther King Jr., Heroism, and African American Literature*. Recent awards include an honorary doctorate, The College of William and Mary; the Richard Beale Davis Award for Lifetime Achievement in Southern Literary Studies; the National Humanities Center Fellowship; and the Clarence E. Cason Award for Nonfiction. Her current book project is "Ungraspable: Depictions of Home in African American Literature."

Amy Lynne Hill is a doctoral candidate at Vanderbilt University, where she is pursuing a joint PhD in German and Comparative Media Analysis and Practice. Her research interests include strategies of disidentification in beauty and body cultures on various social media platforms, particularly in queer communities, as well as gender in criminal discourses. Through the analysis of historical cases, sexological research of the Wilhelmine and Weimar eras and feminist crime fiction from the 1990s, Amy's dissertation focuses on how the figure of the Lustmörderin (sex murderess) interpellates the constellation of gender, subjectivity, and sexual violence as it relates to key crises in twentieth-century Germany

Meighen S. Katz is a public historian, curator, and academic based in Melbourne, Australia. Her research explores public narratives of vulnerability in a transnational context with particular sub interests in the museum and heritage interpretation of experiences of women, and the role of visual culture. Her most recent monograph is entitled *Narratives of Vulnerability in Museums: American Interpretations of the Great Depression.*

Chevelle Malcolm is a recent graduate from the University of New Brunswick: holding a degree in Biology and Philosophy. As a child growing up in Jamaica, her passion for reading Classical and Caribbean literature cultivated a love of writing and storytelling. She began writing poetry at the age of 10 and used her poetry as a means of self-expression. Writing poetry has helped Chevelle to "discover her voice" and gain the courage to use it for empowerment. As a woman of faith, she is very passionate about social justice and morality, writing poetry to champion the cause of the marginalized groups in society particularly, black, and indigenous communities. Chevelle is hopelessly optimistic and as such, she finds pleasure in every opportunity given to use her poetry to bring hope to the lives of others or to lend a new perspective.

Chrissie Andrea Maroulli has a BA in musical theatre from Columbia College Chicago and an MA in Shakespeare and theatre from the University of Birmingham. She is currently pursuing a PhD in English literature and comparative cultural studies at the University of Cyprus. Her research is on the representations of womanhood in English early modern balladry. Moreover, Maroulli is a professional playwright, composer, and performer; she has collaborated with many theatrical companies, including the National Theatre of Cyprus, and several of her musicals have been professionally produced in Cyprus. She currently teaches drama and music in secondary schools.

Anne McGee is an associate professor of Spanish at Arkansas State University, Jonesboro. She teaches courses in Latin American literature and culture and specializes in Mexican literature; her current research focuses on questions of border and regional identities in the literature and cultural production of Northern Mexico and the U.S.-Mexico borderlands. She has published articles on the works of Luis Humberto Crosthwaite, Arturo Pérez Reverte, Nellie Campobello, Sandra Cisneros, and Gloria Anzaldúa, among others.

Sharon Myers is an associate professor in the Department of History and Classics at the University of Prince Edward Island, Canada. Her research and writing has focused mainly on women, children, and their relationship to the state in Maritime Canada in the nineteenth and early twentieth century. In particular, her recent work has focused on the intersections among child welfare, deviance, and the regulatory role of law and policy.

Anna Rocca is a professor of French and Italian at Salem State University, Salem, MA. Her research focuses on contemporary francophone women writers of Africa, diasporic female writers, autobiography, visual arts, post-colonial feminism and transnational feminist movements. In addition to her most recent publications on Tunisian women artists and writers, she is the author of *Assia Djebar, le corps invisible: voir sans être vue* (Paris: L'Harmattan, 2005), and co-edited *Frictions et devenirs dans les écritures migrantes au féminin* (Saarbrücken: EUE, 2011) as well as *Women Taking Risks in Contemporary Autobiographical Narratives* (Newcastle, UK: CSP, 2013).

Georgina Rychner is a PhD candidate at Monash University in Melbourne, Australia. Her dissertation examines public petitioning in capital trials in late-nineteenth and early-twentieth century Victoria, with specific focus on narratives of insanity. More broadly, her research areas include the history of crime and criminal justice, women's history, the history of psychiatry, and historical criminology. Rychner currently teaches criminology at Deakin University. She has published on crime and mental illness in *Lilith*, *Health and History*, and *Law and History* and has been heavily involved in the Australia and New Zealand Historical Criminology Network and the Australian Women's History Network.

Josephine L. Savarese is a scholar from Atlantic Canada. She studied at the University of Saskatchewan and McGill University before completing graduate studies in women's studies at the University of Hawaii at Mānoa, exploring issues related to women's criminalization, feminist theory, justice for marginalized populations, environmental justice, and alternative/ Indigenous research methodologies, among other topics. She is a regular contributor to Demeter publications and is delighted to have been involved in this important and unique text, as well as others.

Andrea S. Walsh, a historical sociologist, is a lecturer in the Comparative Media Studies/Writing and Women's and Gender Studies programs at the Massachusetts Institute of Technology. She has also taught sociology, women's studies, film studies, and writing at Harvard University, Clark University, and Wellesley College. Andrea is the author of *Women's Film and Female Experience: 1940-1950* and various articles on gender, aging, media, writing pedagogy and women's history. She is currently researching the first wave of U.S. women's rights activism in the nineteenth century and is particularly interested in the political role of storytelling within that movement.

Deepest appreciation to
Demeter's monthly Donors

DEMETER

Daughters
Rebecca Bromwich
Summer Cunningham
Tatjana Takseva
Debbie Byrd
Fiona Green
Tanya Cassidy
Vicki Noble
Bridget Boland
Naomi McPherson
Myrel Chernick

Sisters
Amber Kinser
Nicole Willey
Christine Peets